Beyond the Vote: Canadian Women and Politics

This collection of essays focuses on the experiences of women as political activists in twentieth-century Canada, both in the mainstream of party politics and in groups outside the mainstream. The latter include women in the socialist and labour movements, the farm and peace movements, and women active in various ethnic communities. Expanding the notion of politics, the authors highlight the widespread nature of women's activism – particularly at the local level – and challenge the easy formulation that women were primarily interested in the vote and lost interest in politics when they acquired it. Some of the essays suggest that even the suffrage campaign has been misrepresented as solely a middle-class movement.

Women evolved their own styles of political participation shaped by local contexts, class, culture, family, and life cycle. Women often organized at the community level, and worked both in combination with men and in women-only settings. Contributors to this volume explore women's involvement in organizations from the political left to right, and women's efforts to shape Canada's political priorities and activities. Politically minded women often found that their best outlet for commitment and service was through women's organizations, which addressed their needs and provided a base for effective action.

LINDA KEALEY teaches history at Memorial University.

JOAN SANGSTER teaches history and women's studies at Trent University.

Beyond the Vote

CANADIAN
WOMEN
AND POLITICS

162 855612

edited by
Linda Kealey
and
Joan Sangster

UNIVERSITY OF TORONTO PRESS
TORONTO · BUFFALO · LONDON

© University of Toronto Press 1989
Toronto Buffalo London
Printed in Canada

ISBN 0-8020-2677-X (cloth)
ISBN 0-8020-6650-X (paper)

Printed on acid-free paper

Canadian Cataloguing in Publication Data

Main entry under title:

Beyond the vote

Includes index.
ISBN 0-8020-2677-X (bound) ISBN 0-8020-6650-X (pbk.)

1. Women in politics – Canada – History.
2. Canada – Politics and government – 20th century.
I. Kealey, Linda, 1947–   . II. Sangster, Joan, 1952–

HQ1236.5.C2B4   1989   324'.088042   C89-093458-4

Publication of this book has been assisted by
the Canada Council and the Ontario Arts Council
under their block grant programs.

Contents

Acknowledgments

The editors would like to thank the authors for their patience and co-operation in this project. Special thanks are due to Colleen Dalton of St John's for her word-processing skills and her cheerful willingness to make frequent revisions in the manuscript. The editors also thank the *Canadian Historical Review*, *Atlantis*, and the Canadian Plains Research Center for allowing us to reprint the essays by Susan Mann Trofimenkoff, Franca Iacovetta, and Joan Sangster, respectively. Linda Kealey's essay draws upon research funded by the Social Science and Humanities Research Council. Thanks are also due to Virgil Duff of University of Toronto Press for his support of this project from the very beginning, and to Lydia Burton, our copy editor.

PART ONE

Reassessing Women in Canadian Politics

Introduction

Linda Kealey and Joan Sangster

It has long been assumed that once women obtained the key symbol of political equality, the vote, they retreated from the public sphere and political arena, and returned only after a second wave of feminism in the 1970s propelled them back into political action. Indeed, in recent years, under the influence of a renewed feminist movement, mainstream political parties have declared a 'new-found' interest in women and politics; over the last decade all three federal Canadian parties have proclaimed their intentions to seek out female political candidates and consider women's issues in their platforms.

For many feminist historians and political scientists, women's securement of the vote, how (or whether) they used it, and women's participation in the party system have all been the crucial questions for investigation. Canadian historiography has focused heavily on women's campaigns for suffrage and for equal civil, legal, and professional rights; the ideological and 'feminist' content of the early suffragists' agenda has been debated at some length, as has the fate of the women's movement after the suffrage.[1]

In the 1920s, some women worried that their recent suffrage victories had done little to alter Canadian politics. 'Is Women's Suffrage a Fizzle?' asked a disillusioned writer in *Maclean's* in 1928; she went on to argue that women, especially in eastern Canada, had been easily engulfed by the male-dominated party system. Historians have often come to similar conclusions. Carol Bacchi, for example, suggests a certain inevitability to the 'disappearance' of feminism in the 1920s, for the suffragists, she claims, were always more concerned with protecting Protestant family values than revolutionizing gender roles. In a similar vein, Veronica Strong-Boag demonstrated that pre-war feminists either found their moral-reform platform outdated in the twenties, or were easily absorbed into the middle-class status quo.[2] More recently, she has argued that post-war women turned their energies from public to private political questions; thus, 'domestic feminism' and the division of labour within the home became the focus of women's concerns after the vote was won.[3]

From the 1920s to the 1960s, though, the image of women and politics characterized in the Canadian popular press was a more narrow and restricted one, focusing primarily on women's party involvements and election to office. In *Maclean's* and *Chatelaine*, women were expected either to explain their unusual success in the electoral arena or, more often, to justify their failures, as with the eight former women candidates who wrote for *Chatelaine*'s 1930 article, 'Why I Failed to Be Elected.' Historians have often concentrated on similar issues. When women's involvement in twentieth-century politics is discussed, it is often in the traditional form of biography, constructed uncritically around the few successful female politicians who were elected (or appointed) to office,[4] or perhaps around a women of alternate, left-wing politics, who is also presented in a one-dimensional, celebratory manner, well symbolized by the title *She Never Was Afraid: The Story of Annie Buller*.[5]

While some political theorists have been concerned with developing broad, encompassing new theories explaining the origins of women's subordination and oppression,[6] the primary focus for Canadian political scientists has been the empirical investigation of women's 'integration' into the existing political party system.[7] This research has helped to detail when, where, how, and what kind of women joined political parties, what positions they held, and how party structures encouraged, or more often limited, women's political participation. Though useful in explaining women's relative absence from the inner sanctums of party politics, the work of political scientists, like that of historians, has centred its gaze on well-established definitions of politics.

As Jill Vickers argues in her introductory essay, historians and political scientists still need to expand their research in these areas, reassessing women's activities in the suffrage movement and political parties, detailing the interrelationship between the (too often dichotomized) public and private spheres, and developing a clearer understanding of feminists' conception of citizenship and their relationship to the state. At the same time, we also need to develop a more comprehensive definition of politics, searching for and analysing the various methods and local centres of women's political thinking and action, which were situated outside of the suffrage movement and party system, always carefully placing these activities within their appropriate historical context.

If we do develop such a definition, the idea that 'nothing much happened' after women won the vote must clearly be abandoned, for numerous articles in this collection attest to women's vibrant and varied political activities after 1920. As we recover these political activities, special attention to class, ethnic, and cultural differences is required. Although historians and political scientists have been aware of the extent to which women's family identification and concerns moulded women's political work, they have been less cognizant of the powerful forces of class and culture in shaping women's politics. Cairine Wilson's successful career, political loyalties, and 'respectable' style of politics, for instance, had as much to do with class as did the militant, class-conscious protests of working-class Jewish immigrants described by Ruth Frager. Furthermore, as a number of authors in this volume emphasize, ethnicity, in conjunction with class, also determined women's political priorities and activities. There may still have been a distinctive 'female' style of political interaction, shaped by women's socialization and familial identification, as Susan Trofimenkoff hints with reference to Thérèse Casgrain's 'politics of conciliation.' However, women's political priorities and activities were still worked out within an ever-changing historical, class, and cultural context. Finally, although we need to place women's political efforts on centre stage, thus restoring to women their own history, it is important not to neglect the fact that many women were cut off from political power and influence in Canadian society, sometimes even marginalized within their own economic or cultural organizations. As feminists, we need to understand how and under what conditions women became politically vocal, as well as how prevailing ideologies of gender and material conditions circumscribed women's activity in the public sphere.

A reassessment of women's political activity in the early twentieth century should include some discussion of the role played by socialist women in political debate and action. As Linda Kealey's article in this volume points out, historians of the suffrage era have up to now underestimated the activities of labour and socialist women in working for sex equality before the First World War. Socialist women debated how to elevate women's social status and eliminate their economic exploitation, and a significant minority of these socialist women helped build the Socialist Party of Canada and the Social Democratic Party of Canada, though ultimately it was the latter's more flexible, decentralized organization and commitment to reforms like suffrage that allowed women the best possibilities of political participation. Even sexual relationships and issues like prostitution, relates Janice Newton, were scrutinized by pre-war socialist parties, though most socialist men failed to move beyond an economistic political analysis to fully comprehend women's oppression. Indeed, despite the impressive activity of socialist women, gender inequality, Kealey concludes, was never completely understood or embraced by these parties, which remained bound to prevailing views of women's innate maternal biology and to the ideal of a family wage.

Many socialist women carried their organizing skills and political commitment into the post-suffrage period. Although the moderate or liberal feminist tradition was somewhat weakened after the war, left feminism increased its strength and visibility. As Pat Roome shows, Calgary women like Amelia Turner Smith became important participants in western Labor party politics in the 1920s, often simultaneously creating separate women's labour organizations that provided women with moral support and leadership training and publicly addressed pressing issues like equal pay. Similarly, the Co-operative Commonwealth Federation (CCF) women described by Joan Sangster were 'indispensable' party builders in the 1930s, especially in areas like grass-roots organizing and education; CCF women also organized autonomously around women's issues, sometimes promoting a distinct and alternative socialist-feminist perspective within the party.[8]

Even further left, Finnish socialist women, Varpu Lindstom-Best maintains, peaked in their political activity during the 1920s. Since the late nineteenth century, left-wing Finnish women had organized to improve their own communities, aid socialist parties, and promote women's suffrage. Their high degree of political awareness and organization was a result of political precedents and experiences in Finland, high literacy rates, later marriage, and fewer children, as well as the radicalizing influence of working-class life in Canada. Although some of the concerns of the early Finnish socialist women paralleled those of their English-speaking suffragist sisters, such as their temperance crusade, other goals, notably attempts to unionize domestics, clearly marked out the distinct class and cultural allegiances of the Finns. Similarly, the Jewish Fareyn described by Ruth Frager embodied coexisting loyalties to class, culture, and gender. Though primarily dedicated to an ideal of class solidarity promoted by the Communist party, the Fareyn women also organized autonomously and tried to set their own political agenda. Moreover, their campaigns to educate children and protect the working-class family's standard of living reflected long-standing traditions of women's popular political activism. Protests over prices like the kosher-meat boycott questioned the conventional separation often made between public and private spheres, and pushed women into the streets; it is true, however, that such political actions never completely challenged women's traditional and subordinate domestic role.

After the First World War some women did look to the existing, 'old-line' parties as a means of expressing their political views. As Franca Iacovetta points out, the liberal feminist tradition was represented by women like Cairine

Wilson, Canada's first woman senator. Wilson's family background, evangelical sympathies, sense of noblesse oblige, and humanitarianism led her to the Liberal party. One of her accomplishments within the party was her continued support for the National Federation of Liberal Women, officially set up in 1928 but largely inactive until after the Second World War. The federation provided women, unwelcome and ill at ease in the male-dominated Liberal constituency organizations and Liberal Federation of Canada, with an auxiliary devoted to supporting the party and providing a place to discuss women's issues. As Myers argues, however, the Women's Federation was not used as a stepping-stone to greater constituency and party influence, so that most women became isolated as second-class Liberal citizens within their own organization. By the 1970s such party auxiliaries, already condemned by the Royal Commission on the Status of Women, were fast becoming symbols of the past, and in the wake of feminist pressure, both the Liberal and, more recently, the Conservative party have made some attempt to integrate women more directly into the party apparatus.

Myers sees women's auxiliaries as antithetical to women's full political equality; Sangster is more sympathetic, maintaining that, in the CCF at least, women's committees might have exerted a positive, even feminist role. In this social-democratic party, women's organizations traversed the spectrum from coffee-making auxiliaries to socialist and feminist lobby groups. The primary purpose of most committees, however, was to train women for leadership and provide a comfortable forum to discuss women's issues, including gender equality. Before the 1960s, women in both the Liberal party and the CCF often defined women's issues with a strong emphasis on women's homemaking role. Clearly, the dominant social norms prescribing female domesticity influenced the definition of 'appropriate' political issues for women. Shared ideas about gender roles thus shaped the program of both these parties, but it is important to remember that there were still significant ideological differences distinguishing various political parties. Women's role in the party, strategies for social change, views of gender inequality, and the social background of party members differed for the Liberals, Conservatives, and CCF / NDP, as they still do. One of the persistent demands of the Liberal Women in the 1940s, says Myers, was the appointment of women to influential boards and to the Senate. To CCF women this tactic of advancing a few élite women was less important to women's advancement than securing social welfare measures like health insurance.

While the left-wing perspective acknowledged the important role of women in the movement and recognized to a degree that gender inequality was a problem, right-wing political views often admitted only to the first; for example, right-wing women in the Ukrainian community in the 1930s subscribed to a politics shaped by loyalty to the homeland abroad and ethnic consciousness at home in Canada. Indeed, the Ukrainian Women's Organization (OUK) discussed by Swyripa subsumed women's interests to those of the nation, combining nationalist ideals with a strong emphasis on women's base in the home and their sacred maternal role. Right-wing nationalist movements were / are by definition hostile to feminism and the idea of women's equality or autonomy. Often closely tied to a biological view of women's 'natural' role, conservative ideologies tend to glorify the role of mother, glossing over or refusing to recognize the social features of motherhood. This view of woman's 'natural' role lends support to the assumption that change is either impossible or undesirable because it goes against nature. Glorification of motherhood rests on the private sphere of the family. Thus, while the left did not totally escape the biological determinist trap and continued to view women primarily within the family, its internationalist sympathies, class analysis, and the questioning of sex roles by some women within the movement differentiated its views of women from those of right-wing groups.

Commitment to left-wing politics among ethnic women demonstrated the potential for integration of family, community, and political concerns; such integration undercut the separation of public and private spheres as well. The immigrant women studied by Frager and Lindstrom-Best refused to play a passive role in politics, and within their communities they worked to improve the lot of their compatriots. Despite the hindrances imposed by language and culture, these women attempted to bridge the gap between English speakers and non-English speakers, while continuing their activities among their own respective cultural groups. Bridging attempts were not often successful because English-speaking socialists and communists were not always receptive or assumed their own political superiority over the immigrants.

Female styles of politics were clearly in evidence among women from the ethnic minorities as they were among English or French Canadians; these styles were tied not only to class and culture but also to the life cycle. Although Ukrainian nationalist ideology appealed to women as mothers, marriage and motherhood also influenced the direction and definition of political activism for other women. The sexual division of labour within the family, which assigned primary responsibility for children and domestic labour to women, operated to constrain women's political roles. As Roome notes, Calgary's labour and socialist activists tended to be women with older children, childless married women, or single women. Toronto Jewish women who participated in communist-led actions such as the kosher-meat boycotts often included their children in party work in order to remain politically active. Finnish women also struggled to make politics fit with domestic duties, creating their own vehicles for political education and activism in the 'sewing circles.'

Women in mainstream party politics also encountered these problems, but in the cases of Cairine Wilson and Thérèse Casgrain, wealthy family backgrounds and marriages to men with business and professional identities, as well as political experience, altered the impact of gender-role prescription. Both women benefited from privileged social-class standing, including the help of domestic servants; as Iacovetta and Trofimenkoff point out, neither woman, however, was immune from the prevailing notion that politics was really a man's business. Male social-class privileges did not fully extend to women in politics; despite her privileged background, Casgrain never had secretarial assistance until she became a senator late in her political career. Other prominent women in politics, such as Agnes Macphail or Charlotte Whitton, avoided some life-cycle questions by never marrying, viewing marriage as a limiting factor for women in politics, though Whitton certainly derived emotional support for her public life from a long relationship with her partner Margaret Grier. As Vickers explains, women in the post-suffrage period began to reject maternal feminist rationales for the citizen-politician in favour of a more professional model of full-time political commitment.

Marital breakdown and single parenting were hazards for political activists then as now. As Lindstrom-Best and Kealey note, some prominent women organizers in the early socialist movement found that relationships with partners were difficult to maintain, leaving these women with the sole responsibility for the children. Finnish socialist organizer Sanna Kannasto had a son to provide for as well as a mortgage to pay. Sophie Mushkat (later McClusky), organizer for the Socialist Party of Canada and later the Workers' party, brought up her daughter while she was very active in socialist politics. The itinerant organizing model favoured by the socialist cause did not provide for the possibility that women with family responsibilities might be involved. Women's lifecycles and the socially constructed roles of wife and mother varied in their impact on political women; nevertheless, these were considerations that all political women had to negotiate within their respective cultural and class frameworks.

Prevailing ideological notions of womanhood clearly pervaded the lives of all women, not just politically active women. For women political activists the dilemmas raised were even more sharply posed. Although these ideological notions were affected by class and culture, the fundamental outlines of women's roles were similar for all social groups. Marriage and family were central to the definition of womanhood that cut across class ideology; how commitments worked out in practice varied considerably.

Bourgeois ideology about women has been thoroughly examined in the context of early twentieth-century social reform and suffrage.[9] While less dramatic alterations occurred after 1920 for bourgeois married women, at least until the 1960s, single women's roles changed most significantly between the two world wars as women of this class sought education or employment in larger numbers. Veronica Strong-Boag notes in *The New Day Recalled* that post-suffrage hopes for expanded options for young women were only realized in a limited fashion. For political women, the trend to partisanship coexisted with the continuation of women's groups within political organizations and separate from them.[10]

Working-class notions of women's roles also centred around marriage and family; single women's labour-market participation continued to be viewed as a transient phenomenon ending with marriage and motherhood. Even among progressives, socialists, and communists, family obligations were central. The women 'comrades,' to be sure, took on political roles within left-wing groups, but usually within the framework of women's interests, most often assumed to be associated with the home. The result for women on the left was not an avowed feminism, but their views did challenge the private / public division and the separation of family from community and politics. Working-class and ethnic women's experiences and understandings differed significantly from those of bourgeois women. And for ethnic women on the right of the political spectrum, the egalitarian notions of the family espoused by the left, even if not always practised, had little appeal. The patriarchal family and right-wing nationalist ideology provided a different context for these women's political activism.

As Vickers suggests, women's position on the margins of official politics can have advantages. The perception and experience of being on the fringe has the potential for encouraging shared analysis and action. Certainly this can be seen in the case of ethnic or immigrant women isolated by language and culture. Women in the farm and peace movements demonstrably found themselves on the margins of Canadian society earlier in this century. Ontario farm women organized the United Farm Women of Ontario (UFWO) in response to their marginalization as farmers and as women within the male farmers' organization; this phenomenon has repeated itself in the last ten years with the emergence of the new farm-women's groups discussed by Rankin. The economic invisibility of farm-women's work has impeded their political visibility, which became a more pressing issue once women got the vote. Although women's votes counted, their gender-based concerns elicited little attention from the farmers' movement, thus leaving the women little alternative but to organize around their own issues.

Women in the peace movement were even more marginalized, particularly during periods of international tension and conflict. These women cannot be described simply as urban bourgeois progressives, according to Roberts, because of the variety of their backgrounds. What is common to early twentieth-century feminist pacifists is a shared social-gospel philosophy that has persisted down to the present in organizations such as Voice of Women (VOW). Although some groups were not Christian in their orientation and favoured secular and socialist analysis, both radical Christian and secular socialist women's peace groups (such as the Women's International League for Peace and Freedom and the Women's Peace Union) were outnumbered in the 1920s and 1930s by more conservative women's groups and mixed-sex organizations such as the League of Nations Society. The Second World War, and the cold war that followed it, intensified anti-peace-movement initiatives making survival difficult in the anti-Red hysteria of the late 1940s and 1950s. By the late 1950s, radiation hazards and the threat of nuclear weapons mobilized small groups of mothers concerned about radioactive fallout in cow's milk; by 1960 VOW emerged, attracting both previously active women of various political stripes and previously inactive housewives. Originally a non-partisan and 'respectable' middle-class organization, VOW became increasingly militant by the mid 1960s as Canada allied itself more closely to US foreign policy initiatives. The second wave of feminism, dating from the mid to late 1960s, also involved VOW women who developed a broad definition of peace issues encompassing social justice, race, and gender issues.

While women's peace groups became involved in second-wave feminism, other marginal groups of women did not necessarily identify with modern feminism. As Rankin observes, farm women in Ontario, with the exception of the atypical Women for the Survival of Agriculture, find little appeal in an urban-based feminist movement. Feminism appears to espouse a type of politics that excludes farm women and urges public-sphere participation as the answer to women's problems. Unfortunately, the transformative aspect of feminist politics, which advocates a fundamental overhaul of power structures, has been overshadowed by an emphasis on equality with men.[11]

The essays in this collection raise issues of fundamental importance to present-day feminism as well as to our understanding of historical developments in twentieth-century Canada. Revisionist in the understanding of 'politics,' the essays suggest that a much-enlarged concept of politics illuminating women's political activism at all levels of organization is in order; local and community politics, for example, have most often proved to be the primary arenas of women's activism. Politics may thus be defined quite broadly as all organized initiatives by women to change the structure of society.

This would include women's groups espousing changes that affect both the private- and public-sphere experiences of women as well as women's relationships to state structures and state policies. An expanded notion of women's politics must also include the family as an arena of sexual politics, subject to class, cultural, and ethnic variations. As these essays demonstrate, the boundaries between the public and the private are not fixed but shifting; furthermore, the degree of differentiation between them has often been assumed to be greater than historical experience demonstrates.

Women's politics in the past, as in the present, can be characterized as separatist, integrationist, and transformative. Attempts at integration within formal political structures have proved ephemeral and thus the thrust toward separatism has offered, and continues to offer, women a viable alternative. Women working for political change have found women's groups and organizations more compatible in addressing women's issues, in providing support groups, and in training women for political activism. Contemporary feminists have not, however, totally abandoned integrationist tactics in the realm of politics; both have proved necessary because of the variety of issues and forums with which women are concerned.

Any discussion of women's politics must deal squarely with the transformative potential engendered by these politics. Earlier writing on the reform and suffrage movements has stressed the failure of women's politics to transform Canadian society, except in limited ways. These essays suggest that we need to question previous historical certainties and re-examine our assessments. New research indicates that we have not fully comprehended the contributions of ethnic, socialist, and communist women to women's politics and to the general struggle to reshape Canadian society. Not only do we need to be conscious of class and cultural factors in women's politics, we also need to be critically aware of the limitations of the public / private dichotomy that fractures our understanding of women's politics and its transformative potential.

If we begin with the experience of women, particularly at the local and community level, we discover a rich network of women's politics nuanced by class, culture, and ideology. The Canadian political and economic context is itself fragmented and varied, and, thus, any study of women's politics must be sensitive to the nature of Canadian federalism, regional differences, and the cultural duality that structure women's political choices. Such an approach leads to research that documents women's experiences and raises the question of women's relationships with the state at a broader, more comprehensive level.[12] State policies have responded to women's demands at particular, crucial historical moments when these demands could be reformulated in ways that suited the politics of the state; thus, the granting of suffrage to women, the repeal of the Criminal Code provisions on birth control and abortion, and even the funding of women's groups today reflect the complex interaction of women's political activism with state policy. The lack of state commitment to fundamental change for women means that women still find that their double or triple work-loads continue to impinge on women's political activism, as does the prevailing contemporary ideology about women's secondary status in all areas of life. What this suggests is that the need for integrationist, separatist, and transformative tactics has not disappeared even now.

Anti-feminism is a potentially powerful force that needs to be addressed and confronted as these politically active anti-feminists distort women's politics and its history. Basing their stand on 'the family,' right-wing women's groups like REAL women may have provided us with important insights: working within one paradigm or model of the family marginalizes women's experiences, distorts the reality and variety of women's family lives, and assumes a static and innate relationship between women, mothering, and the private sphere. Indeed, such suppositions may also be located outside right-wing groups, even in some areas of the women's movement. As Lynne Segal has recently argued, the development of an 'essentialist' feminist perspective, assuming an unchanging female consciousness, may also provide dangerous guide-lines for women's political activities.[13] Women's reproductive and family roles have often shaped and influenced the content and nature of women's politics, but they remain one variable, albeit an important one, alongside class, gender, and culture, all of which help to shape family experience itself.[14]

Today's women's movement, like that of the early twentieth century, has been the subject of premature obituaries. What these essays convey is the continuation of women's politics in their various formations over the course of the century; although not all forms of women's political activism may be clearly labelled 'feminist,' and some groups or individuals question or reject the label, women's political activism has been and continues to be a source for political change, in the broadest sense of the word. The challenge faced by the women's movement today is to continue to build a broad-based movement that synthesizes the best of our past, recognizing that our task is to reconceptualize women's politics as the basis of action.

NOTES

1 For example, see Veronica Strong-Boag, *The Parliament of Women: The National Council of Women in Canada 1893–1929* (Ottawa 1976); Linda Kealey, ed. *A*

Not Unreasonable Claim: Women and Reform in Canada, 1880s–1920s (Toronto 1979); Carol Bacchi, *Liberation Deferred? The Ideas of the English-Canadian Suffragists, 1877–1918* (Toronto 1983). See also reviews of Carol Bacchi: Ernest Forbes, 'The Ideas of Carol Bacchi,' *Atlantis* 10:2 (Spring 1985), 119–26; Wendy Mitchinson in *Canadian Historical Review* 64:3 (1983) 386–7; and Linda Kealey, 'A Healthy Revisionism?' *Canadian Committee on Women's History Newsletter*, November 1984, 10–13.

2 Veronica Strong-Boag, 'The Roots of Modern Canadian Feminism,' *Canada: An Historical Magazine* 3:2 (1975), 23–33.

3 Veronica Strong-Boag, 'Pulling in Double Harness or Hauling a Double Load: Women, Work and Feminism on the Canadian Prairie,' *Journal of Canadian Studies* 21:3 (Fall 1986), 32–52.

4 For example, Byrne H. Sanders, *Emily Murphy, Crusader* (Toronto 1945); Elsie Gregory McGill, *My Mother the Judge* (Toronto 1981); Margaret Stewart and Doris French, *Ask No Quarter: A Biography of Agnes Macphail* (Toronto 1959). More recently, books like P.T. Rooke and R.L. Schnell, *No Bleeding Heart: Charlotte Whitton, a Feminist on the Right* (Vancouver 1987); Penny Kome, *Women of Influence* (Toronto 1985); C.A. Armstrong, *Flora Mac-Donald* (Toronto 1976). There are also a number of autobiographies such as Thérèse Casgrain, *Une femme chez les hommes* (Montreal 1971); Florence Bird, *Anne Francis: An Autobiography* (Toronto 1974); Judy LaMarsh, *Memoirs of a Bird in a Gilded Cage* (Toronto 1968).

5 Louise Watson, *She Never Was Afraid: The Biography of Annie Buller* (Toronto 1976); Catharine Vance, *Not by Gods but by People: The Story of Bella Hall Gauld* (Toronto 1968); J.F.C. Wright, *The Louise Lucas Story* (Montreal 1965).

6 Such as Mary O'Brien, *The Politics of Reproduction* (Boston 1981).

7 For example, Sylvia Bashevkin, *Toeing the Lines: Women and Party Politics in English Canada* (Toronto 1985); Janine Brodie, *Women and Politics in Canada* (Toronto 1985); Janine Brodie and Jill Vickers, 'Canadian Women in Politics: An Overview,' CRIAW Papers no. 2 (1982).

8 For example, see Susan Walsh, 'The Peacock and the Guinea Hen: Political Profiles of Dorothy Gretchen Steeves and Grace MacInnis,' in Alison Prentice and Susan Mann Trofimenkoff, eds, *The Neglected Majority* (Toronto 1985) 144–59; Joan Sangster, 'The Making of a Socialist-Feminist; The Early Career of Beatrice Brigden,' *Atlantis* 13:1 (Fall 1987) 13–28; Georgina Taylor, 'Gladys Strum: Farm Woman, Teacher and Politician,' *Canadian Women's Studies* 7:4 (Winter 1986), 89–93.

9 See, for example, Kealey, ed., *A Not Unreasonable Claim*; The Clio Collective, *Quebec Women: A History* (Toronto 1987), esp. ch. 11.

10 Veronica Strong-Boag, *The New Day Recalled: Lives of Girls and Women in*

English Canada, 1919–1939 (Toronto 1987), draws attention to the mushrooming number of young middle-class women entering the labour market. Most found their options limited to sales, clerical, and service work. Strong-Boag also downplays the 1920s image of the sexually liberated flapper, maintaining an emphasis on the contradictory sexual expectations young women faced.

11 On this question, see also Angela Miles, 'Integrative Feminism,' *Fireweed: A Feminist Quarterly* 19 (Summer/Fall 1984), 55–81.

12 For essays on women and the state, see Heather Jon Maroney and Meg Luxton, eds, *Feminism and Political Economy: Women's Work, Women's Struggles* (Toronto 1987).

13 Lynne Segal, *Is the Future Female?* (London 1986).

14 On right-wing women in Canada, see Margrit Eichler, 'The Pro-Family Movement: Are They for or against Families?' *Feminist Perspectives*, no. 4a (Ottawa 1985); Karen Dubinsky, 'Lament for a "Patriarchy Lost"? Anti-Feminism, Anti-Abortion, and R.E.A.L. Women in Canada,' *Feminist Perspectives*, no 1 (Ottawa 1985). Right-wing groups also lend legitimacy to homophobia (fear and hatred of homosexuals).

Feminist Approaches to
Women in Politics

Jill McCalla Vickers

[We] must continue to insist on our right to participate fully in public life, but must at the same time challenge its very shape and underlying logic. – Angela Miles

Get into the game and stay in it ... Throwing mud from the outside won't help. Building up from the inside will. – Eleanor Roosevelt

In the past decade, *women-in-politics* has emerged as a research field in the English-speaking world. Most of the scholars involved are women and many are feminists. And yet, the influence of this field has been slight within the social sciences, within the women's movement, and within the male-dominated world of 'official' politics. There are several trends that seem destined to alter this situation. First, the women's movement has begun to mobilize around questions that require insights from feminist theories of politics. The question of why feminists should trust the state to undertake the censorship of pornography is one such question. Second, more than a decade of energetic work by feminist historians has begun to make our collective past more available to us so that we can better understand the dilemmas and choices of the suffrage and post-suffrage generations. Finally, the rise of the New Right with an analysis that makes issues of gender, the family, and the state central requires that we do more than react defensively. This rejuvenation of the old, cold-war political right, feeding on what we believed were 'our issues,' demonstrates the urgency of our task.

In this paper, I discuss feminist approaches to the subject of women in politics. The task is complicated by the fact that what I, and many other feminists, consider to be *political* does not square with either customary or disciplinary definitions of the political. In customary terms, politics is about elections and about the substance of political decision. In customary terms, most social movements are not understood to be political in nature, unless they end up running candidates or forming parties. The discipline of political science involves a focus on the institutions of the state, including bureaucracies, the judiciary, and so on, but is less concerned with the 'what' of policy than with the processes through which it is developed. Moreover, political science deals poorly with social movements that are attempting to reconceptualize the meaning of the political in radical ways. It accepts the existence of a demarcation between the private and the public that assigns the institutions of the state to the public realm and the institution of the family to the private realm. In short, political science continues to work within an outdated paradigm of the political that does not easily recognize what I will call women's politics as political at all.

From our perspective, feminist attempts to remove women's concerns from the private (natural, therefore inevitable) classification to the public (socially constructed, therefore subject to change by political action) classification are too important to be ignored or even muted by accepting either the customary or the disciplinary understandings of what is and what is not political. Methodologically we require *doubled vision*; that is, the capacity to view women's activities through more than one lens – or paradigm – at a time. The lens or paradigm from feminist theories, however, also involves distortions. The notion, for instance, that the personal is the political while central to our current political practice is too broad to guide our research efforts. Our current paradigm does not include feminist theories of citizenship, of the state, or of justice and, hence, does not offer theories of politics per se. If everything is construed to be political, nothing is non-political or private. In actual practice, most feminist theories do retain domains of privacy (the area of reproductive 'rights,' for example) while reassigning other domains (for example, violence against women in the home) to the public / political category. This fact suggests that a new conceptualization of what is political will eventually emerge. What we have now, however, is a set of questions and middle-range propositions from which we can begin to theorize about politics more broadly.

One example of the current state of feminist theorizing about women in politics is found in the debates about participation. Trying to make sense of their virtual absence from the corridors of power, feminists have approached the phenomenon from at least three distinct perspectives. Some have argued that women's ambiguity about power and state politics, and especially the pull to non-partisan movements, have kept women out.[1] Others have argued that women's efforts to participate have been blocked by structural barriers or a virtually unchanged division of reproductive labour.[2] Thelma McCormack's suggestion that there may be a distinctively female 'design for political living'[3] has led others to find women 'doing' politics in arenas previously unstudied and modes generally unrecognized as political.[4]

Even if we were able to demonstrate conclusively which of these arguments best accounts for the present state of affairs, we still would not be much further ahead, unless we had some view of what women *ought* to be doing in political life. Unless we can *locate* these perspectives within a broader framework, of, for example, a feminist theory of citizenship, we cannot tell if urging women to participate is productive or unproductive. Does our participation serve only to legitimize a political order in which women can never be agents on the same basis as men even if we double or triple the number of women in decision-making roles? Can our creation of alternate political modes ever successfully supplant the power politics of the state? Such questions point to the need for feminist theories that take account of the realities of the state and its coercive power, and of the realities of women's lives, past and present.

In this paper, I undertake four basic tasks. First, I examine some historical perspectives on women in politics in Canada. Second, I examine some perspectives drawn from second-wave feminist theories. Third, I explore several contemporary empirical approaches. Finally, I attempt to outline some of the questions we must address to move to the broader feminist framework we require.

PERSPECTIVES ON OUR COLLECTIVE PAST

Our political past, like our political future, is contested ground. The ideological contest to shape and define the meaning of what has happened to women in politics since suffrage has heated up considerably, especially in the United States where the defeat of the Equal Rights Amendment (ERA) and the successes of the New Right have led to acrimonious debates[5] concerning the 'true' feminist meaning of equality.[6]

In Canada, too, our estimation of the success or failure of our suffrage foremothers' choices in politics has been based on our beliefs concerning what women in politics ought to be doing. And our beliefs are drawn from our feminist theories as much as, or perhaps more than, from our society's views of democracy and good citizenship. The fact that our foremothers also worked with some explicit theories about women in politics is worth recalling.

In this discussion I am interested in feminist theory as a potential guide to what I will call, for the moment unproblematically, *political life*.[7] The question of how women ought to act in political life has been problematic to feminists in Canada. The tension between independence and partisanship is viewed by Sylvia Bashevkin as the central dilemma that has limited anglophone women's effective exercise of political power.[8] Bashevkin traces this tension to the ideological pivot of *social* feminism, which, she believes, 'elevated Protestant social reform above demands for legal emancipation and claimed that the granting of the vote to women was essential for general social improvement.'[9] This desire for broad social reform led to a feminist view of politics in which the evils of the existing political structures were to be reformed by the presence of women acting as a purifying influence. It is common now to believe that this theory of politics was 'naïve' or 'sentimentalist.'[10] And yet, in significant ways, the goals of social and political reform that women set for themselves were coherent with their theory.

Women's early political causes included lobbying for everything from clean milk to public education, organizing women into trade unions and peace groups, and voting distinctively for temperance and against war.[11] These activities stemmed from a concept of service performed by women without seriously challenging the private / public split or women's privatization in their home. Women would go into the public realm but the private realm of home and family was to remain intact, none the less. Women's right to participate in the public realm was claimed to allow them to fulfil their obligations. Hence, from a modern feminist perspective, their views show an unresolved tension between rights and obligations.

It is important for us to extract from the suffrage generation their sense of the political, their conceptions of participation, and their comprehension of the processes of political change. Veronica Strong-Boag has identified three major lines of feminist interpretation of the activities of the suffrage generation.[12] First, she identifies the Bacchi view that castigates suffragists for their social reform activities, which make them seem to be conservative defenders of privilege rather than feminists. In this view, first-wave, middle-class feminism failed because it didn't deserve to survive. The second line of analysis identified suggests that 'suffrage was necessary and that its advocates were decent enough people but that it and feminism in general were oversold and died of an acute case of disillusionment.'[13] The third line of analysis is associated with Linda Kealey and Joan Sangster, who argue that radical women attempted to inject a gender analysis into class politics with varying degrees of success. Strong-Boag herself advances a fourth view informed by her research relating to rural prairie women. She argues that these women were excluded from decision-making power and that, lacking a strong tradition of looking to public politics for solutions to their problems, most proceeded to discuss and 'do' politics in arenas apart from and independent of the public world of male politics.

Again, it is clear that a strategy of doubled vision is required. Relying on evidence of women's visible presence in male-created and male-controlled political institutions involves a misleading understanding of political life if we would understand the political lives of our foremothers. We must also look at their participation in community-based groups and organizations where a voluntaristic tradition of politics flourished. The political is not a category fixed for all times in our society. Nor does it involve activities located only in formal political institutions, which direct their interests to the most powerful levels of the state. None the less, the dominant political culture, with its definition of the political, was established by men and has been made to seem 'natural' with the benefit of formal political institutions, laws, and practices that are largely self-perpetuating. Alternative political cultures created by women may be muted and certainly lack the legitimizing institutions men created before women entered the scene. To construct viable feminist theories of politics we must assess whether these alternate modes of doing politics were positive and deliberate creations, or a matter of making a virtue of necessity.

There are, then, a number of conflicting accounts of suffragist women's views of political life. Some of the *questions* we will need to ask in order to construct feminist theories of politics suitable for our own era are already apparent; others are more obscure. Moreover, few of the accounts we have explored to this point take note of the changing nature of political life itself, let alone the changing capacities of women to be involved in it.

First-wave feminism worked with a theory of politics that placed a high value on citizenship but in which claims to it rested as often on perceived obligations as on abstract theories of rights. In their actions, many of these feminists clearly believed in a norm of *service* that involved the Christian duty to help others and in the concepts of self-help and community building. Their views of power and its corruptions are also well known, but, in my view, it would be an error to see them distastefully avoiding political life because they believed that machine politics and liquor-related bossism had corrupted the political institutions men had built. Many viewed it as their obligation to throw the mantle of womanly values over the corruptions of male-created politics.

One further 'view from the past' worthy of our attention is the explicit treatment of the effects of marriage and motherhood on women's abilities to participate in political life. Many Canadian suffragists believed that mothers would be *better citizens* than their menfolk, who were less connected with the altruistic concerns that nurturing fostered. This view existed in an era in which political life was rarely a *professional* affair even for men. The high evaluation of ordinary citizenship went along with an age of largely 'amateur' or citizen politicians. The expansion of state activity and power changed this view, and politics became more and more a profession with limited room for amateurs.[14] But the activities of the average married woman in her community did not run to a profession in political life.

In the first post-suffrage cohort, service and celibacy, long an option for Catholic women, opened a new arena for women to achieve change in the increasingly professionalized social services. Charlotte Whitton's career and ideas illuminate the framework within which, it was then presumed, 'the special force of womanhood – motherly feeling – may be forced into public work.'[15] Whitton represented a new figure in the Protestant tradition of women and public service – the secular, celibate, and unmarried woman. Whitton believed such women bore the 'responsibility for leadership and education of public life.'[16] In Whitton's mind, marriage could not be chosen without motherhood and to her the married woman's involvement in professional politics and professional social service alike would always be half-hearted and limited by divided loyalties and divided energies. She saw her new class of women married to social service and dedicating its energies to thousands of families. Whitton's thesis was that only unmarried women could be involved in political and social life in a fully committed and professional way because they shared married women's 'motherly feelings' but were free to actualize them in public life with singular resolve.

Whitton, herself, was rather scathing about women's 'amateur' efforts in politics. Although her views reflected the conflict of interests between the married and unmarried middle-class women technically 'available' for political work and social service, they also reflected the significant changes that had occurred within Whitton's lifetime in both politics and social service. Both were becoming increasingly professionalized, bureaucratized, and centralized. The *service* to which Whitton dedicated herself now involved a full-time occupation, a professional degree, and a high level of energy and commitment. The helping services, which formed the practical basis of the welfare state, grew out of the 'good works' undertaken earlier by 'amateur' or non-professional women. In rural areas and small centres, however, the older amateur tradition survived, as did the role of religious celibates in Catholic communities. In politics, too, professionalism relegated the 'amateur' to the less powerful arenas and married women's opportunities were affected.

The state addressed by suffrage-era women was vastly less complex than the state we face today. The conceptions of politics held were correspondingly simpler. The vote and the right to exercise it properly seemed like powerful weapons prior to even the modest development and centralization of federal powers during the First World War. Theories of citizenship and of public service were advanced by suffragists primarily in terms of duties, not of rights. That these women's focus was heavily on the improvement of their own communities is hardly surprising in an era of painfully slow and primitive transportation and communication. Not only women but also men cared far less what happened in Ottawa or the provincial capitals until the state at those levels was connected by an exercise of powers to the public life of their communities. It is, of course, to this more complex, more centralized, and more powerful state that we, as second-wave feminists, must respond.

This discussion of our foremothers' views, about which we still know far too little, was intended to highlight a set of themes valuable in framing our debate. Those themes stem in the first place from the very terms of what I temporarily declared unproblematic earlier: political life.

Much contemporary feminist theory revolves around discussion of the private/public split in our society. The terms private and public, however, are difficult to capture. Both are historical concepts that change over time. The private sphere, for example, appears to be captured by the terms domestic and familial, and yet our society talks about private enterprise, which, from the perspective of women, goes on in the public sphere. The terms private life and privacy represent liberalism's view of the limited role its adherents believe the state should have in intimate, domestic matters.

Feminism, whether suffrage-era or second-wave, has tended to support the enlargement of the realm labelled 'public.' If suffrage-era women lacked a strong tradition of looking to formal politics for a resolution of their dilemmas, they had developed instead a strong tradition of looking to *informal community* politics. This tradition of a public but sub-state focus, far from being displaced in recent decades, continues to run parallel to a tradition of increasing support for state-level intervention.

A second theme that emerges is a *service-based* conception of what is involved in political life. Although some contemporary feminist observers are frequently vexed that women have been slow to advance their own political interests within the framework of a theory of rights and entitlements, the older values of duties and responsibilities and the norms of self-help survive.

A third theme is the contradiction between mother-citizens and the demands of political participation at the highly professionalized level of élite decision makers. Instead of working to reconstruct formal political institutions in ways that would permit the continued involvement in decision making by ordinary citizens (citizen courts and office-sharing, for example) post-suffrage women 'solved' the contradiction by remaining celibate or by creating their own grass-roots organizations that made doable demands on their time, lack of mobility, and resources. The character of these organizations (Women's Institutes, for example) has only begun to be explored in detail[17] but suggests that, at both the community and state levels, they provided an arena for political debate and a conduit for political pressure more authentic and meaningful for many women than political parties. In short, women whose circumstances precluded a professional political role nevertheless created organizations adaptable to their life circumstances in which they exercised leadership and engaged in their own form of political discourse informed by domestic and community needs and values.

This brief overview highlights three things. First, while access to formal political institutions was undoubtedly limited both by male hostility and by women's jaundiced views of political life, women's belief in the power of the vote was not 'naïve' in the context of their point of entry. That most women gave little thought to the problems of combining marriage, motherhood, and politics is not surprising in an era of largely amateur citizen-politicians. Second, the option of secular celibacy and a professional career in public life was recognized as legitimate and women's struggles to gain access to higher education and work in the professions supported it as a choice. Third, the tradition of looking to the community for solutions to problems rather than to the state was as much a societal phenomenon as a female disability.

POLITICS AND THE SECOND WAVE: YOU CAN'T GET THERE FROM HERE

What feminist approaches to women in politics emerged in the second wave of the women's movement? First, there were approaches advocated in feminist theories. Second, there were approaches that guided our political practice. In reality, the two were more linked than distinct as new experience-based modes of theorizing emerged.

In this discussion, I am concerned with what feminist theories have to say about women in politics and about the nature of politics. Three themes mark the period: separation, integration, and transformation. Contesting for our attention were theories that argued for a women's politics separate from the inevitably oppressive, patriarchal state, that argued for the integration of women into the politics of the state and existing political parties and movements, and that argued for the need to transform political structures and processes so that women's participation could be authentic and effective.

The three basic traditions of second-wave theory – radical, liberal, and leftist feminisms – offer fewer explicit guides to our subject than do the political practices each has developed. Moreover, these tendencies in our practice were not written on blank slates. Although few of us were familiar with the theories and practices of our suffrage-era foremothers, most of the initiators of the second wave were already politically active and their views reflected prior experiences.

The motive force for most North American women in that first cohort was our experience within other liberation movements. We experienced 'the contradiction of working in a freedom movement but not being very free.'[18] We conceptualized what had previously been understood as private travails as part of a political system of oppression – a system as much experienced within liberation movements as within the society these movements aimed to change. The verity of our conclusion was reinforced for us through the political method of consciousness-raising in small, homogeneous groups. Through this process, we constructed a conception of politics drawn from shared experiences and captioned in the premise 'the personal is political.'

This dissolving of the traditional boundaries between the personal or domestic and the political expressed a 'need for a total politics.' We rejected the proposition held by other movements of which we were (or had been) part that our 'issues' were secondary to, or simply manifestations of, some 'greater' oppressions. We resisted the incorporation of women and women's issues into pre-existing frameworks and organizations. Finally, in our separation we adopted a radical egalitarianism and created groups that rejected the hierarchies, bureaucracies, and professional leadership we attributed to malestream political organizations.

Now you may quite properly be asking 'who is this we?' Is this the gospel according to United States radical feminism or were we also thinking this way in Canada? It is not, in fact, my purpose to examine in this section the empirical facts of Canadian women's political choices at the beginning of the second wave. Rather I will try to outline the political theory that underlay the second great movement of women in this century.

All second-wave feminists have had to respond to the approach of radical feminist political practice. The integration theme, which follows from both Marxist and liberal theories of politics, has been constantly subject to the radical feminist questioning of the efficacy of integrating women into male-defined and male-controlled political frameworks and organizations. Because radical feminist theory demands that women's politics must be based on our specificity, our sexuality, and our role in both physical and social reproduction, the integration of women *on the same basis as men* into existing political structures has also always been accepted as a problematic goal by liberal and leftist feminists. This view has produced a greatly radicalized form of liberal feminism.[19] The picture for leftist feminists is less clear. Certainly the concept of the struggle within the struggle existed earlier and was developed elsewhere without the spur of radical feminist theory. None the less, except in the most orthodox leftist organizations, the substance of the concept of a struggle based on women's sexual and reproductive specificity has been informed by the radical feminist agenda until quite recently.[20]

In short, the political challenge radical feminism represented meant, as Angela Miles has argued, a recognition that 'feminists whose practice is built on a rejection rather than a revaluation of femaleness cannot consciously articulate an alternative, integrative vision rooted in the female-associated values.'[21] Radical feminism, however, although the catalyst that focused our dream of an authentic women's politics, could not provide us with a detailed guide to political life that would transform our world. It certainly wasn't a call to violent revolution and no vision emerged of the sort of political order that would achieve its goals. There are reasons both of theoretical formulation and of organization that help explain women's collective past. But the most fundamental is the conception of the state simply as an artefact of male dominance with little real comprehension of either its character or its power.

Radical feminists, cut off from a knowledge of their collective past, shared no sense of continuity with the history of women's community politics of getting things done. The rather crude conception of politics simply as a coercive instrument serving only the purpose of permitting one group to control the other meant, in fact, that we had bought into a male-generated conception of politics in which the concepts of community and service were cynically manipulated. Those radical feminists who projected all the negative characteristics of politics onto male nature abandoned any hope of a transformation to a shared political life. What is more, the declaration that the personal is political does far more than redefine the boundary between the private and the public; it abolishes it. It leads away from any sense of political action to achieve change but also suggests no limits on political action or state intervention.[22]

Radical feminist organizations were ill fitted to manipulate the political system. And the success of social movements ultimately depends on their organizational abilities to manipulate the political system to get their issues and reconceptualizations heard and legitimized.[23] The stance of total separatism and the limitations of collectivist organizations in sustaining co-ordinated action over time and especially over wide geographic distances militated against such groups playing this role. None the less, radical feminists generated many grass-roots projects conceived as an amalgam of consciousness-raising, political organizing, and theoretical development.[24] This creativity and mobilizing power, moreover, has in no sense been exhausted. As the recent work around pornography and incest suggests, the project of creating a political agenda out of our examination of women's experiences remains a powerful, if flawed technique. Despite the fundamental importance of radical feminism to the creation of an authentic transformative women's politics, however, it is increasingly apparent that its edict of separatism is no better as a guide than the edict that women must simply become integrated on the same basis as men into existing political frameworks and movements.

The theme of transcendence, of rejecting separation and integration alike, is the hardest to capture in this analysis. But Angela Miles's notion of *integrative* feminism comes the closest in theoretical terms. Miles argues that radical feminism cannot be a complete politics and cannot alone guide us to a complete politics because it is ultimately a 'reactive negation' of what is, rather than a blueprint for transcendence. It is from our practice, political or scholarly, that she conceptualizes integrative feminism as a possible guide to a complete politics.

Not enough research has been done at this point to 'ground' my intuition that, in our political practice, we have begun to escape the trap of either separatism or integration. This view can only be an intuition based on participant observation, because we have only begun to explore the ways in which Canadian women try to resolve this tension or contradiction in their own political lives. Miles's suggestive analysis of integrative feminism and such research on our practice as now exists suggest the character of our efforts at transformation. What Sylvia Bashevkin has identified as a *tension* between autonomy and partisanship can also be understood as a tension between separatism and integration. It is a tension that I would argue exists – but not primarily in terms of self-contained streams within the women's movement in Canada. Rather, for many women, it is an internal tension. It is also primarily a tension within organizations in Canada rather than between organizations.

Miles suggests that integrative feminists, motivated by a vision of feminism as a potentially complete politics, are capable of undertaking united action with feminists of different partisan and theoretical orientations. The women interviewed for the women's participation in political life project frequently displayed a *doubled vision* in which they could express the positive value of the 'tension' in their own political activities by seeing value in their own autonomous women-led groups and also in their participation in traditional political structures.[25] If, in fact, the tendencies to both autonomy and integration exist within large numbers of women and organizations, the results could be a transcendence through women's own organizational arrangements and by the demands women make on existing political structures.

At the organizational level, the highly attractive grass-roots groups allow any woman to create her own mode of political competence, however technically limited her resources. The homogeneity of such groups, however, is a major drawback of their character and mobilizing capacity. In addition, we have created heterogeneous political structures that permit the conjoining of energetic small groups, internally dedicated to the political norms of radical feminism, in nation-wide action on specific issues. The motive for sustaining such alliances or umbrella structures is our desire to achieve tangible impacts on the politics of the state. This suggests that the Canadian women's movement is motivated by a desire to participate fully in public life while still challenging 'its very shape and underlying logic.'

In practical terms, how do women manage this apparently impossible juggling act? On the one hand, contemporary feminists are recognizing the need to enter some of the centres from which men exercise institutionalized power. As Iris Marion Young comments: 'Feminists cannot undermine masculinist values without entering some of the centers of power that fosters them ... [otherwise it] can only be a moral position of critique rather than a force for institutional change.'[26]

On the other hand, feminists have created many umbrella groups that link together thousands of small groups both to construct an autonomous politics of women interacting with one another as women and to transmit the insights and energies generated in small groups to the traditional political stage. These umbrella groups designed for coalition formation, public education, and lobbying display more 'normal' or traditional organizational characteristics: some internal hierarchy, leadership individuals, and bureaucratization and professionalization. As a result, the participation costs are higher than in the grass-roots groups but still possible for a rotating contingent from the grass roots.[27] This capacity to create coalition behaviour *within* umbrella organizations capable of significantly affecting the agendas of traditional politics suggests that the tension between separation or autonomy and integration or partisanship can be creative and productive rather than a source of weakness as is often supposed.

Far more research into the nature of women's politics as an autonomous activity would be required to determine the likely future path of the groups and organizations created in the second wave of feminism. Our current political practice as women is suggestive. First, it is clear that women's politics – that is, the politics women create in autonomous organizations, whether small-group collectives or umbrella groups – is as crucial as women's behaviour in the conventional politics of the state. Feminist approaches require a knowledge of women's politics to evaluate the changes needed to allow women to participate in all aspects of political life as women. By examining how we structure political life to suit ourselves when we are free to do so, we can identify the ways in which traditional institutions would have to be altered to allow women to be 'integrated' without loss of those essential values that constitute our specificity.

EMPIRICAL APPROACHES: YOU CAN'T COUNT
WHAT YOU CAN'T SEE

In 1981, Joni Lovenduski wrote: 'In what is one of the minor tragedies of contemporary scholarship, an absorption of a rather constrained branch of women's studies [women-in-politics] by a one-dimensional academic discipline [political science] has taken place.'[28] Feminist scholarship made a late appearance in political science. The discipline itself staggers under the harmful split between American-style 'scientific' empiricism and normative political theory, which emerged in the cold-war environment of the 1950s. In this context, feminist approaches within political science have tended to concentrate on exposing sexism in the discipline's 'sacred texts' and gathering new data within the categories ordained by the dominant paradigm: political behaviour, especially voting frequencies and attitudes; women in political élites, or rather their absence; some analyses of how politics affects women in a general 'status-of-women' framework; and some policy analysis concerning 'women's issues.'

The vibrant feminist work in political theory (Mary O'Brien, Jean Bethke Elshtain, Zillah Eisenstein, and Nancy Hartsock are only four towering examples) largely exists outside the discipline and has little impact within it. The dominant paradigm and its methodological edicts pose a formidable barrier to the development of feminist approaches, although the emergence of the concept of the gender gap suggests that there are some openings to be exploited even within the formidable armour of political science.

In Canada, feminist political scientists have not yet managed to challenge the theoretical and methodological barriers within the discipline to create distinctively feminist approaches to women in politics. Their work contributes in important ways to our understanding of women in conventional political structures such as parties, but it does not yet provide the basis to challenge the discipline's patriarchal character. The discipline, however, is beginning to be aware that the absence of women from élite-level, decision-making bodies requires study and, even if 'you can't count what you can't see,' that you may be required to 'see' or take note of what you can't count.

The dominant approach to the subject of women in politics within political science is best described as the *normal integration model*. It proceeds from the proposition that, over time, women will become integrated into the various arenas of official politics on the same basis as men. The approach leads to a search for barriers to women's integration; psychological, situational, and structural barriers have been explored by various authors to explain the continued marginalization of women in political life. This approach assumes either that there is nothing intrinsic in the nature of liberal-democratic political systems to keep women out on a permanent basis or that any barriers now existing can and will be overcome through the pressure of the increased presence of women in the system.

Gender-gap analysis, which has emerged in the United States, has not been much developed in Canada. The evidence suggests the existence in Canada of attitudinal gender gaps, but it has been argued that these are rarely translatable into electoral gender gaps. Gender-gap analysis, by focusing on the potential electoral leverage of a women's movement that can mobilize votes, is a distinctive feminist approach that does not challenge basic political science norms. It is also part of the normal integration approach because it is assumed that newly integrated groups of voters will gain leverage if they vote as a bloc.

In English Canada, most feminist political scientists have worked within the normal integration approach.[29] Some have also voiced questions that point to the need for alternate approaches which will treat women's political activities as sui generis and develop insights that come from comparing women with one another and comprehending the possibility that women may not want simply to be integrated or may not be, as a mass, integratable.

The normal integration approach reflects and is compatible with the norm of *role equity* within the political system. It does not raise the issue of transforming the political system itself. In fact, it assumes there is something called 'the status of women,' which is syndrome-like in the sense that improvements in one or several variables will result in improvements in political participation. By contrast, Joni Lovenduski demonstrates that it is the characteristics of specific political systems as much as 'the status of women' that permits or inhibits the 'integration' of women into their formal structures: the question is more a matter of mobilization than of integration.[30] Her European data show women less likely to be present in the conventional political arena than men but more involved in the less conventional political arenas of ad hoc politics, community-action movements, peace movements, protest politics, and even terrorist actions. These data may reflect an irremediable inability on the part of existing political institutions to mobilize women effectively across a variety of states. The information also points to the importance of institution building for women's movements so that the mobilization of women over the long haul of a number of generations can be achieved.

Feminist theorists have been little interested in the empirically based explanations for the limited participation of women beyond voting in the formal politics of the state. And yet these approaches do outline the mechanics of male dominance in public policy making that are useful in our task of assessing political strategies. Canadian approaches have focused almost exclusively on the channels of numerical representation: legislatures, elections to them, and the parties that organize the elections. At least four other channels need consideration: agencies of interest representation, institutions of administration, the judiciary, and institutions of enforcement.

The normal integration approach, therefore, can generate information concerning the barriers to women's participation, the capacity of specific institutions to mobilize women, and the channels of participation least resistant to women's involvement. What it cannot do, however, is to generate insights concerning the characteristics of women's politics on its own ground. To pursue Miles's vision of transformation, which retains the positive elements of women's specificity, an approach is required that focuses on women's politics and the norms of women's political culture.

A women's politics approach faces several major handicaps in the current context. First, it requires methods of research quite different from those employed in the integration approach. Women active in women's politics at the grass-roots level are harder to locate than leaders, voters, or aspiring politicians. Working in small all-women, or women-led groups, they are often suspicious of researchers and hostile to 'normal' research methods. Qualitative research methods are required to lay the basis for a profile of activity in women's politics and such methods are expensive and time consuming. None the less, the women's politics approach has already produced insights that illuminate both the reasons women are inhibited in male-centred political institutions and the reasons they are empowered in groups of their own making.[31]

Specifically, women face high participation costs in structured settings that require consistent, geographically distant, and often ritualistic activity.[32] By contrast, the structures women create for themselves permit (indeed are built on the assumption of) sporadic outbursts of activity interspersed with periods of inactivity according to family and work demands.[33] In addition, acts of conventional politics may be surrounded by anxiety and the fear of job loss, loss of housing, and loss of emotional support.[34] That some women perceive that they will be punished even for low-level conventional political acts puts the question of where women should 'go' politically into a different context. These examples of the insights to be gained from a women's politics approach suggest the importance of its further development.

A MUGWUMP MANIFESTO: SOME QUESTIONS
FOR A FEMINIST THEORY OF POLITICS

A mugwump, as the popular press has recently reminded us, is someone with her mug on one side of the fence and her wump on the other. Sitting on the fence is not widely considered a good thing. Perhaps the notion of a doubled vision is less unpleasant. We are, I believe, a long way from conclusively settling the integration / separation debate. We are a long way from determining whether the integration of women qua women is possible, let alone whether it is desirable. We are a long way from understanding what the distinctive characteristics of women's politics are and what sorts of concrete changes in existing political systems would be necessary for women to participate, as women, in political life. Nevertheless, like our suffrage foremothers, we must make choices in the here and now despite our ambiguities and mugwumpish inclinations.

The approaches examined in this paper suggest a number of questions that could form the basis for a more coherent feminist theory of politics and of women's roles in politics. They are questions that we will not find easy to answer and our tentative answers will provoke conflict, but they must be posed if we are, in political life and in research, to move to the next plateau of understanding.

The first question emerging from our examination of feminist approaches to women in politics is the question of the state itself. Second-wave feminists display a profoundly contradictory view of the state. On the one hand, we have the view that 'the state is male in that objectivity is its norm.'[35] On the other hand, most feminists look to the state for the policies and programs we demand. The question of where women should go in terms of politics depends, in part, on some resolution of our ambiguous views of the state.

One central question we must ask is whether we believe the state can ever be transformed into either a neutral agency for the common good or one in which there can be a balance of power between male and female interests. We know that the state as now constructed isn't the neutral agency of liberal theory. But we also know in practice that it enjoys sufficient autonomy to be responsive in some contexts to feminist demands. The answer to this basic question is far from clear. But it would help us to determine if we want to be 'inside' or to remain 'outside,' exercising whatever leverage we have but resolutely refusing to legitimize institutions we believe can never be satisfactorily transformed.

The analyses of Bashevkin and Lovenduski remind us that we must keep in mind the specific structuring of our state in exploring this question. For example, gender-gap or non-partisan strategies may be possible in some state structures but useless in others. We must understand that long-established structural arrangements express and protect the biases within the state. If we conclude that the transformation of the nature of the state is a useful project, we must also recall that seemingly eternal structural arrangements are human creations, subject to change. If we believe that the state cannot be transformed, however, we must work to outline alternate arrangements for its basic functions based on a deeper knowledge of women's politics and its norms.

The second basic set of questions we must consider deals with the character of women's specificity. Most feminists accept the view that the enduring characteristics of women's lives constituting that specificity revolve around sexuality and reproduction. These are elements that may give us a different view on some political matters and that constitute one major barrier to women simply being integrated into the political system constructed by men. Many feminists have assumed that the barriers to women's fuller participation in public life are socially constructed, not intrinsic or natural. Two philosophies of public life have been explored in this paper. The older one was based on concepts of service, duty, and responsibility. The newer one is based on concepts of rights, entitlements, and claims made vis-à-vis society and the state. We need to connect our own specificity to these two philosophies of citizenship and participation.

If we are to continue to be responsible for social reproduction, even jointly with men, can our philosophy of citizenship and participation be based simply on a self-interest framework of rights claims? In Norway, with the best record among the liberal democracies for the involvement of women in politics, the philosophical basis for women's role was the *duty* to share responsibility for public decision making and service. These questions point to the need for theories of citizenship that comprehend responsibilities based on our specificity as well as rights claims based on our commonalities with men. This proposition that we should, as feminists, view women in public life from the sense of the ways in which we both differ from, and are the same as, men is the basis from which we can move to a new theory of justice that comprehends both equality and equity, sameness and difference. Such a view suggests that we must explore more fully the question of *why* women should be involved in politics in various arenas: the politics of the state, of the community, of the workplace, or of women's politics. The suffrage-era answer was that we had something specific to represent and a responsibility to take our values into the public realm. The contemporary answer is often that we have claims to make and rights to advance. To this mugwump *both* motivations seem necessary in our approaches to women and politics.

A third major set of questions I believe we must explore deals with the nature of political institutions and our views of them. I consider political institutions to be structures that survive and pursue coherent goals over time and space.[36] Mary O'Brien, in her brilliant work *The Politics of Reproduction*, argued that men created institutions because they could not be connected to biological time through reproduction.[37] Although perhaps not intended, this insight has led to the conclusion that women have no need of institutions intrinsically and inevitably marked by the tendencies of hierarchy and dominance. Radical feminist political practice attempted to build groups that would refute Michel's 'iron law of oligarchy'[38] by explicitly rejecting leadership, bureaucracy, and professionalism. Many feminist political scientists have recapitulated Michel's perspective by demonstrating that such unstructured groups either don't survive over time, or cannot achieve the co-ordination over geographic distances needed to mount political campaigns even within the realm of women's politics.[39]

Our political practice leads me to be less pessimistic, as the discussion earlier shows. None the less, we must explicitly take hold of the questions concerning institutions, whether we believe women's politics or the politics of the state is the prime arena of concern. This does not mean that we must simply imitate the institutions men have created or be integrated into them. As I have suggested, our political practice, carefully examined, provides important clues about how we can devise institutions of our own making or develop a blueprint for the modification of those made by men.

The point, then, in this mugwumpish summary, is our need to retain our doubled vision until our approaches to women in politics are more informed, both by the history of our collective past and by a fuller understanding of our own political practice. If Angela Miles's vision of an integrative feminism attracts us, we must deepen feminist approaches to women in politics by explicitly addressing these hard questions.

NOTES

1 See, for example, Sylvia B. Bashevkin, *Toeing the Lines: Women and Party Politics in English Canada* (Toronto 1985). While Bashevkin does not reject the existence of barriers to women's participation, she identifies the tension between independence and partisanship as a 'longstanding dilemma.'

2 See M. Janine Brodie, *Women and Politics in Canada* (Toronto 1985), and Janine Brodie and Jill Vickers, *Canadian Women in Politics: An Overview*, CRIAW Papers no. 2 (Ottawa 1982).

3 See Thelma McCormack, 'Toward a Nonsexist Perspective on Social and Politi-

cal Change,' in M. Millman and R.M. Kanter, eds, *Another Voice* (New York 1975), 1–33.

4 See Anne Firor Scott, 'On Seeing and Not Seeing: A Case of Historical Invisibility,' *Journal of American History* 71:1 (June 1984), 17–21. My thanks to Angela Miles for bringing this to my attention.

5 In particular, Zillah Eisenstein's attacks on Jean Bethke Elshtain (and Elshtain's on Eisenstein) suggest that the United States movement's capacity to develop integrative feminism is far less than the Canadian movement's at the moment.

6 Jean Bethke Elshtain, 'Feminist Discourse and its Discontents: Language, Power and Meaning,' *Signs* 7:3 (Spring 1982), 617.

7 Obviously what constitutes political life is as problematic as what constitutes the political. I will develop some aspects of this problem in a later section.

8 Bashevkin, *Toeing the Lines*, 3–33.

9 Ibid., 7.

10 Elshtain, 'Feminist Discourse and Its Discontents,' 617. Elshtain, of course, is not alone in this judgment.

11 Scott, 'On Seeing and Not Seeing.'

12 Veronica Strong-Boag, 'Pulling in Double Harness or Hauling a Double Load: Women, Work and Feminism on the Canadian Prairie,' *Journal of Canadian Studies* 21:3 (Fall 1986), 32–52.

13 Strong-Boag, 'Pulling in Double Harness,' 33. The view is attributed to John Thompson and Allen Seager, *Canada 1922–1939: Decades of Discord* (Toronto 1985).

14 The changing nature of the politician's role has been paid little attention in political science. P.T. Rooke and R.L. Schnell in *No Bleeding Heart: Charlotte Whitton, a Feminist on the Right* (Vancouver 1987) capture quite sharply Whitton's sense that the time for the married women amateurs was past.

15 P.T. Rooke and R.L. Schnell, 'Chasity as Power: Charlotte Whitton and the Ascetic Ideal,' *The American Review of Canadian Studies* 15:4 (Winter 1985), 389.

16 Ibid.

17 Jo Freeman, 'The Women's Liberation Movement: Its Origins, Organizations, Activities and Ideas,' in *Women: A Feminist Perspective*, ed. Jo Freeman (Palo Alto, CA, 1979), and Gwen Matheson, ed., *Women in the Canadian Mosaic* (Toronto 1976), have been useful here. See also *Canadian Woman Studies / Les cahiers de la femme* 7:4 (Winter 1986).

18 Freeman, 'The Women's Liberation Movement,' 559.

19 I find Zillah R. Eisenstein's *The Radical Future of Liberal Feminism* (New York 1981) quite persuasive on this point. I recently reread *The Report of the Royal Commission on the Status of Women* through Eisenstein's 'eyes' and found her thesis generally valid for this key document of Canadian liberal feminism.

20 The pornography / censorship debate is an important watershed in this regard. It is also probable that a more deeply researched analysis would reveal a more complex picture than I have painted here. None the less, I believe the general thrust of my argument will be sustained.

21 Angela Miles, 'Integrative Feminism,' *Fireweed: A Feminist Quarterly* 9 (Summer/Fall 1984), 57.

22 Jean Bethke Elshtain has suggested that there is a fascist or totalitarian tendency in the radical feminist formulation of a boundaryless politics. Although technically correct in terms of political theory, her analysis ignores the absence of any formulation of a plan to capture the state to implement the boundaryless politics implied in 'the personal is the political.' The censorship-of-pornography issue raises the point in a pragmatic way, revealing that some radical feminists would trust even a male-dominated state rather easily.

23 Myra Marx Ferree and Beth B. Hess, *Controversy and Coalition: The New Feminist Movement* (Boston 1985), 116. My thanks to student Roxanne Cooligan for calling this source to my attention.

24 Miles, 'Integrative Feminism,' 60.

25 *Women's Involvement in Political Life: A Pilot Study*, CRIAW Papers no. 16/17 (Ottawa 1987).

26 Iris Marion Young, 'Humanism, Gynocentrism and Feminist Politics,' *Women's Studies International Forum* 8:3 (1985), 182. Again my thanks to Roxanne Cooligan for bringing this source to my attention in her excellent paper 'An Integrative Feminist Analysis of Radical Feminist Organization.'

27 See Christine Appelle, 'The New Parliament of Women,' MA diss., Institute of Canadian Studies, Carleton University, 1987.

28 Joni Lovenduski, 'Toward the Emasculation of Political Science' in Dale Spender, ed., *Men's Studies Modified* (Oxford 1982), 83.

29 Bashevkin, Brodie, Black and Glen, Burt, and Vickers have all begun their work within this approach.

30 See Joni Lovenduski, *Women and European Politics: Contemporary Feminism and Public Policy* (Amherst, MA 1986).

31 My key source is the CRIAW/UNESCO project, *Women's Participation in Public Life: A Pilot Study*, conducted in 1985–6.

32 The concept of participation costs can be very useful in examining the sorts of structures that inhibit or facilitate the political participation of women (or other marginalized groups).

33 See CRIAW, *Women's Participation*, passim. Demands for consistent activity over time characterized the more structured groups and tended to inhibit participation more than for groups based on the 'do what you can, when you can' premise.

34 Ibid., passim. These interviews revealed fears for loss of public housing, loss of employment (secretaries not bosses), and loss of emotional support from spouses

as costs for very conventional political acts, such as putting up a sign, wearing a button or T-shirt, seeking time off to attend a political meeting, signing a petition, or joining a demonstration. The fact that women are more vulnerable to loss for even low-level, conventional political acts is an important discovery.

35 C. Mackinnon, 'Feminism, Marxism, Method and the State: An Agenda for Theory,' *Signs* 7:3 (Spring 1982), 543.

36 I have found the work of Mary Douglas useful in developing my perspective on institutions; see esp. *How Institutions Think* (Syracuse 1986).

37 I am not prepared to assume this meant that women created no institutions defined as structures that can survive and pursue coherent goals over time and space. I do agree with O'Brien that most, if not all, institutions in state societies in historical time are male-controlled and probably male-created. Douglas's view of institutions suggests to me that they were and are a key part of the technology of patriarchy.

38 Joreen's 'The Tyranny of Structurelessness,' in *Radical Feminism*, ed. by Anne Koedt, Ellen Levine, and Anita Rapone (New York 1972), 285–99 and Kathy E. Ferguson, *The Feminist Case against Bureaucracy* (Philadelphia 1984) represent the two sides of the 'iron-law' argument quite well. Michel's argument, of course, based on European left-wing organizations, was that the tendency to hierarchy, control of information by an élite, etc. were inevitably features of groups despite explicit commitment to anti-élitist ideology.

39 See, for example, Joyce Rothschild-Whitt, 'The Collective Organization: An Alternative to Rational-Bureaucratic Models,' *American Sociological Review* 44 (August 1979), 509–27.

PART TWO

Canadian Women and the Old Parties

'A Noble Effort'

The National Federation
of Liberal Women of Canada
1928–1973

Patricia A. Myers

In April 1928, the National Federation of Liberal Women of Canada began auspiciously as over 500 women attended its founding meeting.[1] The event had been long in coming: almost five years before, in June 1923, the Ottawa Women's Liberal Club ordered the formation of a committee to study the possibility of a national federation affiliated with the Liberal party. The federation would consist of a national executive elected at national conventions, of provincial and regional associations, and of local or constituency clubs. Cairine Wilson, who had headed the Advisory Council of the National Federation of Women's Liberal Clubs, an organization that preceded the national federation, accepted the tributes of the Rt Hon. W.L. Mackenzie King, who called the federation a truly 'noble effort.'

It was a 'noble effort,' for in 1928 only Ontario and Nova Scotia had provincial women's Liberal associations. The organizers clearly defined their reasons for establishing a national federation: to devise the best methods for Liberal women to join together and receive political training; and to pursue the study of Canada's history, her current condition, and the principles of Liberalism.[2] In later years, Liberal women would chafe at these limited goals and the constraints placed on their federation. In 1928, however, it was more than many of them had hoped for.

During the 1920s, the diversification of the women's-club movement expanded the outlets for women's broadening interests,[3] and pointed to women's fledgling attempts to make their own way in a male-dominated world. The experience of the Women's Liberal Federation of Canada (WLF) demonstrates how one group of women came to terms with Canadian political culture. Although its particular political reality – Liberal and largely male – exerted a powerful influence on the nature of the women's federation, the WLF's accomplishments and failures are equally the result of the women who served as its presidents and executives and who filled the membership ranks.

The seriousness of the Great Depression curtailed any major attempts at comprehensive national organization. At the 1928 founding meeting, the women set up committees to establish provincial organizations across Canada. Another committee under Cairine Wilson was formed to start a league of youth. In 1930, Liberal women organized Twentieth Century Liberal Associations to provide opportunities for discussion and political activities by young Liberals. They held their second National Assembly in 1933 and elected Mrs W.C. Kennedy of Windsor as president. With her death in 1934, Cairine Wilson, now Senator Wilson, became acting president until 1938, when, at the third National Assembly, she was elected president.[4]

Liberal women did not meet again until 1947. Both the men's and women's national federations had been officially closed during the Second World War in response to the call for non-partisanship and national unity. During 1943 to 1945, however, the Women's Liberal Federation of Canada, commonly known as the WLF, attempted to maintain a low but visible profile.[5] With assistance from Liberal members of Parliament and defeated candidates, the executive drew up a list of potential Liberal women and urged them to organize clubs in their locality. The national office distributed informative articles, copies of some of Prime Minister Mackenzie King's speeches, commentaries on current Liberal legislation (including the government's post-war rehabilitation program), and other material discussing the plight of prisoners of war. Finally, the national office sent out information packages and thousands of circular letters as part of a growing effort to stimulate organization.

When the end of the war signalled the freeing of women from wartime activities, Liberal women could return full time to the support of their federation. They held their first post-war convention in 1947, choosing a president and devising a long list of executive positions.[6] The executive represented and directed Liberal women throughout Canada. It met three or four times a year to report on its committees' activities and to discuss upcoming events. As the direct liaison between the National Liberal Federation (NLF) and the affiliated clubs of the WLF, the executive was the backbone of the Women's Federation. The executive also represented the provincial and local sides of the Liberal women's activities to the national organization.

Ideally, each riding was to have one or more Liberal women's clubs that affiliated with the national federation by paying a nominal fee. Advantages of national affiliation included the right to send delegates to national conventions, the opportunity to submit resolutions for convention discussion, the right to submit nominations for executive positions, and the opportunity to receive material to assist in political education and in the formation of study groups. In addition, affiliated club members received all Liberal party publications.

The size of the mailing list indicated the strength of the federation throughout the country. In 1948, the list boasted 1883 English names and 1140 French names.[7] By 1965, the list had grown to include 15,000 English and 3000 French names. The number of local associations grew steadily as well, from only 100 in 1948 to 450 by 1965.[8]

All members received Liberal party publications, including the WLF's own newsletter, the *Liberal Woman*, which appeared approximately seven times a year from 1948 to 1962, but then not again until 1969. Problems of format and uncertainty about its function plagued the newsletter throughout its periods of publication. Liberal women already received *The Liberal Newsletter*, containing policy statements and debates, news of pending legislation, and other matters of importance from federal and provincial parliaments. To avoid duplicating this function, the *Liberal Woman* became a chatty publication that reported news and events from local clubs and attempted to educate its readership about political life with articles on the steps to election and campaign tactics. Discussion of political issues was mainly limited to themes defined as women's issues.

Many readers, however, were dissatisfied that their publication was often simply a social calendar with a local rather than national focus. They wanted to see women participate more fully in the political process at the national level, and they wanted the *Liberal Woman* to reflect that view by emphasizing policy discussion and political education. A philosophical clash between advocates of the national and local persuasions became increasingly evident: Did the national forum, or the local, offer the best training ground for gaining political experience? The debate was never resolved.

Discussion surrounding the *Liberal Woman* was symptomatic of that concerning the role of women in the Liberal party, a special concern of Liberal women. The debate proceeded on two levels as both the local and the national arenas contained elements to spark controversy. Liberal women hoped that, within the party, their federation represented women as election workers, as part of the electorate, and as party members and politicians. Because the existence of two Liberal federations meant the development of parallel structures, the duties each asssumed had to be different to justify their existence. How Liberal women and the Liberal party interpreted this division by gender determined the roles given and ascribed to women in the three areas of partisan activity identified by the WLF. These responses supply the means to explore the position of women in the Liberal party in the post–Second World War era.

WOMEN AS PARTY MEMBERS

In 1964, Isabel Winkler, then executive director of the Women's Liberal Federation, declared that the Liberal party had a separate women's organization 'because it knows women have a unique role to play in politics.'[9] In 1953, addressing the 25th Anniversary Meeting of the WLF, Jack Pickersgill, then secretary of state, had expressed the same viewpoint, arguing that it was just a matter of convenience that women form their own organizations because they could meet at times that men cannot. He maintained that women can 'do certain kinds of work that men can't do very well,' and insisted that because women had their families as their primary interest, they were more apt to look at questions from the general rather than the specific point of view. This explanation was offered as a contrast to the work of men, he concluded, who are often so caught up in their own private affairs that they lose this general perspective.

Pickersgill was attempting to define the unique role Winkler was to identify eleven years later. Both of them, in advocating a special role for women, clouded the issue of equality of participation in the Liberal party. Winkler, too, maintained that 'our federation recognizes that women can do a number of political jobs better than men.'[10] She mentioned organizing and being poll captains during elections as specific examples. By maintaining that women performed certain duties better than men because of certain common qualities, women's case for equal participation was damaged. This attitude limited women to participating only in areas where those qualities were applicable and deemed as assets, and helped to prevent expansion beyond these clearly defined areas. Members of both Liberal federations were not exempt from these sentiments.

The reason most commonly put forth by the women themselves to explain the existence of a separate women's federation was the need to supply women with a place where they could gain political experience, suggesting that women were not ready to assume an equal partnership with men in Canada's political affairs. This contention persisted throughout the post-war period. Given this seemingly unending state of unpreparedness, women's demands for an equal share of the political sphere seem premature and contradictory.

At the local level, the problem seems to have been mainly one of the division of power. At the 1947 National Convention, the women took part in a session called 'Women's Interest in Constituency Organization.'[11] Here, they concluded that women were not interested in their political clubs because they had no official power. To remedy this situation, the panelists urged Liberal women to be represented in riding associations. This point was still being hammered home in 1960, when an article by Mabel Storie entitled 'One Party —

One Club' appeared in the *Liberal Woman*. 'I do not think,' Storie contended, 'that women should belong to a separate group made up only of women, if it means they are not going to attend and take part in the Riding Association.' That there was little power sharing is evidenced by the fact that membership in the local Women's Liberal Federation did not automatically mean membership in the Liberal riding association. This led to the temptation to view the women's organization as an auxiliary one. In 1969, the WLF's president, Jane MacDonald, reporting to an executive meeting of the National Liberal Federation of Canada, contended that women were being encouraged to join the riding associations 'but they do not receive much encouragement from these associations.'

Pickersgill's 1953 comments apply to the national political forum as much as they do to the local arena, where the parallel party structures again produced separate areas of activity. The issue of representation was a contentious one here as well. In 1966, the executive committee of the WLF passed several resolutions dealing with varying aspects of the inclusion of Liberal women in the top councils of the party.[12] The women resolved that the NLF amend its constitution so that all presidents of provincial women's associations automatically became members of the executive of the Liberal Federation. They also resolved that 'all offices and committees of the Liberal Federation of Canada be filled by men and women on an equal basis numerically.' Finally, they wanted all standing-committee chairmen of the women's organization included as co-chairmen of the standing committees of the National Liberal Federation.

The need to articulate these concerns in 1966 demonstrates that Liberal leaders had not committed themselves to fulfilling their own tenet of equality: in 1945 the Advisory Council of the NLF had passed a resolution supporting the principle of equality of representation by gender in party councils.[13] Party rhetoric did not match party practice. Liberal women did, however, have representation on certain party councils. The WLF was allowed forty-nine delegates to the 1958 Liberal leadership convention; ten years before they had had only three.[14] In 1957 all executive officers of the Women's Liberal Federation were given delegate status with voting privileges at the National Liberal Federation's national convention.[15] These gains, important in setting convention precedents, were much less important in terms of the day-to-day operation of the main association. The women were certainly not excluded completely from the upper echelons of the NLF, for the WLF's president always reported to the Advisory Council meetings of the NLF. She seems, however, to have been little more than a reporter itemizing the activities of the women's federation and does not seem to have had much influence in a policy-forming or advisory capacity.[16]

In 1964, Paul Goulet, the director of publicity for the NLF, outlined in a confidential memo his frustrations with the relationship between the men's and women's federations: 'Well you can't have your cake and eat it too. When there is such a demand that there be a separate women's Liberal organization on a national and provincial scale, should not Liberal women act separately to achieve specialized goals? ... Even while these Liberal women call for greater responsibility and greater authority within the framework of the federal party organization, they call for special consideration through their women's organization – because of the fact that they are women, and because of the contention that they can perform certain political action better than any other group.'[17] The problems of parallel organizations are apparent, as are the problems inherent in calling for special consideration while at the same time actively campaigning for equality. Most women, however, argued that they were not calling for special consideration, but only for what was their due after long years of dedicated service.

Inclusion as members of NLF councils and as delegates to its conventions was only one aspect of the question of representation. The women were constantly campaigning for what they saw as their right to government-appointed positions. Because the WLF felt it was a parallel organization to the NLF, its members believed their work should be acknowledged and rewarded with some of the spoils of office. In 1950, the Honourable Nancy Hodges spoke to the national convention of the 'lip service' men give to the work women do, and argued the time had come when women should share 'in some of the honours which are connected with public life.'[18] At the WLF's 1956 national convention, Prime Minister St Laurent argued that it was 'always difficult' to find women who can assume the extra responsibilities such appointments entail.[19] He listed several places where women held positions, including the United Nations, a royal commission, and in diplomatic posts. St Laurent claimed that the Liberals had demonstrated their 'firm belief in the ability of our Canadian women to fill positions of responsibility.'

To help their case, Liberal women attempted to be more active in recruiting able women with the qualifications necessary to stand for appointment. In 1965, at an executive committee meeting, the members decided to ask the provincial presidents to submit names of prominent Liberal women who would qualify for special appointments 'in an effort to ensure that such women received recognition.'[20] The necessity of having an up-to-date list of qualified women ready to be thrust into the hands of a person having to fill a vacancy in the Senate or on boards and commissions was well known to Judy LaMarsh, who kept such a list herself.[21] Without this prompting, many women felt deserving members of their sex would never be considered as appointees.

The discussion surrounding appointments, however, could not escape the web of contradictions that enmeshed many of the women's endeavours. In 1966, the president of the WLF, Beatrice Asselin, stated that 'persons should be chosen for responsible posts on merits of qualification rather than sex' but then maintained that 'the qualities of women have never been needed more in Canada than they are now.'[22] By making gender a determining factor in the possession of certain characteristics, she defeated her call for equality on the basis of qualifications. It could very easily be argued, and was, that women would be suited for only certain types of appointments in specific fields, or that women were carbon copies of one another, making the appointment of more than one unnecessary.

The theme that one woman was to be taken as a model for all women was a pervasive one. 'It is a heavy responsibility,' commented Mrs A.L. Brown in 1956 after her appointment to the Board of Governors of the National Film Board, 'because there are so few women appointed to these public bodies and any woman appointed to these public bodies must uphold the reputation of her sex and that weighs rather heavily upon us.'[23] In 1970, Jane Macdonald, the president of the WLF, was still contending that a 'clear demonstration of competence' should remove the prejudices concerning women.

Still the Liberal party tended to lump all women together as an anonymous group. Judy LaMarsh related an incident involving Pauline Jewett and Lester Pearson before the 1965 election, when Jewett told Pearson that she hoped she would serve in the cabinet after the election: 'He replied that while she had plenty of ability there already was one women in Cabinet and he didn't think that I intended to leave. It simply never occurred to Pearson that there could be more than one woman in the same Cabinet.'[24] The widespread belief that all women shared the failure of any one of their number, that because of certain shared womanly characteristics one woman could adequately represent all women, and the consequent attitudes that saw women as a group rather than as individuals plagued Liberal women throughout the post-war years.

The debate surrounding the allotment of appointed positions was an important one for Liberal women, who identified one of their major tenets as the improvement of the political status of Canada's women. With each improvement, leading to more women holding positions, the federation hoped to see an accompanying decline in the prejudicial practices that hampered women's access to these positions. The women's uninterrupted stream of memoranda, resolutions, and speeches requesting these changes provides evidence that they were not immediately forthcoming. The Liberal party's reluctance to heed these requests is inextricably linked to its view of women in the party's rank and file as minor performers within the Canadian political arena.

ELECTION: WOMEN AS WORKERS

Liberal women played an important role in the Liberal election machine as campaign workers. This participation was local rather than national in scope and gave a real purpose to the women's constituency organizations. Participation in election campaigns was the most important function of Liberal women's clubs in the local community. Liberal women took seriously the task of electing Liberal governments: 'I know that we are all fully aware that no grass must be allowed to grow under our feet, that the years between elections are only too short to keep up the important work of organization,... [to] build ourselves up to be a greater fighting force when we are again called upon to do practical election work.'[25] The kind of campaign work performed by women, the type of work they were considered to be suited for, and the leadership given by Liberal women to other women both locally and nationally generated constant discussion and much frustration.

At the local level, women were involved with many of the organizational aspects of the campaign. They recruited volunteers, sold posters and pins, and monitored the media's treatment of their candidate.[26] Women's duties could also include checking voters' lists, serving as outside scrutineers, driving people to the polls, and arranging for baby-sitters.[27] During the 1968 federal election campaign, the Liberal party, under the heading 'Woman Power,' sent out many different memoranda to campaign chairmen and candidates alike instructing them on where and how to use women in their campaign. The first bulletin suggested that women could be used in committee rooms, as door-to-door canvassers, and in telephone campaigns because women enjoyed meeting the public and therefore excelled in this type of work.[28] Women were urged to organize noon-hour lunches aimed at 'business girls,' and to have the candidate appear at supermarkets distributing cards with a recipe for good government on one side and his favourite food recipe on the other! 'Let us not be too proud,' Mrs Blair admonished, 'to refuse the most uninteresting job.'[29]

That both male and female Liberals promoted this type of campaign participation is clear. Certainly electioneering gave a raison d'être to the federation's local organizations, and the election to office of a Liberal candidate was the first step to assuring the national triumph of Liberal ideals. Actively participating in local campaigns was also an activity in which the two federations worked together. In his opening remarks to the 1956 WLF national convention, Duncan MacTavish assured his listeners that 'in a federal general election we look forward to the magnificent cooperation of the women's organizations.'[30] As a hopeful prelude to the 1963 campaign, the 1963 election issue of the *Liberal Woman* summarized Lester Pearson's views on the participation of women: 'He realized that the work the Liberal women of Canada did in the 1962 Campaign was largely responsible for the 100% gain in Liberal seats, and he wanted to make sure that this success would be repeated for April 8, 1963.'[31] The article also reported that each province had a liaison member who was to co-ordinate the women's activities with the campaign chairmen in each province.

The contention that the participation of Liberal women was a valuable part of an election campaign was prevalent, and the women were given appropriate doses of praise when victory was secured. Losing an election, however, did not change the praise bestowed upon them. The June 1958 edition of the *Liberal Woman* still maintained, in the aftermath of the great Conservative sweep, that 'there is reason to be tremendously proud of the part our Liberal Women took in the Federal Election. More than ever before our women had opportunities to assist with campaign planning at all levels.'[32] In 1958, more than ever before, the accolades sounded hollow.

However important they were as campaign workers, women still lacked the opportunity to assist in platform formation at the local level. At the national level, attempts had been made to draw women into the campaign strategy sessions. This only happened, though, as the women became discontented with their continual assignment to the menial 'donkey-jobs' in the election campaign. Women in the 1960s and early 1970s were no longer content simply to 'explain the position of the government so as to comand the support of the women of Canada.'[33] They wanted to be directly involved with the formation of new policies to be presented to the electorate, and with the decisions concerning the best way to advertise the Liberal position. It boded ill for the national situation, however, when complaints about the effectiveness of Liberal women's clubs at the local level, women's traditional participatory level, began to surface. A 1963 election memorandum from Keith Davey expressed the need to draw more women into the campaign at the constituency level, but argued that this could not be done through the women's organization.

As an alternative, Davey proposed establishing a women's national advisory campaign committee.[34] The group would meet regularly and submit its recommendations to the National Campaign Committee through its chairman, who would also be a member of the national committee. As well as attempting to include more women in the campaign at a constituency level, this women's committee was to try to discern the woman's point of view in the election campaign. No evidence exists to indicate the importance or actual functioning of the committee, or even to establish whether it was set up. Judging by the literature that exists describing the activities of the 1972 Women's Campaign Committee, it seems doubtful that the 1963 committee got off the ground.

The 1972 Women's Campaign Committee was established by Sen. Richard Stanbury with the president of the WLF, Marie Gibeault, as its director. Other prominent members of the committee included Jan Steele and Muriel Stern, and all members worked closely with Torrance Wylie of the Prime Minister's Office. Stanbury clearly spelled out the objectives and functions of the committee: to involve women in the Liberal campaign and to encourage women to vote Liberal.[35] To accomplish these ends the committee was to serve as a reserve of speakers for women at the constituency level, to encourage media interviews, and to assist constituency organizations with involving women in the campaign. The committee members maintained that the Liberal party was the only party that had acted to improve the status of women in Canada and that this effort went hand in hand with the fact that the Trudeau administration had opened up many social and political activities to women. Another contention – that the Liberal party sought the involvement of women, especially through the Women's Liberal Federation – was a prominent theme. Finally, and perhaps most tellingly, the committee members were assured that the Liberals could win a resounding victory at the polls if women were actively involved in the campaign.

These contentions, however, were not based on any political reality. Liberal women could be quickly thrust aside if the party felt it was to its advantage to do so, as evidenced by the failure of the 1957 Liberal campaign planners to involve the federation in putting the women's folder together. The level of involvement of Liberal women encouraged by the party remained limited, calling into question the sincerity of the avowed Liberal commitment to raise the status of Canada's women.

The 1972 committee did urge all candidates to involve women in their campaigns, and told them it would be particularly advantageous to draw in women at the decision-making level.[36] Still, the fact that women continued to be portrayed by the Liberal party as an amorphous mass is an important comment on the real position of women in the party: even more important is that by the early 1960s the Women's Liberal Federation was no longer seen as the embodiment of that image.

ELECTIONS: WOMEN AS VOTERS

The image of women sharing a mass character is particularly evident in the Liberal party's dealings with women as voters. The necessity of securing the 'women's vote' to ensure the election of a Liberal government was a common rallying cry. What came to be labelled women's issues were identified early by the WLF as potential vote-getters. The fact that these concerns were acted upon very slowly, however, indicates that, until the late 1960s, the political parties did not consider them to be prime material for elections.

The belief that women were almost exclusively concerned with a particular body of legislation persisted during the post-war years. Women's interests were especially linked with health and welfare, and arenas seen as having a direct impact on the home. A women's pamphlet put out for the 1957 election listed several aspects of the Liberal program that appealed particularly to women: family welfare, social legislation, hospital insurance, the building of new homes, and the availability of more consumer goods, including higher-quality foods.[37] In preparation for the 1958 election, the president of the WLF, Mrs Caldwell, informed Senator Connolly that 'particularly if there is material prepared specifically for women, we could assure that some of that is dispersed directly to women's groups, other than Liberal.'[38] 'I would appreciate, too,' she emphasized, 'the opportunity to look over any literature or material which is particularly prepared for women. I know that we could have assisted with the women's folder last year, to advantage.' Liberal women felt they played a vital role in interpreting the concerns of Canadian womanhood to their male party colleagues.

In a 1962 private letter to L.B. Pearson, Sen. Muriel Ferguson charged that the Liberal party had neglected many opportunities to attract women's votes. She maintained that the Conservative appointment of Ellen Fairclough as the first female cabinet minister had given Diefenbaker 'considerable prestige among women voters.' Judy LaMarsh voiced similar charges, although she did not single out the Liberal party: 'No political party in Canada can claim to be particularly sensitive to the women within its own organization, much less to the women of the electorate at large.'[39] Research indicates, however, that there is little difference in the voting patterns of Canadian men and women, especially among those who supported the two main national parties during this time.[40] Liberal claims of their monopoly of the women's vote represent another tactic deployed to convince Liberal women of their worth to the party, and that their loyalty was actually indicative of the loyalty of all Canadian women.

By 1968, and again in 1972, however, the Liberals were making a determined effort to influence the female voter. Candidates were besieged with literature telling them what they could and could not say when speaking with women. A 1968 pre-election bulletin listed national unity, the proposed setting up of a task force to study urban problems, lower drug prices, Canadian travel and exchange fellowships, and the plans to incorporate a charter of human rights into the constitution as safe topics for discussion with women.[41] Citing 'Trudeaumania' as a natural cause of the supposed increased female interest in the 1968 campaign, the bulletin urged candidates to use this opportunity to extend the Liberal appeal even further by turning these enthusiasts into effective campaign workers.[42] Candidates were also told to emphasize the creation of the Royal Commission on the Status of Women, as well as certain issues of a humanitarian nature, including old-age security, student loans, and veterans' pensions.[43]

Although, as chairman of the 1972 special committee, WLF president Marie Gibeault acted in part independently from the Women's Federation, many of her memos to candidates reflect concerns voiced by Liberal women over the years. She urged Liberal hopefuls to do their homework, be properly informed, and treat female questioners seriously.[44] She advised candidates to deal with Liberal achievements in the field of the status of women, but to admit also that the government could have moved faster than it did. Finally, she instructed that a direct appeal for votes should be made to women under 35 because this group had a particular interest in changes in the status of women.

Gibeault also coached candidates on approaches to avoid. She warned Liberal standard-bearers not to be flippant, defensive, or patronizing, to avoid jokes about women, and to avoid condescending remarks such as 'We couldn't win without the hard work of the women.' Although many of these suggestions reveal a sensitivity to some of the condescending manners women encountered as interested voters, the appeals based on issues were still firmly rooted in women's issues: 'In short, in accordance with the campaign theme "The Land is Strong," the major thrust of your campaign effort to the woman voter should be "The Land will Become Even Stronger" when we remove all forms of discrimination and when men and women have equality of opportunity.'[45] Assuming that this literature was read by the candidate and made available to workers in his office, Liberal officials at the local level should have been adequately prepared to deal with questions on the status of women.

The seriousness of the Liberal party commitment to make its part in improving the status of women a national campaign issue is questionable. All the material on this issue originated in Gibeault's office. Just prior to the election, she made this discovery: 'A reading of the Campaign Statement unbelievably had no reference to the Status of Women or to the commitment of the Liberal Government to improve their status. An addition to the campaign statement was therefore suggested. This had been done.'[46] A brochure on the topic was not put out because of the expense; time and expense seemed to be the major difficulties in implementing a status-of-women campaign platform. The reasons behind the original omission are unclear. The most likely cause, however, was the organizational barrier that had plagued the Women's Liberal Federation since its founding day: because there was a separate women's committee to look after the needs of the female electorate, women's issues did not merit inclusion with mainstream political concerns.

Liberal campaign organizers were only too glad to have a fleet of Liberal women sweep into their committee rooms to stuff envelopes and pour coffee. They were less adept at dealing with women as members of the electorate, tending to either ignore them or see them as having very limited concerns. Thus, a women's organization that was increasingly seen as being unable to deliver the women's vote was, in turn, not used to interpret Liberal policy to the female electorate. Liberal women still remained outside the mainsteam election planning. Gibeault's frustrations had been experienced before: they would be experienced again.

ELECTIONS: WOMEN AS CANDIDATES

In 1942, Sen. Cairine Wilson wrote that women have not as yet filled 'a large or prominent place' in our parliaments.[47] Preparing women to run for political office by providing them with political education and experience was the hope underlying many of the Women's Liberal Federation's activities. The women's leaders often compared their federation to a stepping-stone on the path to greater political involvement.

Right from the start, however, women had been faced with trying to operate in the confusing milieu created by the junction of two conflicting ideas. In 1950, Liberal women were cautioned against putting women in Parliament just because they were women.[48] On other occasions women were told that the reason there were so few women in politics was that women failed to support female candidates.[49] Liberal women faced enormous difficulty in reconciling the fact that they were an organization of women representing and furthering women's political interests with the contention that, in some cases, women who supported other women at the polls were doing something wrong. To help overcome this confusing liability, Liberal women chose to stress two main points in their attempts to get women elected: the unfavourable ridings given to female candidates and the need for women's special abilities in Parliament.

Senator Wilson was articulate on both points. 'In Canada,' she argued in 1942, 'I confess that it has been exceedingly difficult for any woman to secure a party nomination where there is a likelihood or even remote possibility of election, and we are usually doomed to carry the banner of a forlorn case.'[50] In 1958, eight Liberal women had stood as candidates, but none had been elected. 'It can be said,' lamented the *Liberal Woman*, 'that each of the eight women contested seats which were conceded to be almost impossible.' This widespread belief surfaced in the Royal Commission on the Status of Women as an indictment of all parties.[51] The most oft-quoted example of this 'forlorn case' on the Liberal side occurred in 1965, when the Liberals ran a woman against John Diefenbaker.

Many women would also charge that, even having secured a nomination, a woman did not receive the help and support given to her male colleagues elsewhere. In 1969, Jane Macdonald, the president of the Women's Liberal Federation, included the following unfavourable comment in her report to the executive committee of the NLF: 'I can speak from experience when I say a woman candidate is entirely on her own once she becomes a candidate. Very rarely do they receive help from the Party.'[52] The perceived abandonment of women candidates by the Liberal party was undoubtedly linked to the equally damaging contention that most women ran in lost or doubtful ridings.

To these serious charges laid against the Liberal party, Judy LaMarsh added another: that the Liberal party did not actively recruit promising women to run for office as it did men who showed political potential.[53] To substantiate her charges she mentioned such prominent Liberals as P.E. Trudeau, L.B. Pearson, and Mitchell Sharp, claiming that 'none of them had a day's association with the Liberal Party before they became candidates; the party or its leadership went after them and persuaded them to run.' Just as Liberal women were supposed to be ever ready with a list of prominent women suitable to fill vacancies on boards and committees, their local ranks were to serve much the same purpose when the party organization was searching for a candidate. This helped to ensure that suitable women were at least considered, and attempted to counter the demonstrated Liberal inability to conceive of women as anything other than a large, amorphous entity.

Ironically, the second of the Liberal women's principal arguments adopted to overcome the numerical imbalance between elected male and female parliamentarians only reinforced the notion of the basic commonality of all women. The contention that women, and here particularly Liberal women, were needed in politics because they possessed special and peculiar qualities served to support rather than defeat the belief that one or a few women could represent the rest of their sex. In 1942, Senator Wilson described her conception of the special characteristics of women, explaining that 'there is a place for women in every parliament.'[54] She claimed that women often enter public life with much more unselfish interests than do men, maintained that 'through long years in office, men have grown accustomed to abuses which we, with fresher minds, may be willing to attack and conquer.' In 1968, the president of the WLF still believed that 'women must continue to be women – using their feminine charms – in their attempts to get elected.'

That confusion reigned supreme, in theoretical and practical situations, is evident. Many of the messages delivered to Liberal women telling them how to remove political injustices conflicted with the rhetoric detailing why they should be removed. This confusion, born of the union of the current reality with the frustration of repeated but unsuccessful attempts to change that reality, cast a pall over the wider political aims of Liberal women.

WOMEN AND POLICY FORMATION

In the post-war decades preceding its amalgamation with NLF, the Women's Liberal Federation did not have a direct role to play in policy formation. Neither did the rest of the rank-and-file party members; but Liberal women were led to believe that their federation fed right into the Liberal leader's office. Many of their direct entreaties, though, were rebuffed. In some instances, party leaders credited Liberal women with the formation of legislation on selected topics to a degree far greater than the women's actual participation would indicate. To women were ascribed powers of influence, persuasion, and inspiration, rather than direct power.

The notion of the 'invisible cabinet' was the predominant image used to describe women's role in policy formation. Liberal women often cast themselves in this supporting role: 'Women should know that their organizations exert a very real power and influence, especially on the members of Parliament. Their M.P.'s should be made aware that they are being closely watched, and that ineffectual legislation will be quickly denounced.'[55] This 'very real power' was neither decision-making nor policy-formulating power but a reaction that could occur only after the decision making had been completed.

To describe this action and its intended results, Liberal women introduced a new image to represent this particular role in determining party policy, that of watchdog: 'It [WLF] regards itself and is regarded by the government [then Liberal] as its affectionate but vigilant watchdog and its trusty organizational right arm.'[56] The widely publicized contentions (prominent in the agitation for the vote) that women's influence would change politics, that they would be ever on the alert to stamp out bad legislation or elements of corruption, that they would purify politics and might even end war were still present in the immediate post-war years. A Liberal woman from British Columbia maintained that women 'are by nature peacemakers,' and urged them 'to work at all times for a high level of ethics within the party.' Emphasis on roles of watchdog and peacemaker that played up to the myths of female moral superiority gradually lessened in intensity during the final years of the federation's existence.

The belief that women's interests centred around the home and family was not as easy to shake off. At the 1952 Special General Meeting of the WLF, several prominent members of the organization addressed the question of why Canadian women are interested in politics. Cecile O'Regan, the president, led off the discussion, claiming that with 'the enormous expansion of social security, surely the women are more than ever concerned with the actual workings of our government. Social security affects our very homes, our children and our older citizens.'[57] The provincial reports presented contained numerous references to this topic. Mrs M. Poupore, president of the Ontario Women's Liberal Association, best defined this bond joining women to politics: 'Our appreciation, our specialization, should be enquiry and mastery of those policies which relate to the welfare of the home. Because, as the home goes, so goes the nation. Further, our duty as women is to propose, advance and protect the ideals of home and family life.' This view formed the most prominent ideology governing women's participation in politics in the immediate post-war years.

From this all-pervasive viewpoint, the leap necessary to attribute the Liberal government's social reforms to the influence of the women was made effortlessly. It seemed a natural corollary to the belief that placed social reform within women's natural sphere. At the 1952 national convention, a member of Parliament, George McIlraith, stressed the point that all social legislation in Canada had been implemented by Liberal administrations.[58] 'If that is so,' he continued, 'then the credit for the fact should be given to the drive and the stimulus of the women's organization.' At the 25th Anniversary Meeting of the federation held one year later, Mrs E. Mooney maintained that the twenty-five years of the federation's existence paralleled the years known as the 'Golden Quarter-century of Social Security.' She attributed the implementations of the Mother's and Family Allowance acts and old-age pensions directly to the demands of the women.

This claim, however, is difficult to substantiate. The fact that the federation was largely inactive during the Second World War suggests that the post-war rehabilitation measures introduced by the King administration were not strongly influenced by the women. Furthermore, Liberal party officials tended to discount the women's petitions more often than they accepted them. Because the ideal Canadian woman was morally superior, unselfish, interested primarily in her home, and essentially powerless in comparison to her male counterpart, her special qualities (which complemented these interests) suited her to be the repository and hence dispenser of virtuous influence, rather than a strident campaigner for change. This type of influence is very hard to measure and in this case would seem almost non-existent. No evidence exists in the women's records to link them directly to the social reforms. King's known interest in social measures, the necessity of planning for a post-war world, and the perceived threat of a socialist take-over were much more important factors in the decision to implement wide-ranging social-reform measures. 'If people were concerned about such questions,' concludes J.L. Granatstein, 'it was a tribute to the effectiveness of the CCF campaign for them.'[59] Cabinet planning and combined CCF and Conservative pressure spurred the creation of the social-welfare program.

By the 1960s this idealistic portrayal of women in politics no longer suited the political reality. Encouraged by the women's liberation movement, and bolstered by the gradual shift to the left in North American society and politics, women's issues were now those concerned with correcting specific injustices affecting women. As Liberal women became more vocal and more unyielding in their demands for improvement of their own position in society and politics, the image of an unselfish being using 'quiet influence' was no longer tenable. Left without the mythical but undoubtedly gratifying power to 'inspire,' Liberal women had no power at all. Resolutions and petitions, traditionally ignored by the party leaders, continued, for the most part, to be ignored.

'I do not think,' intoned Jack Pickersgill in 1953, 'a woman's organization – I hope it is not – is formed for the purpose of promoting the interests of women.'[60] Pickersgill contradicted the WLF's tenet to seek to advance the political and social status of Canada's women, and exposed a time bomb ticking quietly within the federation. As it became a more vocal lobby group, for example in demanding the establishment of the Royal Commission on the Status of Women, the bomb was bound to go off. Although its actual role in policy formation had not changed, the perception of it had: with women's primary functions of inspiring or influencing gone, they were seen to have no wider role than that of a lobby group for women's interests. The frustration of many of the women increased, exacerbated by such occurrences as their exclusion from pre-election discussions on women's issues, a direct outgrowth of the aura of powerlessness surrounding the federation.

By the 1960s it was readily apparent to members of the national executive of the WLF that Liberal women were not successfully scaling the heights of political participation. A pamphlet entitled 'Women ... and the Liberal Party' summarized Liberal women's activities.[61] It was not an encouraging summary: women received credit for influencing social-security legislation, carrying out political education, holding meetings and social functions, and assisting in election campaigns. The political system had proved to be largely unresponsive to Liberal women's demands for fuller participation. Many women were also unhappy with their federation's relationship to the NLF and with its position in the Liberal hierarchy. Their dissatisfaction gradually solidified into a movement calling for the amalgamation of the national men's and women's federations.

The failings of the WLF were not uniquely Liberal problems, but rather the product of separate political organizations for the sexes. Faith in the belief that women's groups prepared women to step into larger political fields flickered and died because no such developments materialized.[62] Deepening frustration over the financial as well as the political neglect of the WLF by the NLF became increasingly evident.

Still, some Liberal women fought to keep their federation a separate organization. At the local level, Liberal women undoubtedly derived some satisfaction and prestige from their positions, helped by the Liberal post-war proclivity for staying in power. Fuelling election victories tangibly reinforced the value of their work. This success points to one of the major factors working against the amalgamation movement: the local / national dichotomy never resolved by the WLF. Local goals, such as women working to elect Liberal candidates, were often realized at the expense of national ones, such as increasing women's level of political participation. Most federation activities were carried out at the local level with little direction from the national office. The first *Liberal Woman* published since 1962 appeared in 1969 and responded to the amalgamation debate by reassuring federation members that the amalgamation plan did not include disbanding the local organizations.[63] 'However,' the article continued, 'everyone thinks that the women of Canada who are interested in the Liberal party should be members of the local riding and constituency organizations.' The thrust of the statement was clear: participation in women's organizations led nowhere. Women were urged to join the real Liberal associations, but they were also urged to retain their memberships in a second local organization. This reasoning was also clear: local membership ensured their participation as women, rather than as Liberals.

The national executive, however, did not see the federation as existing to provide a pool of election workers. The realization that the local organizations, the mainstay of the federation, were not fulfilling any larger purposes figured in the decision to integrate. Many members believed the federation's larger objectives could never be reached if the structure of political organizations continued to emphasize the division of power and non-power between the men's and women's federations. This argument, however well received among the national executive, did not take as strong a hold on the local organizations. Having been rebuffed frequently by the main riding association, many women active locally because of membership in the WLF feared that participation would be lost if the two federations integrated.

From the national standpoint, though, the Women's Liberal Federation was a dead-end street. National leaders were beginning to realize that most Liberal women did not see their federation in national terms, but rather in local ones. The inability of the national executive to give a definite focus and purpose to the federation greatly weakened its claim of being the repository and director of women's political aspirations. In his analysis of the Liberal party, Peter Regenstreif ascribes to the women's federation a very minor local importance, helping in election campaigns, and an even lesser national one, encouraging local activities.[64] Even the ramifications of such national actions were felt locally, and not nationally. The WLF continued to be unattractive to potential recruits because of its purely supportive function.

During the 1960s, various study groups looked at women in the Liberal party, and attempted to decide what to do with them.[65] Finally in 1973, after years of acrimonious debate, the WLF was replaced by the Women's Liberal Commission, a part of the NLF. Liberal women had created a new order by integrating with the men's federation at the national level, but retaining their local structures. They hoped that by removing the parallel structures at the national level, stepping from a local organization to a good position in national politics would be easier. They also hoped to attract more women into the national scene by removing the parallel, and limiting, structure at that level.

Liberal women's 'noble effort' proved unsuccessful in terms of their own organization. In 1973, they had accomplished none of their goals set down in 1928. The Liberal party had continued to encourage the federation to remain a separate organization, and the women found that organizational autonomy did not prove a helpful tool in accelerating their participation in the party's mainstream activities. In terms of the Liberal party, women were somewhat successful as an ever-available pool of local workers to spread the gospel of Canadian Liberalism during election campaigns. Nationally, however, Liberal women grew tired of having their success measured by the standards of others and finally decided to use their own. The amalgamation of the national men's and women's federations resulted: the noble effort had failed.

NOTES

CRW	Cairine Reay Wilson Papers
LBP	Lester Bowles Pearson Papers
LPC	Liberal Party of Canada Papers
LPH	Liberal Party Headquarters
LSSL	Louis Stephen St Laurent Papers
NA	National Archives of Canada
NFLWC	Women's Liberal Federation of Canada
NLF	National Liberal Federation of Canada
WLFC [WLF]	Women's Liberal Federation of Canada

1 Report, First Assembly of the National Federation of Liberal Women of Canada, n.d., LPC, vol. 1175, 3–6, NA; the quotation from King is taken from the same source, 4. In 1963, the organization's name was changed to the Women's Liberal Federation of Canada (WLF). I will use this name throughout the paper.

2 Ibid., 5.

3 Veronica Strong-Boag, *The Parliament of Women: The National Council of Women of Canada 1893–1929* (Ottawa 1976), 116–19.

4 The information in this paragraph is taken from *The Story of the National Federation of Liberal Women of Canada 1928–1957*, n.d., LPC, vol. 1178, n.p., NA.

5 Report of the executive vice-president in charge of the women's division of the National Liberal Federation, 1943–1945, LPC, vol. 1059, 1–2, NA. Information contained in this paragraph is taken from the same source, 1–2. Reginald Whitaker discusses the 1940s and the reasons behind the return to partisanship in his *The Government Party: Organizing and Financing the Liberal Party of Canada 1930–1958* (Toronto 1977), 129–56.

6 Committees had been established to look after organization, the constitution, political education, finances, publicity, the status of women, and convention resolutions.

7 Report of the Women's Division, NLF, 29 November 1948, LPC, vol. 1076, 2; report of the executive secretary to a WLFC executive meeting, 26 May 1965, LPC, vol. 1064, NA.

8 Report of the Women's Division, NLF, to the executive of NLF, 29 November 1948, LPC, vol. 1076, 1, NA. No figures are given for years after 1965; some discrepancy does exist between the numbers on the mailing list and those given as membership figures. Membership figures for the more than 450 clubs operating in 1967 give 31,000, while mailing list figures for 1965 total only 18,000. Many local presidents were lax in sending in the names of new members (report of the executive secretary to an executive meeting of WLF, 26 May 1965, LPC, vol. 1064, NA).

9 'Political Interest Zooms as New Jobs Are Available,' *Ottawa Journal*, 2 May 1964, LPC, series NI1, series C-2, vol. 280, NA; report of NLFWC 25th Anniversary Meeting, 23 November 1953, LPC, vol. 1062, 42–4, NA.

10 'Political Interest Zooms as New Jobs Are Available,' *Ottawa Journal*, 2 May 1964, LPC, series NI1, series C-2, vol. 280, NA. The subsequent reference to Winkler is taken from the same source.

11 Record of NFLWC National Convention, 21–22 October 1947, LPC, vol. 1061, 47, NA. The subsequent information on the 1947 convention is taken from the same source; Mabel Storie, 'One Party – One Club,' *Liberal Woman*, March 1960, n.p.

12 Resolutions passed by the executive committee of WLFC, 5 March 1966, LPC, vol. 1176, NA.

13 *The Liberal News of Canada*, December 1945, n.p.

14 Report of a special meeting of NFLWC, 15 January 1958, LPC, vol. 1063, 26–7, NA.

15 'Important Role for Women at January Liberal Meeting,' *Winnipeg Tribune*, 12 December 1957, LPC, vol. 380, NA.

16 For example, see the report by Mrs A.L. Caldwell to the Advisory Council of NLF, 17–19 November 1958, LPC, vol. 1076, 65–72, NA.

17 Personal commentary on the recent discussion on aims of the Liberal Women of Canada, by Paul Goulet, 5 March 1964, LPC, vol. 1063, 2, NA.

18 Report on the national convention of 1950, LPC, vol. 906, 2, NA.

19 Report of NLFWC national convention, 1–3 May 1956, LPC, vol. 1062, 8–9, NA.

20 Minutes of a meeting of the executive committee of WLFC, 26 May 1965, LPC, vol. 1064, 5, NA.

21 'I soon ran out of women of my own acquaintanceship who might be qualified to hold such responsible positions. I began to compile a black book, the names in it growing from lists sent to me by national women's organizations, from newspaper clippings, and from word-of-mouth recommendations. No one else in the whole of Government, to my knowledge, ever kept such a list, and it was often loaned to the Privy Council office or to one of my colleagues when searching for a likely appointee' (Judy LaMarsh, *Memoirs of a Bird in a Gilded Cage* [Toronto 1968], 293–4.

22 'Women Disregarded, Liberal Official Says,' *Globe and Mail*, 14 January 1966, LBP, series N11, series C-2, vol. 280, NA.

23 Report of NFLWC national convention, 1–3 May 1956, LPC, vol. 1062, 307; 'Challenge Men with Competence,' *The Columbian*, 13 April 1970, LPC, vol. 1078, NA.

24 LaMarsh, *Memoirs*, 292.

25 'Ideals in Action,' Speech by Mrs Douglas Blair on her tour of the western provinces, November 1950, LPC, vol. 905, 1, NA.

26 'Women's Ways (to Help),' WLFC memo, n.d., LPC, vol. 1079, NA.

27 Speech by Mrs Douglas Blair to the Jeanne St Laurent Women's Liberal Club and the Cornwall Women's Liberal Club, 14 October 1954, LPC, vol. 905, 9, NA.

28 The Liberal Party of Canada, Bulletin no. 1, 'Woman Power, Ideas for Involvement,' 17 May 1968, LPC, vol. 1065, 1, NA. The subsequent information is taken from the same source, 2.

29 'Hints for Volunteers in an Election Campaign,' speech by Mrs D. Blair on a lecture trip, April 1961, LPC, vol. 1059, 1–6, NA.

30 Report of NFLWC national convention, 1–3 May 1956, LPC, vol. 1062, 5, NA.

31 *Liberal Woman*, 1963 election issue, n.p.

32 *Liberal Woman*, June 1958, n.p.

33 Speech by the Hon. Stuart S. Garson, in report of the special general meeting, 1–2 April 1952, LPC, vol. 1062, 103; memorandum from Keith Davey to the Hon. L.B. Pearson, 14 January 1963, LBP, series N2, vol. 34, file 391.5.3.2, NA.

34 Memorandum from Keith Davey to the Hon. L.B. Pearson.

35 Memorandum from Fred MacDonald to Marie Gibeault, Muriel Stern, Jan Steele, Senator Stanbury, and Torrance Wylie, re Women's Committee, 21 August 1972, LPC, vol. 1176, 1 and 2, NA.

36 Memorandum from Marie Gibeault to all Liberal candidates, 13 September 1972, LPC, vol. 1091, 2, NA.

37 Pamphlet, *Canadian Women Have Confidence in St Laurent*, 1957, LPC, vol. 832, NA.

38 Jessie Caldwell to Sen. John Connolly, 4 February 1958, LPC, vol. 850, 1, NA. The following quotation is taken from the same source, 2.

39 Sen. Muriel Ferguson to Mr L.B. Pearson, 20 July 1962, LPC, series N2, vol. 34, file 391.5.3.2. NA; LaMarsh, *Memoirs*, 281.

40 Robert Alford has concluded that there seems 'to be little difference in the political behaviour of men and women in Canada' (Robert L. Alford, 'The Social Bases of Political Cleavage,' in John Meisel, ed. *Papers on the 1962 Election* [Toronto 1964], 214). Similarly, John Meisel and Mildred Schwartz contend that 'there is nothing very distinctive or noteworthy about the differences in electoral behaviour between men and women in Canada' (John Meisel, *Working Papers on Canadian Politics* [Montreal 1973], 12). The *Canadian Annual Review* negates even the influence of 'Trudeaumania' on the female voter: 'Despite the widespread publicity given to Mr. Trudeau's impact on the women voter [in 1968], Gallup contended that his percentage increase over the vote received by Lester Pearson in 1963 was approximately the same among women as it was among men' (*Canadian Annual Review for 1968*, 65).

41 WLFC Bulletin no. 4, 'Woman Power,' 7 June 1968, LPC, vol. 1065, NA.

42 WLFC Bulletin no. 2, 'Woman Power,' 28 May 1968, LPC, vol. 1065, 1, NA; the following information is taken from the same source, 1–2.

43 WLFC Bulletin no. 3, 'Woman Power, Achievements of the Liberal Party,' 30 May 1968, LPC, vol. 1065, 2, NA.

44 Memorandum from Marie Gibeault to all candidates, 29 September 1972, LPC, vol. 1176, NA. The following information is taken from the same source, 1–2.

45 Memorandum from Marie Gibeault to all Liberal candidates, 13 September 1972, LPC, vol. 1091, 2, NA.

46 Memorandum from Marie Gibeault to the national campaign chairman, 2 October 1972, LPC, vol. 1176, 1, NA.

47 'Women in the Parliament of Canada,' by Cairine R. Wilson, 28 September 1942, CRW, vol. 6, file 9, 6, NA.

48 For example, see 'What Should the Women of Canada Know about the Liberal Party?' 18 September 1950, LPC, vol. 905, 3, NA.

49 For example, see 'Ideals in Action,' speech by Mrs Douglas Blair on a tour of the western provinces, November 1950, LPC, vol. 905, 10, NA.

50 'Women in the Parliament of Canada,' by Cairine R. Wilson, 28 September 1942, CRW, vol. 6, file 9, 6, NA.

51 *Liberal Woman*, June 1958, n.p.; Royal Commission on the Status of Women in Canada, *Report* (Ottawa 1971), 339 (hereafter referred to as *Report*).

52 Report of the national president of WLFC to the national executive of the Liberal party, 21–22 June 1969, LPC, vol. 1137, 2, NA.

53 LaMarsh, *Memoirs*, 283–5.

54 'Women in the Parliament of Canada,' by Cairine R. Wilson, 28 September 1942, CRW, vol. 6, file 9, 6, NA. The subsequent information is taken from the same source, 6; 'Wants More Say for Women,' Halifax *Chronicle Herald*, 13 January 1968, LBP, series N11, series C-2, vol. 280, NA.

55 Political education committee report by Barbara Perry Stevens, n.d., but approximately early 1950s, LPC, vol. 1061, 1, NA.

56 Report of NFLWC 25th Anniversary Meeting, 23 November 1953, LPC, vol. 1062, 347; report of NFLWC national convention, 29–30 October 1952, LPC, vol. 1062, 29, NA.

57 Cecile O'Regan in the *Liberal Woman* (1952 Special Report summarizing the proceedings of the Special General Meeting of the NFLWC), 3. The following quotations are taken from the same source, 3.

58 Report of NFLWC national convention, 29–30 October 1952, LPC, vol. 1062, 5–6. Subsequent references to McIlraith are taken from the same source, 6; report of NFLWC 25th Anniversary Meeting, 23 November 1953, LPC, vol. 1062, 341–6, NA.

59 J.L. Granatstein, *Canada's War* (Toronto 1975), 251; see esp. ch. 7.

60 Report of NFLWC 25th Anniversary Meeting, 23 November 1953, LPC, vol. 1062, 43, NA.

61 'Women ... and the Liberal party,' n.d., but probably late 1950s, LPC, vol. 1065, NA.

62 See for example, Charlotte Whitton, 'Canadian Women Belong in Politics,' *Chatelaine*, October 1961, 44, 152; Anne Carver, 'The Participation of

Women in Political Activities in Canada,' study prepared for the Royal
Commission on the Status of Women, 27, 46–7; Doris Anderson, 'Desegregating
the Women Scene,' *Chatelaine*, June 1969, LPC, vol. 1078, n.p.; *Report*,
345–6, NA.

63 *Liberal Woman* (n.d., but sometime late in 1969), 1–2.

64 Peter Regenstreif, 'The Liberal Party of Canada: A Political Analysis,' PhD
diss., Cornell University 1963, 188.

65 See, for example, 'Memorandum re Women's Role in Politics' from Ann Booth
to Mrs Winkler, 25 February 1964, LPC, vol. 1063; personal commentary
on the recent discussion on aims of the Liberal Women of Canada, Paul Goulet,
5 March 1964, LPC, vol. 1063, 1–5; 'What Women's Liberal Clubs Do or
Can Do,' questionnaire, no date but approximately 1968 or 1969, LPC, vol.
1064; 'Memorandum re Present and Future Status of WLFC' from Mrs B.
Earle MacDonald to the national executive committee, LFC, 12 November 1969,
LPC, vol. 1137; Senator Stanbury in the *Liberal Woman* (n.d., but sometime in
late 1969), 3–4; 'Proposal to Restructure the Women's Liberal Federation in
Order to Create an Effective Presence for Women within the Party Struc-
ture,' by Marie Gibeault, 29 May 1973, LPH, WLFC papers, 1–3, NA.

'A Respectable Feminist'

The Political Career of
Senator Cairine Wilson
1921–1962

Franca Iacovetta

In February 1930, one year after five Albertan suffragists had established the right of a woman to sit in the Canadian Senate,[1] Prime Minister Mackenzie King recommended the appointment of Cairine Wilson to the Upper Chamber. Apparently relieved that King had not chosen the most likely candidate, feisty Judge Emily Murphy, the Ottawa *Evening Journal* reported: 'Mrs. Wilson is the very antithesis of the short-haired reformer ... that unlovely type which talks of Freud and ... the latest novel and poses as an intellectual.' Rather, Wilson was 'of the much more appealing and competent kind who makes a success of ... taking care of a home and ... family before meddling with and trying to make a success of everything else.'[2] The focus of reporting soon shifted towards predictable discussions about an appropriate dress code for a woman politician, with some columnists encouraging the senator to wear inconspicuous suits and others feminine dresses. Wilson seemed to oblige the columnists by attending her swearing-in ceremony frocked in a stunning powder-blue lace gown, matching satin shoes, and a bouquet of orchids.[3] When addressing the Senate, Wilson similarly felt obliged to reassure her new male colleagues by making clear her intentions to fulfil all the responsibilities of her new position without neglecting her domestic duties.[4] 'I trust,' she stated, 'that the future will show that while engaged in public affairs the ... mother of a family by reason of her maternal instinct will remain the guardian of the home.' Although her comments were neither innovative nor surprising, they probably served their intended purpose. Yet, her next gesture was decidedly bold and dramatic. At the risk of tarnishing her 'appealing' image, Wilson took the occasion to acknowledge the heroic struggles of Canadian women throughout history and, moreover, to link her new honours with the political struggles of earlier feminists in Canada. Specifically, she expressed her indebtedness to the 'five women from Alberta' – Emily Murphy, Nellie McClung, Irene Parlby, Henrietta Muir Edwards, and Louise McKinney – whose victory in the 'person's case' made possible Wilson's appointment to the Senate.[5] So the message was out. The new senator was well mannered and likely would not cause serious trouble; although not as radical as some of her foremothers, she was none the less politically ambitious and a liberal feminist, not afraid to acknowledge the virtues of her predecessors.

Canadian feminist historians have ignored Cairine Wilson, despite her rich and lengthy career. Having dubbed the 1920s and 1930s as the era of the decline of feminism in Canada, scholars have sought to explain why, despite significant legal, educational, and political victories, many Canadian women (though not all, and certainly not the old vanguard) shunned activism after the First World War. Explanations correctly focused on the failure of earlier feminists, who viewed their public activities as part of their maternal responsibilities, to understand that their actions signalled a fundamental break with women's traditional domesticity. Moreover, by forgoing links with a variety of late Victorian reform movements, the campaign for female suffrage became detached from a purely women's rights platform (with its critique of the repressive features of traditional marriage) and from the radical minority that led the campaign for total equality for women. Instead, the suffrage movement became identified with the efforts of moderate, middle-class reformers seeking to preserve the family and Christian values in an urbanizing and industrializing society. By the turn of the century, feminism's earlier link with spiritualism, labour, and democratic radicalism had given way to a narrower notion of maternal feminism that focused on women's motherly contribution to the family and the state. As a result, feminists lacked an analysis of gender as socially constructed and found themselves without a coherent political and economic program for complete liberation. Even the professionally inclined 'new woman' of the post-war period not only accepted the prevailing image of femininity as gentle, innocent, and mildly coquettish, but also sought marriage and family as necessary conditions of womanhood.[6]

Yet, the post–First World War period did not witness a total stagnation of reform initiatives. Women continued to participate in public-health campaigns and long-time suffragists such as Albertan Liberal MLA McClung and United Farmers of Alberta (UFA) representative Parlby remained in politics and progressive movements. Others, including McClung and Lady Aberdeen of the National Council of Women, also turned their efforts towards internationalist and peace campaigns. In light of the earlier defeat of the more radical class- and gender-linked forms of feminism, the kind of feminism that held the best hope of making some inroads on the post-war Canadian political scene was a loosely structured liberal-reformist maternal feminism that called for social and political reforms but did not fundamentally challenge the structural and ideological roots of women's oppression under capitalist patriarchy. Given the reality of the Liberal hegemony over post-war Canadian politics, the respectability of bourgeois feminism probably also depended on its being presented to Parliament and the Canadian public under a Liberal banner.[7]

Cairine Wilson emerged as a feminist politician in this period. She was Canada's first woman senator, a liberal feminist, a peace activist, and a humanitarian. Wilson's social and political philosophy was shaped primarily by two related ideologies. First and foremost was her commitment to a nineteenth-century Gladstonian liberalism, which combined religious and political notions of duty in the belief that Christianity could have a purifying impact on the political process. A staunch Presbyterian, Wilson viewed politics as a way of performing God's work on earth, and she sought to fulfil that objective by supporting humanitarian causes, including world peace, the resettlement of Jewish refugees, and the medical and social work of the League of Nations. Wilson's Christianity and her liberalism, in turn, fuelled her commitment to maternal feminism. She believed that women's public demands were a logical extension of women's maternal responsibility and their moral superiority, as well as the inevitable result of the application of democratic principles to women. Wealthy, professional, politically well connected, and a mother of eight, Wilson strikingly resembled the ideal late-nineteenth-century maternal feminist. She was not a radical; her appeal for Canadians was as an exceptional Superwoman, who could successfully balance a demanding career and a large family. One male senator went so far as to call her the 'ideal Canadian woman and all the best that is in womanhood.'[8]

Still, too much can be made of such conservatism. Indeed, the recent emphasis on the conservative and accommodationist character of the suffrage movement underestimates its truly radical dimension, for the presence of women in the public domain challenged centuries-old traditions. So, too, did women's demands for citizenship, whatever the justification for them. Although feminism did not always occupy a central position in Wilson's politics, she clearly shared with her feminist predecessors a vision of a peaceful and co-operative world purged of masculine values of competition and aggression. Toward that end, she worked for years with various church and reform organizations, including the Presbyterian church and its Women's Missionary Society, the Red Cross, the Victorian Order of Nurses, and the Ottawa Welfare Bureau, as well as the Young Women's Christian Association and the National Council of Women of Canada. In the Senate she supported women's issues, such as more liberal divorce laws, equal pay and equal access to jobs, and welfare measures for working and poor mothers. The significance of Wilson's long career, which spanned the years 1920 to 1962, should not be underestimated. Despite her moderate feminism, Wilson's long-standing presence among liberals and humanitarians in Canadian politics presented an ongoing challenge to conservative administrators. It also illustrated the nature of the contribution that middle-class, professional women could make to politics and to a feminist movement in Canada. Maternal feminism was fraught with ambiguities and political shortcomings, but it also provided an increasingly acceptable ideological vehicle for expanding women's participation in the public sphere.

I

Wilson was born Cairine Reay Mackay on 4 February 1884 in the West End of Montreal. Her father, Robert Mackay, was a wealthy and influential Scottish businessman in Montreal and a Liberal senator. Her mother, Jane Baptist, was a woman of Scottish descent and the daughter of a Trois-Rivières lumber-baron. Cairine grew up as one of four children in the privileged comfort of the anglophone bourgeoisie of Montreal. One newspaper described her childhood in graphic terms: 'She had nurses, governesses, child specialists, tutors, attended private schools, took music, French, painting, learned to ride.'[9] However, she did not go to college. Instead, she attended two private ladies' academies in Montreal where, as she later recalled, 'we were always called "Young Ladies" and heard often of that most desirable attribute, the soft low voice of a woman.'[10] Continuing on a traditional route, in 1909, 24-year-old Cairine married Norman F. Wilson, a wealthy Montreal lumberman and a one-time Liberal MP for Russell County. She was a noted philanthropist, an avid sportswoman, and a popular socialite. Predictably, however, she considered the five girls and three boys to whom she gave birth over the next ten years to be among her greatest personal and social achievements, for as she often noted, 'mother love is the strongest instinct of [woman's] nature.'[11]

Wilson's Victorian upbringing profoundly shaped her attitude towards social and political action. Under the dominating influence of its patriarchal head, the Mackay family was strongly evangelical in its approach to the responsibility of the rich and powerful to perform public service. A public-spirited man, Robert Mackay founded in 1870 the family-operated Mackay Institute for the Deaf.[12] He also impressed upon his children their duty to follow his example and combine a lucrative career with an active Christian life. Defending her father's strict approach to child-rearing,

Wilson applauded his making the same demands of his daughters as he did of his sons. 'Father,' she noted, 'felt that girls should do something purposeful – study, become something, go beyond the fashion magazines.'[13] Following her father's lead, young Cairine became involved in volunteer work in the Presbyterian church. She did charity work for the church's Homes for Unwed Mothers and she supported the overseas work of the Women's Missionary Society. As a senator, she continued to host countless teas and fund-raisers, and she also contributed to *The Presbyterian Record* and the Women's Missionary Society newsletter, *Glad Tidings*.

In the tradition of evangelicalism, Wilson associated Christianity with a commitment to philanthropic and reform work aimed at improving the lot of humankind. 'I'm a Presbyterian,' she informed a reporter in 1930, 'and there's the everlasting job of trying to be of some real use in the world; trying to make life a little brighter, a little more tolerable for the unfortunate.'[14] Elsewhere, she singled out three types of Christians. The first, an insincere Christian, 'stands aside to let somebody else assume the responsibility.' Somewhat better, the next type is at least 'willing to undertake the work if it does not place too great demands upon his or her time and money.' Unfortunately, most fell into this category of 'cosy little Christians' satisfied with their regular attendance at church and uninterested in changing the world. It was the third kind of Christian – the 'active Christian' – whom Wilson admired. She praised such 'militant Christians' as the Presbyterian missionary women for courageously and selflessly devoting their energies and resources on behalf of the underprivileged of Asia and Africa.[15] Similarly, she supported politicians who actively promoted the work of the League of Nations (and later the United Nations) as true Christians devoted to rebuilding a world upon the ideas of 'brotherly love and co-operation.'[16]

Described as 'a Scots Liberal who worshipped at the Shrine of Gladstone and Bright,'[17] Robert Mackay also imparted to his daughter a belief in the superiority of liberalism and the tradition of Gladstone. Although Wilson admitted that growing up in a protective family denied her the opportunity 'to develop a sense of self-expression and independence,' and to 'overcome a great natural timidity,' politics provided an attractive outlet for a young woman reared in a deeply politicized environment.[18] As one newspaper reported shortly after her Senate appointment, 'Mrs. Wilson grew up in an atmosphere redolent with political decision, and [she] cannot remember the time when she did not know intimately the chief political and economic issues in the Dominion.'[19] As a girl, she was read long passages on the philosophies of Liberal Scots, particularly John Fox, John Bright, and William Ewart Gladstone.[20] Under her father's guidance, Wilson associated the tradition they represented with the

Liberal party in Canada. This was reinforced by her family's long-standing connections with prominent Canadian Liberals, including Wilfrid Laurier (whom Wilson idolized as the country's greatest national statesman) and, later, Mackenzie King.[21]

What most attracted Wilson to liberalism was the unity Gladstone perceived between politics and religion. His ideas influenced her desire to combine religious service and reform-oriented politics. This desire involved an almost obsessive devotion to humanitarian and reform causes on behalf of society's underprivileged. Wilson made this commitment the central precept of her public career.[22] She called herself a Gladstonian Liberal, and she shared with her political colleagues, including William Lyon Mackenzie King, a conviction that a liberal democratic tradition, infused with Christian precepts, would ensure conservative and radical attacks against it. Indeed, she viewed parliamentary democracy as the political expression of Christianity. 'The relation between Christianity and self-government,' she observed, 'has long been recognized. Thomas Mann put it thus: "Democracy is nothing but the political name for the ideals of Christianity."'[23] True to the tradition, Wilson believed that the democratic process was premised on intelligent debate and the political education of the masses, 'education in citizenship and political responsibility.' The fate of democracy lay in the 'ideals of its people and the willingness of each individual to serve his or her community or country.' Such commitment went beyond a simple exercise of the franchise and demanded as well that people publicly express their opinions and accept their historic role to keep their elected governments responsible to people. 'If we claim the right to express our opinions,' she explained, 'we must accept responsibility for what [governments] do.'[24]

These convictions gave Wilson a genuine sense of optimism, despite the reality she confronted in her lifetime – a world torn apart by the Great Depression, two world wars, and fascism. Such challenges, she believed, could only be met through the devoted work of true Christians. During a speech on behalf of European Jewish refugees in 1939, Wilson expressed a familiar argument, insisting that Canadians 'cannot yield to despair however grim the prospects ... No matter how dark the outlook, faith and hope are the essence of our religion.' She called upon Canadians to act decisively 'as Christians' and to use their governments to promote a better world. On a more ethnocentric note, she also maintained that the struggle 'for human rights ... justice to the poor, the suffering, and the backward peoples of the world,' was to be led by the educated and propertied citizens of the industrial nations of Western Europe. The wretched and the uncivilized coloured populations of the world's poor countries would eventually come under the enlightening umbrella and the homogenizing influence of Christianity and western modernity – not to mention British customs and institutions![25]

It seems obvious that her father provided Wilson with a role model of committed Christianity and democratic liberalism, but it is not clear when Wilson became a feminist. She did not participate directly in the suffrage movement, although for years she had worked with reform groups that eventually pledged their support for the franchise. Significantly, Wilson did not enter active politics until after she had been married for ten years and had given birth to all her children. Like that of many of her feminist predecessors, her decision to enter public life reflected to a remarkable degree her disillusionment with her dependent existence as an upper-middle-class house-wife. In a 1931 *Canadian Home Journal* article, Wilson admitted:

My marriage brought me great happiness, but deprived me of practically all outside companionship. For ten years I devoted myself so exclusively to the management of three houses [in Montreal, Ottawa, and St Andrews-by-the-Sea, New Brunswick] and the care of my children that a blunt doctor finally brought me up with a start. Never had he seen any person deteriorate mentally as I had, he told me, and from an intelligent girl I had become a most uninteresting individual. I have been grateful since that date for his frank words, for it caused me to realize that the work which I had always considered my duty was not sufficient. At once I made a determined effort not to merit such condemnation and have endeavoured to keep alert.[26]

The sources do not allow us to make definitive statements about why Wilson chose to enter politics rather than some other public career. In a 1930 interview she admitted that her 'social equals' could not understand why a woman of wealth, social prestige, and a large family would want 'to tackle politics in so practical a way.' She simply explained that politics had always appealed to her and that she liked the challenge and excitement. She had not only held her father in high esteem as a politician, but also admired the many politicians she had met during her long years of contact with the Liberal party brass.[27]

A model of maternal feminism supplied Wilson with an ideological justification for entering public life. It also provided her with a political program. Far from accepting cynical denunciations about the failure of women to radicalize the political process, Wilson believed that the women's suffrage movement provided important political lessons. Feminist politicians were obliged to educate, and co-operate with, their more progressive male colleagues so that together they might force the introduction of legal and economic reforms.[28] This effort placed heavy demands on women politicians who were expected to prove their competence in public affairs and push for feminist reforms without alienating their male colleagues. Only then would women receive the attention they deserved as the nation's 'natural reformers.'[29] Stopping far short of any radical platform, Wilson even cautioned women against making rash declarations because they might jeopardize the gains they had made to date. Wilson did envision a future when, as she put it, 'my children will have less and less use for party politics as conducted in the old partizan [sic] lines,'[30] but she also believed that the present task at hand called for reforming the mainstream 'male-stream' Canadian political process.[31]

Soon after she became an active Liberal party worker in 1921, Wilson earned a solid reputation as an efficient organizer and a feminist committed to enlarging women's participation within the party. She organized the women's committee that worked for King's 1930 campaign, and she helped to organize the Young Liberals, in which her daughters were active. She also founded the Eastern Ontario Liberal Women's Association and the Ontario Women's Liberal Club. Her greatest party achievement, the National Federation of Liberal Women (NFLW), elevated the status of Liberal women by making the party's chief policy-making body equally accessible to the women's as well as the men's association, in theory if not always in practice. At Wilson's insistence, the NFLW fostered research into social, economic, and political matters so that it could better offer informed proposals to the party.[32] It also issued a formal request that 'strong women' be encouraged to run as candidates in future elections.[33] These changes were greeted with hostility and resentment from many male party members who believed that women should remain in politically inferior auxiliary committees.[34] Nevertheless, Wilson's patience eventually paid off, as her Senate appointment demonstrates.

Significantly, Wilson's commitment to the feminization of politics cut across party lines. In countless speeches delivered to political, union, and women's organizations, Wilson encouraged women to become politically involved and to pressure their government into legislating progressive social and legal measures. The vote had empowered women, and Wilson called upon them to use their self-sacrificing character to promote social reforms.[35]

The abolition of war was a top priority. Wilson argued that women had a mission to improve the world: 'Women feel impatient of the man-governed world with its succession of wars, and realize that we must discover a way to bring peace.'[36] As a way to combat men's hawkishness, women, she argued, 'must stand for the principle of co-operation and tolerance,' and they must 'promote legislation which benefits women and children.'[37] She believed that women had a special interest as women to promote peace and create a better society for their children, tasks for which women were specially suited by virtue of their nurturing qualities.[38] Significantly, however, men were not excluded from the same responsibility. Going beyond the narrow connection between motherhood and social conscience, Wilson understood that women as human beings shared a fundamental interest with men in the preservation of a healthy, peaceful world. Without the abolition of war, there was no hope for the human race.[39]

There were definite limitations to Wilson's feminism, particularly to the extent that it developed in tandem with her liberalism and its emphasis on slow, evolutionary change. With regard to the role of women in transforming the deeply imbedded material and ideological structures of patriarchal society, Wilson offered a reformist package that would enable women to earn the privileges currently permitted only to men. Although she avoided any explicit discussion of class relations, Wilson clearly believed that well-educated, professional, middle-class, native-born Canadian women were the natural leaders of the feminist movement in Canada. Education and training, as well as the time and money to pursue them, were crucial assets in the struggle against male privilege, but so were respectability and the proper political and social connections. As a by-product of the victories of bourgeois women, feminine values would slowly but irrevocably infiltrate the political and social processes of the nation, indeed of the world.[40]

Notwithstanding such limits, Wilson had an acute consciousness of the reality of women's oppression throughout history. 'For thousands of years,' she noted, 'we have been obliged to accept a man-made estimate of our capabilities and to rely for recognition upon [men's] favour.' As a result, women have been denied their 'natural' capacity for peaceful, collective action and for important and meaningful work. Forced into a state of submission, women were expected to link their fates to the exploits of their men. Indeed, they were forced to compete for the favours of men: 'Each woman strove to supplant the other and we were accused of jealousy and strife.'[41] Wilson observed that even 'famous women' in medicine, law, and education whose accomplishments challenged the gender inequities of their day had failed to develop a feminist and collectivist consciousness around the need to improve the position of women as a group, attesting to the extent to which the dominant values of patriarchal society were deeply imbedded.

This is not to suggest that Wilson did not support the individual exploits of pioneer women, for she frequently reduced women's history to a list of 'first women.'[42] Nevertheless, she paid constant tribute to the past efforts of women to circumvent male prerogative and sexual inequality. With their capacity to endure physical handicaps and demanding domestic duties, the Brontë sisters were special heroines for Wilson, and she described them as writing 'under conditions which would have daunted any ordinary mortal.'[43] She observed how women artists such as Jane Austen and George Eliot were forced to conceal their craft and that even Florence Nightingale was criticized during the Crimean War for stepping beyond her rightful sphere.[44] Closer to home, Wilson repeatedly praised the early pioneer and missionary women of Canada, 'who braved the horrors of the dreadful ocean voyage and the uncertain terrors of the new land to establish homes and bring news of Christ to the Indian peoples and to minister to the sick, both colonists and Indians.'[45] Marie Hébert, the first white child, was usually singled out for specific praise for preaching Christianity to the Indians, and for taking care of the sick and wounded during the early years of the French colony.[46]

It was not merely political opportunism that led Wilson to declare her Senate appointment a significant achievement for Canadian womanhood. Although well aware that Prime Minister King had chosen her as a 'safe' alternative to the more outspoken (and more radical) Emily Murphy, Wilson also felt that she was being fairly rewarded for years of loyal service to the party. During those years it seems that Wilson had also developed a fuller commitment to maternal feminism. Politically, she now associated herself with the suffragists and was careful not to distinguish between the radical advocates of women's rights and the more conservative reformers who had participated in the suffrage campaign. Much later in her career, she even attributed the emergence of the women's suffrage movement to the 'vision and courage of Dr. Emily Stowe,'[47] a natural rights suffragist and founder of the first woman suffrage association in Canada. Upon taking office, Wilson insisted that her new status was the natural outcome of the pioneering efforts of earlier feminists: 'My promotion has come so easily that ... I should like to give credit to the members of my sex, who have struggled so long and courageously for these privileges which we accept naturally today.'[48]

It is impossible to separate the strands of Wilson's feminism from her devotion to a Christian and liberal view of the world. Indeed, liberalism and feminism emerged as complementary and mutually reinforcing elements in her social and political philosophy, and they lay at the source of her tremendous capacity for humanitarian work. Wilson was a humanitarian par excellence and no serious study of her career can ignore the intimate link between her humanitarianism and her feminism. Both grew out of her desire to perform God's work on earth. Among the many causes to which she devoted her energy, Wilson took particular pride in the work she performed on behalf of the League of Nations Society of Canada and its brain-child, the Canadian National Committee for Refugees.

Founded in 1921, the League of Nations Society was devoted to world peace; its members included various liberals and reformers in the country, among them, Rev. C.E. Silcox of the United Church and Anglican Canon W.W. Judd. Veronica Strong-Boag has recently argued that the prominent men who initially chaired the organization eventually turned it over to the women who composed the majority of the society's membership. By the 1930s, the society was primarily a women's peace organization chaired by Senator Wilson.[49] She and her colleagues sought to arouse public support for the League of Nations' international peace-keeping activities, including arms limitation, tariff reductions, and social and health programs. Wilson identified the society's priority as that of focusing attention on the responsibility of Canadians 'to express our wishes and desires as to the kind of peace that we want for Canada and the world.'[50]

Working in close co-operation with church, women's, and veterans' clubs, the society organized disarmament conferences and established local branches across the country. At Wilson's encouragement, NCWC local councils conducted many membership and fund-raising drives.[51] Wilson campaigned vigorously to convince active club and church women to take up the cause of international politics and world peace. Calling on them 'to use their influence to promote a better understanding between nations,' she argued that women were capable of averting the human disasters that men seemed invariably to cause. War grew out of men's greed and ambition, and if women 'who realize the futility of war [and] the suffering it entails' had taken an interest, 'wars would have been a thing of the past.'[52] In an uncharacteristic explosion of anger in the spring of 1933, Wilson castigated armament manufacturers and hawkish national statesmen for engaging in war as a profit-making venture: 'Were the warlords and manufacturers of ammunition required to stand in the trenches, we should not be forced to war for national aggrandizement.'[53]

During the 1930s, as the world moved towards another war, the League of Nations and its Canadian branch came under a great deal of criticism. Staunchly defending the League of Nations against charges that its purpose had become meaningless and irrelevant, Wilson observed that critics and supporters alike stressed only the league's ambitious military objectives without considering its contributions to health and medicine and its attempt to solve social and labour problems. Insisting that the league 'seeks not merely to prevent wars which are looming on the horizon, but to remove the causes of war through the friendly co-operation of the peoples of all countries,' Wilson presented an impressive list of the league's activities. These included its supervision of thousands of prisoners of war returned to their original or adopted home immediately after the First World War, its rescue work on behalf of Turkish and Christian women forcibly evicted from their homes during the Middle East wars of the 1920s, and its creation of an international communications system to detect and regulate the spread of the plague, cholera, and smallpox in Asia, Australia, and Africa.[54]

As the attacks grew, Wilson refused to give ground on the issue. In 1934 she defended the league against a colleague's claim that it had fallen into the hands of extremist pacifists by observing that the Canadian branch of the league included numerous veterans with honourable war records. She again pointed an accusing finger at the 'provocative and sinister influence' of armament manufacturers who were operating at huge profits despite the international depression. The only way to eliminate their insidious presence was to call for 'total discontinuance by nations of the manufacture and sale of armaments.' When another senator supported a motion for Canada's withdrawal from the league on the dubious grounds that modern warfare had become more humane as more soldiers survived the ordeal, Wilson made a mockery of his assertion: 'For the wife or mother who loses a son or husband, it makes little difference that 99 per cent are saved if the loved one loses his life or returns home a helpless cripple.' She added: 'The slaughter and devastation of the late world conflict' had already disproved the assertion.[55]

Despite Wilson's efforts, the League of Nations Society could barely withstand such sustained public attack. Ironically, the Jewish refugee crisis served to revitalize the society and its leaders, and it led to the creation of the Canadian National Committee on Refugees (CNCR) in October 1938. The CNCR emerged as a direct response to Hitler's annexation of Austria and Czechoslovakia and the subsequent Munich Settlement, a sequence of events that resulted in thousands of Jews seeking shelter on the continent and in Great Britain. Its origin also coincided with the decision of the Canadian Jewish Congress (CJC) to endorse a non-denominational anti-Nazi lobby group. The CJC largely funded the CNCR's campaign and helped to establish local branches across the country, although it did so covertly in order to avoid having the committee discredited as a 'Jewish front.'[56] Local church and NCWC councils also organized chapters. Senator Wilson acted as chair of the CNCR.

The aims of the CNCR were twofold. First, it lobbied King's administration for the immediate liberalization of Canada's existing restrictionist immigration regulations in order to permit the entry of substantial numbers of Jewish refugees, particularly skilled workers and entrepreneurs. Second, it embarked on an educational campaign with the hope that by exposing Canadians to the reality of the Nazi horrors and the desperate plight of European Jewry it would 'instil in them a more sympathetic attitude toward the reception of refugees.' Wilson certainly believed that the calamity of the crisis was sufficient to motivate Canadians to offer their homes to Jews. Following the government's decision in the fall of 1938 to accept thousands of Sudeten refugees, she also believed that Canadian politicians would come around on the Jewish question. [57] But neither Wilson nor her colleagues could have anticipated the virtually impenetrable wall of racism erected by the government and the people of Canada to keep out the Jews of Europe. [58] Wilson wrote despairingly to a friend: 'It has been unexpectedly difficult to arouse public sympathy into meaningful action.' [59]

No one was worse off than Jewish children and the CNCR pledged its strongest support on their behalf. Drawing a link between motherhood and child-rescue work, Wilson felt certain that homes could be found for orphaned and separated children because Canadian mothers would rally to the cause. She campaigned vigorously to convince women to take advantage of this opportunity to prove their superior capacity for humane and caring work. [60] But the anticipated response was not forthcoming. While the committee scored a small victory in the summer of 1939 by forcing the government to admit 100 'bona fide' Jewish orphans then residing temporarily in Britain, the outbreak of war disrupted the project. As public support grew for British mothers and children threatened with evacuation during the war, interest in Jewish children waned, and various women's committees, led by prominent social worker Charlotte Whitton, began to organize for a British evacuation movement to Canada. Although Whitton was a key member of the CNCR, she had never been trusted by the Canadian Jewish community and even Wilson, who naturally approved of the British children scheme, now suspected Whitton of collaborating with the director of immigration, F.C. Blair, to destroy the Jewish project. [61] Another attempt to rescue Jewish refugees was aimed at Jewish women and children interned under the pro-Nazi Vichy government of France. It also failed. No more schemes were proposed, [62] although after the war Wilson continued to support child-immigration schemes. [63] In 1950 France made her a Knight of the Legion of Honour for her courageous work on behalf of Jewish refugee children in Europe. [64]

After the war, Wilson continued to support liberal immigration and refugee policies. In the Senate in 1943, she had observed that refugees who entered Canada in wartime had disproved the old arguments about immigrants taking jobs from Canadians, for many had set up new businesses and were making valuable economic contributions to the country. The Koerners from Austria, for instance, had established in British Columbia the second-largest plywood factory in the world. Another Jew, Louis Fischel, initiated a glove-making industry in Prescott County. And the Bata shoe family had created numerous jobs in Ontario. Caught up in the cold-war politics of the post-war period, Wilson also viewed these cases of successful entrepreneurship as victories against the new Communist 'menace,' and she warned Canadians that the only way to repudiate Soviet charges about racial and economic discrimination under capitalism was to provide concrete evidence of the opportunities and freedoms that flourish in a bourgeois democracy.[65]

At the encouragement of Sen. Arthur Roebuck, a liberal progressive and long-time supporter of immigration, Wilson headed the Senate Standing Committee on Immigration and Labour from 1946 to 1948. With the support of various ethnic groups, many of whose compatriots included refugees and displaced persons currently languishing in camps on the continent and in Britain, the committee enthusiastically endorsed an expansionist and non-discriminatory post-war immigration policy.[66] To Wilson, this recommendation was a logical extension of her wartime refugee work. Now, however, she found herself in the company of such unlikely allies as humanitarians, cabinet ministers, ethnic leaders, and big business. Indeed, the recommendations of the Senate committee reflected a dramatic shift among business and political interests toward large-scale immigration. Led by the minister of reconstruction, the powerful C.D. Howe, Canadian immigration officials became interested in recruiting young, hard-working labourers from Europe to replenish the country's labour supply, particularly in the extractive industries. The displaced-persons camps emerged as a major source of labour, but immigration officials continued to exclude Jews, although they now did so covertly by advising their overseas inspection teams to reject Jewish applicants.[67] Whether Wilson was aware of this exclusion or not is uncertain, but she did support the Department of Labour's official campaign to recruit able-bodied refugees and displaced persons. By 1951 she had also turned her attention to the provision of adequate language and work-skills programs for new immigrants. That these programs provided the country with an opportunity to mould 'new Canadians' out of old foreigners did not go unnoticed by Wilson. Indeed, she even likened the task to the civilizing efforts of Christian missionaries overseas.[69]

II

For over three decades the harsh political realities of the day overshadowed the potency of women's issues in Canadian politics. Even Wilson's loyalties were divided between war-related calamities that required immediate attention and legislative reforms on behalf of women's legal and economic rights, although she would have argued that both sets of issues required feminist and humanist solutions. Whatever might be said of Wilson's cautious brand of feminism and of the questionable influence of the Senate on Parliament and public opinion, the Senate record reveals her consistent support for measures designed to improve the economic independence and career opportunities of Canadian women, and to upgrade the health and welfare benefits available to poor and working women. Unlike many senators, who tend to recede into public oblivion soon after their appointment, Wilson deliberately publicized her position and openly campaigned for the causes she supported. She set out on countless speaking tours during which she addressed not only women's clubs but political, religious, and reform organizations, as well as such obviously male-dominated groups as veterans' associations and monarchist leagues. In addition, numerous women's columns and magazine articles chronicled her political career.

Wilson championed her bourgeois model of the ideal woman as an efficient household manager and active club woman devoted to public affairs. In speeches across the country she advised women to embrace the new labour-saving devices so that they would be free to pursue careers and public work. She also lamented the arresting impact of femininity on women, especially those embarking on professional careers. By constantly reaffirming the trait of 'womanly patience,' she noted in a 1939 speech to domestic-science graduates, many women have remained unconcerned with achieving independence, even failing to design the very tools that have eased the burden of their domestic duties.[69] Yet, Wilson did not reject totally the prevailing stereotypes of women. In a 1930 speech to the Toronto Women's Teachers' Association, Wilson opposed the feminization of teaching because she felt that children's constant exposure to women's peculiarly feminine qualities, especially 'too much sentimentality,' might have adverse effects on the students, particularly the males. Later, during the cold-war politics of the post-war period, she maintained that education should first and foremost promote patriotism.[70]

Two issues of central importance to Wilson concerned women's access to career opportunities and liberal divorce laws. Her philosophical justification was premised on liberal precepts: women, too, had a right to equality of opportunity, property, and happiness. Early in her career, Wilson even denounced the League of Nations for failing to comply with Article Seven of the Covenant under which all posts were open to men and women. Women were virtually excluded from all but the junior and non-political posts, and no attempt had been made to replace retired women with new female appointments. In what amounted to a proposal in favour of affirmative action, Wilson insisted that the league actively recruit qualified women to head important committees.[71] Several decades later, she recounted with obvious pride her own experience as Canada's first woman delegate to the United Nations Fourth General Assembly in 1949, when she worked on the committee devoted to the status of women and the International Save the Children Fund (UNICEF).[72]

Similarly, she supported the decision of the 1947 Liberal party convention to endorse the appointment of a woman to the Civil Service Commission and to the Unemployment Commission. She felt that the appointments could not be more appropriate given the large numbers of women employed in the civil service and dependent on welfare benefits. Later that year, she also applauded the government's plans for a women's bureau in the Department of Labour to be headed by a woman. Although these were small gestures, Wilson acknowledged such administrative changes as significant advances in women's struggles to be considered as competent professionals, and she hoped that such government trends would expand into the private sector.[73]

For over three decades Wilson consistently and courageously supported the liberalization of divorce laws on the grounds that women had a right to a respectable and non-stigmatizing way out of a miserable, even life-threatening, marriage. During the 1930s, when much of the Senate debates revolved around the issue of expanding legitimate grounds for divorce, Wilson advocated adding men's desertion and the threat of violence as valid grounds for divorce, and she denounced the suggestion that desertion exceed seven years before an abandoned wife could file for divorce. She stood firm in her condemnation of the views expressed by her male colleagues, who, predictably, equated the 'loosening up' of rigid divorce laws with the breakdown of traditional Christian values and the moral decay of Canadian society.[74]

In their presentations, male senators portrayed women seeking divorce as scheming villainesses taking undue advantage of lax legal codes in order to gratify their carnal desires and to escape the duties of wifery and motherhood. In response, Wilson dismissed simplistic correlations between divorce and social decay and insisted that married people, herself included, had no right to impose marriage on others as the ideal arrangement because it ignored the sexual inequality upon which the institution was premised and the plain fact that many women suffered miserably unhappy marriages. No woman, she added, should be forced to submit to cruel and unfair treatment at the hands of her husband. Commenting on the harsh experiences of a young woman friend abandoned by her husband for over eight years, Wilson dismissed any sexist notions that might lay the blame on the woman's undesirable character: '[A] young woman had a right to lead a happy life ... it was not her fault that her husband ran away.'[75]

By 1955 Wilson's tone became sharper as she argued that marriage laws reflected the fact that 'for centuries women have been treated as a piece of men's property.' 'A woman today,' she added, 'demands a goodness of her own making upon a new set of values, for she realizes that since the early days of patriarchal society, morality laws have been framed for her subjugation.'[76]

These were strong words and they indicated Wilson's increasing frustration with the chauvinist ethos of the 1950s and the moralizing male politicians. Although she believed that many divorced women might find happiness in a second marriage, Wilson acknowledged the growing number of single mothers forced to enter the labour force without any marketable skills and without day-care facilities for their children. Consequently, she also advocated alimony and child-custody payments. To Wilson's credit, for she certainly considered herself a happily married woman, she understood that the central issue in divorce was a feminist one, that women had the right to control their lives and those of their children. For the same reasons she opposed the Naturalization Act that made it obligatory for a Canadian woman who married a foreign national to accept her husband's nationality. Such legislation was as harmful to women, she observed in 1959, as the outmoded property laws of Quebec where, only forty years earlier, married women had been 'classed with inmates of mental institutions, minors and Indians, and not permitted to vote even in municipal affairs.' At that time, her husband, a resident of Ontario, had received the voting papers for property she owned in her home town Montreal.[77]

Wilson's feminism stopped far short of a critique of industrial capitalism and its exploitation of wage-earning women. Her genuine concern for the daily struggles of poor and working-class women, as well as rural women, was tainted by the paternalism common to her class. However, she did acknowledge that 'women in industry were not working for a few luxuries, but were forced outside the home in order to help support their husbands and children.'[78] Subscribing to stereotypical images of the urban lower orders as susceptible to idleness and potentially destructive behaviour, Wilson believed that working-class children often came from broken or unhappy homes. It was therefore up to the state and members of the respectable stratum to help workers 'maintain their morale [and] keep their families together.' But she also encouraged middle-income and wealthy housewives, as well as professional women, to support government welfare and social-service schemes and to pressure their MPs into endorsing improved unemployment and health services.[79]

As the Second World War came to an end, Wilson wondered how the transition from a wartime to peacetime economy would affect the status and earning power of Canadian women, especially those who had been employed in war industries and who were now expected to turn over their jobs, and their new-found independence, to returning veterans. She was particularly concerned with establishing a post-war national health organization in co-operation with all the provincial governments, whose functions would be to subsidize mothers, especially poor and working single mothers, and to develop infant health care as a way of combating infant mortality, which she understood to be a class as well as a gender issue. She also insisted that health services be extended to the sick and elderly.[80] These demands were costly. They were also progressive, humane, and courageous, words that might well describe Sen. Cairine Wilson.

III

The class and gender limitations of Wilson's liberal feminism should not detract from the importance of her lengthy career as the first woman senator in Canada and as a respected humanitarian politician and active feminist. Faced with the hostility of colleagues, the difficult political realities of the day, and the general ambivalence of Canadians towards women's rights, it is not surprising that Wilson did not make impressive political gains for feminism. Despite these obstacles, she effectively used her influence within the Liberal party and government to pursue progressive reforms on behalf of the disadvantaged, including women, and to promote peace. Her efforts did not go unnoticed. In 1960, a woman friend and colleague wrote to Wilson to express her admiration for the senator. 'You have always been,' wrote Margaret Wherry, 'a person of such great integrity ... To so many refugees you have become a friend ... To us who worked with you on various Committees you were always a great source of sound and considered judgement ... thanks for the trail you have blazed for Canadian women.'[81] At the time of her death in March 1962, CJC vice-president Saul Hayes wrote to Wilson's daughter: 'The Canadian Jewish Community has cause to mourn the death of your esteemed mother whose actions on fundamental freedoms and ... rights has [sic] illuminated the pages of recent Canadian history. It was one of the rich experiences of my life that I knew senator Wilson so well and looked upon her ... as a great resource in the great humanitarian work which we were called to do ... Her life work should be the best tribute to the memory of a grand and great woman.'[82]

Humanitarianism was the essence of Wilson's feminism and it grew out of her intense commitment to an evangelical Christian tradition and to an English liberal tradition that stressed self-sacrifice and godly work in politics. It also reflected her belief that well-educated and enlightened middle-class women could make a fundamental contribution to the women's movement by entering the political sphere and promoting reform, particularly social reforms aimed at addressing the disadvantaged position of society's victims. Significantly, she understood that women deserved special treatment in this regard, and in the Senate she gave women's issues her undivided attention. The length of her career and the admiration she had earned by the end of it contradict the notion that, after the suffrage victory, women fell into the category of either passive femininity or, as the reporter of our opening story put it, an 'unlovely type' of brash feminism. Wilson presented the Canadian public with a model of respectable feminism. Although that image would often be unfairly used against more radical women, it also played an important role in making feminism and the presence of women in public positions acceptable to Canadian men and women.

NOTES

I would like to thank Ruth Compton Brouwer, Ruth Frager, Craig Heron, Susan Houston, Linda Kealey, and Ian Radforth for their helpful comments on earlier drafts of this paper.

1 On the person's case, see Catherine Cleverdon, *The Woman Suffrage Movement in Canada* (Toronto 1974), 141–55; Eleanor Hartman, 'Five Persons from Alberta,' in Mary Quayle Innis, ed., *The Clear Spirit* (Toronto 1966), 240–59.

2 *Evening Journal*, 12 February 1930; *Ottawa Citizen*, 12 and 15 February 1930; also cited in Mary Lowry Ross, 'First Lady of the Senate' *Saturday Night*, 11 June 1955; *The Gazette* (Montreal), 22 February 1980.

3 Cited in Ross, 'First Lady,' 51.

4 Wilson was so intimidated by the hostile reception she received that she remained silent during the opening session (*Senate Debates* [hereafter SD], 20 February 1930). See also W. Kunz, *The Modern Senate of Canada* (Ottawa 1965), 54–6.

5 SD, 21 February 1930.

6 On Canada, see Carol Bacchi, *Liberation Deferred? The Ideas of the English-Canadian Suffragists, 1877–1918* (Toronto 1983); Linda Kealey, ed., *A Not Unreasonable Claim: Women and Reform in Canada, 1880s–1920s* (Toronto 1979); W.R. Morrison, 'Their Proper Sphere: Feminism, the Family and Child-Centred Social Reform in Ontario,' *Ontario History* 68 (March and June 1976), 45–74; Veronica Strong-Boag, *The Parliament of Women: The National Council of Women of Canada 1893–1929* (Ottawa 1976), and her 'Canadian Feminism in the 1920s: The Case of Nellie McClung,' *Journal of Canadian Studies* 12:4 (Summer 1977), 58–68.

On the United States, see, for example, Jill Conway, 'Women Reformers and American Culture 1870–1930,' *Journal of Social History* 5 (Winter 1971–2), 164–77; Carl Degler, *At Odds: Women and Family in America from the Revolution to the Present* (New York 1980); Ellen DuBois, 'The Radicalism of the Women's Suffrage Movement: Notes toward the Reconstruction of Nineteenth-

82 Franca Iacovetta

Century Feminism,' *Feminist Studies* 3 (Fall 1975), 63–71, and her
*Feminism and Suffrage: The Emergence of an Independent Women's Movement in
America, 1848–1869* (Ithaca 1978).
7 Recent studies have dealt with a variety of women involved in social and political
action. See, for example, Gwynneth Buck, 'One Woman's Campaign for a
New Social Order, Beatrice Brigden,' MA Major Research Paper, York Univer-
sity 1981; Katherine McCuaig, '"From Social Reform to Social Service."
The Changing Role of Volunteers: The Anti-Tuberculosis Campaign, 1900–30'
Canadian Historical Review 61:4 (December 1980), 480–501; Joan Sangster,
'Women in Radical Politics and Labour in Canada,' PhD diss., McMaster
University 1984; Veronica Strong-Boag, 'Internationalism and Peace: The
Efforts of Canadian Women, 1919–1939,' paper presented at the Conference
on Women and Education for Peace and Non-Violence, OISE, Toronto, 29
September 1984; John Manley, '"Women and the Left in the 1930s": The Case
of the Toronto CCF Women's Joint Committee,' *Atlantis* 5:2 (Spring 1980),
100–19.
8 *SD*, 13 March 1962.
9 John L. Scott, 'Our New Woman Senator,' *Maclean's*, 1 April 1930, 16.
10 Speech to the Toronto Women's Teachers' Association, 22 November 1930,
Cairine Wilson Papers (hereafter WP), vol. 5, National Archives of Canada
(NA).
11 Speech to the League for Women's Rights, Montreal, 28 February 1931, WP,
vol. 2, file 31.
12 Scott, 'Woman Senator,' 16, 97–8; Jean Graham, 'Among Those Present,'
Saturday Night, 18, June 1932, 5; M.H. Halton, 'Canada's First Woman
Senator,' *Canadian Home Journal*, July 1931, 139 in scrapbook, WP, vol. 6;
notes on Wilson, Charles Clay Papers, vol. 3, NA.
13 Scott, 'Woman Senator,' 16. In addition to his very successful Mackay
Brothers' dry-goods wholesale business, Mackay also held influential positions on
the Montreal Board of Trade, Montreal Harbour Board, Bank of Montreal, and
the Montreal General Hospital.
14 24 February 1930, scrapbooks, WP, vol. 8.
15 Speech Notes to St Stephen's Presbyterian Church, 14 January 1955, WP, vol. 6.
16 Trans-Canada Broadcast: World Day of Prayer, 8 February 1951, WP, vol. 6.
17 Halton, 'First Woman Senator,' 139.
18 Wilson, 'Home and Love Life's Boons,' *Canadian Home Journal*, May 1931,
in scrapbooks, WP, vol. 8.
19 *St. Croix Courier*, 4 January 1934 in scrapbooks, WP, vol. 8.
20 Scott, 'Woman Senator,' 16; Halton, 'First Woman Senator,' 139.
21 See scrapbooks, WP, vols 7 and 8. They are filled with clippings documenting
Laurier's political career. On King, see *Ottawa Citizen*, 21 March 1932.

22 24 February 1930, scrapbook, WP vol. 8. On Gladstone, see Phillip Magnus, *Gladstone: A Biography* (London 1970); see also J.T. Saywell's introduction to *The Canadian Journal of Lady Aberdeen, 1893–1898* (Toronto 1960).

23 Speech on Christian Youth Week, 24 January 1957, WP, vol. 6.

24 Canadian Girls in Training and Truxis Trail Rangers, 11 February 1951, CFRA Broadcast, WP, vol. 6.

25 World Day of Prayer, 8 February 1951, Trans-Canada Broadcast, WP, vol. 6.

26 Wilson, 'Home and Love.'

27 Scott, 'Woman Senator,' 16; Wilson, 'Home and Love.'

28 See, for example, *Saskatchewan Liberal*, 8 June 1933 in scrapbook, WP, vol. 8: SD, 18 May 1943, 13 March 1947, 18 February 1949, 17 March 1955, 4 April 1960.

29 Speech to the League for Women's Rights, Montreal, 28 February 1931, WP, vol. 5.

30 Evelyn Tufts, 'One of the Most Useful Members of Parliament,' in scrapbooks, WP, vol. 8.

31 See, for example, the Twentieth-Century Association Luncheon, 5 June 1933, WP, vol. 8.

32 National Federation of Liberal Women, Constitution, 14 and 15 November 1945, Catherine Cleverdon Papers, NA.

33 *Ottawa Citizen*, 21 March 1932.

34 Reginald Whitaker, *The Government Party: Organizing and Financing the Liberal Party of Canada, 1930–58* (Toronto 1977).

35 See, for example, *Ottawa Citizen*, 13 March 1933; Brief Message to the Mothers of Georgian Bay, Radio Station CFOS, Owen Sound, 12 May 1950, WP, vol. 1.

36 World Day of Prayer, 8 February 1951, Trans-Canada Broadcast, WP, vol. 6.

37 Quoted in *Ottawa Citizen*, n.d. in scrapbooks, WP, vol. 6.

38 Speech to the League for Women's Rights, Montreal, 28 February 1931, WP, vol. 5.

39 League of Nations Society, National Executive Meeting, 22 January 1943, Charles Clay Papers, NA; *Ottawa Citizen*, 13 March 1933; speech to Peace Action Week dinner, Ottawa, 9 November 1937, WP, vol. 6; speech to the Women's Organizations, League of Nations Society, Toronto Branch, 26 June 1935, WP, vol. 6.

40 *The Globe*, 2 March 1933; *Saskatchewan Liberal*, 8 June 1933; speech to the Empire Club, 20 November 1930; SD, 13 March, 1956, WP, vol. 5.

41 Speech to the Empire Club, 20 November 1930, WP, vol. 5.

42 See, for example, ibid.; speech to the Halcyon Club, Ottawa, 16 May 1931; Wilson, 'The Present Status of Women,' *The Canadian Bar Review*, no. 1014 (April 1932), 217–21; speech to Eaton's Girls' Club, Toronto, 10 April 1931, WP, vol. 5.

43 Wilson, 'Women's Opportunities,' n.d. in scrapbooks, WP, vol. 6.
44 Ibid.; speech to the Empire Club, 20 November 1930, WP, vol. 6.
45 Speech to the Women's Canadian Club, Quebec City, 22 January 1931, WP, vol. 5.
46 See for example speech to the Halcyon Club, Ottawa, 16 May 1931, WP, vol. 5; SD, 17 December 1945.
47 *Glad Tidings*, March 1957, 2. Wilson also praised MP Agnes Macphail for supporting reform measures in Parliament and for initiating the Archambault Commission on Penal Reform.
48 Speech to the Empire Club, 20 November 1930, WP, vol. 5.
49 For details, see Irving Abella and Harold Troper, '"The Line Must Be Drawn Somewhere": Canada and Jewish Refugees, 1933–39,' *Canadian Historical Review* 15:2 (1979), 179–209 and their *None Is Too Many: Canada and the Jews of Europe 1933–1948* (Toronto 1983), Strong-Boag, 'Internationalism and Peace.'
50 Executive minutes, First General Meeting, 6 and 7 December 1938, Canadian National Committee on Refugees [hereafter CNCR] collection, vol. 6, file 24, NA; An Appeal on Behalf of Refugees, 29 December 1938, WP, vol. 6.
51 See CNCR correspondence between executive secretary Constance Hayward and local branches located in CNCR collection; Hayward to Edmund Walker, 6 June 1941, CNCR; vol. 4, file 31; Hayward to G.W. Simpson, 22 January 1944, CNCR, vol. 6, file 10.
52 *Montreal Daily Star*, 15 December 1932.
53 *Ottawa Citizen*, 13 March 1933.
54 SD, 12 March 1931; 16 January 1932.
55 SD, 16 May 1934.
56 Abella and Troper, "The Line," 198, and *None Is Too Many*, 44–6; Gerald E. Dirks, *Canada's Refugee Policy: Indifference or Opportunism?* (Montreal 1978).
57 Executive minutes, First General Meeting, 6 and 7 December 1938, CNCR.
58 For details see Abella and Troper, *None Is Too Many*.
59 Cited in Dirks, *Refugee Policy*, 71; on Wilson's efforts, see CNCR, vol. 6 and WP, vol. 6, file 6, 2, 4.
60 CNCR, vol. 6, file 24. See also correspondence between Hayward and Wilson.
61 Abella and Troper, *None Is Too Many*, 101–2.
62 Ibid., 102–5.
63 1 November 1954, WP, vol. 1, file 3; Mrs R.T. Tanner to Wilson, 6 July and 22 December 1954 and C.E.S. Smith to Wilson, 12 May 1954, WP, vol. 1, file 5. Canada Save the Children Fund, WP, vol. 1, file 5; SD, 15 August 1946.
64 Gwynneth Evans, *Women in Federal Politics: A Bio-bibliography* (Ottawa 1975).
65 SD, 4 April 1960. See also SD, 14 December 1953, 20 February 1951, 13 May 1947.

66 Senate Standing Committee on Immigration and Labour 1948; SD, 4 April 1960, 28 March 1946, 25 June 1948.

67 Abella and Troper, *None Is Too Many*, 238–79; SD, 5 March 1943, 3 February 1944. See also D.C. Corbett, *Canada's Immigration Policy* (Toronto 1976); Alan C. Green, *Immigration and the Post-War Economy* (Toronto 1976); R. Bothwell and W. Kilbourn, *C.D. Howe: A Biography* (Toronto 1979).

68 *Glad Tidings*, 19 January 1951.

69 Speech to the domestic-science graduates, Macdonald College, Quebec, 8 June 1932, WP, vol. 5; Wilson, 'Women's Opportunities.'

70 Speech to the Toronto Women's Teacher Association, 22 November 1930; speech to the Twentieth-Century Liberal Club of Ottawa, 27 October 1932; address to the Kiwanis Club, 6 February 1951, WP, vol. 5.

71 Speech noted, n.d. WP, vol. 2, file 13.

72 SD 14 December 1953; Dirks, *Refugee Policy*, 71.

73 SD, 14 December 1953, 3 February 1944.

74 SD, 15 March 1938; Wilson, 'Present Status of Women,' 217–21.

75 SD, 15 March 1938.

76 SD, 17 March 1955.

77 SD, 17 July 1959.

78 Quoted in *Evening News*, New Glasgow, Nova Scotia, 3 August 1933, scrapbooks, WP, vol. 8.

79 Ibid.; SD, 3 February 1944, 17 December 1945.

80 SD, 5 March 1943; address to the Kiwanis Club, 6 February 1951, WP, vol. 5.

81 M. Wherry to Wilson, June 1960, WP, vol. 3, file 27. Another woman, Theresa E. Thomson, wrote a poem entitled 'Honourable Lady (Cairine Wilson),' located in WP, vol. 3, file 27.

82 Saul Hayes to Miss Wilson, 22 March 1962, WP, vol. 13, file 2.

PART THREE

The Co-operative
Commonwealth Federation

Amelia Turner and Calgary Labour Women

1919–1935

Patricia Roome

I think, on every occasion, that you appeared before the public, whether on the radio or on the platform, that you made friends. And not merely because of your fine presentation of socialist theories, but because of your dignity and modesty. One of the Stanley Jones teachers said of you, after the Sunday meeting, she looked so sweet and modest. We all owe you a great debt and we will surely try to repay it in loyalty and greater appreciation.[1]

When Edith Patterson wrote this note to Amelia Turner on the evening of her defeat in a Calgary provincial by-election (20 January 1933), she was articulating the widely held expectation that women politicians must be 'sweet and modest' both in their style and their politics. Consistent with the maternal feminism and ethical socialism that the Calgary Dominion Labor party (DLP) espoused, it was also a confining ideal under which many labour women chafed, but only a few, like Jean McWilliam of the Women's Labor League (WLL) and Communist Sophie McClusky, rejected. As a Calgary School Board trustee from 1926–36 and as a Cooperative Commonwealth Federation (CCF) candidate in the 1933 and 1934 by-elections, Amelia Turner fulfilled these expectations of feminine respectability; at the same time, her career symbolized the ambitious, committed, and important work of socialist women who built the Women's Section of the Dominion Labor party.

Influenced by William Irvine and the experiences of the British Labour party, Turner believed that women's socialist and feminist agenda could best be achieved through political action and success at the polls; however, from 1919 to 1925, Calgary labour women sought greater involvement in the labour movement beyond their traditional participation in union auxiliaries; they created the Women's Labor League to achieve these goals. Throughout this period a fruitful partnership flourished between women in the DLP and WLL; but, as this essay will demonstrate, the mid 1920s witnessed an erosion of this co-operation as the Alberta section of the Canadian Labor party moved to end alliances with communists and encouraged women to achieve their goals within the confines of the Women's Section of the Labor party. As a result, the later period from 1925 to 1935 became a more partisan era of consolidation for women.

A study of Amelia Turner's career and relationship with Calgary labour women challenges the assumption made by standard historical accounts of the period that the women's movement collapsed and post-war feminists retreated into their private lives after winning the vote.[2] That labour women rejected private domesticity for socialist politics is easily demonstrated: more difficult to answer are questions regarding their effectiveness within the labour political movement. Were they marginalized within this movement; or, despite tacit acceptance of the image of sweet, modest, and dignified woman, were women able to effect change consistent with their vision of socialist feminism?

I

Amelia Turner's passion for social justice was rooted in her family milieu and their experiences.[3] Born on 11 February 1891, she was the eldest of ten children born to Letitia Keefer Turner, a physician's daughter and United Empire Loyalist descendant, and Henry James Turner, the only child of a British tailor and his wife who immigrated to Canada in the 1860s.[4] Grandfather Thomas Turner and Amelia's father owned a store in Tottenham, Ontario, where Amelia spent a comfortable childhood. In 1898 the Turner families travelled west to the booming mining town of Fernie, British Columbia, where Henry Turner bought and managed a hotel, the Victoria. In Fernie, Amelia attended school, studied music, and enjoyed the excitement of a frontier town until her father became disenchanted with the saloon business, sold his hotel, and moved the family onto a southern Alberta homestead.[5]

During these financially troubled farming years, Amelia continued her education, tutored by her grandfather and father ('an intellectual snob'). Although isolated, their pioneer homestead provided Amelia with a stimulating environment through its extensive library, many newspapers, and visitors.[6] Eventually the Turner home became the centre for education in the Ewelme community, with Amelia acting as the teacher. Between teaching and domestic duties, Amelia wrote, published a bulletin for her family, and took correspondence courses in shorthand, bookkeeping, and typing, which qualified her for a job in Fort Macleod with the *Macleod Advertiser* in 1911.[7]

Her working experiences over the next five years in a variety of newspaper offices paralleled those of many Canadian girls, but Amelia was not typical. Even before she moved to Fort Macleod she proudly called herself an agnostic, suffragist, and socialist. After reading Robert Blatchford's *Merrie England* at the age of twelve, Amelia became a devoted socialist, as did her brother Hereward. Initially, the immediate homesteading experiences of economic discrimination were the focus of numerous family discussions.[8] But socialism also exerted a lifetime influence on Letitia Turner and the eldest Turner children, especially Amelia, who emerged as the leader determined to become a journalist, a newspaper publisher, and an activist.[9]

Amelia moved to Calgary in 1913 and worked at a series of 'dull office jobs' while she assisted her sister Donata through high school and normal school. She spent her leisure time in the stimulating company of members of Calgary's 'labor group,' which coalesced around William Irvine, pastor of the Unitarian church in 1916.[10] Involved in this closely knit labour group were most of the future leaders of the Dominion Labor party and Women's Labor League, whose political lessons were learned through participation in the People's Forum, the Unity Club, the Non-Partisan League, and the Labor Representation League (LRL). In the June 1917 election, the LRL entered provincial politics and candidates William Irvine and Alex Ross contested two seats.[11] Amelia was invited by Edith Patterson to hear Irvine speak at Unity Hall in 1916 and identified immediately with his Fabian socialism.[12] Within months, Amelia and her sister were boarding with the Irvine family, marking the beginning of a lifelong and intimate friendship.[13]

The Irvine family provided congenial companionship for Amelia, and, perhaps more important, William Irvine encouraged her intellectual development and supervised her political apprenticeship. Throughout the years 1916–20, Amelia attended the Unitarian church and the People's Forum, joined the LRL, and campaigned for Irvine. Employed as his secretary at the Non-Partisan League's office, she later moved with Irvine to the *Western Independent* newspaper.[14] Amelia's apprenticeship deepened her knowledge and commitment to the farmers' movement, building on strong sympathies developed on her father's homestead before the war. When the United Farmers of Alberta (UFA) decided to enter politics and the Non-Partisan League was dissolved, Turner naturally progressed to the UFA office in 1920 and joined the staff of the UFA magazine in 1922.[15]

Amelia was deeply convinced by Irvine's argument articulated in *Farmers in Politics* (1920) that organized workers and farmers must enter politics and co-operate to revise the democratic structures of government in order to facilitate the creation of a new egalitarian social order with radically altered economic and social structures. Co-operation and evolution were key elements in the Fabian-like philosophy espoused by Irvine and explained to Calgary audiences like the members of the new Labor church, who heard Irvine label the One Big Union tactics as anti-democratic, destructive, and counter-productive. For him, the new social order would 'be an equilibrium of all conflicting forces ... a society in which every class will have expression and be allowed to function.'[16] To realize this co-operative commonwealth, Irvine and Alberta UFA MPs entered into an uneasy alliance with provincial UFA leaders like Henry Wise Wood. Although Amelia's association with the UFA was closer than Irvine's, she also built strong friendships in the Calgary labour community, the 'Ginger Group' of the federal Progressives, and the CCF. Though attempts at group government in the 1920s ultimately failed, both Irvine and Turner remained firm in their commitment to a co-operative commonwealth.[17]

Amelia was drawn initially to socialism by the ideas of Robert Blatchford and Keir Hardie, but the ideas and style of middle-class intellectuals like Sydney and Beatrice Webb and George Bernard Shaw deeply influenced her. Later in life she wrote: 'I was, I think a congenital Fabian.'[18] Turner's optimism sprung from her belief in the inevitability of socialism, the necessity of moral reform, education for citizenship, and the civilizing role of the middle class. Far more than Irvine, who was a popular agitator, Turner was the genteel idealist armed with a cheerful practicality reminiscent of Beatrice Webb though, in contrast to Webb, both Irvine and Turner were concerned with feminist issues.[19]

Bourgeois respectability with its ideal of gracious womanhood was Amelia's family legacy, as much as was socialism. Although few of the labour women leaders she met in Calgary during the First World War became socialists as early in life as did Amelia, they came from similarly cultured and politically literate middle-class families that encouraged women's involvement in social reform and politics. Sisters Marion Carson and Rachael Coutts, who were Amelia's elders, were from a comfortable Ontario family; influenced by the social-gospel movement, they were led to socialism by their pacifism and experiences in the Alberta Temperance and Moral Reform League. For these two women, political literacy had developed gradually, influenced by the experience of Marion Carson's husband, who was a Calgary alderman in 1905.[20] Edith Patterson's Nova Scotia father, a long-time school trustee and Conservative MP, gave her a model of community service, but her commitment to social justice came through her own experience of poverty when teaching miners' children in Glace Bay, Nova Scotia. Conversion to socialism and political action initially precipitated a personal crisis for

Patterson, who had to make a decisive choice 'for or against a new political party, in harmony with the social gospel' as preached by Irvine.[21]

II

What role did the young and ambitious Amelia Turner play in the Calgary labour community between 1919 and 1925? Involved in the birth of the Dominion Labor party and influenced profoundly by William Irvine, Amelia believed partisan political action was integral to achieving socialism. Nor did her experiences during these formative years alter her stand, even though most of her more experienced female colleagues believed in co-operation among women and held joint memberships in the non-partisan Women's Labor League and the DLP. This section focuses on the organizational work of senior activists who were Turner's mentors. Through the independent WLL and the Dominion Labor party, these Calgary women laid the foundation for women's political action and determined its direction in the later decade, when Amelia easily dominated electoral politics. This section also examines the relationship between these two organizations. Was the WLL, with its political independence, more outspoken on gender and class questions and able to steer a more radical course than the DLP?

The genesis and early years of the Calgary Labor party are a story of coalition politics, left-wing factionalism, and idiosyncrasies. In Calgary, LRL activists formed the nucleus of a labor-party local in April 1919 and called it the Dominion Labor party (DLP). Although the DLP local eventually affiliated with the Alberta section of the Canadian Labor party (CLP) and joined the Calgary Central Council of the CLP, labourites refused to change their name partially because they disliked the influence communists held in the CLP. Until the expulsion of the communists in 1928, Calgary members insisted they were 'The Dominion Labor party.' After 1928, usage of the name Canadian Labor party gradually gained acceptance. Trivial as it may appear, the Calgary conflict over labels was symbolic of deeper tensions within the labour political movement.

In 1917 the Alberta Federation of Labor Convention endorsed the principle of establishing a labour party, and the trade unions played a major role at the founding convention, in January 1919, of the Alberta branch of the CLP. Alvin Finkel argues union support was crucial to the CLP success and signified a departure from 'pure labourism to ethical socialism as the official ideology of the labour movement.' In contrast to working-class Marxists with whom they formed an 'unholy' alliance through the central councils of the CLP, ethical socialists accepted change at ballot boxes. 'Rather than speaking of the inevitable hostility between an exploiting class and an exploited class, they stressed moral superiority of socialism with its emphasis on production for use over capitalism with its emphasis on production for profit.' Although the Alberta party formally adopted the British Labour party's post-war program, implementation proved impossible: the CLP gradually sacrificed these socialist principles to accommodate the more conservative and strictly labourite demands of its craft-union membership.[22]

Women played an important role in this debate and also within the structures of the Calgary DLP, where they formed over 50 per cent of the membership, joined the executive, contested elections, and worked as politicians on both city council and the school-board. Throughout the 1920s, the Dominion Labor party maintained a core of fifty to seventy-five active women who were primarily of two types: single working women, usually teachers or journalists, and married women, often union auxiliary members (such as Mary Corse). Not all these labour women maintained as high a profile as did Marion Carson; instead, many, like Adelia Irvine herself, supported socialism but centred their lives on their families and thus were 'not the type' for leadership. Women labour leaders were usually ambitious, experienced, and older, with both freedom and finances to pursue a political career.[23]

As a young woman of 28 years, few of these characteristics described Amelia's situation. Despite a strong commitment to ethical socialism, gender, inexperience and youth prevented Amelia from rapidly assuming a leadership role. 'It was an ordeal,' she remembered, 'for me to say "present" at a study group.' Ironically many progressive and socialist women found that, despite their shared goals, socialist politics remained a male world. Amelia's political education in the DLP took place among senior female activists, who encouraged Canadian and British labour women to visit Calgary and share their experiences. Important as these links were, Amelia firmly believed that separate women's organizations were essential also for training women who lacked a tradition of political participation. Equally confining for Amelia were family and career pressures, for in the small office of The UFA magazine, she worked long hours learning a variety of jobs. When her father died in 1921, Amelia's mother, with her younger sons, moved to Calgary, re-established the family home, and relied upon Amelia's salary for support.[24]

Although Amelia concentrated on the Dominion Labor party and municipal election campaigns, her female colleagues created organizations like the Women's Labor League, which was born in April and May 1919, the child of experienced activists Mary Corse and Jean McWilliam. As Linda Kealey has demonstrated, the First World War's differential impact on Canadian women radicalized progressive women, who formed organizations devoted to advancing the cause of social justice for working-class women. In Calgary, for example, the Next of Kin organization founded by outspoken Scots immigrant Jean McWilliam advocated increased mothers' pensions and pensions for soldiers' dependants.[25] Inflation, wartime profiteering, and conscription of labour further radicalized these women, whose reform agenda was echoed in other organizations like the Local Council of Women.[26] When Calgary experienced a wave of strikes between 1918 and 1919, labour women found themselves directly involved, supporting women restaurant and hotel workers on the picket line, assisting striking husbands, joining union auxiliaries, and sitting as delegates on the Trades and Labor Council.[27]

Mary Corse's advocacy of both industrial unionism and political action made her one of Calgary's more radical socialist women. By 1919 she was the labour trustee on the Calgary School Board, a voting delegate for the Typographical Women's Auxiliary on the Calgary Trades and Labor Council (TLC), and their delegate to the Western Canadian Labor Conference held in Calgary 13–15 March 1919. Here she met and heard Winnipeg Labor League women Helen Logan and Helen Armstrong assert to the male delegates that neglect of their wives' political education and working women's issues had weakened the labour movement. Following the conference, Mary Corse joined the Alberta executive committee of the One Big Union. As the Calgary General Strike developed, she encouraged McWilliam, who was her frequent partner on TLC committees, to help develop a WLL similar to the Manitoba model. While the league's primary aim was to support the families of striking workers, they also endorsed collective-bargaining strategies and strike action for all workers, especially working women.[28]

Born in crisis and independent of political affiliation, the Calgary WLL differed substantially from the WLLs that the British Labour party created from 1906 to 1918 to encourage women's participation in the Labour party.[29] Most labour women who joined the Calgary League had worked in the movement since 1916, attended Irvine's Unitarian and Labor churches, and developed high hopes for the creation of a new, but vaguely defined, social order. This social-gospel tradition carried over into the WLL, whose motto was 'Deut. 3:16. Be strong and of good courage, fear not nor be afraid of them, for the Lord thy God He will go with thee. He will not fail thee nor forsake thee.'[30] Although not always consonant with the image of sweet and modest womanhood, this motto still promoted a religious perception of socialism.[31] When Mary Corse was president of the WLL and active in the Dominion Labor party, the WLL executive included DLP women. Although some league women remained aloof from affiliation and some DLP members did not join the WLL, throughout this period the two organizations complemented each other and allowed labour women to be articulate on gender and class issues.[32] In contrast to the league's independence and commitment to support industrial action, the DLP worked on annual civic elections, groomed women politicians like Amelia Turner, and supported a platform in which women's issues were secondary.[33]

Conscious of working-class women's grievances, Corse and McWilliam gave testimony at the Calgary hearings, 3–5 May 1919, before Justice T.G. Mathers's Royal Commission on Industrial Relations. As the women's representative from the TLC, in her speech Corse outlined problems of high rent, low pay, and poor working conditions. Her case rested on evidence she had gathered during the April 1918 strike of waitresses and hotel employees. Bourgeois indifference and class inequalities, she said, were a source of unrest that encouraged women 'to join the socialist parties.'[34] While assuring the commission that she was a reformist, Corse emphasized Calgary women's growing radicalism and resentment at not 'getting a square deal' and at being 'kept in the background,' even though 'women have been the backbone of the labour movement.'[35] She explained that her viewpoint had 'utterly changed' since 1917, when her union-organizing activities exposed her to prostitution, poverty, and exploitation of working girls.[36] A 'living wage,' not merely a minimum wage paid to young girls, was her solution to female labour unrest.

Jean McWilliam's fiery testimony presented additional information that she had gathered while organizing laundry workers and investigating conditions of hotel and restaurant employees.[37] Unionization of women and a fair minimum wage were McWilliam's solution to the crisis. Exploitation by capitalists and government, along with the callousness and bourgeois apathy of the Local Council of Women, represented for her examples of liberalism's failure. She broadened her analysis of women's problems to include hardships experienced by soldiers' wives and widows, advocating generous widow's and mother's pensions as a partial solution in the redistribution of income.

Neither McWilliam nor Corse presented a critique of the family and the problems of working-class wives; instead, they opposed the right of married women with employed husbands to work. Corse felt obliged to use maternal feminist arguments to justify her volunteer political work, explaining that 'it is the duty of every mother who has girls to find just how employers ... are keeping house for our children.'[38] For her, political work was a logical expression of womanhood, 'militant mothering' as Joan Sangster defines it.[39] Guided by Corse and McWilliam, the Women's Labor League infused maternal feminism with a strong class consciousness. Within the first year they organized the Calgary Defence Committee with McWilliam as president, raised $1200 for strikers, sent protests to Ottawa regarding deportation of strikers through amendments to the Immigration Act, and organized a petition demanding that the federal government reinstate the postal workers. Convinced that women's organization and education assisted the struggle, McWilliam travelled widely in southern Alberta encouraging women to form leagues.[40]

Throughout the immediate post-war period, the WLL defended the general strike weapon and OBU supporter Alderman Broatch.[41] Later, McWilliam encountered stiff opposition to the WLL's position when she requested that the May 1920 United Mineworkers of America Convention pledge support for the jailed Winnipeg strikers. When a struggle ensued, *The Searchlight* claimed that McWilliam discovered 'her mistake in thinking she had got into a bunch of labor men' and as she departed accused them of being 'just like a bunch of old women.'[42] While such naïvety and pugnaciousness won McWilliam paternalist amusement and notoriety, the incident also illustrates her disregard for the complexities of union politics when issues of social justice were involved. Likewise, despite Mary Corse's position on the OBU, she maintained an amiable relationship with the Calgary Labor Council, which tolerated her politics because, like McWilliam, she lacked membership in a powerful union, and therefore could exercise marginal influence.[43]

By 1922, the WLL had politicized many women voters and awakened some to 'a realization that organization is necessary to remove the economic shackles now bearing so heavily upon them.'[44] But in the adverse labour climate of 1921–4, the WLL relied more heavily on protection of working women through adequate minimum-wage legislation than on union organizing. In 1919 it proposed an amendment to the Alberta Factory Act creating a Minimum Wage Board with a woman representative from the 'labouring classes' – subsequently Edmontonian Harriet J. Ingam, president of the Garment Workers' Union. The league successfully pressured the Calgary Labour MLA and Minister of Labour Alex Ross to create a Women's Bureau and campaigned for a board of women to assist Margaret Lewis, the factory inspector, in enforcing the Factory Act. Despite some successes, the league's strategy was a failure, as demonstrated by the experience of three league women who represented domestic workers of the Housekeeper's Association in 1920 before the Minimum Wage Commission hearings. Regardless of their protest, domestic workers were not granted an eight-hour day and wages of $25 monthly, nor were they likely to be covered by future legislation. Although in 1922 some women won a new minimum wage of $14 and a maximum work week of 48 hours, the UFA government even delayed its implementation of these changes for several years.[45]

Focusing on the needs of working-class families, the WLL created task forces and accumulated data to demonstrate that ill health, prostitution, and malnutrition were rooted in economic inequality. Reflecting Marion Carson's involvement in the campaign for free hospital treatment for tuberculosis patients, the league championed this cause as part of state-funded medical services.[46] Eager to challenge the establishment, Jean McWilliam 'crossed swords' with a Presbyterian minister, the Reverend McRae, over malnutrition among children. Publicly she ridiculed both his characterization of working-class fathers as 'scalliwags' and his belief that charity was a substitute for economic justice. The WLL assigned delegates to attend meetings of the hospital board, city council, and school-board as watchdogs on labour women's behalf.[47]

Between the Women's Labor League's goal of 'principles before party – measures before men' and the Dominion Labor party's need for party discipline, a chasm existed that women bridged by fragile alliances. McWilliam opposed women joining political parties; rather, she believed the best strategy was lobbying, support of collective bargaining, and union organizing. In sharp disagreement with McWilliam's philosophy, Mary Corse (like Amelia Turner) argued that elected representatives meant power for the labour movement.[48] Although DLP women played an active role in the party, they were rarely as free as the WLL women to concentrate on gender issues; party commitments meant they served on the DLP executive, organized the women's vote – especially in 1921–4 elections – supported women candidates, and encouraged ladies' auxiliaries to support the DLP. When the Calgary TLC finally voted to affiliate with the Canadian Labor party and to create a central council in 1924, DLP women created a Women's Section that joined CLP. If Mary Corse had remained in Calgary, the WLL might have dissolved and encouraged its members to work through the Women's Section, but McWilliam's leadership meant labour women were forced to choose. Most opted for membership in the DLP Women's Section, where many were already active on the DLP, filling every position but president.[49]

Although the need to achieve workplace equality was high on labour women's agenda, there was disagreement within the labour movement on this issue. Some male DLP colleagues, like school trustee Harry Pryde, did not endorse the Calgary TLC's 1921 decision to oppose the employment of married women with working husbands and argued that 'self-determination for women is the slogan being used in the women's forward movement and they take the stand that a woman has as much right to hold down a job as a man.'[50] Ironically, the WLL in 1923 petitioned the Calgary School Board to reduce married women on staff, supporting instead the concept of a family wage and married women's duty to raise a family.[51] Throughout this period, a married woman's right to work was a contentious issue for labour women, who usually avoided public debate. Generally, the league advocated measures like the 1919

Mother's Allowance Act as a solution to female poverty, subsequently sponsoring several admendments requesting inclusion of women whose husbands were invalids, in mental asylums, or had deserted the family. In 1922 a WLL delegation appeared before Premier Brownlee to address these changes.[52] Whereas most of the younger generation tacitly shared Amelia Turner's view that married women's rights included the opportunity to employment, equal pay, and access to birth control, elder leaders like Marion Carson strongly opposed married women working and refused to place birth control on the agenda of the DLP Women's Section meetings.[53]

In contrast to the WLL, the Dominion Labor party worked closely with teachers supporting the new Alberta Teacher Alliance's (ATA) attempt to achieve collective bargaining and representation on the school-board. In 1920, the DLP adopted a labour educational policy, which supported ATA wage demands, recognized experience, required representation from the ATA in dismissal cases, ensured more independence for principals, extended part-time classes, set a pupil maximum of thirty-five, supported the principle of free school supplies, and argued for the extension of school clinics. Later, the DLP supported the Public School Ladies Association and endorsed the feminist principles of equal pay and advancement to principal's position. Radicalized by the organizing work of the ATA and the 1921 strike, many women teachers joined the DLP.[54] As a young activist, Amelia Turner identified primarily with this group, which included her sister Dorothy. Initially she received emotional support and intellectual stimulation from female teachers, and later, as a trustee, she championed their cause for a decade. Thus, while the WLL could afford to ignore the issue of equality for teachers, the Dominion Labor party could not and on this issue demonstrated greater consciousness of discrimination.

A characteristic of both DLP women and the WLL was their contribution to labour's cultural cohesiveness through fund-raising tag days, whist drives, and family events like Christmas concerts and May Day picnics. The WLL and DLP women (and often it was the same women serving in different capacities) sponsored speakers whom they entertained royally. Through the 'Women's Page' of the *Alberta Labor News* (ALN), labour women in Alberta maintained a lively forum for discussion of local and international events. Considerable solidarity with women involved in the United Farm Women of Alberta (UFWA) and networking developed, mirroring the alliance of the Dominion Labor party with UFA government.[55]

In her study of Canadian women's political involvement, Bashevkin argues that 'early women's groups were attracted toward a position of political independence, which would guarantee both organizational autonomy and purity: on the other hand, they were drawn toward conventional partisanship, which might better ensure their political influence and legislative success.' The British Columbia example of combining partisan alliances, 'including the election and cabinet appointment of an active feminist woman, with politically independent and effective women's organizations,' she argues, 'became the exception rather than the rule for many years following 1918.'[56] However, the experience of Calgary labour women in the WLL and DLP until 1924 provides another example of successful co-operation. These women shared a similar commitment to elements of maternal feminism, regarded the vote as a democratic right, and wanted to increase labour's political power. While neither group viewed women as its exclusive constituency, both were articulate about gender and class issues – though each group was sometimes cautious, even contradictory in its perspective. The WLL championed the working girl but rejected the right of married women to work, while Dominion Labor party women, despite their labour loyalties, focused on professional women's issues like equal pay and promotions.

Two significant case studies from the early 1920s demonstrate the fragile nature and limitations of co-operation. The first revolves around the WLL and DLP women's role in the unemployment struggles of the early 1920s; the second concerns the controversy over rehiring part-time teacher Sophie McClusky, a well-known communist, active in organizing the unemployed. These two struggles are important because they marked a turning-point for Amelia Turner and Calgary labour women. After 1924, labour women increasingly chose partisanship over independence as the latter became synonymous with a communist alliance. By the mid 1920s, the communist presence on the Calgary Central Council of the CLP had become barely tolerable to the moderate elements of Calgary's labour community.

The link between the Women's Labor League, the DLP, and the Committee for the Unemployed occurred at two levels. Many of the committee's organizers lived at Jean McWilliam's boarding-house, where radicals were welcome and able to enlist her support. Through the Central Council of the Unemployed (CCU), which was communist-dominated, other labour women became directly involved. Over the tough winter of 1921–2, the CCU lobbied the Calgary City Council to centralize the administration of relief by placing it under the management of a city council committee composed of aldermen and representatives of labour and of the unemployed. After the December elections, the presence on the Calgary City Council of five DLP aldermen provided the Council of the Unemployed with allies. Militancy grew among the unemployed, who were housed over the winter at Calgary Fair Grounds, and culminated in a march to occupy city hall on 7 April 1922.[57]

Since November 1921, the WLL had pressured city council to accept greater responsibility for unemployment. During the demonstration, the WLL's involvement increased beyond fund-raising drives, when the president Alice Corless interceded with the mayor following the police dispersal of the marchers. An earlier emergency meeting at the Labour Temple revealed many labour women assembled to prepare resolutions for city council, but with a Dominion Conference on Unemployment planned for 3–4 August 1922, the city administration remained intransigent and, even in August, the municipalities failed to persuade the federal government to finance relief.[58] The WLL and another organization called Women of Unemployed Committee, which McWilliam founded, contributed two unsuccessful resolutions to the conference demanding the dismissal of the city relief officer for 'offensive treatment' to wives of the unemployed and reallocation of monies from the Canadian Patriotic Fund to families of disabled soldiers.[59]

During the spring of 1922, solidarity on the unemployment problem crumbled when conservative trade unionists withdrew their delegate from the CCU and told the unemployed to affiliate with craft unions. While the presence of One Big Union and Workers' party organizers alienated conservative trade unionists, the WLL continued to 'vigorously protest the present administration of relief,' requesting the firing of board of welfare officer McKillop.[60] Although Dominion Labor party women held five executive positions in the WLL, they maintained support for the CCU and championed other politically explosive causes, despite pressure from craft unionists. Through McWilliam's influence and connections with Drumheller miners, who often came to Calgary to work during the turbulent years before 1925, the WLL had successfully petitioned for a retrial for miner Gallagher who was first found guilty of murdering a mine manager but acquitted in 1922.[61]

One of the CCU organizers objected to by the conservative trade unionists of the TLC was Sophie McClusky, who applied to the Calgary School Board to teach English to immigrants in 1921, but was refused employment because of her political activities. McClusky vigorously protested her treatment in the press, arguing that her socialist ideas were not relevant to her teaching credentials. According to McClusky, Marion Carson, the only trustee who accepted her invitation to observe her teaching, 'did not hear me teach Bolshevism or socialism. I taught English to a class of anxious Ukrainians who were bright and willing to learn but unable to pay rent and a teacher's salary.'[62] Superintendent Melville Scott of the Calgary School Board wrote that opposition to her politics was 'shared by all members of the Board but one and is especially strong, apparently among the Labour members on the Board.' Was Marion Carson the one sympathetic supporter of McClusky? Although it is difficult to answer this question with certainty, Carson was the only trustee involved in the Council of the Unemployed. Regardless of McClusky's protest and reapplication in later years, the blacklisting was effective.[63]

Despite common interest in the unemployed, McClusky never identified with women's issues or joined the Calgary WLL. Instead, McClusky organized unemployed single men, headed a delegation to the mayor and commissioner in 1925, and requested work at union wages and accommodation instead of charity. For spreading communist ideas among the unemployed, she earned the wrath of police magistrate Colonel Sanders, before whom she appeared over a dispute with her husband. Accusing her of leading single men astray, Sanders recommended McClusky be taken down to the river and given 'a good ducking.' Colonel Sanders's treatment drew a formal protest from the Calgary Trades and Labor Council to the Attorney General's department in 1925, but a surprising silence from labour women who obviously knew her well. This lack of response foreshadowed future problems in the late 1920s.[64]

By 1925 the heyday of co-operation among labour women had ended. Following Margaret Bondfield's visit in 1924, the DLP women created a 'ladies section,' withdrawing support from the WLL, which affiliated with the eastern-based Federation of Women's Labor Leagues. Remaining in the WLL were women whose husbands opposed the Dominion Labor party or those whose views, like McWilliam's, favoured non-partisanship.[65] In later years Amelia Turner expressed her contempt for Jean McWilliam and the league, with its 'Communist connections.' Increasingly, DLP women bowed to party discipline, though many abandoned their other alliances with reluctance. In an address to the 'wives of labour men' at Marion Carson's home on Elbow Drive, British Labour party representative Ethel Snowden counselled: 'The best type of Labor woman ... was the one who was able to keep her ideals and yet to find in others of different views, some point of contact and always to be kind.'[66] Although it described Amelia Turner and Dominion Labor party women and was compatible with their ethical socialism, this conservative version of womanhood certainly excluded women like McWilliam and McClusky, who found that bourgeois respectability contradicted and compromised socialist goals.

III

Political maturity for Amelia Turner and Calgary labour women characterized the 1925–35 era as the DLP Women's Section developed a common analysis of women's role in politics and a strategy to accomplish socialist goals. Through study groups, networking within other labour parties, participation in the peace movement, and political action, these women sought to develop the co-operative commonwealth. Within the world of politics, however, they found 'male elite power' to be 'well and truly guarded.' Although many labour women challenged these barriers, as Veronica Strong-Boag explains, often they 'were effectively marginalized' and experienced 'great difficulty in translating their individual successes into a transformation of the political agenda of the public realm to reflect more fairly women's needs and experience.'[67] Amelia Turner and Edith Patterson were exceptional women; significantly, their success came because they had developed a partnership with a committed women's network, which was a product of women's separate culture.

Amelia Turner and other DLP women shared a vision of women's role in the socialist movement and accepted Agnes Macphail's challenge that 'a woman's place is any place she wants it to be,' but few Calgary labour women questioned the supremacy of motherhood. Instead, they expected women to make marriage and children their primary commitment. According to this view, the barriers to women's participation in labour politics were simply a lack of education and the absence of leisure time. Labour women accepted that political activism would be primarily the responsibility of single, career, and elder married women, who would be backed up by the women whose domestic work limited their involvement.[68] Although Amelia Turner managed to combine marriage and a career, even her case demonstrates this accepted division of labour: she married W. Norman Smith at the age of 45, when her political and advertising careers were secure; motherhood was not an option. Accepting these familial limitations on women's activism as 'natural,' labour women often confused their party's success at the polls and the achievement of social reforms with gender equality and access to power within their own movement.[69]

After the DLP women withdrew from the Women's Labor League, the league continued to have a strong focus on the problems of the working girl and solidarity with labour struggles, but by 1926 its activism seemed spent and its membership was confined to a few faithful crusaders.[70] By contrast, the DLP Women's Section became a vigorous group with an expanding membership. Its unchallenged president, Marion Carson, shepherded the group over the next decade of educational inquiry, networking, lobbying, and political victory. Established in 1926, the Women's Section's study group was often led by one of the studious Turner family and included articulate teachers like Rachael Coutts and Annie Campbell, who gave formal papers like 'The Birth of the Labour Movement' and 'The Causes of War.'[71]

As DLP's participation in the peace movement reveals, the purpose of education was to inform activism. After Laura E. Jamieson addressed their group in October 1927, DLP women affiliated with the Canadian branch of the Women's International League for Peace and Freedom. Over the next decade their participation was based on the assumption that although 'peace would not come under the present economic system,' nevertheless peace campaigns were essential to political change.[72] 'The maintenance of world peace is eminently women's work,' Carson argued, and 'the maternal instinct, which is strongest in women who are not mothers, finds outlet in extending protection ... and preventing suffering.'[73] This concept of womanhood was a great unifying force and the 'intellectually rigorous, rational discourse' of women peace activists influenced members of the inter-war generation and 'conditioned the way they approached their careers.'[74] As illustrated by Amelia Turner's political work and Rachael Coutts's teaching career, which focused on promoting internationalism and pacifism, DLP women promoted a peace agenda that unified much of their thought and work.

To achieve these goals and break their isolation from male structures, the DLP Women's Section became adept at networking, linking up with both a national and international support groups such as the Women's International League for Peace and Freedom. Although birth control advocates like Emma Goldman and Margaret Sanger also spoke in Calgary, it was the tours of the more 'respectable' British Labour party women that most influenced labour women. They were avid readers of the British *Labour Woman*, later the model for Patterson's column named 'The Alberta Labor Woman.' On the national level, Calgary DLP women affiliated in 1927 with the Western Labor Women's Social and Economic Conference (LWSE Conference) when it held the fourth annual conference in Calgary.[75] While the Calgary WLL organized the meetings, Dominion Labor party women actively participated also in debating resolutions.[76] On the provincial level, when the Alberta CLP met in Calgary in 1928, Calgary DLP women organized a luncheon for women delegates featuring J.S. Woodsworth as speaker.[77] Invited to attend were executive members of the United Farm Women of Alberta, a connection the Calgary women carefully nurtured by inviting Cabinet Minister Irene Parlby to address their members on a regular basis. When the UFA government created a Woman's Bureau under the Department of Agriculture, president Carson attended the convention as a delegate.[78]

Because winning yearly elections was a formidable challenge for the DLP, the Women's Section provided its share of organizers and candidates. Prior to 1925, Mary Corse and Marion Carson had represented DLP women on the Calgary School Board. When Carson resigned, she recruited Turner, who had expressed confidence in handling the difficult board chairman. Although she was unsuccessful in the December 1925 municipal election, when the new school-board met in January 1926 and voted to discontinue supplying free textbooks, Turner received another chance. The Dominion Labor party organized a mass meeting to protest the move and passed a resolution requesting the school-board at its January meeting to call for a plebiscite within twenty days or face recall proceedings against the mover and seconder of the motion. When the board refused to hold a plebiscite on the issue, the DLP swung into action. On 31 March 1926 a recall election resulted in the defeat of both men by DLP candidates Amelia Turner and W.E. Turner.[79]

This famous recall election established Amelia's reputation for independence and provided the opportunity for her to advance the Dominion Labor party's education agenda, which involved providing free milk, dental and medical services, classes for the handicapped, greater access to technical education, and the abolition of cadet training from schools. From 1918 until 1936, at least one woman labour trustee sat on the Calgary School Board and supported collective-bargaining rights for the ATA and equality for female teachers. Both these issues earned strong support and recruits for the DLP.[80] Over the next decade, Amelia Turner and other labour trustees, who hammered away at Citizens Government Association trustees' opposition to their agenda, often controlled the vote and succeeded in implementing much of their program. A popular and respected politician, Turner was also an able administrator and financial manager: she demonstrated strength and independence when serving as board vice chairman with F.S. Spooner, who openly opposed her politics and disliked her partnership with the DLP Women's Section and the Ladies Public School Local of the ATA. Despite such opposition from within the board, Turner chaired the school-board for two terms and the school management and health committees many times.[81]

Dominion Labor party women scored another success in the election to the Calgary City Council of alderman Edith Patterson, Amelia Turner's closest friend. Although a colleague predicted Patterson would 'take great interest in those things which come closer to the scope of the female part of the community ... hospitals, clinics, unemployment and all social legislation,' Patterson also showed an interest in issues of public ownership and taxation. During her aldermanic term, 1927–32, and in her newspaper column 'The Alberta Labor Woman,' Patterson championed feminist networking; but, she also challenged women to oppose both privatization of garbage collection in Calgary and taxation on publicly owned utilities. Although anxious for increased female participation on city council, she wrote: 'Though we greatly desire representation of women on the governing bodies, more fervently do we desire greater representation of labor.'[82] Though sensitive to gender inequality, Patterson none the less approached divisive gender issues (including birth control) by cautiously urging working-class unity above all else.

As models of bourgeois respectability, Amelia Turner and Edith Patterson knew the rules, kept their frustrations private, and never challenged the CLP or the newly formed CCF on feminist issues. Reporting on the women's luncheon at the 1933 Regina Conference, Turner conceded there was 'a suggestion of "feminism" here and there, since many of the women had been "keen feminists"'; however, she concluded, 'talk of fair play for women was quite unnecessary ... all are working together for great ideals.'[83] Although Amelia wanted to downplay conflict, not all CCF women were prepared to overlook gender inequality in politics.[84] In Calgary conflict was muted: women who served on the DLP executive during the 1920s assumed a supporting role, reproducing the societal sexual division of labour in politics. As activists and candidates, women represented women's concerns and won their votes, but few Dominion Labor party members expected women to direct the future of the movement. Neither Amelia Turner nor Edith Patterson was consulted on questions of policy or strategy in these years.

What, then, did Amelia Turner's candidacy in the provincial by-election campaigns of January 1933 and January 1934 mean? Following the 1932 Western Conference of Labour Political Parties, the CLP selected Amelia to run as a joint CLP/CCF candidate. Not only popular and able, she was also trusted by the new CCF party establishment, who knew of her long-standing connections to radical Progressives through Irvine and W. Norman Smith, *The UFA* magazine's editor. Amelia's ideological identification with this group rather than with the conservative and discredited UFA government of Premier Brownlee meant she would challenge the Alberta UFA and support attempts to force its program leftward.[85]

Between 1933 and 1935, Turner contested two provincial by-elections and Patterson a federal election. These elections are significant because Turner was the first CCF candidate in Canada and polled the largest percentage of votes ever received by a Calgary labour candidate. Furthermore, both by-elections featured a high turn-out of women voters, demonstrating the activist and party-building role that Calgary women had played over the last decade. Finally, the elections revealed serious problems within the alliance of labourites and the UFA, as well as labour's vulnerability to the Social Credit movement. When Edith Patterson contested the 1935 election, a new era had arrived: it was characterized by the disorganization and demoralization of the former Dominion Labor party and its new CCF ally. In 1935, Amelia refused to 'carry the banner in some hopeless ridings,' sensing the exploitation of women candidates as 'sacrificial lambs.'

In the January 1933 election, Amelia Turner polled 12,301 votes to her opponent Norman Hindsley's 14,128. She was billed as the people's favourite, and an impressive team waged a tough fight on her behalf. But Turner battled with party fragmentation, and her defeat foreshadowed the future problems of the Alberta CLP and the CCF. When long-time Calgary labour alderman and MLA R.H. Parkyn entered the race as an Independent Labour candidate, the Calgary CLP group refused to endorse him and instead nominated Turner; however, Parkyn's candidacy spoiled labour's chance of a victory and communist John O'Sullivan's candidacy completed the defeat.[86] Both candidates viewed with hostility Turner, the new CCF, and the CLP's partnership with the UFA government. Former political enemies like school-board chairman F.E. Spooner, now Hindsley's campaign manager, tried to damage Turner's credibility. Although these problems cost her the election, they did not prevent working-class women from turning out in record numbers to vote for her.[87]

Analysing the demise of the CLP in 1935, Finkel argues that by the depression era the party had become the preserve of a small group of union bureaucrats who commanded little public support. What then is the explanation for Turner's electoral support? In the 15 January 1934 by-election, she gave a repeat performance in a closer contest, winning 44.9 per cent of the popular vote, but losing to W. Harry Ross who received 10,968 votes to Turner's 9065. Again, a former DLP member and school trustee, E.H. Starr, who resigned from the party to run as an independent Progressive-Labor candidate, opposed Turner. Some dissatisfied party members argued that the Labor party MLAs had become apologists for the reactionary UFA government and pushed for an 'independent' labour party.[88] Brownlee's suppression of the 1933 Hunger March in Edmonton with support of a Canadian Labor party mayor and labour councillors made it difficult for the party to maintain discipline, and confusion over the nature of the CCF affiliation also compounded the problem.

Yet Amelia Turner's supporters did not seem alarmed by her UFA connections, nor did they appear troubled by relief strikes in Calgary during 1933. Audiences were impressed with her explanation of the 1933 Regina Manifesto's support for a planned economy, banking reform, public ownership of essential services, socialization of health services, and free education.[89] An astute politician, Turner viewed with alarm the Social Credit movement with its brilliant organizing tactics and growing following of working-class voters. To please her audience she presented social credit positively by supporting its creation at the federal level and promising to prod the UFA government to fully investigate social credit.[90] Without fragmentation from CLP members, Amelia could have won both elections, but such a victory would have been bittersweet.

After 1934 the Canadian Labor party and the CCF followed a disastrous course, unable to undermine the appeal of the Social Credit movement by adopting a 'populist discourse as well as class discourse.' Voters reacted swiftly to the populism of Social Credit, for by the 1935 federal election the CLP's vote went from 44.9 per cent for Amelia Turner to 4.5 per cent for Edith Patterson.[91] Between 1934 and 1935, Social Credit rapidly captured the CLP's Calgary working-class base, striking hard at the ageing labour group. Under siege from unemployment and declining union membership, the CLP/CCF collapsed. Women felt the political chaos keenly: many, like Amelia, could not adjust to political failure and retired from active politics. Nor did Calgary develop such a cohesive group of socialist women until the 1970s.[92]

IV

Yet from 1919 to 1935, Calgary labour women had politicized women to support a socialist and feminist agenda. From radical roots laid in the First World War, the labour women's groups blossomed and matured into the Women's Labor League and the DLP Women's Section. The WLL maintained a consistent emphasis on gender inequality; in the DLP Women's Section, class issues dominated over incipient interest in women's equality. Ultimately, non-partisan alliances were forsaken by Dominion Labor party women for power and influence within their own organization, where women's presence helped prevent the party from being solely the expression of craft-union leaders.

Because female activists were primarily either single professional women or married women with grown families, who volunteered time for a 'second' career, they did not encounter the contradictions of 'hauling a double load,' nor did they advance a feminist analysis of women, work, and the family. Even for labour women, married women with small children could hope for neither a political career nor paid employment. Married women in the labour political movement began to 'mother the world' when they had the energy, leisure time, and support from their husbands. Problems of rivalry were avoided because many politically active wives were widows or had a husband indifferent to politics, as Mary Corse and Jean McWilliam's careers illustrate.

Successful female politicans were rare in Alberta as elsewhere in Canada, so Amelia Turner occupies a unique place in provincial politics. Along with Liberal MLA Nellie McClung and UFA cabinet minister Irene Parlby, she experienced gender discrimination. Although personally successful, her career represents neither a transformation of political structures to include women nor a significant broadening of the agenda in a feminist direction. At the same time, her municipal and provincial campaigns were grounded in the DLP women's own agenda of international co-operation and peace, democratization of education, availability of free medical and dental service, unemployment insurance, fair minimum wage, mother's allowances, and pensions for women. These 'mothering issues' formed the nucleus of the Canadian Labor party's program, but movement on these issues was equally the goal of Dominion Labor party women, who organized and promoted women politicians specifically to implement this agenda. Amelia Turner spoke clearly for her constituency and received their full support. Her career demonstrates that women failed to penetrate the inner sanctum of labour politics, but it also illustrates that women were a significant political force. Calgary labour women rejected the image of passive apolitical women, and utilized their new political power to effect change consistent with their earlier maternal feminist and socialist vision. A continued focus on male élites keeps hidden from analysis the structural barriers and contradictions that women faced, and precludes an understanding of the solutions they developed.

NOTES

The author wishes to acknowledge the critical reading and useful comments of Linda Kealey and Joan Sangster on an earlier draft of this paper.

1 Edith Patterson to Amelia Turner, 20 January 1933, Norman Smith Papers (NS Papers) AS5663 f. 215, Glenbow-Alberta Institute (GAI).

2 See, for example, John Herd Thompson with Allen Seager, *Canada 1922–1939* (Toronto 1985), 69–75; and Alvin Finkel, 'The Rise and Fall of the Labour Party in Alberta 1917–42,' *Labour/Le Travail* 16 (Fall 1985), 61–96. For an insightful discussion of feminism in 1920s, see V. Strong-Boag, 'Pulling in Double Harness or Hauling a Double Load: Women, Work and Feminism on the Canadian Prairie,' *Journal of Canadian Studies* 21:3 (Fall 1986), 32–52; and Sylvia B. Bashevkin, *Toeing the Lines: Women and Party Politics in English Canada* (Toronto 1985), ch. 1.

3 For a more detailed biographical sketch, see P. Roome, 'Amelia Turner: Alberta Socialist,' in Max Foran and Sheilagh Jameson, eds, *Citymakers: Calgarians after the Frontier* (Calgary 1987).

4 Frederick Turner to P. Roome, 2 August 1985, and photocopy 'Turner Family Tree,' 17 July 1969, at family reunion, Calgary, Alberta; wedding certificate of James Turner and Amelia Dyke, GAI.

5 E. Silverman interview with Amelia Turner Smith, 10 December 1975, typescript 1–9, Provincial Archives of Alberta (PAA). On financial problems see Henry J. Turner, file 10 May 1902–1 June 1921, Homestead Records, PAA.

6 Silverman interview, 1975, 5–9.

7 Ibid., 12.

8 Ibid., 12–14. Letter, A.T. Smith to Isa Grindlay Jackson, 14 January 1966, NS Papers, AS5663, file 27, GAI.

9 Hereward Turner farmed at Alliance, Alberta, and was active in UFA/CCF. Donata married Frank Irvine; both were active in UFA/CCF. Dorothy, Amelia, and Mrs L. Turner lived together in Calgary, working in the DLP. See *Alberta Labor News (ALN)*, 28 April 1928, for notes on Mrs L. Turner's leadership of a study group; Elise Corbet interview with Amelia Turner Smith and Dorothy Smith, n.d., RCT–475, GAI. Amelia described herself as different from other girls, with more drive, knowledge of the world, and desire for a different life.

10 For insight into this period see Diary 1913–1917, Amelia Turner Smith Papers (ATS Papers) AS5663, file 12, GAI. See also G. Lowe, 'Women, Work and the Office: The Feminization of Clerical Occupations in Canada 1901–1931,' *Canadian Journal of Sociology* 5:4 (1980), 376–8; and 'Class, Job and Gender in the Canadian Office,' *Labour/Le Travail* 10 (Autumn 1982), 1–37.

11 Anthony Mardiros, *The Life of a Prairie Radical: William Irvine* (Toronto 1979), ch 3. See also J.E. Cook and F.A. Johnston interview with Amelia Turner Smith, 28 May 1973, PAA; J.E. Cook interview with Dr A. Calhoun, 28 May 1972, PAA. On the Unity Club, see Rachael Coutts, *Voice*, 7 September 1917 and 27 July 1917. There was also a Women's Alliance of the Unitarian church affiliated with the Local Council of Women for 1919–20. Minute Book 1919–1921, Local Council of Women, M5841, file 24, p. 192, GAI.

12 P. Roome interview with Amelia Turner Smith, 21 July 1982, typescript 1. See also Edith Patterson, 'Memories of William Irvine,' *The Commonwealth*, 27 February 1963.

13 Roome interview, 1–2. Often Nattie Turner baby-sat the Irvine children while Amelia and Mrs Irvine attended movies or played cards with friends like Kate Clark or Edith Patterson.

14 Silverman interview, 1975, 16; Cook and Johnson interview, 1973.

15 Silverman interview, 1975, 15.

16 *ALN*. 25 September 1920.

17 See Allen Mills, 'Cooperation and Community in the Thought of J.S. Woodsworth,' *Labour/Le Travail* 14 (Fall 1984), 103–20.

18 Amelia Turner Smith, autobiographical notes, n.d. GAI.

19 See Norman and Jeanne Mackenzie, *The Fabians* (New York 1977).

20 Mr and Mrs William Carson clipping file, GAI. Marion Carson (1861–1947?) came to Calgary in 1898 with husband William (d. 1924), who became the successful owner and manager first of Calgary Milling Co. and then of Western Milling Co. During the First World War, he was in the grain-commission business. Marion, mother of six children, co-founder with Rachael

of the Tuberculosis Society, joined the Unitarian church in 1913 and became a pacifist, strongly active after the death of her son overseas in 1917. She was the most socially prominent labour woman, able to bridge the gap between women on Local Council of Women and labour women in DLP, as demonstrated by her position as Convenor of Peace and Arbitration (renamed many times) for the LCW for more than a decade, president of DLP Women's Section, and trustee 1920–4; Rachael Coutts clipping file, GAI. Rachael Coutts was teacher, charter member of ATA, active on LCW, the Unitarian church, and executives of WLL and DLP, League of Nations clubs, and WILPF.

21 Edith Patterson to Mr Cook, William Irvine Papers (WI Papers), 83, 115/15, PAA; Edith Patterson clipping file, GAI; 'East Calgary Nominates Former Labor Alderman,' ALN, 5 October 1935. E. Patterson (1876–1967) taught in Calgary 1913–40, served on the executives of WLL and DLP and became DLP president after Carson in the 1930s. Patterson was an alderman (1928–32, 1937–8) and CCF candidate in 1935, president of the Alberta Education Association, and, in 1934, president of ATA. She edited the column 'Alberta Labor Woman' in ALN between 1927 and 1935. Some of Edith Patterson's brothers, sisters, and their children – all Conservative party supporters – lived in Calgary. One nephew was Judge H.S. Patterson.

22 Finkel, 'The Rise and Fall,' 67–8. While the Canadian Labor party was formed in Alberta in 1921, factionalism prevented Calgary from setting up a central council until 1924.

23 'Alberta Labor Woman,' ALN, 17 September 1927 and 3 March 1928; see notes 20, 21 above. Kate Clark was a teacher who lived with Patterson for over twenty years and served on WLL and DLP executives in the 1920s. Mary Corse was a mother of six, resident in Calgary sporadically from 1916–24, member of Women's Auxiliary Typographical Union No. 449, a DLP school trustee 1918–20, on the executive of DLP, president of WLL. Her husband was a linotype machinist on the *Morning Albertan*. Elizabeth Broatch (d. 1944) was a mother of seven, on the executive of WLL, member of the Women's Auxiliary of Machinists (with a husband who was a machinist), OBU member, and alderman. Mrs M.L. Parkyn was a mother, active on the executive of WLL, Sunnyside PTA, Sunnyside Community Club, and wife of carpenter and activist R.H. Parkyn – DLP member, alderman, MLA. On types of women, see Roome interview with Amelia Turner, 21 July 1982. Marion Carson's upper-middle-class position set her aside from most of these women and gave her an unquestioned position of power.

24 Roome interview with Amelia Turner, 21 July 1982; Frederick Turner to P. Roome, 2 August 1985.

25 Linda Kealey, 'Prairie Socialist Women and WWI: The Urban West,' unpublished paper 1986, 15–16.

26 Minute Book 1919–1921, Local Council of Women; Jean (McWilliam) McDonald Papers, A.M135B, file 1, 2, GAI. Jean McWilliam (1877–1969) came from Scotland to homestead near Calgary in 1907, with husband William McWilliam. She ran a boarding-house from 1912 to the 1930s, and supported radical socialists and communists like John Reid and John O'Sullivan. She was president of WLL, president of Local Council of Women 1927–8, and active on LCW throughout the 1920s and 1930s. In the 1940s she formed the National Social Security Association. Mrs F.W. Grevett was later president of WLL, active on LCW from 1919 onward, becoming second vice-president in 1929 and Convenor of Immigration 1927–32. Her husband was a clerk at CPR in 1920.

27 Elizabeth Ann Taraska, 'The Calgary Craft Union Movement,' MA thesis, University of Calgary 1972: Calgary TLC Minutes (CTLC Minutes), 27 April 1918, M4743 file 6, GAI. Mrs J. McWilliam is recorded as a voting delegate for Federated Workers Union and Mrs George Corse for Typographical Auxiliary, 5 July 1918.

28 Western Convention Report, Western Canada Labor Conference, Calgary, 13–15 March 1919, Alfred W. Farmilo collection, 72.159, PAA. For Corse/McWilliam roles on the TLC, see CTLC Minutes, 5 July 1918, 19 July 1918, 2 August 1918, 30 August 1918, 22 November 1918, GAI.

29 On the British WLLs see Lucy Middleton, ed., *Women in the Labour Movement* (London 1977) 25–35; Caroline Rowan, 'Women in the Labour Party 1906–1920,' *Feminist Review* 12 (October 1982), 74–91.

30 'People's Church in Calgary,' *Searchlight*, 9 April 1920. 'Work of the Women's Labor League in Calgary,' *Searchlight*, 3 September 1920.

31 'Women's Labor League of Calgary,' *Searchlight*, 28 November 1919.

32 E.g. Elizabeth Broatch, Alice Corless, Kate Clark, Rachael Coutts, and Edith Patterson.

33 See note 23 above. Mrs A. Corless (d. 1942), mother of a large family, husband a janitor at Earle Grey School, both active in Unitarian church, later Labor church, until about 1925 when they moved to the United States (A. Corless to William Irvine, January 1945, WI Papers 83.115/2, PAA). Other WLL executive members: Mrs Elizabeth Petrie, secretary of Bridgeland PTA 1928, husband a lawyer; Mrs J.H. Sprague, mother, husband a traveller for Drumheller Coal; Mrs G.H. Gerrad, WLL's vice-president 1922, president 1923–7, treasurer of Canadian Council of Child Welfare 1926; Mrs R.H. Parkyn; Mrs E.E. Antis, husband a carpenter, active in Machinists, Women's Auxiliary.

34 'Mrs. George Corse, Representative of Trades and Labor Council,' *Royal Commission on Industrial Relations, 1919 Testimony*, Calgary 3 and 5 May 1919, Department of Labour Library, 35.

35 Ibid., 41. For a more rigorous critique, see Florence Custance, 'Why the Women's Labor League Movement?' *Woman Worker* 1:2 (August 1926).

36 'Corse,' *Royal Commission*, 279.

37 'Mrs. Jean McWilliam, representing no organization but appearing as a citizen,' *Royal Commission*, 182–6.

38 'Corse,' *Royal Commission*, 279.

39 Joan Sangster, 'Canadian Women in Radical Politics and Labour, 1920–1950,' PhD diss., McMaster University 1984.

40 'Work of the Women's Labor League,' *Searchlight*, 3 September 1920; Georgia Baird and Karl Kaesekamp interview with Molly (McWilliam) La France, 3 May 1972, PAA. See also Royal North West Mounted Police Report, re: One Big Union, Strike in Calgary, dated Calgary 27 May 1919, signed S.R. Waugh, Det.-Corpl, copy in Warren Carragata Collection, BO 218, box B, PAA. Waugh falsely accuses McWilliam of being a member of SPC because she supported OBU and was on the Central Strike Committee with R.H. Parkyn; also, Waugh reports, a member of the SPC.

41 'An Appreciation of Alderman Broatch,' *Searchlight*, 2 January 1920.

42 'Speaker Called Them Bunch of Old Women,' *Searchlight*, 28 May 1920.

43 CTLC Minutes, 2 July 1920, GAI. Mrs G.S. Corse was presented with a purse of money by the council and its locals on behalf of her 'able services as a delegate and representative of Council.' She was leaving for Vancouver but returned, 1922–4.

44 'The Woman's Vote in Calgary,' *ALN*, 4 November 1922.

45 'Women's Labor League Active,' *Searchlight*, 23 January 1920. '$25 Per Month Minimum for House Workers,' *ALN*, 25 September 1920. 'Mrs. McWilliam Asks Minimum Wage of $21.48,' *ALN*, 9 October 1920. See also *ALN*, 10 September 1921 and 11 November 1922. 'Women's Labor League 40 Protests Delay in Minimum Wage Law,' *ALN*, 1 December 1923. Alice Corless to His Worship the Mayor and Councillors, 2 July 1919, Calgary City Clerk Papers (CCC Papers) box 161, file 971, GAI. Bessie Petrie to J.M. Miller, 23 August 1920, CCC Papers, box 176, f. 1036. Elise Corbet, 'Alberta Women in the 1920s: An Inquiry into Four Aspects of Their Lives,' MA diss., University of Calgary 1979, ch. 1. See also Linda Kealey, 'Women and Labour during World War I: Women Workers and the Minimum Wage in Manitoba,' in Mary Kinnear, ed., *First Days, Fighting Days* (Regina 1987), 76–99. Margaret E. McCallum, 'Keeping Women in Their Place: The Minimum Wage in Canada 1910–1924,' *Labour/Le Travail* 17 (Spring 1986), 29–56.

46 'Women's Labor League Active,' *Searchlight*, 23 January 1920. Mrs George Corse argued for socialized medicine during her testimony in 1919, *Royal Commission*, 281: 'During the war the Government has proven that the nationalization of one medical profession is a possibility.'

47 'Children Starve in This City,' *Searchlight*, 20 February 1920.
48 'The Woman's Vote in Calgary,' ALN, 4 November 1922. See also P. Roome interview with Amelia Turner. Autobiographical notes by Annie Gale, 9 July 1919, Annie Gale collection, M402, GAI. Annie Gale (1867–1970) was an English woman who organized the Calgary Women's Consumers League, became president of the Women Rate Payers Association, alderman 1918–24, school trustee 1924–5. As an independent, she supported labour's goals, serving for two years as treasurer of People's Forum.
49 Although Lethbridge WLL did affiliate with the Central Council of CLP, there is no existing evidence that the Calgary WLL did. Because Mary Corse was absent from Calgary from 1920 to 1922, returned 1922–4, then left permanently, Jean McWilliam was able to dominate the league and oppose affiliation with CLP ALN, 14 April 1923 and 20 September 1924.
50 ALN, 26 March 1921.
51 Calgary School Board Minutes, 10 April 1923, Calgary Board of Education (CBE). Bessie Petrie to Mr D. Bayne, secretary school board, 19 September 1924, CCC Papers, file 9E, box 35C, GAI.
52 Corbet, 'Alberta Women in the 1920s,' 18.
53 Corbet, interview with Amelia Turner.
54 ALN, 20 November 1920, 2 April 1921, 16 April 1921, and 30 April 1921.
55 Ibid., 11 June 1921: 'I like the idea of all women's organizations getting together on a plane of usefulness.' On behalf of WLL, Mrs A. Corless argued this view at a tea given by Calgary women for Mrs Sears, president UFWA.
56 Sylvia Bashevkin, 'Independence vs. Partisanship: Dilemmas in the Political History of Women in English Canada,' in Veronica Strong-Boag and Anita Clair Fellman, eds, *Rethinking Canada: The Promise of Women's History* (Toronto 1986), 248.
57 E.R. Fay to the mayor and alderman, 23 December 1921; E.R. Fay to Mr Miller, 2 January 1922, CCC Papers, box 217, file 1228, GAI. Special committee membership: Mrs Sprague, Mrs McWilliam, E. Croft, A. Davidson, Mrs Carson, A. Allison; see also interview with Molly La France.
58 E.R. Fay to J.M. Miller, 3 April 1922, CCC Papers, box 217, file 1228, GAI. Central Council of Unemployed Petitions and Resolutions, CCC Papers, box 211, file 1192, GAI; 'Calgary Unemployed Occupy City Hall,' ALN, 8 April 1922. See also Judith B. Bedford, 'Social Justice in Calgary: A Study of Urban Poverty and Welfare Development in 1920s,' MA thesis, University of Calgary 1981.
59 Resolutions no. 12 and no. 13, CCC Papers, box 202, file 1145; report of Unemployment Conference held in Calgary, 4 and 5 August 1922, CCC Papers, box 207, file 1175, GAI.

60 'Trades Council Will Organize Workers,' ALN, 10 June 1922; E.R. Fay to
   J.M. Miller, 3 April 1922, CCC Papers, box 217, file 1228. Mr Cassidy and
   Mr Lessey were OBU organizers whom TLC opposed. On Cassidy, see David J.
   Bercuson, *Fools and Wise Men* (Toronto 1978), 227–33. A.J. Boulter was
   the Worker's party organizer on CCU. Boulter, a miner from Drumheller who
   worked as labourer at CPR yards, was very hostile to craft unions. In 1927 he
   secured CLP nomination for alderman and was supported by the General Worker's
   Union. Calgary organized this first local of ACCUL with Boulter as a key
   person. The Boulter family were friends of McWilliam, who supported other
   miners. Resolution re case of P.T. Thompson, Jean McWilliam to city
   clerk, 22 May 1922, CCC Papers, box 203, file 1151. WLL protested police
   harassment of Thompson, who was an unemployed Drumheller miner active
   in CCU.
61 'The Women's Vote in Calgary,' ALN, 4 November 1922.
62 Sophie McClusky was a Russian immigrant, SPC organizer, and provincial
   secretary for Alberta, known in 1913–14 in Calgary as Sophie Mushkat. She
   taught English to immigrants at Riverside School and was active in the Unemployed Committee (Calgary Protestant Public School Board Minutes, 20
   January 1913, 13 January 1914, CBE); Warren Carragata collection, 80.218,
   box A, PAA; See Kealey, 'Prairie Socialist Women,' 8–9.
63 Dr Scott to Mr G.F. McNally, 3 November 1921, Calgary School Board
   Papers, box 40B, file 1921 L–Z, GAI. On reapplication, see Calgary School
   Board Minutes, 19 September 1925.
64 Sophie McClusky file, GAI; ALN, 14 February 1925. See also T. Thorner and N.
   Watson, 'Keeper of the King's Peace: Colonel G.E. Saunders and the Calgary
   Police Magistrate's Court 1911–1932,' *Urban History Review* 12 (February
   1984), 45–55.
65 For example Mrs M. Parkyn, Mrs G.H. Garrad, and Mrs F.W. Grevett.
66 ALN, 24 January 1925.
67 Strong-Boag, 'Pulling in Double Harness,' 33.
68 'Reply to Address of Welcome, Mrs. M. Lowe,' ALN, 6 April 1929 and 'By the
   Way,' ibid., 1 December 1928.
69 'Alberta Labor Women,' ALN, 17 December 1927, 26 January 1928, 3 March
   1928.
70 A full discussion of the demise of the Calgary WLL lies beyond the scope of this
   paper. McWilliam, Parkyn, Hunt, and Grevett continued to be involved. The
   WLL hosted the 1927 Women's Social and Economic Conference in Calgary and
   Mrs D. Hunt joined the executive. In 1928 it helped A.E. Smith raise money
   for the Canadian Labor Defence League. By 1930, the WLL was affiliated with
   the Local Council of Women, because of McWilliam's and Grevett's partici-

pation from 1919 onward. They both served on the executive with McWilliam as president (1926–8) giving lectures on Russia (February 1927) at Central United Church (see Minutes of Local Council of Women, 21 January 1927, M5 841, file 24, GAI; *Alberta Labor News*, 28 March 1927, 2 April 1927, 9 April 1927, 28 April 1927, 28 February 1928).

71 'Alberta Labor Woman,' *ALN*, 17 September 1927, 15 February 1928, 28 April 1928, 26 May 1928, 20 October 1928.

72 Ibid., 17 September 1927; 'Mrs. Jamieson Has Message for Calgary Women,' *ALN*, 22 October 1927.

73 'Internationalism Means Loyalty to Human Race,' *ALN*, 17 September 1927. Marion Carson, 'Some Peace Movements Other than League of Nations,' *Alberta Labor Annual*, September 1921; Carson, 'The Growing Revulsion toward War,' *Alberta Labor Annual*, September 1928; Carson, 'Women and the Peace Movement,' *ALN*, 20 October 1928.

74 Francis Early, 'The Historic Roots of the Women's Peace Movement in North America,' *Canadian Women Studies/Les cahiers de la femme* 7:4 (Winter 1986), 47; Thomas P. Socknat, 'The Pacifist Background of the Early CCF,' in J. William Brennan, ed., *Building the Co-operative Commonwealth: Essays on the Democratic Socialist Tradition in Canada* (Regina 1984), 57–68.

75 'Our Labor Leagues at Work,' *Woman Worker*, May 1927; 'Mrs. McArthur Heads Labor Conference,' *ALN*, 2 April 1927; 'Agnes MacPhail,' *Alberta Labor News*, 9 April 1927 and 'Labor Women Discuss Many Vital Matters,' *ALN*, 9 April 1927. On LWSE Conference, see Joan Sangster, 'Communist Party and the Woman Question 1922–29,' *Labour/Le Travail* 15 (Spring 1985), 31. On founder of LWSE Conference, see B. Brigden, 'One Woman's Campaign for Social Purity and Social Reform,' in Richard Allen, ed., *The Social Gospel in Canada* (Ottawa 1975), 36–62.

76 'Alberta Labor Woman,' *ALN*, 10 March 1928, 21 April 1928, 5 May 1928, 17 November 1928, 16 March 1929, 23 March 1929, 30 March 1929, 6 April 1929.

77 Ibid., 10 November 1928, 17 November 1928.

78 'Fine Spirit Prevailed at Conference,' *ALN*, 12 May 1928.

79 Calgary School Board Minutes, 25 January 1926 and 13 February 1926, CBE; *Calgary Herald*, 30 March 1926, 31 March 1926. For a more detailed analysis, see P. Roome, 'Amelia Turner: Alberta Socialist.'

80 Annual reports, Calgary School Board 1927–1936, CBE.

81 Calgary School Board Minutes, 8 June 1926, 25 June 1926, CBE.

82 'Alberta Labor Women,' *ALN*, 29 October 1927, 5 November 1927, 12 November 1927, 19 November 1927, 10 December 1927, 17 December 1927, 26 January 1928, July 1928.

83 *The UFA*, 1 August 1933.

84 For example, the Women's Joint Committee; see John Manley, 'Women and the Left in the 1930s: The Case of the Toronto CCF Women's Joint Committee,' *Atlantis* 5:2 (Spring 1980), 100–19; Joan Sangster, 'Women of the "New Era": Women in the Early CCF,' in Brennan, ed., *Building the Co-operative Commonwealth*, 69–98.

85 Irvine/Smith correspondence, 1933–4, WI Papers, 83.115/199, PAA; also Irvine/Smith correspondence, NS Papers, box 2, file 22, GAI. DLP and its Women's Section formally adopted the Canadian Labor party label in 1930.

86 *Calgary Herald*, 13 January 1933. For detailed analysis of 1933, 1934 by-elections, see P. Roome, 'Amelia Turner.'

87 Robert M. Stamp, *School Days: A Century of Memories* (Calgary 1975), 59–63.

88 *Calgary Albertan*, 5 January 1934, 9 January 1934, 11 January 1934.

89 Ibid., 11 January 1934, 12 January 1934, 13 January 1934.

90 Ibid., 15 January 1934.

91 Larry Hannant, 'The Calgary Working Class and the Social Credit Movement in Alberta 1932–1935,' *Labour/Le Travail* 16 (Fall 1985), 97–116; Alvin Finkel, 'The Obscure Origins: The Confused Early History of the Alberta CCF,' in Brennan, ed., *Building the Co-operative Commonwealth*, 99–122.

92 Alvin Finkel, 'Populism and the Proletariat: Social Credit and the Alberta Working Class,' *Studies in Political Economy* 13 (Spring 1984), 109–35.

The Role of Women
in the Early CCF

1933–1940

Joan Sangster

At the founding convention of the CCF in Regina, 1933, the women delegates were far outnumbered by the men in the conference hall. Despite their small numbers, they were a determined and dedicated group, many of whom, like the men, had to improvise and economize to reach Regina that summer. Dorothy Steeves and Mildred Osterhaut Fahrni, from Vancouver, shared a bumpy car ride to Regina with frequent tire blow-outs. They had feared that the car would not make it through the mountains. Lorna Cotton-Thomas, a well-educated but unemployed graduate of the University of Toronto, made illegal use of a friend's CPR pass, despite the disapproval of her boy-friend, who tried to persuade her that in this case the end did not justify the means. Elizabeth Morton, an Ontario SPCer, drove from Toronto, sharing a car with four other delegates and raising money for her expenses with speaking engagements along the way.

These women, along with the other female delegates at Regina, symbolized the important presence, although less influential role, that women were to play in this new party. Women who joined the CCF were deeply moved by the economic upheaval of the Great Depression, and had found their despair with the social system answered in socialist literature by Edward Bellamy, Marx, and the British Fabians. But once active in the party, they were rudely awakened to a less than ideal socialist division of labour. Women were to be found primarily in grass-roots work, but rarely in the leadership. Drawing on traditions of earlier labourite or farm groups some women set up their own organizations, which were encouraged by the party, though it did not, as a rule, view the woman question as a priority issue. Indeed, only a small minority of women became involved in the CCF with feminist goals in mind. These early socialist feminists recognized that despite the egalitarian principles of the CCF, in practice the party, like the society it strove to change, upheld distinct, and sometimes unequal, roles for women.

I

The CCF was an alliance of socialist, labour, and farm groups united against the economic inequalities of capitalism, which had been greatly magnified by the 1930s depression. The precise analysis of capitalism, however, varied among the CCF's constituent groups, as did their remedies for change.[1] Agrarian groups and intellectuals from the League for Social Reconstruction (LSR), moderate labourites, and Marxists made for an eclectic and sometimes uneasy alliance. Many women who joined the CCF in 1933 had already been active in the LSR, labour parties, or farm groups; women like Beatrice Brigden, prominent in the Manitoba Independent Labour party in the 1920s, brought organizational experience and a well-developed socialist perspective to the CCF. A second generation of CCF women, who grew up in the 1930s, often came from highly politicized, progressive families. Hilda Kristiansen, for example, was the product of a prairie farm family well versed in co-operative and socialist ideas: her father was active in a local Saskatchewan co-op and in the United Farmers of Canada; he attended the CCF's historic Regina Convention, while her mother was 'quietly supportive' of these causes. After moving to British Columbia to work, Hilda joined the Young Socialists and eventually became an important leader in the BC CCF Women's Committee.[2]

Still, the commitment of women to the CCF cannot be explained simply by the inheritance of family politics. What, then, were the motivating forces behind women's interest in socialism? Underlying women's activism lay certain common themes; women's experience of working-class or farm life, or witnessing of social inequalities, combined with exposure to new socialist ideas, led them to the CCF. Economic insecurity and arduous working conditions were the lot of most working-class and farm women in the 1920s; the Great Depression only worsened their lot. Single and married women working for wages faced wage reductions, speed-ups, and job loss; women workers were often forced to resort to the only alternative open to them – despised and poorly paid domestic work. The depression experiences of friends, relatives, and even strangers also raised the political consciousness of many women; Irene Biss, a university professor and an LSR member, for example, was moved by the poor conditions of the Toronto garment workers whom she investigated and wrote about. Unemployment and relief – either experienced at first hand or viewed at second hand – were also radicalizing forces for many women. In East York, a Toronto municipality hard hit by unemployment, relief recipients, aided by local socialists, organized collectively into a self-help and action-oriented organization, the East York Workers' Association (EYWA). Women in the EYWA constructed their own women's Marxist study group as well as aiding the association's anti-eviction and lobbying campaigns. Some of these women subsequently joined the CCF.[3]

Nor was the relief experience limited to urban Canada. In the west, and particularly in Saskatchewan, depression and drought carved out a path of poverty: income levels plummeted and some families, if not forced off their land, were reduced to the most meagre subsistence or the 'humiliation' of relief. These years, according to many women who became CCFers, left an indelible mark on their memories. Women were forced to leave school early to support their families; they were faced with the fear – and the reality – of crop failure; they were given no alternative but relief; they scrimped and compromised on their family budget, and they saw brothers or friends leave to ride the rods or head off to the relief camps. In the midst of such social upheaval, it is hardly surprising that some women began to question the status quo. Although the depression did not 'cause' the emergence of the CCF, it did encourage some women to reflect on the social order and it stimulated their search for an alternative system. 'It seemed by 1933,' recalled Sophia Dixon, 'as if the capitalist system was simply crumbling before us and our task was to find and build a new system which could replace the old.'[4]

Radical ideas, along with material realities, also led women to the CCF. For many, progressive Christian politics and groups like the Fellowship for a Christian Social Order (FCSO) provided an introduction to socialism. Young CCFers like Marjorie Mann had their early education in the Student Christian Movement (SCM), a progressive student organization founded in the 1920s. Avis McCurdy, who came from a middle-class Maritimes family, was also schooled in the SCM's Christian politics: 'I came straight to the CCF because I was convinced I had to be my brother's keeper. It was right out of my religious background – CGIT and SCM. I had also worked in business in my summers, and was overcome with the injustice and inequality. But mainly, it was my moral, religious background.'[5] Women like Louise Lucas, Beatrice Brigden, and Mildred Fahrni also found the CCF a logical extension of their Christian belief in the brotherhood and equality of humankind.

Mildred Fahrni, who grew up in a religious household, found her eyes opened to the inequalities and waste of capitalist society during the depression, and particularly when she worked with single unemployed women in Vancouver. At the same time, her intellectual growth as a Christian and pacifist was also integral to her activism. The influence of her university studies at Bryn Mawr and the London School of Economics, of her travels to

Russia and later India, and of her life at London's Kingsley Hall Settlement House shaped her socialism, which was ethical, humanist, and Christian in nature. 'We CCFers were evangelists,' she remembered, 'out to build a new world order, out to build the Kingdom ... and we felt it could be done!'[6] Even CCFers who did not participate in organized Christian groups often described their politics as 'applied Christianity.' 'To many of us,' commented Nellie Peterson, 'socialism was simply the practical expression of Christian ideas about equality.'[7] In a society still receptive to the moral language of Christianity, many CCFers culled their metaphors from radical Christian ideals, just as earlier socialists had used these metaphors to plead for social justice.

For CCF women like Mildred Fahrni, Christian ideals were inextricably intertwined with pacifist ones, and for many CCF women, the new party had appeal because of its commitment to international peace. Behind Fahrni's pacifism lay both a materialist analysis of war as a means of economic aggrandizement and, perhaps more predominantly, a Christian belief that under no circumstances was taking a human life justifiable. Although other CCF women subscribed to different variations of anti-war and pacifist ideals, most saw some connection between their socialism, pacifism, and feminism, and a great number of CCF women found common cause for these ideals in the Women's International League for Peace and Freedom (WILPF), popularly known as WIL. In the 1920s, the WIL had branches in Vancouver, Winnipeg, and Toronto and was affiliated to some women's farm groups; it was led by women like Violet MacNaughton, editor of the women's column of the popular *Western Producer*, and Laura Jamieson, a Vancouver suffragist and social reformer who became a CCFer. The WIL's campaigns against cadet training in the schools were supported by many socialists, and by the early 1930s the local leadership of the WIL and CCF women's groups sometimes overlapped. Although the WIL also included liberal pacifists, it did have an important appeal to socialist women, with its calls for the elimination of social, economic, and sexual inequalities, as well as violence, from all societies.[8]

For women like Rose Henderson, Laura Jamieson, and Lucy Woodsworth, who had been influenced by the maternal feminism of the suffrage era, WIL principles and the CCF's pacifist connection had a special attraction. Not only did the WIL speak to the economic causes of war, but it also spoke to women's 'maternal' aversion to violence and war. Henderson's anti-war pamphlet of the 1920s, for example, argued that the basic causes of war were 'hatched within capitalism,' but that women, as the bearers of life, should combine with the working-class (inevitably used as 'cannon fodder') to work for peace. Because of women's mothering experiences, she emphasized, they better understood the

value and sanctity of human life.[9] Henderson's pacifism was a unique b.
of socialist and feminist ideas that was not uncommon to other CCF wom.
Drawing on both a materialist analysis of imperialism and an idealized view c
women's (maternal) commitment to non-violence, many women came to see
peace as a socialist issue *and* a women's issue, and they eagerly embraced the CCF
as a party promoting the peace alternative.

There were other important ideological traditions, such as Marxism,
stimulating women's interest in the CCF. Although the CCF did not rely
predominantly on Marx and Engels in their educational work, as did the
Communists, Marxist books were offered for sale through many provincial
literature committees, and where a strong tradition of Marxism existed, as in
British Columbia, Marxists within the party were certain to share their
viewpoint with newcomers. George Weaver, for instance, a self-educated
Marxist from BC, who was a regular party speaker and columnist for the
Federationist, used Marx's writings and Engels's *Origin of the Family* as key
texts in his columns on women. Though Weaver always tended to stress
women's primary class oppression, his writing represented, for the times, a
fairly sophisticated attempt to construct a dialectical understanding of the
class and sexual oppression of women.[10]

Women whose radicalization crystallized around Marxist ideas saw the
economic devastation of the depression as a sharp reminder of the inherent
contradictions of a capitalist economy, but not all party Marxists shared
Weaver's interest in the woman question. Like Eve Grey Smith, some
downplayed women's secondary status in the party and emphasized the need for
class solidarity. 'The problem [of gender inequality] was not a sexual one, but
an economic one,' concluded Smith, 'and the economic problem makes a
sexual one.' In 'retrospect,' continued Smith, 'my enthusiasm for working-
class unity made me somewhat tactless in the eyes of other women less
comfortable in the male-dominated Party.' She added: 'At the [1938] National
Convention the women asked me to speak to them ... I said why do you have a
women's group? Why do you not have a mixed group? They said women can
more easily attend day meetings, and at mixed meetings, women don't like to
talk in front of the men. I said, "well you just *have to* get up and talk at mixed
meetings!"'[11] Of course Marxist ideas may have also sensitized women to
problems ignored by others: Eve Smith was also active in the Single Women's
Unemployment Association and, in her brief turn as women's columnist for
the *Federationist*, stressed some of the urgent problems of women wage-earners.

The intellectual development of women in the CCF did not emerge only from
Christian or Marxist principles, for the ideological traditions influencing the
young party crossed the spectrum from Fabian ideas of efficient state

planning to the powerful influence of Edward Bellamy's utopian and co-operative socialism described in *Looking Backward*. Moreover, some founding CCF members combined selected Marxist ideas with Fabian or Christian concepts in an eclectic socialist philosophy. And in a young political movement offering discussion in weekly club meetings, educationals, and summer camps, the intellectual options open to new members were constantly broadened. The precise way in which women's personal experiences and intellectual development mixed to form a radical view of the world was also an individual process. Sympathy for feminist ideas, for instance, varied, even among women with similar backgrounds. In British Columbia, Dorothy Steeves was less interested than Laura Jamieson in organizing separate women's groups, yet they both came from middle-class backgrounds, were well-educated, and had had some contact with the suffrage movement. Quite naturally, the way in which women entered politics also varied according to region and class: farm women were more likely to come through the co-operative movement, working-class women through relief organizations.

Whatever their background, once active in the party the majority of women gravitated towards 'female' areas of political work, revealing the existence of a political sexual division of labour within the CCF similar to that in Canadian society. Although a few notable women like Grace MacInnis and Dorothy Steeves became party leaders, most women were active at the grass-roots level of the party. It is axiomatic that, in political parties, women were called on to 'make the coffee and lick the envelopes,' yet it is important to remember that this day-to-day support work was essential to the life of the party. As one Saskatchewan CCF woman succinctly put it: 'The CCF was made in the kitchen and you didn't find too many men in the kitchen!'[12] To some extent, the party encouraged women to fulfil these supportive but less powerful roles. In an article in the *Ontario New Commonwealth*, one writer described 'How to Organize a Successful CCF Unit,' explaining that the social committee, an essential unit of the party, should be at least two-thirds women because they were 'perfect jewels' at raising funds and loved 'playing amateur salesladies at bake sales.'[13] Such exhortations for women to remain the drones in the movement were not, of course, part of a conscious design to segregate women in inferior roles, but they did reflect the party's unthinking acceptance of prevailing sex roles and the male-dominated power structure of society.

Election time usually found CCF newspapers discussing the role women could and should play in politics. Like the more radical Communist party, democratic socialists often assumed that women were predominantly home-makers, and that they had little inclination for politics. As a result, CCF articles indicated ways in which government decisions affected women's domestic labour and the lives of their children. Politics do not simply involve abstract principles, they would say, for government decides whether or not your husband will have work, how much you will pay for milk, what kind of education your children receive, and whether your family will get adequate medical care. On the one hand, these appeals promoted the conception that women, isolated amid diapers and dishes, were less knowledgeable and more apathetic than men about politics. On the other hand, the party's approach also reflected pragmatic thinking: the CCF put important emphasis on electoral politics and because many women were homemakers, the party felt it must convince this large constituency of the need for socialism by speaking to the immediate, daily concerns of women in the home. And such appeals to a woman's maternal concern for her family's welfare were often effective, for many women explained their attraction to socialism in terms of the humanitarian answers it offered to the problems that took up women's daily realities. As one Saskatchewan woman put it: 'The CCF may have had a special appeal to women ... the appeal of humanity, of health services, educational opportunities, and so on ... because most mothers wanted the best for their children.'[14]

Women were also asked to take an active role in party work, and to many CCFers, this attitude signified a more egalitarian approach than that of the Liberals and Conservatives. As one male CCFer commented (and not in jest), 'in clubs, women not only fold and stamp literature, they also go out door to door with male comrades to distribute it ... whereas under the old parties, women are almost disenfranchised.'[15] And certainly it does appear that CCF women played a more active role than women in the old-line parties. Many CCF women did their door-to-door work only during election time; others remained actively involved all year round. In Winnipeg, Edith Cove became known as the efficient manager of election victories in Woodsworth's riding of Winnipeg North Centre, while in Saskatchewan, women like Gertrude Harvey, Florence Baker, Eve Pfeifer, and Elsie Gorius all developed respected reputations as membership and campaign organizers. 'Those Saskatchewan women,' remembered Grace MacInnis, 'they were organizers! ... many MPs were only in Parliament because of the women's organizing skills.'[16]

Women like Elsie Gorius in Saskatchewan and Nellie Peterson in Alberta were able to work as travelling organizers for the party, not only because of their proven organizing talents, but also because of the essential aid of a supportive family, including someone to do child care. Nellie Peterson, for instance, had a sympathetic mother who helped look after Nellie's son and a politically supportive husband – the latter in particular an essential element in the career of a married woman organizer. Other women found that long absences from home were not tolerated by their husbands, who shared the community's suspicions of such 'wandering wives.'[17] For women who could not travel, there was still an immense amount of on-the-spot local organizing – such as gathering memberships, raising funds, and preparing for elections – to be done. One local publicity organizer in Fort William described her normal day, aptly revealing the kind of work women did, and the way in which married women integrated domestic and political labour: 'Up at 8, feed family of 5, make lunch, send boy to school, do report on meetings, draw up ads, numerous phone calls. 9:00, dress baby, wash dishes, answer phone, make beds, sweep and dust, answer phone. Sell potatoes donated by country CCF units. Write letters and notes for tonight's speech. Dishwashing, cleaning, calls, dress baby for outdoors, odd jobs, supper, prepare kids for bed, go to meeting.'[18]

At the local and provincial levels, women were also prominently represented in educational work. Within a constituency CCF club, women were often put in charge of local libraries, or they sat on provincial education committees that ordered books, drew up reading lists, and organized discussion groups and summer schools. The high profile of women in educational work may have been partly the consequence of the widely held notion in the party that women were eminently suited to such practical tasks, as well as of the fact that women, who were not encouraged to see themselves as leaders and therefore lacked self-confidence, opted for behind-the-scenes work. Also a key factor was the duplication within the party of occupational roles found outside it. In the 1930s one of the only professions truly open to women was teaching; women's educational work in the party was thus described as logical and natural. Because women were suited to teaching, it was said, they could put their talent to use in socializing new members to socialist ideas: 'Women teachers worked with youth and this helped them to realize that we had to reach the younger generation. Their mind was turned to the channels of education – how to get ideas across, that is why women were involved in education.'[19] And, of course, many CCF women, especially on the prairies, had worked as teachers and were probably eager to use their skills in party work. Although women's participation in educational work thus emerged from a traditional definition of women's sphere, we can't lose sight of the fact that education *did* have a vital role to play in the party. Because the CCF was a new socialist party, which opposed the dominant ideals of competition and free enterprise, it desperately needed the committed and well-informed recruits that good educational work might produce.

As part of their mandate to recruit new socialists and re-educate old ones, educational committees established CCF summer camps, and women often worked as camp organizers. This activity took considerable time, for camps lasted for a week or more; and besides the provision of educational material, the mundane essentials of accommodation, cooking, and cleaning all had to be attended to. Gertrude Telford, who oversaw the Saskatchewan Crystal Lake Camp from 1937 to 1942, recalled her long list of duties: 'We had educational programs – lectures, speakers were brought in; we had discussions on economics, debating and also recreational activities, swimming, games and campfire programs.'[20] CCFers recall the camp experience fondly, for learning and discussion took place in an atmosphere of camaraderie and common purpose sustaining a strong socialist 'counter culture.' Women who were homemakers, like Telford, could again integrate political work with family responsibilities, for provisions were made for children's tents and programs. Within camp life, however, women were never limited to domestic tasks: because camps were organized as a microcosm of the communal socialist future, everyone shared in the dishwashing, a fact commented on so emphatically by the women that one suspects it was not the practice outside camp life.

Some women who were on provincial education committees did eventually get elected to the provincial council, or even to the provincial executive. Women's degree of under-representation in the leadership varied over time and by region. In the 1930s, in Saskatchewan, women sometimes composed up to one-third of the provincial leadership, a high percentage, which might be explained by established traditions of female participation in the farm movement. And in British Columbia, three women – Laura Jamieson, Dorothy Steeves, and Grace MacInnis – were elected as members of the legislature, and had a high profile in the party: Dorothy Steeves eventually became vice-president of the BC party, while Grace MacInnis later became a national political figure.

No simple generalization can characterize women in leadership positions, for female notables held differing political perspectives and had different styles of doing politics. Steeves, for example, was known as a sharp-minded (and sometimes sharp-tongued) debater, who once said that 'she was as good as any man.'[21] Saskatchewan's Louise Lucas, in contrast, had a very different persona. Not an intellectual, but a charismatic, religious-minded woman, Lucas was a never-tiring evangelist for the movement, and her popular title, 'Mother of the CCF,' indicated a different reputation, which stressed the feminine attributes of her leadership. Although women who became leaders could be as different as were Steeves and Lucas, one wonders if they were assigned stereotypic images, stressing either their maternal and feminine qualities or their similarity to men. One CCF newspaper, for example, had the audacity to publish an article pigeon-holing women into three stereotypes – the 'clinging vine,' the 'aggressive, mannish' women, and the 'normal' woman, who was 'neither superior or inferior but interested in children, home and career.' Needless to say, similar pseudo-psychological pronouncements on men's character types did not appear in the paper.[22]

Whatever their style of politics, it was simply more difficult for women to reach the leadership. Women's economic dependence and double burden of work, as well as the influence of prevailing sexist ideas about gender roles, were fundamental causes of women's secondary status in the party. Not only did women have less money, and work longer hours than men – leaving them with fewer material resources or even the energy so necessary to political participation – but the dominant ideology of gender presented women as private beings whose lives centred on marriage and family, rather than as public beings whose interests should be politics and government. Women in politics were considered an oddity: mass magazines, on the rare occasion they addressed the subject, treated women politicians as 'freaks,'[23] as Agnes Macphail so frankly put it, and such publications invariably assumed that a political career and family were almost incompatible. But also at fault were socialists themselves, who failed to challenge these traditional ideas and inequalities within their own ranks. Unfortunately, within the party many members (including some women) stubbornly held that, as a socialist party, the CCF *was* egalitarian – and they refused to see any evidence to the contrary. Yet, evidence indicates that women were channelled into social committees; that women's feminine character was often described as emotional and sensitive, implying a female inability to cope with the 'rational' world of politics; and that women were seen as more apathetic and politically backward than men. Perhaps most important of all, because women's primary responsibility for the family was never questioned, an essential barrier to women's whole-hearted participation in politics remained unchallenged and unchanged.

Nowhere was women's secondary role in the party more glaring than in the selection of candidates for election. Although the CCF often fared better than its Liberal and Conservative counterparts, women were still placed in unwinnable ridings or given inadequate support in their bids for CCF nominations. After Agnes Macphail's election defeat in 1940, Jean Laing lamented that so few women were seriously considered as candidates by the party: 'In Toronto, in all the Parties, the men were doing all the contesting as candidates and the women were doing all the work ... We expect of the old line Parties that they will nominate all men candidates, but for the CCF we look for equal recognition of the women. Yet, in Ontario, the only woman CCF candidate was Mrs. Dymond, and she was nominated because one of the man candidates was sick.'[24]

In Saskatchewan, Gertrude Telford lost a provincial nomination to a man whose attack on her candidature, she said privately, was 'on her *as a woman*.'[25] Telford had for years done the hard leg-work in the riding and justifiably felt unhappy when an outsider (who assured her he was not going to run) threw in his hat at the last minute. Despite some unusual circumstances surrounding the nomination meeting, the case was not investigated by the party. Telford was later considered as a potential replacement to Louise Lucas in the federal riding of Melville, but again she was bypassed. Lucas expressed her sympathy to a disappointed Telford, and voiced her anger about men's tight control of the party: 'There is no need to tell you how chagrined I am over B's nomination. If it had been Mrs. Baker, Mrs. Strum or you, I would have felt reconciled – in fact elated, but you know what I think of this ... I had written to Mr. J.C. from the conference pleading that he think of Christ and the women's cause in their deliberations. Replied that he agreed we need more women in the Party but said they would have to take a more *prominent* part. These men don't seem to be able to grasp that they are not *allowed* to take these prominent parts. You know what I mean.'[26] Out of loyalty to the party, Lucas's criticisms, like those of Laing and Telford, were voiced privately, rather than in the columns of the CCF newspaper. Dedicated to their party and to an ideal of socialist egalitarianism, they always hoped that women would be accorded the same opportunities as men. Privately, however, they sometimes shared their bitter disappointment as women were held back from nominations or discouraged from advancing into the leadership.

II

Women's committees in the CCF emerged, in part, to counteract women's secondary role in the movement, for committees were seen as a training ground for female leadership, as well as a medium through which women's special concerns might be addressed. Some provincial newspapers also sponsored women's columns that included everything from sophisticated political editorials to news of local CCF women's groups and even household hints. Within the party there was always a running debate over the desirability of such 'special' appeals to women. Even the women's columnist for the *Ontario New Commonwealth* revealed ambivalence about her task – well symbolized by her name for the column, 'Fairly Feminine' – for she explained that, on one level, she 'disapproved of women's pages ... for women should read all articles in the paper.' On another level, she added, 'women are rather backward about expressing their ideas in print, especially in competition with the masculine point of view.'[27] She concluded more positively, urging men to acquaint themselves with the column, but overall, her puzzling remarks seemed to combine a negative view of 'backward' women with an honest desire to help women become more vocal and powerful in the movement. Although the column only ran for a short time, it did contain informative articles on women's history, the activities of CCF women, the peace movement, and women on relief. Its author was sometimes daring enough to challenge some of the staples of 'bourgeois' women's pages, such as her 'Behind the Paris Gowns – the Dressmakers Strike,'[28] an exposé of the deplorable conditions for women workers in the fashion industry. On other occasions, however, the column itself reverted to fashion tips and recipes.

Within the *New Commonwealth* and other CCF papers, women were addressed primarily as homemakers, and secondarily as wage-earners. Major strikes involving women invariably got substantial and sympathetic coverage, but women's domestic concerns were seen as the meat and potatoes of their political existence. The women's columnist in the *Saskatchewan Commonwealth*, for example, argued that women 'who were practical and realistic, although perhaps not theoretically inclined,' should turn their thoughts from household tasks – more patching, crimping, planning' – to tidying up the outside world. 'So who is in a better position to understand the economic system than the person who is a consumer for the family?' she asked. 'To whom is the threat of war terrible and the appeal of peace ... more significant?'[29]

In all the provincial newspapers, women's columns appeared and disappeared through the 1930s, taking on a different flavour according to which CCF paper they were in, and who the author was. In British Columbia, for example, the *Federationist*'s column was written in the early years by Eve Grey Smith, and it concentrated on economic issues, such as women's role in the class struggle and the situation of unemployed women. When Elizabeth Kerr, who had a long association with feminist and socialist causes, took over in 1937, the column also began to address more 'feminist' concerns, such as women's role in the family, the need for better divorce laws, and the imperative of increasing women's participation in the CCF. In her column written after the 1938 provincial convention, Kerr lamented the small number of female delegates present, blaming 'family responsibilities and male prejudice' for their absence, and she objected strenuously to the male paranoia expressed at the convention, that three women on the CCF executive would spell 'feminist control' of the inner party sanctums. 'We have not shown feminist views,' she retorted angrily, 'but we have examined a broad range of problems from a human perspective, but ... even if we were stay-at-home types, without a broader view, why shouldn't that womanly view be expressed in our movement?' For a movement 'boasting no differences in sex, race and creed,' she frankly concluded, 'some of our Marxian socialists are pitifully mid-Victorian.'[30]

Not all the women's columnists were as bluntly feminist as Kerr; none the less, women's columns, even those with recipes and sewing patterns, enhanced the discussion of a wide variety of women's issues – from birth control to rising prices – within the party. Without them, a feminist point of view, like Kerr's, might not have been heard at all.

Like the newspaper columns, women's committees had different political outlooks and activities, ranging from fund raising to socialist education and feminist social action. Although women's organizations existed in almost every province, three short examples can illustrate some of their aims and accomplishments.[31]

In Saskatchewan there was some debate in 1936–7 within the party executive and the Provincial Convention over the small female membership in the movement, and it was proposed that women's 'study clubs' be established and given voting status at the convention.[32] This rather radical proposition was rejected, but as a consolation prize it was agreed to appoint a part-time provincial organizer, Minerva Cooper, to help set up new women's CCF clubs. In her short term as organizer, Cooper aided the formation of sixteen new clubs, boosting the number of provincial CCF women's groups to forty-two. Her aim was to orient the clubs to women's need for a social contact as well as for political development. Her assumption was that women needed different, indeed extra, education geared to their isolated and less knowledgeable approach to politics. 'We can use the time-honoured custom of afternoon tea,' she explained, 'to have a programme for the tried and true worker and the new rank and filer, combining business, study and social time. In the meeting we can start off with slogans and anecdotes ... we should avoid dull papers on economics.'[33]

The problems of organizing women, Cooper soon found, were generated primarily by the vast geographical area she had to cover, and by the CCF's limited economic resources. The central office could not afford to hire a full-time women's organizer, nor could local clubs afford to pay transportation costs to bring Cooper in. Gas shortages prohibited some women from attending regular meetings, and study materials were expensive for the women to buy and for the central office to supply. Despite all these difficulties, local clubs did flourish; indeed, one dynamic activist in northern Saskatchewan, Dorise Nielsen, helped to establish six new clubs in the space of a year. Cooper believed that local organizers, with a feel for the community, often had the best results. Success was also scored, she maintained, when the women's clubs gradually evolved into mixed ones. New people were thus drawn into the movement and the women, already fortified with executive and speaking experience, still tended to 'hold executive positions in the mixed setting, not taking a back seat'[34] as they did in other clubs.

In Saskatoon, the Nutana CCF Women's Club followed the socialist study program prepared by Minerva Cooper, as well as knitting socks and fund raising for the Mackenzie-Papineau Battalion in Spain, and holding regular social events. Another Saskatoon women's club sprang up spontaneously out of a working-class neighbourhood where many families were on relief: on one street, women who shared common worries and advice were persuaded by a CCF supporter to form a political discussion group. Margaret Benson, an original member of the group, recalled that their first political actions were whist drives and other fund raising, but the women also found time to study *The Case for Socialism* and *Looking Backward*, analyse newspaper articles, and present their own opinions on political issues. Ridicule from other neighbours about their 'red flag' meetings, says Benson, 'just made us more determined ... for we were militant, unlike [other] ladies auxiliaries.'[35] These women's groups met within the bounds of a culturally sanctioned institution – the women's auxiliary – but they did not limit themselves only to whist drives, for they also tried to make themselves and their neighbours more conscious of the need for socialism. Their political discussions often centred on family-related issues, but these concerns were located in a political context qualitatively different from the thinking of the earlier suffragists. In the 1930s, CCF women addressed social and economic issues only skirted by these earlier reformers: the economic struggles of farm women, women on relief, and wage-earning women were the catalysts for their politicization, and their solution to social ills was the replacement of private with co-operative ownership. Rather than the patchwork reform efforts to improve the morals of society, CCF women proposed to improve family life by effecting an entire reordering of the economic system.

Women's family-centred concerns were also the focus of CCF women's groups in Winnipeg. There, women's ILP groups, already constituted on a neighbourhood basis and since 1932 federated into a city-wide Women's Labor Conference, became the foundation for a women's CCF network. In the small neighbourhood CCF clubs, fund raising and political education were the main activities. At the monthly meetings of the city-wide Women's Labor Conference, delegates discussed current issues and pooled their resources on campaigns like the Minimum Wage Committee or the Education Committee. By the late 1930s, some thirty-six groups were affiliated, and the conference was vocal on local and international issues, urging the federal government, for example, to allow a generous immigration policy for Jewish refugees fleeing Germany. The conference saw education as a key to women's socialist conversion, and so they set up small study groups, using books like *Social Planning for Canada* or *The Cooperative Commonwealth*, and drawing on the guidance of the conference's leaders, Beatrice Brigden, Lucy Woodsworth, and Edith Cove. The commitment of these women to the separate organization of women emerged from their experience with women's labourite groups in the 1920s and from their shared belief that, within the socialist movement, women's needs and concerns were sometimes different from men's. Brigden, for example, saw women's primary social role as housewife and mother, though her columns in the *Manitoba Commonwealth* also emphasized the need to fight for women's right to employment and economic opportunity. She resolutely decried the depression-initiated hostility to working women, labelling efforts to force women back into the kitchen as akin to 'feudalism.' The hope for women's emancipation, she believed, would come from an alliance of women with the socialist movement. Co-operation and working-class unity would pave the way to the New Jerusalem: 'If humanity is to advance,' she once wrote, 'then all must march together; no lagging behind by one group, no suppression of one sex for the benefit of the other.'[36]

Still, in the long march towards socialism, women's groups provided a useful focus and sometimes comforting retreat for women activists. In 1937, under Brigden's leadership, the Winnipeg women organized a conference to discuss how to organize from a woman's viewpoint and how to express the particular needs of homemakers and rural women. Brigden had already carried these concerns to the national convention the year before, making a long report on the Winnipeg Women's Labor Conference and urging a more concerted national policy on enlarging the party's female constituency.

Clearly, not all the delegates took these 'ladies' groups seriously, nor did the party leadership see any pressing need to discuss women's issues. Indeed, when Brigden described how Winnipeg women had established groups to discuss birth control, her report was greeted with 'chortles of amusement.'[37]

A small enclave of women delegates listened sympathetically to Brigden's speech, then spoke in defence of her crusade to integrate women into the party. Two Toronto delegates, Jean Laing and Rose Henderson, were particularly vocal. 'We must point out to women,' Henderson declared, 'that every aspect of their lives is affected by politics ... [and] we must directly address socialist issues.'[38] Henderson and Laing were active in a short-lived but significant Toronto women's CCF group, the Women's Joint Committee (WJC). Prominent activists in the WJC, including Henderson, Laing, Elizabeth Morton, and Alice Loeb, brought to this group their experiences of both socialist and feminist causes. Henderson, for example, had been involved in the suffrage movement and labour politics in the 1920s, Loeb was involved in birth-control issues and the WIL, while Laing and Morton had had their political schooling in the trade-union movement, especially in the union auxiliaries.

The feminist-socialist aims of the Toronto WJC were twofold: first, to address 'social problems, particularly those of women' and second, to 'act as a training school' for CCF women.[39] John Manley has pointed out that to the WJC, addressing the social problems of women primarily meant addressing the problems of the family: because most of the WJC were married women, 'the family and its fate during a period of intense socio-economic crisis became a central preoccupation of the WJC.'[40] The committee, for instance, aided the establishment of a progressive summer camp for inner-city children, even bringing old pots, dishes, and towels to a meeting as donations, and jokingly referring to this as a 'shower for the camp.' The committee drew on other aspects of female culture, especially women's maternal concerns: they organized a Mothers' Committee to visit youths imprisoned in Mimico Jail after a relief strike; planned a Mothers' Day peace program with the WIL; and sponsored a conference on unemployment, focusing on relief 'in relation to the home and children in the home.'[41] As well, the committee wrote letters protesting the plight of the single unemployed woman and expressed some interest in organizing around the birth-control issue. Elizabeth Morton brought the director of the East York Parents' Clinic to speak to the WJC, and in response to her talk, the committee immediately suggested that Margaret Sanger be brought to Toronto. This plan, however, never materialized, as Brant suggested building more community support for the clinic first, and CCF women soon found that within their own movement 'the clinic idea was well received by the women ... but not by the men.'[42]

The second purpose of the WJC – to train women for leadership – was a less threatening issue, because WJC feminists could argue that, in increasing women's self-confidence, the party as a whole would benefit. As the WJC secretary explained: 'Women are very diffident about engaging in discussion at a meeting where men are in the majority. As women in the future will plan an important role in the building of Socialism and have a real contribution to make, they must be trained and encouraged to take their place.'[43] To give women more expertise and confidence, the WJC rotated its own position of chair, and it made plans to draw in a wider network of CCF women across the city. The WJC, however, did not live long enough to fulfil its hopes, for it was debilitated by conflicts with the party leadership over united-front work with Communists, and over what WJC women caustically referred to as the party's opportunistic 'vote catching policies.'[44] In 1936, acrimonious debate over co-operation with Communists openly split the party and resulted in the expulsion of Laing and others by the CCF leadership. The WJC's protests over these expulsions may have only exacerbated their tense relationship with the leadership. Although the WJC visited the provincial executive to try to 'explain the WJC's function,'[45] it was unsuccessful in reversing executive disapproval and it disappeared from existence shortly afterwards. Although the WJC had a brief history and a minimal impact on the national CCF, its existence indicated the presence of a small but dedicated group of socialist feminists within the party. At the time, though, many women and men in the CCF did not attach a priority to women's issues or understand why these women felt the need to organize autonomously. Lacking a stronger feminist awareness among the party's membership or in society as a whole, a more significant feminist revolt within the party had to await a future date.

III

Late into the July evenings, delegates to the CCF's inaugural convention in 1933 avidly debated the party's statement of principles, the Regina Manifesto: was reform or revolution, private or public ownership, centralization or local control to characterize this new party? Feminism, however, was not a significant part of this political terrain. Though it advocated equal opportunity and pay, the CCF's founding document did not devote substantial attention to women's oppression, and throughout the 1930s women's issues took a secondary place in party strategies. Although some Marxists within the party were well aware of women's economic subordination, competing intellectual traditions within the party, such as Fabianism and Christian socialism, did not, as a rule, stress gender inequality. Moreover, many CCF women were drawn to the party because of their experience of economic and social inequality in general, not because of their concern for women's inequality in particular. These women, the younger of whom were newcomers to politics after the intense feminist experience of the suffrage movement, were principally influenced by the economic upheaval of the depression, and they simply failed to see women's issues as primary concerns. As one woman reflected: 'The question of women just never came up. Economics and war overshadowed everything else. I never thought about the woman question ... except for resenting always being the stenographer of the group.'[46]

Despite this lack of interest in gender inequality, the party firmly held that women had a distinct political outlook shaped by their domestic and maternal roles. Women wage-earners were a subject of concern – the party tried to intervene in strikes and alter labour legislation – but working women figured less prominently than homemakers in the CCF's electoral strategies. Because many women did work in the home, the CCF's appeal was a pragmatic one, shaped by and oriented to women's day-to-day material concerns, but it also remained a barrier to women's full integration into political life. Women had difficulties carrying the double burden of family and political obligations; they probably had difficulties moving from the social committees into which they were channelled to the centres of decision making; and they may have had difficulties convincing themselves and others that their 'maternal' qualities really suited them to positions of power in the 'important' policy-making areas of economics and defence.

Despite women's under-representation in the leadership, they comprised an indispensible army of local educators, organizers, and electioneers, who created the supporting edifice that allowed the socialist movement to build upwards. Their political work contradicted the more pessimistic charges that women had simply retreated to the home after the vote was won. Furthermore, women's secondary position in the party did not go unnoticed and unchallenged: women's committees were sometimes set up with the distinct purpose of training women for leadership and augmenting women's participation in the party. CCF women's groups ran the gamut from fund-raising auxiliaries to more militant socialist-feminist action groups. Even committed feminists, however, shared many of society's prevailing notions of womanhood and agreed that women's issues should focus predominantly on women's family-related concerns – thus echoing one of the contradictions that kept women isolated from the mainstream of the socialist movement. But at the time, neither the women's auxiliaries nor the more vocal women's committees saw their efforts as marginal or limited by a maternal mystique, and they quite honestly saw their politics as militant and unique. And indeed, with their connection of class and gender issues and with their radical socialist solutions, CCF women did fashion a more militant brand of political mothering. Perhaps Beatrice Bridgen, who personally travelled the path from the suffrage-era maternal feminism to the 'new era'[47] of militant mothering, best articulated this difference: 'Yes, the CCF woman does differ from others. Chiefly in this, we think, she has separated herself very largely from the prejudices and fallacies of the capitalist order. She repudiates the system of competition ... She has accepted the cooperative principle, the well-tested recipe for success in her own home-making: each giving according to her ability and each receiving according to [her] need. The CCF woman proposes to apply this same kindly, enduring fundamental to the social order?[48]

NOTES

1 Some critics from the left describe the CCF as 'liberals in a hurry.' See Gary Teeple, '"Liberals in a Hurry": Socialism and the CCF/NDP,' in Gary Teeple,

ed., *Capitalism and the National Question in Canada* (Toronto 1972).
Norman Penner is more sympathetic to the CCF, seeing the Regina Manifesto
as 'reformist,' though 'anti-capitalist' (Penner, *The Canadian Left*
[Toronto 1977]). Many writers also presume that the CCF changed over time,
either from a 'movement to a Party,' or from a socialist party to a more
moderate social democratic party. See Walter Young, *The Anatomy of a Party:
The National CCF* (Toronto 1969) for the first view, and Leo Zakuta, *A
Protest Movement Becalmed* (Toronto 1964) for the second view.

2 Interview with Hilda Kristiansen, 8 December 1980.

3 Irene Biss, 'The Dressmakers' Strike,' *Canadian Forum* 11, July 1931, 367–9;
Patricia Schultz, *The East York Workers' Association: A Working Class
Response to the Great Depression* (Toronto 1975).

4 Interview with Sophia Dixon, 1 November 1980.

5 Interview with Avis McCurdy, 30 May 1982.

6 Interview with Mildred Fahrni, 3 December 1980.

7 Interview with Nellie Peterson, 21 November 1980.

8 On the WIL, see G. Bussey and M. Tims, *Pioneers for Peace* (London 1965), and
Tom Socknat, 'Witness against War: The Canadian Pacifist Movement,' PhD
diss., McMaster University 1980. The league's statement of purpose called for
a far-reaching transformation of the social order: 'We work for universal
disarmament, the solution of conflicts by human solidarity ... and the establishment of social, economic and political justice for all, without distinction of
sex, race, class or creed' (*Pax Internationale* 5:6 [April 1930], Flora M. Denison
collection, University of Toronto Rare Book Room).

9 Rose Henderson, 'Woman and War,' n.d., Kenny collection, University of
Toronto Rare Book Room.

10 Examples of Weaver's articles are found in later *B.C.Federationist/CCF News*, 22
June 1946, 29 July 1948.

11 Interview with Eve Smith, 19 July 1981.

12 Interview with D.L., 9 November 1980.

13 *Ontario New Commonwealth (ONComm)*, 27 April 1935.

14 Interview with Sophia Dixon.

15 *ONComm*, 10 August 1935.

16 Interview with Grace MacInnis, 17 July 1981.

17 Interview with L.M., 29 November 1980. Other women also referred to social
disapproval of wives who spent long periods away from home, travelling and
organizing for the party.

18 *ONComm*, 23 November 1935.

19 Interview with Mildred Fahrni.

20 Typescript, 'Memories,' vol. 31 and education files, vol. 20, Gertrude Telford Papers, Saskatchewan Archives Board (SAB).

21 Interview of Marlene Karnouk with Dorothy Steeves, 4 April 1975, University of British Columbia Archives.

22 *ONComm*, 25 May 1935. Some oral evidence also supports this contention; see interview of Georgina Taylor with Gladys Strum, 14 August 1981, SAB.

23 *Maclean's* magazine, 15 September 1949, 16, 71–3.

24 Jean Laing to Agnes Macphail, 28 March 1940, Agnes Macphail Papers, MG 27 III C4, vol. 2, National Archives of Canada (NA).

25 Gertrude Telford to C.M. Fines, 12 June 1944, Gertrude Telford Papers, vol. 32, SAB (her italics).

26 Louise Lucas to Gertrude Telford, 5 May 1945, ibid.

27 *ONComm*, 18 May 1935.

28 Ibid., 8 June 1935.

29 *The New Era*, 28 January 1938.

30 *B.C. Federationist*, 7 July 1938.

31 I have omitted discussion of other local and provincial women's committees not because they were less important but for the sake of brevity. A longer discussion of women's committees in Ontario and the west is presented in Joan Sangster, *Dreams of Equality: Women on the Canadian Left, 1920–50* (Toronto 1989).

32 This debate took place over a period of time. See Minutes of CCF Provincial Executive, 1936, and Provincial Convention, 1937, SAB.

33 *The New Era*, 28 January 1938.

34 Minerva Cooper to 1938 Provincial Convention, SAB.

35 Interview of Georgina Taylor with Margaret Benson, SAB.

36 *Manitoba Commonwealth*, 22 February 1936.

37 See David Lewis, *The Good Fight* (Toronto 1981), 101–2.

38 Rose Henderson to National Convention, 3 August 1936, CCF Papers, MG 28 IV 1, vol. 10, NA.

39 Women's Joint Committee Minutes, 6 March 1936 and 20 March 1936, Woodsworth Memorial Collection, University of Toronto.

40 John Manley, 'Women and the Left in the 1930's: The Case of the Toronto CCF Women's Joint Committee,' *Atlantis* 5:2 (Spring 1980), 112.

41 Women's Joint Committee Minutes, 12 May 1936.

42 Ibid., 7 April 1936.

43 *ONComm*, 21 March 1936.

44 Women's Joint Committee Minutes, 9 June 1936.

45 Ibid. United-front work was an issue of some contention in the CCF in the 1930s. After 1935, the Communist party tried to co-operate with the CCF in a

'Popular Front,' but the CCF leadership was opposed to a Popular Front, as it was suspicious of the Communists' motives and wished to maintain the CCF's organizational and ideological autonomy. At the local level, however, CCFers and Communists sometimes did work together on specific issues or protests. On this issue, and also for an analysis of the similarities and differences in the kind of roles socialist and communist women played in the CCF and Communist party during the 1930s, see Sangster, *Dreams of Equality*, ch 4 and 5.

46 Interview with D.L., 9 November 1980.
47 Beatrice Brigden, *Weekly News*, Labour Day Supplement, September 1933.
48 Beatrice Brigden, *Labor Annual*, September 1934.

Thérèse Casgrain and the CCF in Quebec

Susan Mann Trofimenkoff

From Paris, Thérèse Casgrain cabled her acceptance of the leadership of the party.[1] It was the second time she had been elected in absentia and by acclamation to prominent positions in the Co-operative Commonwealth Federation (CCF). Three years earlier a national convention of the CCF chose her as one of the two national vice-chairmen, while she summered in Point au Pic.[2] Now, in the late spring of 1951, while she was in Europe to attend meetings of the Socialist International in Frankfurt (and to keep an eye on the latest Paris fashions[3]), she took on the provincial leadership as well.

She thus became the first woman to head a political party in Canada. Doubtless, her own and the party's eccentricities account for the mutual attraction. For here was a wealthy and well-connected upper-class French-Canadian widow, known for her charm and her advocacy of women's rights, involved, during the years of Duplessis's *grande noirceur*, with a minuscule and moribund socialist party, one that was tarred with an English-Canadian brush and feathered with clerical suspicion. What on earth was she doing?

To explain Casgrain's link to the CCF and her role within such a party requires an approach somewhat different from that of standard political history. For a number of reasons Casgrain slips through the conventional net of political analysis. She was a woman and hence her political options were different from those of men. She had a husband (at least until 1950) and thus her political timing was as much family as personal timing. She had no secretary (at least until she became a senator in 1970), so her 11 boxes of papers at the National Archives of Canada sit rather forlornly, in contrast to the 250, for example, of a male contemporary, Brooke Claxton. She is not even mentioned in the one study of Quebec left-wing political development since the 1950s.[4] To see her through the obscurity thus requires another vantage point, for she does not appear to lend herself to what might be called the strategic-studies approach to political history: an investigation of the ideas, actions, and impact of an individual.

The vantage point that seems appropriate to Casgrain's involvement with the CCF is that of her feminism and her nationalism. A combination of the two as filtered through her own personality, training, and experience are what brought her to the CCF in the mid 1940s. Then for the sixteen years (six of them as provincial leader) during which she played an active role in the party, her feminism and her nationalism, filtered this time through the expectations the party had of her, took a decided buffeting. That experience, in turn, may well be part of the explanation of the failure of the CCF in Quebec. Instead of becoming the first socialist premier of Quebec, Thérèse Casgrain served as midwife to the Quiet Revolution.

Little in Casgrain's personal background foretold her joining the CCF at age 50 in 1949. She brought to the party a heritage of wealth, social standing, and public prominence that are normally associated with certain members of the Conservative or Liberal party. Because her financier father – Sir Rodolphe Forget, Conservative MP for Charlevoix from 1904 until 1917 – was reputedly one of the richest men in turn-of-the-century Montreal, with a palatial summer house at St-Irénée, she was used to a life of ease. Even if much of the family fortune disappeared in the stock market crash in 1929,[5] there was always enough to make daily life very comfortable indeed. Long before the 1930s, of course, the Forget daughter had ensured the continuation of such a life-style by marrying the independently wealthy lawyer Pierre Casgrain, Liberal MP for Charlevoix-Saguenay from 1917 to 1940, speaker of the House of Commons from 1936 to 1940, secretary of state in Mackenzie King's early wartime cabinet, and subsequently judge of the Quebec Superior Court. Neither the inherited nor the acquired connections marked out Thérèse Casgrain for anything but the most pampered of female existences. The only oddity was the political difference between father and husband, a difference that suggests some independence of thought within the family.

If her male connections determined Casgrain's class and social standing, her activities as a child and young woman conformed to the pattern designed for an infant born female in privileged surroundings in 1896. She had the best of convent educations from the Dames du Sacré-Coeur at Sault-aux-Récollets outside Montreal, along with other daughters of the political and financial élite.[6] Like them she was expected to marry well: the education and the subsequent carefully controlled introductions to appropriate young men ensured her an excellent position in the marriage market. The purpose of marriage was also perfectly clear to the young Thérèse. One of her love-letters to Pierre is embellished with her drawing of the two of them and three childish heads to represent their future family.[7] But her social obligations would be just as demanding as the maternal ones and she probably knew that, too. Volunteer social service was a necessary undertaking of wealthy wives. As untrained, unpaid, and unprofessional social workers, such women were expected to finance and organize charitable and patriotic endeavours. The list of Casgrain's social services, including the Ligue de la jeunesse féminine, Fédération des oeuvres de charité canadiennes-françaises, Canadian Welfare Council, and Consumers Branch of the Wartime Prices and Trade Board, indicates just how seriously she took the obligation. For all their disparate character, the common feature of the activities is their timing: each one could be organized around the functions of wife and mother. In Casgrain's case, of course, the presence of domestic servants in both her father's and her husband's household facilitated all her endeavours. But, none the less, the pattern for her childhood and young adulthood was firmly established for her, and she appears to have absorbed it. The only oddity was her chafing somewhat at the educational restrictions placed upon her. She had wanted to pursue her studies towards an eventual law degree, but her father had made it quite clear that her task as a convent graduate was to learn how to make cakes. And she did.[8]

There is little, therefore, in Casgrain's upbringing or family connections to suggest active political involvement with a socialist party. Indeed, most people absorbing such class- and gender-determined functions would shun such a party. Might there be something in the personality, then, that would suggest unusual behaviour? Casgrain claims to have been contesting things since she was born, although any evidence beyond her own recollections is hard to come by.[9] Similarly it is difficult to document her recollected dismay as a child when limitations were placed on her activities because she was a girl.[10] However, she did refer to herself as a *tigresse* in her courtship correspondence with Pierre, and she worried lest the tenderness she felt toward him absorb her independence.[11] Without quite recognizing it, she may also have been warning him that hers was a strong personality, needing scope and action. She certainly objected to the ceaseless round of entertainment and frivolity that she observed among her social peers.[12] And she also measured her distance from the Catholic church: she was, she claimed, less obedient than other women in the early feminist movement and she refused to have a Catholic chaplain for the Ligue de la jeunesse féminine, which she founded in 1926.[13] Perhaps this independence was already known when Lady Julia Drummond and Marie Gérin-Lajoie approached her in 1921 about becoming involved in the suffrage campaign just as the Fédération nationale Saint-Jean-Baptiste was obeying clerical orders to drop the issue.[14] Casgrain's own public undertakings were all strictly secular. And she went at them with verve: she was self-confident, optimistic, proud, witty, humorous – and charming. Sometime in the 1930s, she recognized her own political ambition, and many of the organizations that she founded (and subsequently deserted) show the clear mark of someone who rather enjoyed being in a position of leadership. She liked to run things. At the same time she was aware that being a woman made a difference. 'Had I been born a man,' she stated in 1970 as she became a senator, 'either I'd be prime minister of Canada or in jail. What a choice!'[15] She implied that the difference was an advantage, giving her far more range for more varied activities but there is, perhaps, room for some healthy scepticism. In terms of her eventual link to the CCF, one can fairly assume that had she been a man hoping to be prime minister, she would not likely have joined that particular party. In any case, from the personality alone there are definite hints of someone who may well do something unusual.

Before that something unusual can be specified as the 'queer sort of organization' that was the CCF in its early years,[16] Casgrain's feminism and her nationalism have to be considered. The feminism was an advance on that of her mentors in the Fédération nationale Saint-Jean-Baptiste; her nationalism remained in the mould of Henri Bourassa. Both feminism and nationalism coloured her increasing alienation from the Liberals (a party she seems to have adopted on marriage, thus altering the last word of the adage *qui prends mari prends pays* to *parti*). Both led her in the direction of the CCF.

As a feminist, Casgrain clearly distinguished herself from the first generation of feminists in Quebec.[17] Whether by design or belief, that generation had stressed women's duties: women needed educational or political opportunities in order to further the exercise of their familial and social functions. They simply needed more scope to continue fulfilling a socially (and largely male) prescribed role. Casgrain appears to have been uncomfortable with these restrictions although she never discarded them entirely. She believed, for example, as did her predecessors, that women did have specific areas of social concern in public life. Education, health, housing, the cost of living – all were of particular interest to women.[18] But in order to take part in public life, women needed equality of opportunity. Casgrain's feminism stressed women's rights and thus is much more individualistic than the earlier version. Even the name of her feminist organization emphasizes the difference: Ligue des droits de la femme in contrast to the Fédération nationale Saint-Jean-Baptiste. Where the latter harboured a murky mixture of aims and methods and kept a now-wary / now-benevolent eye on the clerics in its midst, the former had clearly defined political goals by means of secular action. Votes for women, access to the professions, equality before the law were the aims;

petitions, delegations, meetings, submissions, speeches, and the radio were the means.[19]

From such a stance, Casgrain began to have her doubts about the Liberal party. For almost two decades she had used every one of the means to achieve only one of the aims. Votes for women in Quebec provincial elections came only in 1940, twenty-two years after the federal vote had been accorded to all Canadian women. In the meantime, neither the illogic of the situation nor the absurdity of election campaigns that had federal politicians assiduously courting the female vote, and provincial politicians just as carefully shunning it, impressed itself on male – and Liberal – minds.[20] Only when the Liberals found themselves out of office in the late 1930s did they begin to look with some interest at the question of votes for women. Well might Casgrain be sceptical. The party actually added female suffrage to its program in 1938, but with fourteen seats to the Union nationale's seventy-six in the legislative assembly, it could be fairly sure that implementation was a long way off. Casgrain was elated by the addition but wary of the promise.[21] When the Liberals did, in fact, regain power a year later and passed a suffrage bill in spring 1940, other issues were leading Casgrain elsewhere.

During the lengthy struggle for the vote, she had other occasions to be dismayed with the Liberals. In the late 1920s, the Taschereau government had appointed the Dorion commission to investigate possible changes in Quebec's civil code regarding matrimony. Casgrain and other feminists had hoped both for a woman commissioner and for some substantive recommendations for change. On both grounds, they were disappointed. Within a year, commissioners Charles-Edouard Dorion, Ferdinand Roy, Victor Morin, and Joseph Sirois produced three reports to substantiate their view that, by and large, the legal status of married women in Quebec was quite acceptable. Perhaps married women could control their own salary if they were engaged in the public labour force, but otherwise they had no need to bypass the authority of their husbands in the signing of contracts or the guardianship of children. Nor should they complain about their husband's behaviour (let alone request separation because of it), unless he actually housed his 'concubine' in the same household as his wife and family. Relations between the sexes were just fine, intoned the commissioners, as Casgrain and others barely contained their annoyance.[22]

The disillusionment with the Liberals extended to federal politicians as well, and, when combined with Casgrain's developing interest in the CCF and with her nationalism, resulted in the definitive break in the mid 1940s. Casgrain had thought, for example, that a grand gesture on the part of Mackenzie King would have been the appointment of one of the 'Five Persons' to the Senate.[23] The question of a woman's eligibility for a senatorship had been carefully dodged by the Liberal government throughout the 1920s. Hiding behind the British North America (BNA) Act, which stated that only persons could be named to the Senate, the male politicians seriously wondered whether women were persons. And they went on wondering as five women from Alberta challenged them through the courts. Even the Supreme Court justices, federal appointees all, could not accept the challenge. It took a final appeal – admittedly financed by the federal government – to the Judicial Committee of the Privy Council in London before the law recognized women as persons in 1929.[24] What better way to celebrate (or to acknowledge defeat gracefully) than to name one of the five to the Senate? It didn't happen. The appointment went instead to Cairine Wilson, a Liberal party activist. If feminists could rejoice at the public admission of equality, they could also murmur that it was not recognized in quite the right manner.

Years later the federal Liberals were prepared to make another gesture that Casgrain considered not quite right. In 1945 the first family allowance cheques were to be sent out, addressed to mothers in most of Canada and to fathers in Quebec! On the grounds that money in the hands of mothers would undermine paternal authority in the family as sanctioned by the Civil Code, Mackenzie King was prepared to support discriminatory treatment of Quebec women – until Casgrain told him not to. She set her own political machinery to work and deluged the prime minister with protests from all over Quebec; she drew on her own and her husband's friendship with King to persuade him of the insult to Quebec women that such a gesture would represent.[25] She won her point, but a year later she joined the CCF.

During the same time that feminist doubts about the Liberals were forming in her mind, Casgrain was increasingly interested, again for feminist reasons, in the CCF. Here was a party out of western Canada, the source of the most progressive ideas about women's rights. Votes for women had first come in the three Prairie provinces; the most outspoken feminist in Canada, Nellie McClung, was a westerner, and the persons' challenge had come out of Alberta. Moreover, the CCF was advocating social-welfare measures of just the kind that were of particular interest to women, not just as recipients but, in the case of Casgrain, as care-givers and organizers as well. Instead of leaving such tasks to the good offices of well-intentioned and well-financed women working in an ad hoc and piecemeal fashion (even if they did gain a certain public role thereby), the CCF insisted on universal, state-organized, and state-financed social-welfare programs. And it did so during the dark years of the 1930s, when both Liberals and Conservatives were saying little could be done on a public scale to alleviate such social ills as unemployment, poor health, inadequate education, slum housing, wage differentials for women, and infant mortality. Casgrain was concerned for each of these issues; the only political party visibly sharing the concern was the CCF.

Through the inter-war years Casgrain had occasion to observe two of the more striking politicians in Ottawa, each of whom ended up with or was supportive of the CCF. One of them was a woman. As a political wife in the capital, Casgrain spent many hours in the Commons' gallery. From there she was particularly taken with Agnes Macphail and J.S. Woodsworth. Macphail stood out as the sole woman, Woodsworth as the sole socialist.[26] Each of them expressed Casgrain's own social concerns; each of them had an independence of political spirit that intrigued her. It seems, indeed, that the admiration she felt for Macphail was mutual: a photo of Casgrain as Quebec's women's rights leader adorned the walls of Macphail's office.[27] No doubt Macphail's parliamentary presence inspired Casgrain, for sometime during the 1930s she began to envision being the first woman MP from Quebec. She had not yet settled on the CCF, but Macphail certainly implied the direction by her own Farmer-Labour support for the seven MPs that the newly formed party produced in the election of 1935. Casgrain watched them, too, with increasing curiosity. At their head was J.S. Woodsworth, comfortable for a while in party ranks and stamping the group with his own impeccable moral qualities, but ultimately ill at ease with an issue of great concern to feminists in the 1930s. The advent of war in 1939 led to a break between Woodsworth and his party: as a pacifist he could not sanction Canada's entry into the war and he said so to an awed but somewhat disbelieving Commons. Casgrain, in the gallery, was moved.[28]

However, it was not just Woodsworth's expression of a feminist interest in peace that moved her; there were French Canadians in the House that day who were also very uneasy. Though none captured the attention of the Commons as Woodsworth did, three of them objected openly to Mackenzie King's carefully planned state-of-war readiness.[29] The war summoned up French-Canadian sensibilities, and Casgrain felt that pull, too. For all her distaste for contemporary nationalists, with most of whom she had to battle over the question of votes for women, Casgrain harboured nationalist sentiments of her own. More like those of Henri Bourassa at the turn of the century, Casgrain's views were anti-militarist and anti-imperialist. Like Bourassa, she envisioned Canada as a country of French / English equality, free of colonial ties to Great Britain. Her worries were thus similar to his: the status of the French language, imperialism, war, and conscription. Casgrain would encounter the first worry later within the CCF; the other three she had to confront in the early 1940s, and they constituted the final rupture of her links with the Liberals.

Indeed, political ruptures over such questions were not new to Thérèse

Casgrain. Her own father had distanced himself from the Conservatives in 1917. After thirteen years as an independent Conservative, he had decided not to run in the election that was to test the popularity of the government's conscription law, a law against which he had voted.[30] Casgrain's husband ran in his stead, but as a Liberal supporting Laurier and opposing conscription. His political career thus had its origin in a nationalist cause. It also came to an end – judging by the timing – over the same cause. Late in 1941 Pierre Casgrain resigned from the Liberal cabinet to become a judge. His health may have been a consideration (he died less than nine years later), but the timing was just too fine for total credibility. The resignation came very shortly after the death of Ernest Lapointe, the self-styled barricade against conscription and a close friend of Thérèse and Pierre. It also came just a few weeks before King's announcement of a plebiscite on conscription in the Throne Speech in January 1942. The Casgrains shared their political lives intimately; the resignation and the reasons for it must have been the subject of lengthy family conversations. Certainly the political consequences affected Thérèse. After voting 'non' in the conscription plebiscite in April,[31] she decided to run in the by-election called for November to fill the now-vacant Charlevoix-Saguenay seat. Her excitement at the prospect was palpable in her diary: 'Je me présente, rien ne m'arrêtera. J'aimerais tant aller sur le parquet de la Chambre des Communes, dire tout haut ce que je pense tout bas depuis si longtemps.'[32] But she ran as an Independent Liberal in order to distinguish herself from what was beginning to look like a conscriptionist Liberal party. Of all the prominent party members with whom she had been associated for over twenty years, not one of them assisted her campaign and she lost to the Independent candidate Frédéric Dorion. Louis St Laurent, successful in his own by-election campaign to replace Ernest Lapointe in Quebec East earlier in the year, later apologized for the slight,[33] but by then Casgrain was national vice-chairman of the CCF. In 1942 the defeat was a great blow to her, for she had expected her family connections with the riding to ensure victory. So, too, was the aftermath, when all manner of people turned against her: 'Pour les adeptes de la Laurentie, je suis trop anglifiée, pour les impérialistes, je suis une nationaliste, une isolationaliste.'[34]

As a political outcast, Casgrain then had to ponder her future. Might the CCF, increasingly capturing popular fancy during the mid-war years, and acceptably uneasy on the conscription issue (it had advocated a 'yes, but' response to the plebiscite), offer a home for her? There she could advocate her own Canadian nationalism and thus avoid the clash of nationalist (bordering on separatist) and imperialist views. There she could find a political program to match her feminist social concerns, a program that stated the same thing to Canadians in all parts of the country. There she would certainly find the challenge of making such a party and such concerns acceptable to the Quebec electorate. And there, just perhaps, she might find scope for her own political ambitions as an equal-rights feminist.

During her years with the CCF, this latter ambition may well have been the most satisfied. In spite of repeated electoral defeats – in two provincial and five federal elections – she none the less gained a prominent place within the party. She was fully aware that such positions were not so easily obtained in the other parties;[35] moreover, she was used to and enjoyed the stature that went with the positions. That they were also firsts for women pleased her, too. She was national vice-president of the party from 1948 to 1963, the first and only woman. She was provincial leader from 1951 to 1957, the first and only woman. She was the sole woman member of the national committee for the New Party from 1959 to 1961. And she was one of the prominent founding members of the New Democratic Party in 1961. The enjoyment she drew from being a woman in a man's world[36] she kept carefully controlled by her concern for social action, which allowed her to make a link to her feminist predecessors and to her feminist successors. 'Comme chef provincial du CCF mes responsabilités absorbaient tout mon attention et donnait libre cours a mes préoccupations sociales. S'il est vrai que le travail satisfaisant libère, j'étais donc devenue une femme vraiment libre.'[37] Her role within the CCF, however, had its less exalted moments. The party had certain expectations of her, many of which hinged on the fact that she was a woman. While attempting to fulfil those expectations, Casgrain encountered a number of difficulties, the result of which was a bruising of both her feminism and her nationalism. Had they not been so bruised, the political outcome in Quebec might well have been different.[38] As it was, Casgrain's years with the CCF constituted part of the burbling of the 1950s towards the Quiet Revolution. Once she had served as midwife for that revolution, she departed on another feminist mission, that of peace.

Casgrain's interest in the CCF was reciprocated by the party. Here was someone who would surely bring stature and stamina to a party sorely in need of both. Barely 100 French Canadians were members of the Quebec CCF in 1950, less than a quarter of the entire provincial membership.[39] Few candidates could brave federal or provincial elections when there were no funds and even less organization. Perhaps Casgrain could work some magic. She certainly had the funds, but she also had leadership and organizational abilities, both amply illustrated during the lengthy battle for votes for women. Indeed, the CCF in the late 1940s looked like as much of a hopeless cause as did woman suffrage in the inter-war years. Like woman suffrage, the CCF suffered from nationalist disfavour, the party being considered a creation of English Canadians, westerners at that, advocating a strong central government. Like woman suffrage, too, the CCF suffered from political disfavour, the party being considered idealistic and impractical. To emphasize the point, opponents had only to mention the name of David Côté, the sole CCF member ever elected to the Quebec legislature, who had deserted to the Liberals within a year of his startling Rouyn-Noranda victory in 1944.[40] Worse still, the party, like the campaign for votes for women, suffered from the disfavour of the popular press: journalists considered the CCF at best insignificant and at worst communist. Where woman suffrage might destroy the family, the CCF would surely destroy society as a whole. By and large, the press had the backing of the Catholic church in its attitude to the CCF. Just as the church frowned upon votes for women, so too did it take a dim view of the CCF. In the 1930s it had actually condemned the party, through the pen and voice of Mgr Gauthier, the archbishop of Montreal, and had thrown some of its weight behind the Ecole sociale populaire and its formulation in 1933 of a Programme de restauration sociale as a middle ground between the visible horrors of laissez-faire capitalism and the imagined horrors of interventionist socialism. By 1943 the church had softened its stand sufficiently to accept that Catholics could support a party such as the CCF, but some journalists disputed the leniency and were still doing so as late as 1956;[41] many Catholics thus continued to harbour suspicions about the party's proximity to communism. With a provincial premier ready to bait the good journalists of *Le Devoir* with bolshevism, it was easy enough to relegate the CCF to the outermost limits of respectability. Besides, in contrast to the Union nationale, or the Liberals, the CCF did appear odd: it actually sold membership cards and expected its members to raise money for the party. No rewards were promised or forthcoming at election time. Well might one wonder just what kind of party this was. And yet none of this popular, clerical, journalistic, political, or nationalist disfavour was new to Thérèse Casgrain. She had experienced them all while campaigning for votes for women. Moreover, she had eventually overcome them all. Perhaps she could do the same for the CCF.

In order to achieve what the CCF expected of her – the great breakthrough in Quebec – Casgrain had to take on the role of intermediary, a role usually assigned to, and performed by, women in families. She was expected to be the liaison between the English- and French-speaking members of the party, soothing family squabbles and ensuring a minimum of domestic harmony. She was expected also to enlarge the CCF family in Quebec by linking it to her own numerous contacts across the province. If she could not count on everyone she knew, certainly everyone who counted in Quebec knew of her. She had links to politicians, to the media, in volunteer agencies, and among the socially prominent, and she cultivated those links in a feminine fashion of individual concern and social receptions along with a provocative combination of duty, charm, wit, and style. To a party concerned for respectability, a respectable woman was the greatest of boons. She could move in any circles and hence serve as liaison between the party and the new groups it hoped to attract in the labour and co-operative movement, among middle-class professionals, and in the business world.[42] She mothered and nagged and shamed a lot of them into at least thinking about the CCF and sometimes even acting and voting for it. On top of those purely domestic duties concerning the Quebec CCF, Casgrain was also to serve as liaison between the Quebec party and the national CCF. In that role she was more than just a Quebec voice on the national council of the party; she was an essential part of the CCF dream of the time, of forming 'a socialist equivalent of that historic working partnership between the two great races on which this nation has been built.'[43] That the statement should be made while a woman was national vice-president and provincial leader perhaps has some significance. The partnership was as much a marriage as a business arrangement, and Casgrain was the go-between. She would facilitate the linking of French Canadians and the CCF.[44]

It was a rather tall order, even for a woman, and Casgrain was only able to fulfil the expectations in part. She did serve as liaison; she did make the CCF visible; she did increase its membership and its votes. But she could not resolve all the difficulties of a socialist party in Quebec in the 1950s. Moreover, her own experience as liaison added to the difficulties. In her relations with middle-class intellectuals, the labour movement, and the national CCF, she served as much as an intermediary to the Quiet Revolution as to 'a socialist equivalent of that historic working partnership.' In part that outcome was a result of what happened along the way to her feminism and her nationalism.

Just why the CCF looked first to urban middle-class intellectuals as sustenance for the party remains a mystery.[45] The intellectual tradition within the party was of course a strong one, with a branch of the League for Social Reconstruction flourishing in Montreal during the 1930s. One of the league's more prominent members, Frank Scott, was, in fact, a friend of Casgrain and persuasive in having her join the party. But the leanings of the CCF towards intellectuals may also have something to do with its English-Canadian background: both language and religion stood in the way of any meeting with other than bilingual, and perhaps even slightly anti-clerical, French Canadians. Scott, David Lewis (the national secretary of the party), and Bill Dodge (the provincial president during the 1950s), all Montrealers, may well have been fluent in French but few other CCFers were, so the party had to count on Québécois willing to meet it more than half-way. Until 1955, meetings of the party were held in English and the minutes recorded in that language.[46] Within the party, too, lurked the suspicion that the Catholic church had far too much influence over Quebec voters; it was thus necessarily in search of people willing to stand up to the church.

People of that very type were appearing in the post-war years and the CCF considered them to be the most promising source of new recruits and new ideas.[47] Emerging from Quebec's universities with social-science training, complemented frequently by post-graduate studies in the United States or France, an increasing number of young people were looking for interesting and challenging careers outside the traditional mould of law, medicine, or the priesthood. Many of their career paths were, in fact, blocked by the presence of clerics in education or social services. And in the political realm they encountered Maurice Duplessis and the Union nationale, solidly in power thanks to an over-represented rural electorate and extensive patronage. Duplessis referred to intellectuals as 'poètes' and they reciprocated the disdain. Nor did they have much use for a nationalism which they associated with a rejection of modern ideas and external influences.[48]

In their search for ideas and action, a number of these young people brushed up against the CCF. They may have been flattered by the attentions of someone as prestigious and outspoken as Thérèse Casgrain, who put them in touch with each other and invited them to her home for intense political discussions.[49] Or they may have been attracted by ideas of social organization that had nothing to do with religion. Even the notion of an interventionist state, planning, organizing, and directing, was an appealing idea. When it combined with the offer of jobs, the attraction was often irresistible and a number of these very people disappeared into the federal civil service in the 1950s. But before then, such people may have been intrigued by a political party actually soliciting the opinions of intellectuals. Whatever the source of the interest, it aroused a great flurry of excitement in CCF ranks in 1949. There seemed to be a 'Quebec LSR [League for Social Reconstruction] or a Quebec Fabian Society' in the making.[50] With CCF backing and Casgrain facilitating, the group formed an Equipe des recherches sociales to engage in systematic inquiry into such questions as the social doctrine of the church, the economic structure of the province, the organization and functions of the state, health insurance, housing, and education.[51] The outcome was supposed to be a provincial program for the Quebec CCF.[52] However, the people involved – Gérard Pelletier, Pierre Juneau, Maurice Sauvé, Guy Rocher, Maurice Lamontagne, Jean-Charles Falardeau, Maurice Tremblay, Albert Faucher, and Pierre Trudeau – all subsequently shied away from the party. When some of them began *Cité Libre* in 1950, the CCF continued to hope that here might be a vehicle for French-language expression of the party's ideas.[53]

But the accent on Quebec eventually undermined any possible benefit for the CCF. An analysis and a critique of the institutions of Quebec society took precedence over the formation of some socialist alliance between French and English. Some of the original équipe disappeared into academic neutrality to produce such early sociological analyses as *Essais sur le Québec contemporain*, some of whose chapters and authors reflect the research program of the Equipe des recherches sociales.[54] Others worked for unions and acquired the political reserve that went with their jobs.[55] Still others who may have found the accent on Quebec too confining moved into the federal public service (and hence political anonymity) to exercise their social-science training in a modernizing bureaucracy. Those who did maintain an active political interest spotted Duplessis as the real block to social progress in Quebec. Once he was gone, anything could happen. But in the meantime and to ensure his departure, allies of any political stripe were welcome.

From that standpoint, it was easy enough to attract all manner of Duplessis opponents to the Rassemblement in 1956. The pet idea of Pierre-Elliot Trudeau, who at the time was being courted by Thérèse Casgrain to take over the provincial leadership of the CCF,[56] the Rassemblement brought together people disturbed by the overbearing, anti-democratic, and conservative presence of Duplessis. Individual CCF members joined the Rassemblement in the hopes of finding allies: the democratic structures of the CCF and its advanced social policies were there for all to see and Trudeau himself acknowledged them.[57] But the party itself was uneasy about any formal presence within the Rassemblement, and Casgrain appears to have been at the centre of an internal row over the link. Accusations of running the party 'as her own private and personal property' were hurled at her by one of her prize catches for the party, Jacques Perrault, the brother-in-law of André Laurendeau.[58] Just what the basis of the accusation was is unclear, but it may well be that Casgrain was wary of any formal endorsement of the Rassemblement, which desired to be a 'mouvement d'éducation et d'action démocratique.'[59] It shunned the label of political party and yet obviously wished to see the end of Duplessis. The danger Casgrain may have foreseen was exactly what happened: instead of the CCF attracting new members via the Rassemblement, those CCF members who supported it were swept up in the anti-Duplessis tide, a tide which ultimately benefited the provincial Liberals.

Much of Casgrain's cosseting of middle-class intellectuals thus headed them in the direction of the Liberal party. Whether they would have gone there anyway without the prodding of the CCF is a moot point. Certainly her facilitating – an invitation here, a chance encounter there, a telephone call elsewhere, a dinner, a luncheon, a salon discussion – brought people together and kept political ideals alive. But that it should be done by an elegant woman (fast approaching 60) of Quebec's financial and social élite may well have been increasingly upsetting to the new young men that she had attracted to the party. It was perhaps not surprising that in 1957 she relinquished the leadership to Michel Chartrand, an outspoken young man who spanned the gap between middle-class intellectuals and the labour movement.

The labour movement was also the object of CCF interest through the late 1940s and 1950s. As Catholic unions gradually sloughed off their clerical coloration and international unions followed the North American trend toward amalgamation, both took an increasing interest in the question of direct political action. One of the eventual affiliates of the Fédération des travailleurs du Québec, the Fédération des unions industrielles du Québec, was, because of its link to the Canadian Congress of Labour, sympathetic to the CCF. Many CCF members came from its ranks. Among labour groups in general the need for political action became increasingly clear through the 1950s as the Union nationale indicated its anti-labour bias in legislation and during strikes. Whether that political action would take the form of support for the Liberals, the CCF, or a new political party fostered by the labour movement was debated at great length in union circles throughout the 1950s.[60]

Casgrain ensured a CCF presence in that debate. The provincial CCF, and Casgrain personally, joined the picket lines of major and minor strikes in Quebec from Asbestos in 1949 to Murdochville and Arvida in 1957. She gave speeches of support and encouragement, while the strikers admired, albeit in a deferential manner, her presence among them. With her prodding, the national council of the CCF sent statements of support (and sometimes money as well) to striking workers.[61] Her own flair is quite noticeable: she used donations from CCF members of Parliament to fill a truck with food and toys for the families of the Asbestos strikers in 1949.[62] Casgrain was also a prominent figure in the many demonstrations against Duplessis's labour legislation, in 1949, 1954, and again in 1957.[63] Whether her presence actually attracted political support or merely aroused paternal appreciation is open to debate. For on one occasion, when she was being hassled by an inebriated demonstrator returning to Montreal from Quebec City by train, another working man gallantly put a stop to her discomfort with the remark, 'Laisse la "petite mère" du Québec tranquille.'[64] Casgrain was not, in fact, a petite woman but her maternal presence may well have served some political purpose. Certainly her feminine – and feminist – concern for such questions as housing, health, education, and cost of living brought her close to working-class worries. And her leadership of the CCF indicated her belief that political solutions had to be found for such worries and that the CCF was the party to do so.

Casgrain's presence and CCF policies seem indeed to have attracted individual people from the labour movement. She talked with workers on picket lines and attended labour conventions. She issued press releases from strike-bound communities and wrote special Labour Day editorials for the CCF publication *Le social démocrate*. From private pleas – Jean-Robert Ouellet of the Confédération des travailleurs catholiques du Canada was attracted by a combination of her charm, his chivalry, and the CCF constitution[65] – to public statements, Casgrain argued that 'les principes et le programme de PSD [CCF] ... sont la réponse tout indiquée au besoin de justice et de démocratie qu'exprime avec de plus en plus de force le mouvement syndical.'[66] People such as Roger Provost, Michel Chartrand, Emile Boudreau, Louis Laberge, Roméo Mathieu, and Gérard Picard were increasingly willing to agree with her and make the CCF their political home.[67] There they found policies that an ever more politically conscious labour movement was willing to sanction. Each one of the policies, from hindsight, had an assured political future in Quebec, but not by means of the CCF: a ministry of education, free access at all levels of the educational system, health and medical insurance, economic planning by the government, provincial control of natural resources with hydroelectricity as the most important one, bilingualism in the federal civil service, and full Canadian autonomy by means of an amending formula to the BNA Act so that Canada need no longer seek British approval for constitutional changes. The policies were gradually put into place in the CCF provincial program through the 1940s and 1950s: Casgrain was both attracted to them and instrumental in their formulation at the annual conventions of the party.[68] But each one of the policies was subsequently implemented by a Liberal government either in Quebec City or in Ottawa. That outcome was less the result of direct CCF influence than of the political meanderings of the labour movement. From the mid 1950s it hesitated over the desirability of political action and whether that action ought to be linked to the CCF or not. The Rassemblement took its fancy momentarily, as did the idea of a new party, which the Canadian Labour Congress and the national CCF were pursuing as of 1958. But eventually the labour movement in Quebec succumbed to the charm of proximity to political power that the provincial Liberals offered after 1960. What had been CCF policies became Liberal action, and in return for labour support, the government facilitated the expansion of the labour movement, notably among its own employees. Justifying much of the activity and the rhetoric of the Quiet Revolution was the notion of *rattrapage*, or catching up. The notion, if not the word, had in fact long been part of Casgrain's political speeches, as she and the CCF argued that Quebec had been slow in undertaking modern social-welfare measures.[69]

By the time the labour movement was lending visible support to the Liberals, however, Casgrain was no longer provincial leader of the CCF. It appears that she was somewhat summarily pushed aside in 1957 to make room for a leader coming from the labour movement. Until just a few weeks before the provincial convention in autumn 1957, Casgrain had had every intention of being a candidate once again for the leadership.[70] But suddenly she withdrew and proposed instead Michel Chartrand, a fiery union employee, for the leadership. At the time she stated that his leadership couldn't be more fitting because 'the party was gaining headway among members of the Quebec labor movement.'[71] But later she added another element. On radio in 1970 she recalled the time: 'J'ai démissionné en faveur d'un homme ... [at which point her voice hesitated and she did not name Chartrand] je trouvais que c'était plus facile pour lui de lutter puis je me faisais pas d'illusions sur des préjugés.'[72] Only in 1981 did she commit to paper what she may have been thinking all along: that she had withdrawn from the leadership because a number of people attributed the party's lack of electoral success to the fact that she was a woman.[73] In her autobiography she refrained from making that connection but did record the 'triste satisfaction' of hindsight that gave the CCF its brightest public image during her leadership.[74] That there was a certain tension between her and Chartrand is obvious from a radio interview in 1957. Chartrand dominated the discussion with a language and manner not only different from hers but also indifferent to her.[75] Quite clearly he had little use for the social (and perhaps female) powers she represented; a political party that meant business should have a man at its head. Casgrain's very success as an intermediary between the CCF and the labour movement entailed her own disappearance as leader.

The disappearance seems to have been particularly unpleasant. Insults were flung about; her contribution and devotion to the party were ignored; she was not even invited to certain meetings of the executive.[76] It was all a great blow to her. And yet she did not fight back,[77] almost as if her style of feminism did not entail personal combativeness for her own position. She would gladly pour all her energies into nagging political figures to implement some cause she held dear, but she would not use her tremendous powers of persuasion, organization, and stamina to further her own career. Perhaps she was not yet willing to confront the question of male power; that confrontation came only with the feminism of the 1970s, a feminism about which Casgrain had reservations. Or it may be that only in the CCF did she encounter any questioning of her leadership *as a woman*; the many other organizations with which she was involved never questioned the sex of her leadership: it was either appropriate or irrelevant. Perhaps as the CCF expanded during the 1950s and took on the appearance of something more significant than a mere fringe party, the question of the sex of the leader became relevant and her sex in particular inappropriate.

If Casgrain was unwilling to take on a feminist struggle involving her personal position, she was willing to fight when her nationalist sensibilities were aroused. And in her relations with the national CCF those feelings were not only aroused but heightened. Having come to the party sharing with its English-speaking leadership a sense of national unity based on common social policies, she none the less experienced a growing awareness of Quebec's special place within the federal CCF. That awareness became so strong that, according to party leader M.J. Coldwell, she was the one who convinced the founding convention of the New Democratic Party in 1961 to adopt a policy of two nations.[78]

Along the way she had had to engage in a number of battles with the national CCF. The party had hoped that her presence would bring more funds into provincial coffers so that the Quebec CCF could at least pay its own provincial secretary and perhaps even a provincial organizer. It never happened and support from the national office, based on Quebec's special needs, was always necessary. Although Casgrain kept promising donations from her many socially prominent friends, few of them contributed to the party and it was chronically short of money.[79] In spite of (or perhaps because of) her lengthy experience with voluntary organizations financed by private donations, she did not easily make the transition to a political party operating in the same way but requiring much more sustained and organized funding. Indeed she found the whole question of money 'tiresome'[80] and expressed little enthusiasm for a planned national campaign of fund raising.[81] Thus, when the situation became particularly desperate, she dipped into her own resources. In 1952, for example, she paid the deposits for most of the twenty-five candidates the party needed to muster in order to have free radio time during the provincial election campaign.[82] But obviously she could not sustain the party single-handedly, nor was it interested in having her do so. She thus had to make pleas to the national party using her own privileged position as vice-chairman on the national executive. And the pleas were based on Quebec's special status. It had particular needs that justified special grants from party headquarters.[83] Moreover, it held the key to the party's desire to show itself as a national entity; if for that reason the Quebec CCF had to appear stronger than it really was (by, for example, fielding more candidates than it could sustain), then surely it deserved more dollars from the national office in Ottawa. CCF leaders were uneasy about the situation: there were so few electoral returns for the money invested and the national party itself rarely had funds to spare.[84] It tried on occasion to have ephemeral CCF publications in Quebec, such as *Le Canada nouveau* and *Debout*, serve a double purpose and print material of interest to francophones outside Quebec. In return, the national office would pay part of the cost. But the co-ordination was complicated and no one was ever entirely satisfied.[85]

In 1954 a similar question of money, federal/provincial haggling, and Quebec's special place in Canada found Casgrain supporting Maurice Duplessis, of all people, against her CCF colleagues in Ottawa. That year, the Quebec government introduced a provincial income tax in order to raise the funds it claimed it was losing because of the refusal to sign a tax-rental agreement with the federal government. Duplessis took a calculated risk that the federal government would permit the deduction of the provincial tax from federal taxes paid by Québécois and thus he could avoid the politically damaging accusation of double taxation.[86] But the national CCF saw even greater harm in the provincial tax. Besides being unconstitutional, it was a sure means, CCF MPs contended, of undermining national standards of social services. Duplessis would do as he pleased with the monies he collected and he could certainly not be trusted to do anything very progressive. If he had his way on deductibility, other provinces might well follow suit and thereby destroy the entire purpose of the tax-rental provisions – to redistribute the wealth of the rich provinces to the poorer ones so that they could meet their constitutional obligations.[87] The Quebec CCF was divided on the question, some members agreeing with federal MPs that a provincial tax was contrary to the BNA Act, others thinking some federal / provincial agreement could be arranged to allow for deductibility.[88] No one wanted a public difference of opinion with party leader M.J. Coldwell, but everyone recognized the political popularity of autonomy in Quebec. There the CCF could only harm itself by insisting, in effect, on the supremacy of the Ottawa government. The compromise suggested by the provincial CCF, and eventually adopted by the national council, recognized the right of Quebec to impose a tax on personal income and proposed that the tax be deductible from federal tax paid in Quebec, up to an amount equal to that which the province would have received had it entered into a tax-rental agreement with the federal government.[89] Privately, Coldwell thought the party had gone too far,[90] but the compromise did allow Casgrain and the provincial party to defend Quebec's autonomy, while the national party was able to tie concessions to Quebec to the tax-rental arrangements with the other provinces. If all seemed smooth on the surface, Casgrain's increasing defence of Quebec's special place in Canada was becoming obvious.

Just as the national council was adopting the Quebec CCF's position on provincial income tax, an even more disturbing question threatened to disrupt the CCF irrevocably. Early in 1955, four CCF MPs, all from western Canada, made disparaging remarks about Quebec, the French language, minority rights, and separate schools. Erhart Regier spoke of Quebec as 'the sore spot in the matter of Canadian unity'; Hazen Argue attacked the federal government's eventual allowing of a 15 per cent deductibility of the Quebec provincial income tax from federal taxes as 'sacrificing the well-being of fifteen million Canadians on the altar of ultra-nationalism'; Harold Winch was then provoked into suggesting to the press that French-speaking MPs should really use English in the House; Angus MacInnis in turn rejected the notion of minorities in British Columbia having any right to separate schools financed by public funds.[91] French-Canadian MPs baited their CCF opponents, the press lapped it all up, and Casgrain was appalled. Here was the national party giving credence to all the notions that too many French Canadians harboured about the CCF: that it was hostile to the very institutions that kept French Canada distinctive and alive. Casgrain threatened to resign from the party. So did most of her executive, and the party was faced with one of its greatest crises.[92]

With 'the cause of socialism ... set back for God knows how long,'[93] the party attempted to patch things up. The resignations were postponed and most of them eventually withdrawn as federal MPs and members of the national executive rushed to Montreal for 'long and difficult conversations' in order to head off the suggested formation of another socialist party in Quebec, free of CCF shackles.[94] From the meetings emerged a carefully worded press release regretting the remarks of the MPs and reiterating CCF commitment to 'the equal status of our country's two official languages' and to 'provincial authority in the fields reserved to the provinces, particularly education.'[95] The Quebec CCF acquiesced, but some of the members wanted a public admonition of the wayward MPs.[96] It was not forthcoming. Many long-time CCFers left the party, newly persuaded ones turned their back in disdain, and French-speaking Canadians outside Quebec 'were just as agitated and incensed.'[97] 'It will take eons of time to heal the wounds,' remarked one of the key negotiators, Stanley Knowles, in reply to Frank Scott's prescription: every CCFer should read Mason Wade's new book, *The French Canadians*; the national office should hire a full-time French-Canadian secretary and 'not even the word QUEBEC be uttered by any western member (Ontarians are trained) without prior clearance with said French secretary.'[98]

In spite of her anger, Thérèse Casgrain maintained her personal and political charm throughout the fracas. She had, for example, not even raised the matter at the national council meeting in mid January; at that point only Regier had made his damaging remark and Casgrain had apparently felt sorry for him.[99] By the end of January when she was ready to resign, she could comment jocularly: 'We can now get more votes in the west by capitalizing on the anti-French sentiment.'[100] But it was a western CCFer who was able to persuade her to stay with the party. She had wired her resignation threat to the premier of Saskatchewan, T.C. Douglas, and he had hastily penned a lengthy reply, hoping to dissuade her: 'I am terribly sorry that you have been caused so much heartache at a time when I know the CCF movement in Quebec has all the problems it can handle without any of us increasing the load which you are carrying.' Susceptible to the kindly voice of an old friend, Casgrain acquiesced in his argument that the CCF had been consistently favourable to the rights of French Canadians and that policy had not changed; if it did, many non-Quebecers would leave the party, too. Douglas suspected a 'clever newspaper campaign' of denigration[101] and Casgrain picked up this very note in a radio broadcast ten days later:

Il est assez curieux de noter que toute cette campagne contre le CCF s'est précisément déclenchée au moment ou notre Parti se déclarait officiellement en faveur de la déductibilité complète de l'impôt sur le revenu, reconnaissant ainsi les droits de la province de Québec dans le champ fiscal. Evidemment, cette attitude n'a pas eu l'heur de plaire au parti libéral qui, dans ce domaine, n'a pas admis le principe de l'autonomie provinciale dont Monsieur Duplessis se sert très habilement d'ailleurs pour promouvoir ses fins politiques. Dans le but d'empêcher notre population de se rendre compte que le parti CCF lui, était soucieux de reconnaître et de défendre les droits constitutionnels de notre province, on s'est servi de quelques discours pour jeter le discrédit sur un parti susceptible de devenir extrêmement dangereux pour ceux qui détiennent les monopoles dans le domaine économique, et les ficelles dans le domaine politique.[102]

And yet how heavy her heart must have been. For she had to assure her listeners that the CCF was doing everything possible 'afin de créer entre les deux groupes ethniques de notre pays cet esprit de bonne entente et de véritable collaboration sans lequel il est impossible de travailler effectivement aux réformes sociales qui s'imposent pour assurer le bien-être des citoyens du Canada.'[103] She was a veteran politician; she had decided not to resign; and she said what had to be said in public. Privately, however, she continued to fume: 'I am still in very bad humour against the guilty M.P.s of our side they better not try any more stunts all of us down here are fed up and don't forget *we did not start it*, but we must pay for the repair job and how [*sic*].'[104]

Whether the national office would assist in the repair job remained to be seen. By mid March, Casgrain had informed David Lewis that she was thinking of resigning both as provincial leader and as national vice-chairman 'in the very near future, unless some proper action is taken to help our section in our work.' With some very specific grievances – no full-time paid person for the French section of the CCF, no attempt to provide French-language support for the forthcoming Ontario election, no one in the national office with knowledge and understanding of Quebec[105] – Casgrain linked the financial question to that of Quebec's status in a national association. The solution, she threatened, might have to be separation.

Later that same year, the Quebec CCF actually did take an independent stand of its own. Since the early 1950s the party had been toying with distinguishing itself from the national CCF and also giving itself a more appropriate name. CCF was quite untranslatable and on at least one occasion had been confused with the radio station CFCF! But no agreement had ever been reached on just the right name, and the issue dragged on for years. [106] By winter 1955 the impetus was clearly there: the provincial party not only had to differentiate itself from the national party, it also had to head off its breakaway members who were about to form a Ligue d'action socialiste. Hence, in late summer 1955, the provincial convention adopted the name Parti social démocratique (PSD) and merely informed the national party of the fact. [107] The national secretary, the national executive, and the subsequent national convention duly endorsed the change, but even had they objected, the PSD would have continued on its autonomous route. Well might the national executive claim that the change of name involved no change in the constitutional relations between the provincial and the national party; [108] within three years the CCF was contemplating a new party of which the Quebec wing would be virtually independent.

While Casgrain was leader of the Quebec CCF, she and the party had a foretaste of the kind of wrenching the entire country would experience in the 1960s. Just as Quebec would then insist on more money, status, and autonomy during the Quiet Revolution, so did the provincial party vis-à-vis its federal colleague in the 1950s. Anyone within, or even close to, the Quebec CCF would not have been at all surprised by the developments of the next decade. Casgrain had even prodded the national secretary into specifying the equal protection a CCF government would give to the two languages and cultures in Canada; she also wanted CCF MPs to demand a royal commission on bilingualism in federal government positions. [109] Both suggestions became part of the federal Liberal response to the Quiet Revolution a few years later. Casgrain may even have contributed, by her activities and experiences in the CCF, to the linking of socialism and nationalism. The link appeared in a very mild form during the Quiet Revolution, when many middle-class intellectuals were hired as bureaucrats for the new interventionist state. It appeared again in a much more dramatic form in the late 1960s, as rebels and revolutionaries formed new political parties or engaged in kidnappings and common fronts. Casgrain had been surprised to note the happy combination of socialism and nationalism among Asian socialists in 1956. Attending a conference in Bombay as a 'fraternal observer' for the CCF, she reported that 'those two doctrines are perfectly compatible and serve as the expression of their aspiration towards liberty and social justice.''¹⁰ She obviously considered the combination quite foreign to Canada. And yet her own experience within the CCF had presaged just such a combination. While advocating socialist policies, she had encountered situations that provoked a nationalist reaction from her. Perhaps the two were not so foreign after all.

But when the link became evident on the Quebec scene in the early 1960s, Casgrain withdrew from any active involvement. Perhaps the implications were not to her liking, even though she may have fostered them. Perhaps she, too, like many progressive Québécois, began to feel the pull toward the provincial Liberals, although she assured the federal NDP, on her resignation from the national vice-presidency early in 1963, that her political sympathies had not changed.'¹¹ In 1970, however, she accepted a Senate appointment from the Liberals and marked her break with the NDP by supporting the federal government's use of the War Measures Act.'¹² But in the meantime she seemed more swayed by her original kind of nationalism, with its fear of imperialism (now centred in the United States), and by an old feminist issue, that of peace. Significantly enough, she chose to pursue those issues through an organization of women, one in which she could once again play a leadership role. The Voice of Women was to many people, including some in the NDP, an even 'queerer sort of organization' than the CCF had seemed in its early years. But it gave women positions of public leadership and it focused attention on the dangers of nuclear warfare. While Casgrain thus took another leap into political eccentricity – something she had been doing all her life – the CCF, transformed into the NDP, was effectively stillborn in Quebec'¹³ as the Quiet Revolution got lustily under way.

NOTES

A skeletal version of this article was delivered as part of my duties as Seagram Lecturer at the University of Toronto in January 1984. A published version appeared in the *Canadian Historical Review* 66 (June 1985), 125–53.

1 Jacques-V. Morin (provincial secretary) to Lorne Ingle (national secretary), 21 June 1951; press release, 24 June 1951, CCF Papers, National Archives of Canada (NA).
2 Telegram from Thérèse Casgrain to Frank Scott (national president), 18 August 1948, CCF Papers.
3 Her own appearance, and that of others, was always very important to Casgrain. In 1937, during a European trip (the only time, it seems, when she kept a regular diary: after July 1937 there are only seven scattered entries to

1943), she recorded in Paris: 'Je me lance à la dépense ai acheté deux amours de robe. Décidement ça coûte cher pour être chic mais cela en vaut la peine' (diary entry, 31 mai 1937, Thérèse Casgrain Papers [hereafter Casgrain Papers] NA). In 1970 an interviewer tried to have her acknowledge a certain disappointment after nine electoral defeats. 'Mais non,' she replied in both a surprised and matter-of-fact manner. But later in the same interview she did admit to a certain vague hope, to the point of wondering what 'belle robe' she might wear the day of her entry into the House of Commons (taped recollections of T. Casgrain for the radio program 'L'expérience des autres,' 21 mai 1970, Archives de Radio Canada [ARC, Montreal).

4 Roch Denis, *Luttes de classes et question nationale au Québec 1948–1968* (Montreal 1979).

5 Thérèse Casgrain, *Une femme chez les hommes* (Montreal 1971), 175.

6 Among her school friends at Sacre-Coeur were the daughters of Rodolphe Lemieux and Sen. Napoleon Belcourt (ibid., 29 and taped recollections of Thérèse Casgrain for the radio program 'L'expérience des autres,' 21 mai 1970, ARC).

7 Thérèse Forget to Pierre Casgrain, 19 août 1915, Casgrain Papers, NA. The Casgrains, in fact, had four children.

8 Taped recollections of Thérèse Casgrain for the radio program 'Le grand carousel du samedi matin,' 22 mars 1980, ARC. In recounting the story, Casgrain added: 'Pour me venger, je me suis mariée ... puis j'ai fait des gâteaux,' the intonation alone suggesting more than sixty years of recollected revolt.

9 Ibid., 'L'expérience des autres,' 21 mai 1970. Commenting on the young *contestataires* of the 1960s she remarked: 'Ils n'ont rien inventé. Moi, je conteste, je crois, depuis que je suis au monde.'

10 As recounted to Robert Rumilly in his published interview with her. *Chefs de file* (Montreal 1934), 30.

11 Thérèse Forget to Pierre Casgrain, 27 juin 1915 and 6 juillet 1915, Casgrain Papers.

12 During her European trip in 1937 to attend the coronation of George VI, she was caught up in a whirl of social engagements in London. She could tolerate them for a while but not to the extent of her friends Pauline Vanier and Alice Massey, who seemed to thrive on such activities: 'Moi cela me rendrait folle' (ibid., diary entry, 4 mai 1937).

13 A four-part series of videotaped recollections for the television program 'Propos et confidences,' part I, 18 mai 1980, ARC; Casgrain, *Une femme chez les hommes*, 101–2.

14 Casgrain, *Une femme chez les hommes*, 72. On the FNSJB, see Marie Lavigne, Yolande Pinard, and Jennifer Stoddard, 'La Fédération nationale Saint-Jean-

Baptiste et les revendications féministes ou début du 20e siècle, *Revue d'histoire de l'Amérique française* (RHAF) 29 (decembre 1975), 353–73, reprinted in Marie Lavigne and Yolande Pinard, eds, *Travailleuses et féministes: Les femmes dans la société québécoise* (Montreal 1983), 199–216. An English version of the article is in Linda Kealey, ed., *A Not Unreasonable Claim: Women and Reform in Canada, 1880s–1920s* (Toronto 1979), 71–87.

15 Press clipping from *Montreal Star*, 8 October 1970, Casgrain Papers.

16 So defined by Grace MacInnis in a telephone interview from Vancouver, 30 December 1983.

17 See, for example, the articles of Lavigne, Pinard, and Stoddart, 'La Fédération nationale Saint-Jean-Baptiste,' of Yolande Pinard, 'Les débuts du mouvement des femmes à Montréal, 1893–1902,' in Lavigne and Pinard, eds, *Travailleuses et féministes*, 177–8, of Marta Danylewycz, 'Changing Relationships: Nuns and Feminists in Montreal 1890–1925,' *Histoire sociale/Social History* 14 (November 1981), 413–34 and ch. XI of Le Collectif Clio, *L'Histoire des femmes au Québec depuis quatre siècles* (Montreal 1982).

18 'Propos et confidences,' part II, 25 mai 1980, ARC.

19 The papers of the Ligue des droits de la femme from which this assessment is drawn are in the Salle Gagnon of the Bibliothèque municipale in Montreal.

20 'Propos et confidences,' part II, 25 mai 1980, ARC.

21 Casgrain was one of forty women delegates in attendance, for the first time, at the Liberal convention (Casgrain, *Une femme chez les hommes*, 124–5). Her suspicion of Liberal leader Adélard Godbout's motivation is also recorded in 'Propos et confidences,' part II, 25 mai 1980, ARC.

22 Casgrain, *Une femme chez les hommes*, 88–95; Jennifer Stoddart, 'Quand les gens de robe se penchent sur les droits des femmes: le cas de la commission Dorion, 1929–1931,' in Lavigne and Pinard, eds, *Travailleuses et féministes*, 307–35.

23 Her own preference was for Emily Murphy ('Propos et confidences,' part II, 25 mai 1980). Each of the five appellants was, however, from Alberta, and at the time there was no Senate vacancy for that province.

24 See, for example, Eleanor Harman, 'Five Persons from Alberta,' in Mary Quayle Innis, ed., *The Clear Spirit* (Toronto 1966), 158–78; Sandra McCallum and Anne McLellan, 'The Persons' Case: A Beginning Not the End,' Proceedings of the Third Annual Meeting of the Canadian Research Institute for the Advancement of Women, *Resources for Feminist Research*, Special Publication 9 (Fall 1980), 76–9.

25 Casgrain, *Une femme chez les hommes*, 170–4; Ligue des droits de la femme, Rapport de la secrétaire pour l'année 1945–46, Casgrain Papers.

26 Casgrain, *Une femme chez les hommes*, 178–9. Woodsworth also stood out as the desk-mate of another striking individual, Henri Bourassa. Casgrain fre-

quently observed the two taking an evening stroll together around the Parliament buildings. 'Je songeais alors que s'ils avaient travaillé ensemble, ces deux hommes auraient pû bâtir un Canada vraiment fort,' ibid., 150.

27 Ibid., 179.

28 Ibid., 150.

29 Maxime Raymond, Luguori Lacombe, and Wilfrid Lacroix in the Debate on the Address in Reply to the Speech from the Throne, 8–11 September 1939 (House of Commons, *Debates*, 7–13 September 1939).

30 He recorded his opposition during the vote on second reading of the Military Service Act (House of Commons, *Debates*, 6 July 1917, 3085) but was not present for the vote on third reading (ibid., 24 July 1917, 3736–7).

31 Casgrain, *Une femme chez les hommes*, 152.

32 Diary entry, 9 juillet 1942, Casgrain Papers.

33 Ibid., Louis St Laurent to Casgrain, 5 juillet 1949. At least one Liberal expected that she might do something politically odd after her husband's resignation. Brooke Claxton suggested she be named to the Senate in order to head off 'some change in the direction or extent of her own political activities' (Claxton to W.L.M. King, 16 December 1941, Claxton Papers, NA). Thanks to David Bercuson for drawing this reference to my attention.

34 Diary entry, 12 août 1943, Casgrain Papers.

35 For example, she remarked in her autobiography: 'Je doute fort que pareille occasion de servir m'aurait été offerte dans un des vieux partis politiques' (*Une femme chez les hommes*, 195).

36 The English title of the translation of her autobiography, published in Toronto in 1971.

37 Casgrain, *Une femme chez les hommes*, 203.

38 Just before she died in 1981, Casgrain completed a book-length manuscript, 'Les raisons pour lesquelles le Québec a dit non au CCF,' a copy of which can be found in her papers at the National Archives. The manuscript is a disappointment because Casgrain keeps herself well hidden throughout the account. Her own reaction to things is camouflaged; even her own participation is minimized by her use of the third person. The manuscript is obviously a draft, for there are numerous errors and repetitions; it also draws heavily on secondary accounts of Quebec's antipathy to the CCF and repeats many of the clichés about the failure of the left in Quebec. Hence, it was not a source of inspiration for the rather different approach and interpretation in this article.

39 J.-V. Morin to Lorne Ingle, 3 October 1950, CCF Papers; Report of the Provincial Secretary to the Provincial Council, 17 December 1950, Frank Scott Papers, NA.

40 David Lewis has an interesting, if unconsciously sexist, account of Côté's

financial difficulties, which apparently forced him into accepting a Liberal offer (*The Good Fight* [Toronto 1981], 209–11).

41 In the pages of *L'Action catholique*, 20 mars and 9 mai 1956, editor Louis-Philippe Roy wondered whether the CCF had evolved sufficiently to be free of the episcopal condemnation once formulated against it. Casgrain protested to Mgr Roy, archbishop of Quebec, and, when *Montréal Matin* reproduced the first article from *L'Action catholique*, she also complained to Cardinal Léger, archbishop of Montreal (copy of letter from Casgrain and J[acques] P[errault] to Mgr Roy, 15 mai 1956; copy to Cardinal Léger, 17 mai 1956; Maurice Roy to Casgrain, 2 juin 1956, Casgrain Papers).

42 Jacquest Perrault, 'Rapport d'une rencontre CCF' (at which Casgrain is present), 18 decembre 1948, Scott Papers.

43 Report of Donald MacDonald, 'The State of the Movement,' to the national council, November 1953, Scott Papers.

44 This portrayal of CCF expectations of Casgrain stems from what my French literary colleagues term a 'lecture au féminin' of the sources.

45 Desmond Morton raised this question in the discussion following my lecture on which this article is based.

46 Manuscript 'Les raisons pour lesquelles le Québec a dit non au CCF,' 61, Casgrain Papers.

47 As Donald MacDonald commented: 'Until we get French Canadians to take the lead in these matters [research, publications] we will not get very far in Quebec' (D. MacDonald to Louise Parkin, 23 October 1948, CCF Papers).

48 Gérard Pelletier's memoirs, *Les années d'impatience* (Montreal 1983), provide a delightful personal view of trends and people of the 1950s. Casgrain merits two paragraphs (130–1).

49 Copy of a letter from T. Casgrain to Reginald Boisvert (provincial secretary), 10 aout 1949, Scott Papers; G. Pelletier, *Les années*, 130.

50 Boisvert to Lewis (national secretary), 21 December 1949, CCF Papers.

51 The CCF Papers contain a detailed program of research with certain tasks assigned to certain people (unsigned 'Report on meeting of l'Equipe des Recherches sociales,' Quebec City, 10–11 Sept. 1949). The September author of the report, Eugene Forsey, adds his, Trudeau's, and Pelletier's uneasiness about the projects being too theoretical: 'But I think the whole lot are valuable allies, and once we get to work things will develop towards more practical and concrete action.'

52 Boisvert to Lewis, 16 August 1949; Lewis to Forsey, 29 August 1949, CCF Papers.

53 Boisvert to MacDonald, 23 May 1951; MacDonald to Trudeau, 7 February 1953; MacDonald to Boisvert, 7 February 1953, CCF Papers.

54 J.-C Falardeau, ed., *Essais sur le Québec contemporain* (Quebec 1953).

55 Gerard Pelletier refers to the 'devoir de réserve qui obligeait les permanents syndicaux' (*Les années*, 130). The author of the 'Report on meeting of L'Equipe des recherches sociales' states that [Jean] Marchand had to be somewhat circumspect in the support he none the less thought was forthcoming from his employer, the Confédération des travailleurs catholiques du Canada (CCF Papers).

56 G. Pelletier, *Les années*, 130–1.

57 Casgrain quoted his reaction on attending, as an observer, a CCF convention in Toronto: 'Je ne croyais jamais voir ainsi la démocratie en action en terre d'Amérique' ('Les raisons pour lesquelles ...' 203, Casgrain Papers).

58 Perrault to Casgrain, 13 septembre 1956, Casgrain Papers. He was furious with her because she did not pass on to the Rassemblement a resolution that the party had adopted unanimously earlier in September. Perrault had joined the party in spring 1956 and there was great excitement about his membership. 'Jacques Perrault's public adherence to the Party is almost equivalent to your inducing say, David Crowl [*sic*] to join the CCF' (Scott to Stanley Knowles, 19 April 1956, Scott Papers).

59 The constitution and aims of the Rassemblement were published in *Le Devoir* under the front-page headline 'Il faut doter Québec d'une démocratie,' 14 septembre 1956.

60 See Roch Denis, *Luttes de classes et question nationale*, 162–8; Louis-Marie Tremblay, *Le syndicalisme québécois; idéologies de la CSN et de la FTQ 1940–1970* (Montreal 1972), 54–60, 165–8; 'Les raisons pour lesquelles ...' 205–6, Casgrain Papers.

61 Minutes of meeting of national executive 30 April–1 May 1949; minutes of meeting of national council, 24–5 January 1953; minutes of meeting of national council, 24–5 January 1959, CCF Papers.

62 Lewis to Morin, 6 April 1949, CCF Papers; 'Les raisons pour lesquelles ...' 192, Casgrain Papers.

63 'Les raisons pour lesquelles ...,' 189, 190, 193.

64 As recalled by Casgrain, *Une femme chez les hommes*, 197.

65 Typescript interview by T. Casgrain with J.-R. Ouellet, Casgrain Papers.

66 Press release quoting Casgrain, 3 septembre 1957, CCF Papers.

67 Casgrain lists some twenty union cadres but admits the party had difficulty reaching the workers themselves ('Les raisons pour lesquelles ...,' 194–202, Casgrain Papers).

68 Fonds Nouveau Parti Démocratique de Québec, Programme provincial du parti CCF (1940s), Archives de l'Université de Québec à Montréal; Ingle to Fred Thatcher, 8 October 1948; provincial program, 1951; draft program,

1955; Ingle to Edward Bantey, 4 July 1951; [Ingle] to Casgrain, 9 March 1953, vol. 90, CCF Papers. The radical education policies were added at the party convention in 1956.

69 For example, taped radio broadcast by Casgrain for the series 'Les affaires de l'état,' 24 janvier 1950, ARC; press release, 3 février 1957, Casgrain Papers.

70 SDP Quebec, press release, 5 July 1957, CCF Papers.

71 Ibid., press clipping with an account of her resignation, Montreal *Gazette*, 15 October, 1957.

72 'L'expérience des autres,' 21 mai 1970, ARC.

73 'Les raisons pour lesquelles ...' 180, Casgrain Papers.

74 Casgrain, *Une femme chez les hommes*, 214.

75 Taped interview with Thérèse Casgrain and Michel Chartrand by Jean-Marc Léger for the radio program 'Les affaires de l'état,' 25 fevrier 1957, Radio-Canada (National Film, Television and Sound Archives [NFTSA], NA).

76 Marie-Ange Gill to Lorne Ingle, 7 May 1957; Norman Allen to Carl Hamilton, 23 November 1958, 8 Dec. 1958; Hamilton to Allen, 18 December 1958, vol. 40, CCF Papers.

77 Grace MacInnis claimed that Casgrain was 'shunted aside' in 1957 and that 'she never got over that.' She was, said MacInnis, 'too ladylike to fight back' (interview, 30 December 1983).

78 Notes of an interview with M.J. Coldwell (by Shirley Thomson?), 11 November 1969, Casgrain Papers. Coldwell added that he did not agree with the policy but 'there was a feeling within the convention, that if this was what the French section of the CCF wished, they should comply.'

79 Morin to MacDonald, 20 Dec. 1950, CCF Papers. There is a series of incomplete and somewhat scrambled financial statements in the Fonds NPD Québec (UQAM). They suggest that the party was operating on annual amounts varying from $2000 to $11,000 (the latter during election years), with debts accumulating between 1952 and 1957.

80 'It seems such a pity that the wonderful work to be done is held up all the time by this tiresome question of money' (Casgrain to Ingle, 14 May 1951, CCF Papers).

81 Morin to MacDonald, 20 December 1950, CCF Papers.

82 Ingle to Durocher, 17 June 1952; Durocher to Ingle, 2 July 1952; Casgrain to [Ingle], 14 June 1952, CCF Papers.

83 Minutes of meeting of national council, 29–30 January 1949; minutes of meeting of national executive, 20 March 1949; Ingle to Casgrain, 19 February 1954; Ingle to Pauline Dodge, 16 September 1955; minutes of meeting of national executive, 26 June and 24 November 1957, 24 January 1959, CCF Papers.

84 Copy of a letter from Lewis to Bill Dodge, 24 January 1950, Scott Papers; minutes of meeting of national executive, 9–10 December 1950, CCF Papers.

85 Minutes of meeting of national executive, 15 February 1948; Roger Provost to Lewis, 29 June 1948; Lewis memorandum to Ruth Cook, 4 August 1948; Lewis to Provost, 4 August 1948, CCF Papers.

86 Aspects of the provincial income-tax question are dealt with in C. Black, *Duplessis* (Toronto 1977), 434–42; G.-E. Lapalme, *Le vent de l'oubli* (Montreal 1970), 170–9. The CCF Papers contain a file on the subject: 'Quebec: Income Tax 1954–1955.'

87 Coldwell to Paul King, 13 April 1954; Coldwell Papers, NA; M.J. Coldwell in House of Commons, *Debates*, 12 April 1954, 3996–7.

88 Roméo Mathieu to Casgrain, 25 avril 1954, Casgrain Papers.

89 Minutes of meeting of national council, 15–16 January 1955 (CCF Papers), at which Casgrain, Scott, Bill Dodge, Roméo Mathieu, and Michel Chartrand were present from Quebec. See also report by Lorne Ingle, 'Federal Provincial Tax Rental Agreement,' Scott Papers.

90 Coldwell to Lewis, 5 February 1955, Coldwell Papers.

91 Ingle to Andrew Brewin, Morden Lazarus, Henry Weisbach, and George Bothwell, 3 February 1955, CCF Papers. For the statements in the Commons, see House of Commons, *Debates*, 1955, 12 January 1955, 120; 19 January 1955, 346; 27 January 1955, 597.

92 Casgrain devotes only one paragraph of her memoirs to this question (*Une femme chez les hommes*, 205–6). In her later evaluation of the CCF in Quebec the incident merits two pages. But archival holdings are more revealing of the depth of the crisis: press release from national executive, 1 February 1955; Ingle to Brewin et al., 3 February 1955; press release from Quebec Provincial Council, 3 February 1955; T.C. Douglas to Casgrain, 7 February 1955; Ingle to Bill Dodge, 15 February 1955; typescript of radio broadcast by Casgrain for 'Les affaires de l'état,' 18 février 1955; Ingle to Casgrain, 24 February 1955; Casgrain to Lewis, 15 March 1955; Casgrain to Ingle, n.d. (between 3 February and 9 March 1955); minutes of meeting of national executive, 12 February 1955, CCF Papers. Lewis to Angus MacInnis, 4 February 1955; Coldwell to Lewis, 5 February 1955; Douglas to Coldwell, 8 February 1955, Coldwell Papers. Scott to Knowles, 6 February 1955; Knowles to Scott, 8 February 1955; copy of a letter from D.H.F. Black to Casgrain, 8 February 1955, Scott Papers.

93 Scott to Knowles, 6 February 1955, Scott Papers.

94 Ingle to Brewin et al., 3 February 1955, CCF Papers.

95 Press release from national executive, 1 February 1955, CCF Papers.

96 Press release from Quebec Provincial Council, 3 February 1955, CCF Papers.

97 Lewis to Angus MacInnis, 4 February 1955, Coldwell Papers.

98 Knowles to Scott, 8 February 1955; Scott to Knowles, 6 February 1955, Scott Papers.

99 As reported by Knowles to Scott, 8 February 1955, Scott Papers.

100 As reported by Scott to Knowles, 6 February 1955, Scott Papers.

101 Copy of a letter from Douglas to Casgrain, 7 February 1955, CCF Papers.

102 Typescript of Casgrain's radio broadcast for 'Les affaires de l'état,' 18 février 1955, 4–5.

103 Ibid., 6.

104 Casgrain to Ingle, n.d. (late February 1955), emphasis in original, CCF Papers.

105 Casgrain to Lewis, 15 March 1955, CCF Papers.

106 Casgrain to Scott, 3 June 1951; undated list of proposed names signed by Morin, Scott Papers; 'Les raisons pour lesquelles ...' 62, Casgrain Papers; Bantey to Ingle, 25 June 1951, CCF Papers.

107 Dodge to Scott, 30 August 1955, Scott Papers; Ingle to Lewis, 2 August 1955; Ingle to Michel Forest, 2 September 1955, CCF Papers; interview with Casgrain and M. Chartrand by Jean-Marc Léger, 25 février 1957, NFTSA.

108 Minutes of national executive, 10 September 1955, 1–2; report of the national secretary to the national council, 13 January 1956, Scott Papers; interview with Casgrain and Chartrand by Léger, NFTSA.

109 [Ingle] to Casgrain, 9 March 1953, CCF Papers; copy of a letter from Black to Casgrain, 8 February 1955, Scott Papers.

110 Report of Casgrain on her attendance at the Asian Socialist Conference, November 1956, to the national convention of CCF, 23–25 July 1958, Casgrain Papers.

111 Michael Oliver to Casgrain, 14 January 1963, CCF Papers.

112 Canada, Senate, *Debates*, 4 November 1970, 108–9.

113 Denis traces the many abortive attempts to found the NDP-Québec (*Luttes de classes et question nationale*, chs 12–14). Casgrain's own account appears to draw heavily on Denis ('Les raisons pour lesquelles ...' 222–31, Casgrain Papers).

PART FOUR

Labour, Socialist, and Communist Women

Women in the
Canadian Socialist Movement

1904–1914

Linda Kealey

The names of Canadian women in the socialist movement are seldom mentioned in existing histories of the left, for narratives of the socialist movement in Canada have tended to concentrate on the political experiences and organizations associated with male socialists. In the published studies, English and Scottish socialist immigrants, especially those in the skilled trades, usually emerge as the most important leaders of socialism in this country. Recent work has begun to investigate the roles of non-British workers and women in both the labour and socialist movements. This essay focuses on the role of women in the Canadian socialist movement in the critical decade 1904–14. Leaving aside the Christian socialist roots of the movement in the late 1890s and early 1900s, it concentrates on the major socialist parties of the early twentieth century and the women in their ranks.[1]

This essay examines women's issues and the roles women played in the Socialist Party of Canada (SPC) and the breakaway movement that resulted in the Social Democratic party of Canada (SDP). The analysis suggests that the issues of suffrage and autonomous women's activities, and male socialist perceptions of these issues (as well as of woman's place in society generally) inhibited the development of a recognized women's presence in the socialist movement. Male socialists encouraged women to join the movement, but their attitudes and policies towards women's issues effectively undermined women's participation. Viewed as wives, mothers, and daughters only, socialist women were able only exceptionally to challenge male dominance within the movement. Although individual socialist women won some respect and recognition, gender issues were to remain secondary. For ethnic women, language barriers and cultural expectations created further obstacles; even the outspoken Finnish women who came to Canada and joined the socialist movement were hindered in their attempts to become full-fledged, independent socialist women.

With the founding of the Socialist Party of Canada in late 1904, a new stage of Canadian socialism began. Unlike earlier Christian socialist groups, the SPC stressed the 'irrepressible conflict of interest between the capitalist and the worker ... culminating in a struggle for the possession of the reins of government.' Political action was of paramount importance, while industrial or trade union activities were downplayed. In economic terms the party stood for the 'transformation of capitalist property into the collective property of the working class,' management of industry by workers, and production for use rather than profit. The party pledged its office-holders to support only that legislation that benefited the working class. Dubbed 'impossibilists,' SPC members consistently stressed the need to overthrow capitalism through class-conscious propaganda and rejected 'immediate demands' as compromising this goal, a position which eventually led to discontent and the creation of new socialist parties. [2]

Between 1907 and 1911, several breakaway movements were launched, the first in Vancouver in 1907. The Social Democratic party of Vancouver (SDP) was created in that year after Ernest Burns and Bertha Merrill Burns were suspended from the SPC for arranging speaking engagements for Walter Thomas Mills, a 'reform socialist.' The Burns and sixty others left to form the new SDP. Bertha M. Burns had noted rising discontent within the SPC as early as summer 1906. In a letter to Britain's Mrs Ramsay MacDonald she wrote: 'Matters are going on in the same old way here, the Impossibilist element in full control, but there is a strong movement among the foreign comrades, led by the Finns, who outnumber the English speaking members of the SP of C, for a reconstruction of the constitution along more rational lines, and for a platform of Immediate Demands.' She wrote Mrs MacDonald the following year that the SPC had lost many of its former supporters to the new SDP; E.T. Kingsley, editor of the *Western Clarion*, was 'left with only a few ranters to support him – lip revolutionists but utterly incapable of any organized activity.' She also noted that the new party had 'a good percentage of women ... and we mean to so conduct it that we shall keep them there.' SPC antipathy to women's issues formed a significant part of the SPC's anti-reform policy. [3]

Toronto's Finnish socialists were also pressing for changes in the SPC. At the 1908 Ontario provincial convention of the SPC, the Finnish branch appointed a committee to draft a broader program. The Finns wanted practical measures included to accomplish political reforms. They proposed the inclusion in the program of universal suffrage without regard to sex, municipal ownership of land and utilities, municipal housing, a stand against contract work on government projects, and municipal responsibility for employing the unemployed. The convention vote split along ethnic lines and the Finns lost by one vote. [4]

In British Columbia the Finnish comrades had by this time set up a separate ethnic executive, which they defended as necessary within the SPC to strengthen ties among their compatriots and to carry out propaganda work. By spring 1909, Port Arthur (Ontario) Finns passed a resolution aimed at securing a party referendum on affiliation to the Second International, opposed by the Dominion executive of the SPC. A similar resolution was sent by the Toronto local. Winnipeg's ethnic socialists passed resolutions regretting the SPC's refusal to hold the vote and asked for a reconsideration and referendum of the SPC's membership to decide on the question. By the late summer of 1910, most of Winnipeg's Jewish, German, Ukrainian, and Latvian members had defected to the SDP, as did those in Ontario. In October 1910, Port Arthur Finns and others called for yet another referendum, but this time the purpose was to organize a new socialist party, the SDP.[5]

Among the English-speaking members in Ontario chaos and discontent also reigned. The Dominion Executive Committee's (DEC) refusal to affiliate with the Second International and its refusal to countenance a referendum led to the eventual revocation of the charter of Toronto Local Number 1 and the reorganization of the ethnic branches into separate locals. A new English-speaking Toronto local (Number 24) that sided with the DEC emerged and claimed jurisdiction over all the English-speaking comrades. The dissidents of Local Number 1 protested this move, the expulsion of around 200 comrades (146 Finns, 30 Jews, 22 English, 10 Italians) from the party, and the high-handed manner in which the DEC interfered in Ontario. The ousted members drafted a pamphlet to explain their position in late 1909; it suggested that the SPC was not growing because the most outspoken English-speaking members, now in Local 24, attacked religion, maligned the trade unions, insulted people, and talked wildly about guns. The prime culprit named was George Weston Wrigley, aided by two others.[6]

The Dominion executive dissolved the Provincial Executive Committee (PEC) in Ontario and the dissidents responded by organizing a convention in Toronto in May 1910 initiated by the Galt, Guelph, and Berlin members. This convention endorsed changes in the platform, instructing the national and provincial executives on when referenda must be held, and it passed another resolution asking for a vote on affiliation to the Second International. The Ontario dissidents called for a Dominion convention and chose Berlin as the new provincial headquarters. If the SPC as a whole refused to recognize this meeting, the dissidents resolved to continue to meet. At the 1911 convention, the independent socialist newspaper *Cotton's Weekly* noted the new spirit of 'hopeful enthusiasm and practical work' that contrasted sharply with the gloomy meetings of 1910. SPC intransigence in the face of demands for change resulted in the creation of a rival party by 1911–1912 – the SDP. The membership of the new party was dominated by the Finns, Ukrainians, Jews, and Poles, who were organized in language (ethnic) locals. English-speaking members were in the minority, but tended to assume leadership positions.[7]

The role of women's issues in these developments has been little commented upon. Issues such as woman suffrage and the place of autonomous women's groups within the SPC were never major preoccupations for male socialists, but these issues touched on the major difficulty between the SPC and the SDP – the place of immediate demands and practical reforms for the working class. Each issue reveals the major ambivalences felt by male socialists toward women in the movement and helps to explain why women's activities within the movement were largely confined to the supportive activities discussed below. Ethnic women, especially the Finns, were supportive of women's issues within the socialist movement, but they, too, experienced some difficulty in making their presence felt, even in their local communities; moreover, because of language barriers they were isolated from English-speaking women socialists as well.

WOMAN SUFFRAGE

In May 1911 the *Western Clarion* printed a letter from Lena Mortimer of Vancouver commenting on an overheard conversation after an SPC meeting on the 'woman question.' The men were heard to say, let the women remain home and leave the voting to the men, to which Mortimer replied, 'To me it was the same old yarn.' If we're fit to be mothers and the educators of children and to occupy a variety of positions in life, then we should be able to vote, she wrote. Mortimer reiterated what many working-class women felt on the suffrage issue – that the franchise would give the working-class woman recognition and the means to affect legislation pertinent to herself as a worker, a wife, and a mother. 'The vote is only a means,' wrote E.M. Epplett, a Toronto woman socialist. Dora Forster Kerr of British Columbia pointed to the absence of women in the legislature and the resulting injustices women suffered as mothers unable to obtain custody over their children; the vote was the first step toward justice for women. Despite these arguments, the SPC remained ambivalent toward the franchise for women, even in its early years when socialist MLA J.H. Hawthornthwaite introduced private member's bills to extend the vote to women. In 1906 Hawthornthwaite warned, however, that women would find that the franchise did not cure all ills and that economic independence was needed for real freedom. The second attempt, in 1909, prompted him to remark that the average woman was just as qualified as a man to vote, but that she was 'necessarily more conservative than man,' a remark that neatly summed up socialist anxieties about women. In response to a 1911 fund-raising letter from the middle-class BC Political Equality League (PEL), the *Western Clarion* sarcastically replied that it did not oppose the PEL women obtaining the vote, although it would be used against the working class; the latter knew only two kinds of people – masters and slaves – not men and women. Later in 1911, a woman member of the SPC reiterated this position after attending a PEL meeting: 'You claim that votes for women will change conditions under which women work! And yet you talk largely of upholding private property interests and dower laws ... the vote will not then seriously touch on the majority conditions of women. They, like the men, are the proletariat or property-less class ... to a Socialist there is no inequality between the sexes. Rather is the inequality in prevailing economic conditions.'

The SPC's negative attitude toward woman suffrage hardened after the creation of the SDP, its major rival; the latter's support for the enfranchisement of women confirmed the SPC's suspicions that the movement represented a reformist approach that would enable wealthy women to participate in a system which only oppressed the working class. As for the much-touted regeneration of society through women's virtues of compassion and love, SPC spokesmen denied that the vote would change capitalism, but rather only dress it up 'in the frills and laces of feminine sentimentality.' By aligning itself to reform, the suffrage movement supposedly proved its reactionary nature.[8]

Not all socialists agreed with this condemnation of the suffrage campaign. Within the SPC itself, some members supported woman suffrage, as did correspondents and writers to the independent socialist newspaper, *Cotton's Weekly*. Mary Cotton Wisdom, editor of the women's page in *Cotton's Weekly*, often supported the franchise as necessary for working-class women and rejected commonplace assumptions that the female franchise was unnecessary because women could influence men's votes. Echoing the suffrage movement's vision of women cleaning up and purifying politics, Wisdom associated the women's vote with improvements in legislation affecting women and children. More generally, however, women's political clout would assist in the repeal of legislation that condemned many to marginal existence because of laws favouring the propertied and wealthy. As a critic of government and as a 'real suffragette,' she admired the courage of British women militants in the movement, 'though I must admit they express their opinions a little forcibly at times.'[9]

Ethnic women, particularly the Finns, also supported suffrage almost as a matter of course, having won the vote in Finland in 1906; Finnish women were sometimes puzzled by the divided opinions within the socialist movement

on this question. Their highly visible presence in the SDP, along with
Ukrainians and Jews, confirmed support for suffrage because the SDP, in
general, also supported the female franchise in its platform and active SDP
women participated in suffrage meetings and organizations across the
country. Vancouver's SDP, for example, under the leadership of Bertha
Merrill Burns, sponsored meetings on the topic in the pre-war period. During
the war years, other SDP women also assisted in the suffrage campaign,
including Vancouver's Mary Norton who also belonged to the Political
Equality League, the Local Council of Women, and the Women's International League for Peace and Freedom (WILPF). The PEL, in particular, worked
for suffrage and drew in women of various political stripes; Norton recalled
that tensions between socialists and non-socialists in the PEL and the WILPF
caused some problems and Norton herself claimed that she never mentioned her
socialism to the PEL. Working women who identified with the suffrage
campaign were urged to join the BC Women's Suffrage League by labour leader
Helena Gutteridge, who also edited the women's column of the *BC Federationist*, organ of the BC Federation of Labor. Gutteridge found the PEL too
conservative and founded the suffrage league as an alternative that would also
deal with issues of concern to working women. These activities, she argued,
were supplementary and necessary to each other, if the economic freedom of
women was to be obtained. 'The economic value of the ballot is one of the
strongest arguments in favour of votes for women,' she concluded in 1913.
Despite Gutteridge's prominent role in the labour movement and particularly
in the Trades and Labor Council of Vancouver, the outbreak of war and male
workers' anxieties about the threat of cheap female labour undermined the
support for woman suffrage that had characterized pre-war labour meetings. [10]

In other major urban centres, the SDP gave support to the suffrage issue,
although in cities such as Winnipeg, the prominent spokeswomen of the
middle or upper-middle class tended to dominate. Winnipeg's PEL, formed in
1912, took up the cudgels for the franchise with the talents of women
journalists and writers such as Frances Marion Beynon and her sister Lillian
Beynon Thomas. As editor of the woman's page of the *Grain Growers' Guide*,
Frances Beynon utilized her column to muster support for a number of causes,
including woman suffrage. Beynon's Christian socialism linked her to the
reform community in Winnipeg, which included moderate socialists and
labour party activists such as Fred Dixon, R.A. Rigg, and Winona and Lynn
Flett, among others. The PEL actively supported Dixon's campaigns as an
independent progressive in 1914 and 1915 because of his pro-suffrage and
reform views, which included support for compulsory education, prohibition
of child labour, and efficient factory inspection. Winona Flett married

Dixon in the fall of 1914 and continued to campaign for Dixon, as well as supporting the suffrage and, later, women as political candidates in the Dominion Labor party. Dixon's arrest during the Winnipeg General Strike in 1919 also involved her in Defence Committee activities in 1919–20. Her sister Lynn became prominent in the Women's Labor League of Winnipeg in 1918 and 1919, eventually also serving as the league's representative on the Minimum Wage Board, created in 1918.[11]

Some Toronto socialists still in the SPC in 1909 also favoured woman suffrage, defending it as a weapon against capitalism in the hands of women workers. A resolution favouring suffrage was endorsed and the Socialist Women's Study Club co-operated with the Canadian Suffrage Association (CSA) in lobbying the Ontario government to extend the ballot to women on the same terms as men. The dissidents from the SPC who formed the SDP passed a resolution in December 1910 supporting amendments to Toronto's election by-laws that would permit any citizen, property owner or not, to run for civic offices and that included married women in the electorate. The latter resolution echoed demands made nearly twenty years previously in the *Labour Advocate* and by the Local Council of Women, both arguing in particular for women on school-boards and for the extension of the municipal franchise to married women. By 1909, the suffrage work of Flora MacDonald Denison in Toronto, particularly through her column in the *World*, had begun to bear fruit; the labour newspaper, the *Lance*, noted with approval the increased agitation for suffrage that repeated early arguments for woman suffrage on the basis of justice and representation of women taxpayers. By 1910 the Toronto suffrage movement had launched a campaign to interest working women in the movement, realizing the potential benefit of good relations with labour; by early 1914 the ties were strengthened as labour supported the woman suffrage referendum, led by Dr Margaret Gordon and Harriet Dunlop Prenter, to change the municipal by-laws to allow married women to vote. Despite the two to one majority in favour, the provincial legislature rejected a proposed bill on the topic in 1914. The labour movement continued to support the franchise issue throughout the war, sending representatives to meet with the government and using the pages of the *Industrial Banner* to promote labour support of woman suffrage. Labour's support for suffrage, however, was tinged with ambiguities at times; many viewed women through the lens of maternalism, expecting women to clean up politics and promote industrial reforms. At the same time as it touted the women's vote as a progressive force, the labour movement also viewed women workers as a threat to male workers because women were a source of cheap labour. These fundamental ambiguities undermined and weakened the links between the groups. As for co-operation between socialists and feminists, despite the resolutions in favour of woman suffrage, socialists were not the main actors in the suffrage campaign. The presence of support from the SDP and individual socialists, however, cannot be dismissed as insignificant, particularly at the grass-roots level. Social-democratic women in urban areas publicly supported woman suffrage as a basic democratic right. Toronto's Women's Social Democratic League, an autonomous organization with ties to the SDP, supported the female franchise, as did the Independent Labor party in Ontario. Montreal's SDP activist Mrs R.P. Mendelssohn defended socialist support for suffrage, noting that it was unrealistic to expect economic changes without the political participation of women voters. Mendelssohn also promoted the recently established Equal Suffrage League of Montreal as a positive step. At the local level, then, labour and socialist women consistently demonstrated their commitment to political as well as economic change for women.[12]

SEPARATE WOMEN'S ORGANIZATIONS AND ACTIVITIES

Socialists were also divided on the question of separate women's organizations and activities. Although the SDP accepted that various interest groups within the party would band together, the SPC treated such attempts with suspicion and hostility; the 1908 controversy over a women's column in the *Western Clarion* highlighted SPC difficulties with separate women's activities within the party. A request for a women's column in August prompted editor D.G. McKenzie to respond in such a way as to touch off a debate that encompassed not only the column, but also the role of women in the party itself. In response, the editor wrote: 'So far as women are concerned while we have a few women comrades, some of who are second to none and a leap or two ahead of most of the men, yet as a general rule, a woman who is a socialist is a socialist because some man is.' By mid September McKenzie had retreated, as women wrote in to denounce him. McKenzie referred the matter to E.T. Kingsley, former editor and financial supporter of the paper, claiming it was his decision to make. At the same time he bluntly stated his scepticism of female abilities to keep up with the pace of producing a regular column and warned against modelling any column on the bourgeois press. B.O. Robinson of Toronto condemned the editor for his 'narrow-minded egotism,' warning that male opposition and intolerance would defeat the ultimate goal of socialism, 'for women with the spirit of revolt aroused in them can never be encouraged to join such an obvious man's movement.' Robinson pointed out that socialist propaganda did not appeal to women, especially women workers; she further asserted that 'it is just as ridiculous to ignore their [women's] position as it would be, say that of the miners or any one particular line of industry.' Thereafter Robinson became involved in organizing a Socialist Women's Study Club in Toronto, which gave support to woman suffrage, as noted above. [13]

Edith Wrigley of Toronto connected male socialists' indifference to women's problems to women's lack of political power. Until women could vote for socialism, she argued, no energy would be expended by the SPC on women. Wrigley criticized socialist men because they did not encourage their wives and daughters to participate in SPC activities; the men never took them to meetings, nor did they pay their dues for them. Tackling McKenzie's assertion that women only joined the party because of their relationships with socialist men, Wrigley chided McKenzie: 'I have come in contact with women full of the spirit of revolt and very often it is not because some man is a socialist but because of some man she is working for.' She closed her letter with a plea for more equality and democracy in the socialist movement. [14]

Others wrote to the *Clarion* to protest as well. 'A Worker' suggested that socialist men stay home with the children and let their wives go to propaganda meetings. As a socialist woman, she challenged McKenzie's estimation of socialist womanhood and concluded: 'We want common sense and logical revolution but we want it to include the working woman's field.' Prominent SPCer George Weston Wrigley wrote in to urge a change in party attitudes toward women and noted that he had to recommend the United States publication, *Socialist Woman*, to the working-man's wife for lack of other alternatives. Men and women were needed in the party to make it 'a two-sex working class movement,' he added. Ada Clayton of Victoria, commenting on the correspondence over the women's column, noted that she, too, recommended the US publication to show the part women could play in the movement and urged women to send material to the *Clarion*. Clayton suggested that socialism had to address not only the needs of working women, but also the position of married women who received no wages and resented dependence on husbands' wages; she criticized socialist speakers who ignored this current of unrest among women by promising merely that men would be able to support their wives and families under socialism. [15]

While the SPC declined to act on the agitation for a women's column, the independent socialist newspaper *Cotton's Weekly* began a women's column in fall 1908 that continued to appear for nearly a year. Published in Cowansville, Quebec, by William U. Cotton, lawyer, prohibitionist, and Christian socialist intellectual, *Cotton's Weekly* remained independent until the war when it became the official organ of the SDP. Its women's column combined articles on domestic topics with commentaries on the roles of women at home and in the work force, and with appeals for socialism. Mary Cotton Wisdom wrote and edited much of the material and reprinted articles from US and European socialist newspapers. In one of her early pieces, Wisdom appealed 'To the Wives of Workingmen' to recognize the importance of understanding politics and the need for female activism if any change in women's position was to occur. Women no longer needed to follow the conservative idea that men should run their affairs: 'It is time for the women of the working class, and all women who sell their labour power, anyhow, anywhere, to rally to the sides of their fathers, of their brothers, of their husbands.' Her columns encouraged women to speak up for themselves as well as for their men, and they also documented social conditions under capitalism that she felt might be changed if women had the vote. In May 1909 she recommended that men change places with women for a few years. If women were the only enfranchised group, they would begin government house-cleaning immediately and concentrate on issues relating to the home, children, sanitation, housing, and property. In the spirit of Christian socialist and temperance advocate Frances Willard, Mary Cotton Wisdom stressed suffrage as integral to socialist and feminist activism.[16]

The attitude of *Cotton's Weekly* toward women sharply contrasted with that of the *Western Clarion*. Both newspapers, and the debates carried on in their pages, reflected the ferment over the 'woman question.' The years 1908–9 marked a crisis point for public discussion of women's roles within the socialist movement. The divisions over woman suffrage and the women's column were also part of a larger debate on the nature of the socialist movement. This debate was also furthered by the influx of ethnic groups into the ranks of the SPC; the visible participation of ethnic women in party activities raised the general isue of women's participation in socialist politics.

ETHNIC WOMEN IN THE SOCIALIST MOVEMENT

Women in the Jewish, Ukrainian, and Finnish communities played important, if heretofore little understood, roles in their ethnic socialist milieus. The activities of these women socialists remain largely undocumented, with the exception of the Finnish case. These women's important contributions, however, cannot be ignored; although the leadership figures of these various ethnic socialist groups were primarily male, activism among the women took shape in various forms: in drama groups, sewing circles, ethnic organizations, trade unions, study clubs, and in the male-dominated socialist parties. I discuss Ukrainian women's roles in the socialist movement to illustrate ethnic women's contributions to the radical socialist movement, turning then to the early career of Sophie Mushkat, a Polish-Russian Jew, to suggest the difficulties women organizers faced within the socialist movement.

The Ukrainian community in Canada was sharply divided along left/right political lines just as the Finns were. As Swyripa's article in this volume indicates, a segment of the Ukrainian community adhered to a conservative, nationalist ideology after the First World War that stressed women's roles as mothers to work to free Ukraine from Russian domination. A significant Ukrainian socialist movement also existed in Canada in the decade before the First World War and continued to exist during the war, albeit with considerable difficulty in the wake of repressive wartime measures against 'dangerous foreigners' suspected initially of support for the Austro-Hungarian Empire and later of bolshevism. Socialist politics among Ukrainians were dominated by men, who assumed the leadership positions; evidence remains, however, that Ukrainian women took active roles in their communities, some urging Ukrainian women to participate in the movement. Most Ukrainian settlement occurred in the west and it was here that women's activities were most visible in the pre-war period.[17]

Ukrainians first formed a branch of the SPC in Winnipeg (simultaneously with Portage La Prairie and Nanaimo) in 1907, where the first Ukrainian socialist newspaper appeared in November 1907 under the title *Chervony Prapor* (The Red Flag). The newspaper reported in December 1907 on an SPC meeting of the Winnipeg local dealing with municipal elections; the local stood for the eight-hour day, minimum-wage legislation, equal suffrage, and municipal ownership of electrical power. Support for women's rights, especially suffrage, appeared from time to time in Ukrainian papers. The arrest of members of Winnipeg's Local Number 2 prompted a public address by Antonia Jacks at a protest meeting in which she called on the working women of the city to help in the cause. A week later, in early January 1908, 'H. R-kivna' wrote in to rouse the Ukrainian women of Winnipeg to action, noting that about 500 Ukrainian women were employed in factories, laundries, and restaurant kitchens at poor wages. The answer, she wrote, did not lie in marriage and upward mobility through English husbands, but in working with Ukrainians and abandoning scornful attitudes toward Ukrainian men. Occasionally women from small towns, like Mariyka Osadchuk from Sarto, Manitoba, wrote to urge women to join in the movement. Larger centres like Winnipeg provided more evidence of a female presence: Hanna Stechyshyn (wife of Myroslav Stechyshyn) took on responsibilities in the Federation of Ukrainian Social Democrats (FUSD), on committees and on the advisory council of the Ukrainian Socialist Publishing Association.[18] Hanna also carried the red flag in Winnipeg's May Day parade in 1909. As new locals of the FUSD were organized, *Robochy Narod* (Working People) often reported on the sex composition of the new local, noting with approval the presence of women. The newspaper, in 1911, carried articles on prostitution, child-raising, and other issues that appealed to the female readership. The minimum-wage laws of Oregon provided an opportunity for the discussion of women's real work, that is house and children, and Ukrainian women were urged to join the SDP to protect the home. The lack of protection for women workers was also commented upon in the Ukrainian press, which urged organization to obtain better legislation. Thus, Ukrainian women were encouraged to become involved in politics, particularly socialist politics, in order to change oppressive conditions for women workers and to exert greater influence over those areas that affected home life.[19]

The connection between women's domestic roles and politics appeared in the Ukrainian press on the eve of the war. A number of writers linked child-rearing, cooking, and cleaning to larger political questions, such as the need for involvement in schools, municipal health, and even issues of national importance, such as tariff policies, because all such issues affected home life: 'The house isn't an island hidden away from the world, but a part of society.' Yavloha Pynduse, a young Montreal Ukrainian woman, wrote *Robochy Narod* in early 1914 stressing that the working class 'doesn't consist only of men, but of whole families ... they're all sufferers and they all need to fight for a better future.' Pynduse criticized a socialist movement without women because it lacked the rage, the emotion, and the family love that motivated the struggle for change: 'We women, we girls are those who pour the magic potion of courage into these fighters' hearts,' she wrote. Urging women to join social-democratic organizations, she claimed that it was 'the only organization which wants to free women from their right-wing, family, and our social enslavement.' Women who ignored the struggle became enemies of their class and of themselves; because women 'are stamped on by the capitalists a hundred times worse than men,' their place should be in the ranks of social democracy with men. This theme of indifference about the struggle also informed Anna Novakovska's 1914 letter to *Robochy Narod*. The letter contained a call to women workers to recognize their servitude and recognize the importance of their labour power as a source of strength. Novakovska urged women workers to stand on an even footing with male workers by abandoning religious reading to take up socialist and educational works, including *Robochy Narod*. Because women 'even play a bigger role in life than do men, ... we should prove we're really equal to men,' she wrote, adding: 'We'd have more respect.'[20]

Despite these urgings, women were not highly visible in the Ukrainian socialist movement at the leadership levels. Exact figures for female membership are lacking as well, although reports of newly organized locals suggest that women's involvement varied substantially from place to place.

Other activities undertaken by women remained largely invisible, although clearly there were supportive tasks that women performed. In April 1914, women in Winnipeg participated in the founding and running of an amateur theatre circle that presented plays on topics of working-class interest. Cultural activities were important features of ethnic working-class life and politics. Concerts, choral recitals, and theatrical performances reinforced group identity and also carried political messages to the audience. Anne Woywitka had described such cultural activities in Cardiff, Alberta, in the early war period, noting the important leadership given by Teklia Chaban, a miner's wife. Winnipeg's Ukrainian theatre no doubt served similar purposes in Ukrainian socialist circles; other ethnic groups such as the Finns and the Jews also organized cultural events in which women were very active participants.[21]

Women organizers were rare in the socialist movement; for ethnic women, language and cultural barriers proved to be formidable obstacles when added to gender ideology that placed central importance on the role of the working-class mother within her family. The role of itinerant organizer also did not mesh easily with women's domestic responsibilities. Despite these obstacles, a few ethnic women emerged as prominent organizers for the socialist movement. Lindstrom-Best discusses one such Finnish woman organizer in her article; Sanna Kannasto of Port Arthur organized for the Finnish socialist movement across Canada, but her efforts were largely confined to the Finns because of language barriers. Sophie Mushkat, a contemporary of Kannasto's, began her organizing career in the Maritimes, armed with both a fiery style and proficiency in several languages including English. Born in Warsaw, Poland (then part of Russia), Mushkat immigrated to Canada in 1903 or 1904, appearing on socialist platforms in Moncton and other nearby locations in 1909–10. She assisted SPC organizers and spoke on public platforms, expounding on temperance and prohibition, trade unionism and socialism to her audiences. Several times in 1910 she spoke in the strike-bound mining town of Springhill, Nova Scotia, earning her the title of 'Mother Jones of the Canadian Socialist movement.' In 1910, for unknown reasons, Mushkat left the Maritimes, travelled west, and eventually settled in Alberta, where she continued to organize for the SPC.[22]

For almost twenty years Sophie lived in the west, first going to Winnipeg, where she taught English to immigrants; by 1913 she had commenced an organizing tour for Alberta's SPC that covered the mining towns of southern Alberta and British Columbia. Between 28 April and 10 June 1913 she reported speaking at thirty-three English and ten 'Polish' meetings. That fall Mushkat spoke in the Fort William, Ontario, area before proceeding east to New Brunswick for a visit. By early 1914 she had returned to the west, touring northern and central Alberta in February, visiting settlements with a strong Russian composition. In farming areas, she attended fourteen meetings, speaking on the hardships of homesteading and the farmers' relationship to the working class. By fall 1914, Mushkat had settled in Calgary, earning her living as a teacher and acting as provincial secretary of the SPC. At this time she became involved in an organization of the unemployed that worked in conjunction with the Calgary Trades and Labor Council. The economic slump of 1913 continued in the early years of the war and unemployment increased in most urban areas. The Unemployed Committee in Calgary resembled similar committees formed elsewhere in the country, serving as an umbrella coalition for labour and social-reform groups intent on pressuring the various levels of government to provide work. Sophie represented the Unemployed Committee in November 1914 at a conference called to discuss the unemployment situation with business and government representatives. This conference passed resolutions that demanded that public-works projects and relief funds from the federal and provincial governments should be administered by the municipalities during the coming winter. Mushkat was vocal in her arguments that the federal government should levy taxes for relief, just as it did for war; the government needed recruits, she noted, inquiring 'where are you going to get them if you are going to starve them?' Mushkat continued to work as an SPC organizer, while teaching English to immigrants. On her Christmas holidays she travelled between Calgary and Edmonton speaking for the SPC; this pattern continued until August 1915, when the Dominion executive of the party confirmed the Alberta provincial executive's decision to expel Sophie for her part in the Alberta prohibition campaign. Her expulsion did not slow her down, because in September the *Western Clarion* reported on her activities in the mining towns of Hillcrest and Bellevue, organizing for the John Reid Defence Fund. Sophie's marriage to socialist William (Wallace) McClusky in January 1916 and their move to a homestead at Berry Creek diminished her activities, however, as did the birth of daughter Laberta. After the war, in the early 1920s, Sophie's activities for the SPC, the Workers' party, and later the unemployed brought her to the attention of the RCMP. From later RCMP reports, it appears that Sophie remained outspoken in her views, often alienating those who disagreed with her; a tenacious fighter for socialism, she maintained a critical relationship with the Communist party in later life.[23]

Mushkat's organizing experiences, the failure of her marriage, single parenthood, and her struggles to obtain employment illustrate the difficult circumstances faced by women socialists who pursued active roles. In

Mushkat's case, political involvement contributed to a strained relationship with her husband and, eventually, the disintegration of her marriage. These obstacles faced other women organizers as well; Sanna Kannasto's experiences were quite similar in the Finnish socialist community. For ethnic women, language and cultural barriers sometimes proved extremely limiting as well. For most women socialists the life-style of the peripatetic organizer clashed with both social expectations and the structures of women's roles.

WOMEN'S ACTIVITIES IN THE SPC AND SDP

Between 1904 and 1914, the major role for women socialists was a supportive one involving key activities that contributed to the growth of the movement. Fund raising and soliciting subscriptions to the socialist press occupied women in every party of the country; ethnic women's voluntary organizations often resorted to dramatic or musical performances, as well as sponsoring sewing circles and sales of women's crafts, to raise money. These techniques were also used by native-born and British women, and socialist women usually provided organizing skills and domestic talents for social events sponsored by the local socialist community. Whatever the general social events – dances, whist drives, summer picnics, or special celebrations to commemorate May Day, Labour Day, or the anniversary of the Paris Commune – women pitched in to help. Occasionally a social event was aimed specifically at recruiting more women comrades. Reports of socialist meetings often noted with approval the presence of 'ladies,' or pointed out new female members of the local. Visiting speakers, often from the United States, attracted both men and women, the latter responding particularly to the novelty of a woman orator. Well-known women socialists and social reformers such as Elizabeth Gurley Flynn, May Wood Simons, and Charlotte Perkins Gilman attracted women to meetings.[24]

Women organized study groups and reading circles in both parties to provide women with a basic socialist education, but also to discuss the position of women, past and present. Toronto's SPC women organized a Socialist Woman's Study Club in September 1908 that continued to meet until the next summer. E.M. Epplett spoke for the group in two letters outlining the work of the study group; in order to understand the position of women in capitalist society and their status in previous stages of development, the group began with Engels's *Origin of the Family, Private Property and the State*, later reading other socialist works. A dozen women attended regularly once a week, contributing funds to buy books. Epplett noted that 'as working women we have double chains to lose.' A similar undertaking occurred in Vancouver, and

Toronto's Women's Social Democratic League later sponsored a reading circle for its members.[25]

Toronto's SDP women were active participants in the creation of the organization; at the 1911 Ontario convention, three of thirty-two delegates were Toronto women. Edith Bellemare, former secretary of Toronto Local 1, SPC, had taken part in the debates of 1910 over the Dominion Executive Committee's action in expelling a large number of SPC members. Of Mrs Crawford, the second delegate, little is known. The third, Elizabeth Nesbitt, was associated with the Socialist Sunday School, which taught English, Jewish, Finnish, and Italian children to think critically about economics, science, history, and evolution. Another Socialist Sunday School activist, Elizabeth Crockett, contested several elections for the SDP. In late 1912 she ran for alderman on the Political Action Committee's ticket, a group composed of the SDP, the ILP and the Toronto TLC; in 1914, the SDP nominated Crockett for Board of Education in ward 1 and Florence Fraser in ward 5. The SDP, unlike the SPC, encouraged women to organize their own branches of the party, thus allowing women more scope to develop their own agendas. While Toronto women formed their own separate Women's Social Democratic League, in other cities and provinces women created female branches of the party; women's branches of the BC SDP were widespread enough to require a provincial secretary. In fall 1913, Bertha M. Burns was elected provincial secretary of the women's organizations and all locals were instructed to elect their women's organizations' committees. A 1914 publication of the SDP in British Columbia listed Mrs Helen Christopher of Victoria as the Provincial Women's Organization secretary, as well as Vancouver's Mrs Edmonds as the provincial secretary for the Young People's Socialist League. Ada Clayton and Bertha M. Burns were secretaries of the Victoria and Vancouver locals respectively in that year.[26]

Toronto's Women's Social Democratic League was formed in September 1914 to aid in propaganda and educational work among women in the socialist and labour movements. The executive included Edith Bellemare, Mrs May Young, and Mrs Lucy MacGregor; Young later ran in ward 4 for school trustee and MacGregor became involved in the Toronto Women's Labor League and helped organize women workers into unions. The league was officially launched in October with a speech by the Reverend W.E.S. James in which he outlined why the organization was necessary. Women were needed, he claimed, to be the wives, mothers, and sweethearts of socialists primarily, but they were also needed to organize and articulate working-class demands and to help realize the ideal of woman in the co-operative commonwealth. The league co-operated with James's Church of the Social Revolution, using its facilities for a reading circle; the group also maintained ties with the Christian Socialist Fellowship group in Toronto. Optimistically, the Toronto group envisioned itself as the nucleus for similar groups 'to be extended into every town and city in Ontario.' Writing in 1916, Gertrude Mance noted that the Toronto Women's Social Democratic League began with thirty members and was open to all progressive women because it was not a party branch. Debates sponsored by the group were not open to men, although lectures, socials, and fund-raising events were; the league's efforts cleared the party's debts in 1916 and a Christmas bazaar that same year provided funds for the party newspaper, the municipal election campaign fund, and various Jewish organizations, as well as for the league itself. The organization carried on a vigorous schedule of activities throughout the war and beyond.[27]

Socialist views of women and women's issues were coloured not only by the philosophies and programs of socialism, but also by widely accepted notions about biology, evolution, the family, and women's roles. While socialist writers acknowledged some of the inequalities and the exploitation experienced by women, their projections concerning a socialist transformation of society left the realm of reproduction improved, yet completely separate from the world of production. This fit well with the notion that dramatic changes in production would have to precede any alterations in the home or family.[28]

Even the notion of the equality of women with men proved problematic. Common to socialist writing about women, especially in the SPC, was the denial that women could be equal to men because of biology. An unsigned article on 'Sex Equality' in 1911 insisted that there is 'no foundation in fact to the sex equality upon which the feminists insist and no reality to the sex war as some of them proclaim.' The same writer stated baldly that women made slow progress not only because of their upbringing and environment, but also because of 'the deeper reason of their biological femaleness,' which condemned them to passivity and conservatism. Although emancipation from wage slavery would probably benefit women more than men, W.W. Lefeaux wrote, because of training and acquiescent nature, women would be slower to grasp change. For Lefeaux, women might accept the benefits of a new social order once they understood it, but certainly would not lead the fight for such change. These biological and evolutionary views permeated the socialist movement, affecting socialist attitudes not only towards woman suffrage and women's autonomous organizations, but also towards women's work in the home and in the labour force.[29]

According to the socialist view, women and children were driven from the home into the labour market because the male wage-earner could not support the family. The need for several incomes to maintain the family allowed capitalists to lower wages and thus women and children competed in the labour market with men. Socialists repeated this theme over and over again in defending their beliefs against charges of 'free love' – that capitalism and not socialism was destroying the family by making female and child labour necessary; wages were thus lowered to the point where marriage for many men and women remained an impossibility. In reply to the often-asked question concerning the position of women under socialism, writers in the socialist press stressed that women would be economically independent in a socialist system and that this independence would alter the relations between men and women, thus raising women to the status of comrade and equal partner. But the socialist application of economic independence for women apparently varied according to marital status and whether or not a woman had children. Family responsibilities were pre-eminent in the case of married women. [30]

While some socialists defended married women's paid work as integral to her independence, most commentators stressed the evils of married women's work and child labour and accepted the family wage ideal, that is, the male bread-winner's primary responsibility to provide for all members of the family. 'Gourock,' for example, stated this position most clearly in 1908: 'Socialists don't believe in mothers working at all. They hold that under a sage industrial system wherein the worker would obtain the full value of his products, the man could earn sufficient to raise and maintain his family under proper conditions and that various exigencies which may arise, such as sickness and accident, be provided against by the community.' Another writer promised that 'your wife will no longer have to leave the baby at the creche on her way to the factory.' While some allowed women a choice in the matter, the expectation was clear that married women would not choose to work. Given the conditions and wages for women in pre-war Canada, the socialist position is understandable; the emphasis on marriage, motherhood, and the family wage, however, served to restrict female potential. Motherhood was presented as woman's true vocation, and freedom of choice as to marriage partner emerged as the socialist conception of women's future economic independence. Women need not marry for bread, as they did under capitalism; once women were economically independent they would marry on the basis of love and free choice and 'Let the Best Men Win!' [31]

In the socialist future, maternity would be elevated to its proper place and the state would provide the best possible care. A number of writers speculated that married women would cease to be drudges once municipal or state-run laundries, bakeries, kitchens, and kindergartens were in place. Mary Cotton Wisdom noted the double burden of working-class women: while the men were agitating for the eight-hour day, their wives often put in sixteen-hour days and had to deal with the needs of infants in the evenings. She urged men to pitch in and help their wives and she described socialism as meaning honour for mothers and a lightening of their work-load. A clerical advocate of socialism described the true home under socialism in terms of 'love ... innocent childhood ... work enough ... leisure for reading and study and recreation ... all the comforts and none of its harmful luxuries.' The ideal socialist home and family also included children, brought up with collective values and freed from the necessity to labour.[32]

From these views, it followed that socialist concern with the plight of single working women was secondary and fraught with ambivalence. On the one hand, such women represented a threat to men's jobs, yet, on the other hand, the expectation that single working women would marry and leave the labour market provided some comfort and undermined attempts to organize these women. Labour and socialist women, however, although divided on the question of married women's work, sought to organize working women, realizing that union representation might benefit the primarily young single women who worked in factories, shops, laundries, and offices for low wages. These women and some male supporters viewed unions as one means of political education and economic protection. Women's labour leagues, employment organizations, and other groups were formed to address the needs of working women, complementing efforts at industrial organization. The longer story of their efforts, however, comprises a separate chapter in the history of labour and socialist women.

Between 1904 and 1914 the socialist movement grew and altered its shape, spawning two major parties, with clear-cut differences of approach. The SPC basically hardened its impossibilist position on issues that it viewed as 'reformist.' The SDP, in contrast, identified itself with British and European social democracy, from which many of its members originated, and constructed a platform and party structure more favourable to the inclusion of issues such as suffrage, trade unionism, legislative change, and other ameliorative reforms. While the SDP's structure allowed for some input from special-interest groups – whether that of ethnic groups, youth, or women – the SDP (like the SPC) placed primary emphasis on the overthrow of capitalism. Although the SDP allowed more scope for women's autonomous groups and opinions than did the SPC, women's issues were still subordinate to the larger struggle, rather than integral to it. Thus, although both major socialist parties could boast of outspoken women speakers and organizers, the material and ideological paradigm within which women operated provided limited support for their activities and underutilized their potential. Some women drew attention to the necessity of making socialist organizations responsive to the needs of women, but they had varying degrees of success. They did so to advance the women's cause, but also because they appreciated the need for a 'two-sex movement.' They realized that a socialist movement that ignored the problems and potentials of women was a flawed socialism at best.

NOTES

Thanks are due to Bohdana Dutka of Winnipeg and Orest T. Martynowych of Edmonton for translation from Ukrainian to English and for research assistance.

1 For material on the earlier period, readers can consult my earlier 'Canadian Socialism and the "Woman Question," 1900–1914,' *Labour/Le Travail* 13 (Spring 1984), 77–100 and works cited therein.

2 See Carlos A. Schwantes, *Radical Heritage: Labor, Socialism and Reform in Washington and British Columbia, 1885–1917* (Seattle 1979), 109.

3 Schwantes, *Radical Heritage*, 180; Bertha M. Burns to Mrs Ramsay MacDonald, 26 July 1906 and 29 April 1907, J.R. MacDonald Papers, National Archives of Canada (NA), Ottawa. The *Western Clarion* (WC) was the SPC's newspaper.

4 WC, 26 September 1908; the vote was 18 to 17.

5 WC, 29 August 1908; *Cotton's Weekly* (hereafter CW, Cowansville, Quebec), 27 May 1909; WC, 17 July 1909, 7 August 1909; CW 26 August 1909, 2 September 1909, 20 August 1910, 29 October 1910.

6 WC, 30 October 1909, 6 August 1910. The pamphlet 'Facts for Ontario Socialists,' was reprinted in WC, 22 January 1910. Wrigley was a prominent SPC organizer from Toronto.

7 See WC, 9 April 1910, for Local 24's resolution to dissolve Ontario's PEC; see also 22 April 1910. The 1910 Ontario convention proceedings are reported in WC, 19 June 1910, and CW, 16 June 1910. By August 1910, Local Berlin's charter was revoked by the Dominion executive; see WC, 6 August 1910. For the 1911 Ontario convention, see CW, 4 May 1911. Still using the name Socialist Party (of Ontario), the dissidents reported a membership of 20 locals with 625 dues-paying members. H. Martin of Berlin was the new provincial secretary (CW, 9 February 1911). A smaller breakaway group, the Socialist Party of North America (SPNA), emerged in the winter of 1910–11. Some of its members eventually helped form the Worker's party, later the Communist party of Canada.

8 WC, 27 May 1911; CW, 8 April 1909, 22 April 1909. On Hawthornthwaite, see WC, 20 January 1906, 1; 10 February 1906, 1–3; 7 July 1906, 4; 20

March 1909. See *WC*, 22 April 1911 for the response to the PEL. 'A Lady's View' appears in *WC*, 2 December 1911.

9 *CW*, 25 February 1909, 1 April 1909, 23 September 1909.

10 See K. Marianne Wargelin Brown, 'Trailblazers in Finland for Women's Rights: A Brief History of Feminism in Finland,' in Carl Ross and K. Marianne Wargelin Brown, eds, *Women Who Dared: The History of Finnish American Women* (St Paul, MN, 1986), 11; *CW*, 14 November 1912 (public meeting on votes for women held by the Vancouver SDP); on Mary Norton, see 'Great-grandma Still Does Battle,' Vancouver *Sun*, 24 November 1969, 23, and Mary Norton interview transcript, 21 February 1973, 141–1, Provincial Archives of British Columbia, Victoria. On Helena Gutteridge, see Susan Wade, 'Helena Gutteridge: Votes for Women and Trade Unions,' in Barbara Latham and Cathy Kess, eds, *In Her Own Right: Selected Essays on Women's History in BC* (Victoria 1981, 2nd printing), 187–203 and 'Helena Gutteridge's story,' *Pacific Tribune* (Vancouver), 8 March 1957, 11–12; see also Gutteridge's column, 'Woman Suffrage,' *BC Federationist*, 1914–15. The column disappeared in 1915, as did discussion of the suffrage issue from the newspaper.

11 On the Winnipeg SDP's support for equal suffrage, see *Voice* (Winnipeg), 21 September 1917, 8. On the PEL, see Catherine Cleverdon, *The Woman Suffrage Movement in Canada*, 2nd ed. (Toronto 1974), 55–6; Political Equality League, Minute Books, 1912–14, Provincial Archives of Manitoba (Winnipeg). On Dixon's 1914 and 1915 campaigns, see various issues of the *Voice*, including 6 March 1914, 8 (platform). Nellie McClung campaigned vigorously for Dixon as well; see, for example, *Voice*, 24 April 1914, 1. For Winona Flett's marriage and a brief biography, see *Voice*, 14 and 16 October, 1914, 8. Dixon's election reported in *Voice*, 17 July 1914, 1. On Frances Marion Beynon, see Barbara Roberts, *'Why Do Women Do Nothing to End War?': Canadian Feminist-Pacifists and the Great War*, CRIAW Paper no. 13 (1985). On Dixon, see also Allen Mills, 'Single Tax, Socialism and the Independent Labour Party of Manitoba: The Political Ideas of F.J. Dixon and S.J. Farmer,' *Labour/Le Travailleur* 5 (Spring 1980), 33–56.

12 On Toronto's SPC, see *WC*, 3 April 1909; *CW*, 29 December 1910. Early comments supporting suffrage can be found in the *Labor Advocate* [LA] (Toronto) 2 January 1891, 36; 16 January 1891, 52; 17 April 1891, 156; 24 April 1891, 166. For LCW resolution, see *LA*, 6 February 1891, 77. On Denison, see Deborah Gorham, 'Flora MacDonald Denison: Canadian Feminist,' in L. Kealey, *A Not Unreasonable Claim: Women and Reform in Canada, 1880s–1920s* (Toronto 1979), 47–70, and especially 57 for Denison's role as columnist for the Toronto *World*; see also Wayne Roberts, "Rocking the Cradle of the World": The New Woman and Maternal Feminism, Toronto

1877–1914,' in Kealey, *A Not Unreasonable Claim*, 24, 37. The *Lance* (Toronto), 30 October 1909, 1, noted coverage of increasing suffrage agitation in the *World*; the *Voice*, 3 June 1910, 12, noted that suffragists in Toronto were becoming interested in organizing women workers; 'some of the leaders are very friendly to organize labour,' noted the *Voice*, 28 October 1910, 3. The 1914 referendum is covered in *Industrial Banner* [*IB*], 2 January 1914, 1; 9 January 1914, 1; and 16 January 1914, 4. James Simpson presented labour's case for woman suffrage at a meeting with the government; see *IB*, 4 February 1916, 6. On WSDL support for the franchise, see *IB*, 18 December 1914, 6; and 2 March 1917, 4. For early ILP support of suffrage, see *Lance*, 10 June 1911, 3; 16 September 1911, 3. On Mendelssohn see *CW*, 9 January 1913, 3.

13 *WC*, 22 August 1908, 12 September 1908.

14 *WC*, 12 September 1908.

15 *WC*, 12 and 28 September 1908. *Socialist Woman* was begun by Josephine Conger-Kaneko in 1907 and changed its name to *Progressive Woman* in 1909; see Mari Jo Buhle, *Women and American Socialism 1870–1920* (Urbana 1981), 148.

16 *Cotton's Weekly* [*CW*] began as the *Observer* on 17 September 1908. The name was changed in December and the paper shifted from local news to the discussion of ideas. In the issue dated 21 January 1909, Cotton described the editor and manager of the paper as members of the SPC. See *Observer*, 17 September 1908; *CW*, 3 December 1908, 27 May 1909. For a more detailed look at Wisdom's column, see Janice Newton, 'Women and *Cotton's Weekly*: A Study of Women and Socialism in Canada, 1909,' paper presented to the Annual Meeting of the Canadian Research Institute for the Advancement of Women, Edmonton 1980. *CW* was succeeded by the *Canadian Forward* [*CF*], organ of the SDP in the early years of the war.

17 Peter Krawchuk, *The Ukrainian Socialist Movement in Canada (1907–1918)* (Toronto 1979), gives an overview of the movement and discusses centres of activity; see also Frances Swyripa, 'Outside the Bloc Settlement: Ukrainian Women in Ontario during the Formative Years of Community Consciousness,' in Jean Burnet, ed., *Looking into My Sister's Eyes: An Exploration in Women's History* (Toronto 1986), 155–78, especially 157. Swyripa notes that, even as late as 1931, the Prairies claimed 85.7 per cent of Canada's Ukrainians.

18 *Chervony Prapor* (Red Flag), 12 December 1907, 26 December 1907; on suffrage, see *CP*, 6 February 1908. *CP* folded after 18 issues in 1908; in 1909, *Robochy Narod* (Working People) began to publish from Winnipeg, lasting until 1918. The letter from 'H. R-kivna' appeared in *CP*, 5 January 1908; Osadchuk's letter appeared in *CP*, 13 February 1908. Stechyshyn's activities are noted in Krawchuk, *Ukrainian Socialist Movement*, 11, and in *Robochy Narod*, 2 June 1909 and 9 February 1910. The FUSD was formed in 1909 in response to

discontent with the SPC and to unite all Ukrainian socialists under one umbrella. Myroslav Stechyshyn was the editor of *Robochy Narod* and became secretary of the general executive of the FUSD in 1910 (see Krawchuk, *Ukrainian Socialist Movement* 13–19. The FUSD joined the SDP of Canada in 1910 while a rival organization, the Federation of Ukrainian Socialists, aligned with the SPC.

19 Membership figures with sex breakdown appear in various issues of *Robochy Narod* from 1912 on: see 1 March 1911 on morality, 1 May 1911 on children, 15 October 1913 and 10 December 1913 on minimum wage laws and protective legislation.

20 Ibid., 22 January 1914, 22 January 1914.

21 Women members of the FUSD in Ontario and Quebec benefited from a lower membership fee after the 31 January convention; because women earned less, their fees were half the men's; see *Robochy Narod*, 11 February 1914, 28 January 1914. See also Anne B. Woywitka, 'A Pioneer Woman in the Labour Movement,' *Alberta History* 26:1 (Winter 1978), 10–16.

22 Biographical information on Sophie Mushkat comes from the socialist press and the Canadian Security Intelligence Service, RCMP Personal History files, Sophie Lindsay (McClusky), 1921–68. Sophie married twice, the first time William (Wallace) McClusky in 1916, and the second time in 1944 in Halifax, where she died in 1954. See also Linda Kealey, 'Sophie,' *New Maritimes* 6:3 (November 1987), 12–13. Her CSIS file lists two conflicting immigration dates, one in 1903 and another in 1904. Although not a Ukrainian, Sophie sometimes spoke to Ukrainian audiences (see *Robochy Narod*, 21 April 1915).

23 Mushkat's presence is recorded at a Winnipeg WLL meeting in 1910; on her activities in Alberta, see *WC*, 5 April 1913, 15 March 1913 (report of the Alberta executive of the SPC for 1912 states there are 21 locals and 362 members); 2 August 1913, 27 September 1913, 11 October 1913, 28 February 1914, 11 April 1914, 10 October 1914. *CW*, 11 and 25 September 1913 note her speeches in New Brunswick in late August and September. Information on the unemployment conference is found in PAA (Edmonton) Warren Caragata collection, 80.218, 59, box 2. On 1915, see *WC*, 16 and 30 January 1915, 1 March 1915, July–August 1915, and September 1915. John Reid, SPC candidate for Red Deer, was arrested in summer 1915 for sedition. See *WC*, February 1916 for a report of his sentencing to 15 months. Sophie's marriage is mentioned in her personal history file, p. 92, Oscar Coderre to the Commissioner, RCMP, 19 September 1933. For her activities in the early 1920s, see the personal history file, pp. 1–32, January–November 1921; on her unemployed activities in the 1920s, see GAI (Calgary), 'McClusky, Sophie,' clipping files. These clippings also reveal that sometime in the 1920s Sophie separated from McClusky.

24 See, for example, issues of *WC* and *CW* between 1909 and 1914 for
mention of women subscription hustlers; some, like Mrs M.A.
Owen of Fernie, BC, sent in scores of subscriptions. For social events, see, for
example, *WC*, 18 June 1904, 21 October 1905, 27 January 1906, 15 February
1908, 9 May 1908, 20 February 1909. Visiting lecturers included C.P. Gilman
(*WC*, 24 June 1905), May Wood Simons (*WC*, 30 September 1905, 23 May
1908, and *CW*, 26 January 1911), Lena Morrow Lewis (*WC*, 18 and 25 November 1905), Irene Smith (*WC*, 3 February 1906), Elizabeth Gurley Flynn (*WC*, 24
April 1909). British women leaders, such as Sylvia Pankhurst, sometimes visited
Canada, too.

25 On the study club, see *CW*, 4 February 1909 and *WC*, 20 February 1909; see also
B.O. Robinson's letter on the study club in *WC*, 15 May 1909. Whether the
Vancouver study group materialized is not clear; see *WC*, 29 August 1908 for a
mention of the planned study group.

26 *CW*, 4 May 1911; see Nesbitt's report in the *International Socialist Review* 12
(1911–12), 884; for Crockett, see *Globe* (Toronto), 28 November 1912;
CW, 26 November 1914; on BC, see *CW*, 6 November 1913; *The Social Democrat*
(Victoria), 1914 fragment provides a directory with names of secretaries.
Winnipeg also had a women's branch of the SDP, which is mentioned in *Canadian
Forward* (formerly *Cotton's Weekly*), 27 December 1916; when it was founded is
not clear.

27 *IB*, 11 September 1914, 5; 2 October 1914, 4; *CW*, 15 October 1914 (James'
speech); *IB*, 6 August 1915, 7; 28 May 1915, 7; quote from *CW*, 12 November 1914, 3; *CF*, 28 October 1916, 8; *IB*, 1 December 1916, 7.

28 Socialist ideas about women's roles were derived from the writings of Marx,
Engels, and Bebel, who recognized that women were subordinate in nineteenth-
century society and found the origin of this inequality at that point in history
when private property and the monogamous family appeared and 'mother-
right' ended. The emancipation of women thus depended on the destruction of
private property and the disappearance of traditional marriage and the family
that could only occur within a socialist revolution. In general the 'woman
question' was viewed as secondary to the general problem of overthrowing
capitalism.

29 'Sex Equality,' *WC*, August, 1911, 17–20; for Lefeaux, see W.W.L., 'Morality,'
WC, July 1911, 40–4. At this time *WC* published only monthly.

30 *WC*, 4 November 1905; *CW*, 17 June 1909, 1 July 1909, 23 September 1909.
Comments on married women's freedom to choose a partner appear in *WC*, 14
December 1907, 26 December 1908, 19 April 1913; *CW*, 11 February 1909, 8
April 1909, 30 June 1910, 13 November 1913.

31 For a fuller discussion, see L. Kealey, 'Canadian Socialism and the "Woman

Question.'" On the family wage, see Michele Barrett and Mary McIntosh, 'The "Family Wage": Some Problems for Socialists and Feminists,' *Capital and Class* 11 (1980), 51–72 and Michele Barrett, *Women's Oppression Today* (London 1980); *WC*, 26 December 1908; *CW*, 17 June 1909; *WC*, 14 December 1907 and 19 April 1913; *CW*, 11 February 1909, 30 June 1910, and 19 January 1911.

32 *CW*, 19 January 1911, 4 May 1911; *WC*, 13 January 1906; *CW*, 13 May 1909, 11 November 1909, 3 April 1913.

Finnish Socialist Women
in Canada

1890–1930

Varpu Lindström-Best

I never thought I was a radical. I have just always supported the worker's movement. But then one day the mounties came and searched through my house, took my books, even went through my letters and called me a 'damn red.' The same year my husband got blacklisted from the mine. That's when I realized that in this country the workers who tried to help each other were radicals. I have been proud to be called a radical ever since. [1]

To this disgruntled immigrant woman, radicalism was a relative term. She came from Finland, where the socialist movement had spread rapidly around the turn of the century until it became numerically the largest political force in the country and, proportionately, the strongest socialist party in the world. To her, workers' activism was a necessary part of political life, not an aberration to be punished by the invasion of her privacy and unemployment. Significantly, all Finns, men and women, had gained full political rights, including suffrage, in 1906. In 1907 Finnish women were the first in the world to hold public office when nineteen women were elected to the parliament, nine of whom were Social Democrats; as well, workers' involvement in politics was by then an established fact in Finland. [2]

In Canada, however, the political mood was less favourable to both women and workers. Yet, as the most recent research into the history of women's political participation in Canada indicates, some groups of working-class women were deeply involved in social and political debates. Many of these were immigrant women from a variety of different cultures, often working in relative isolation because culture and language posed restrictions on their ability to communicate. The same restrictions later hampered historians eager to discover more information about their valuable and often vigorous activities.

Among the most enthusiastic supporters of the socialist and later communist movements in Canada were many Finnish women whose political activism has evoked some interest among North American scholars. Joan Sangster has noted that in the 1920s Finnish women were 'extremely active' in the Women's Labor Leagues and that their 'consistent activism ... in auxiliary socialist and union organizations was impressive.'[3] Linda Kealey agreed that these women were 'particularly prominent in North American socialism.'[4] Finnish women have received the most glowing accolades thus far from Mari Jo Buhle, who claimed that the achievements of the Finnish women were so impressive that other socialist women would 'frankly consider [them] utopian.'[5]

Despite the Finnish women's enthusiastic activism and heightened sense of class consciousness, they seemed to have remained largely separate from their Canadian sisters, failing to produce strong national leaders beyond their own communities, and thus limiting their influence on the Canadian socialist women's movement. In order to explain this anomaly it is necessary to probe deeper inside the Finnish-Canadian communities and to try to view the Finnish immigrant women's brand of socialism through their own eyes and actions. In doing so, we should remember that Finnish radical women, like their Canadian socialist sisters, were not free of the patriarchal traditions or the influence of the capitalist labour market. Despite their few personal victories, they also suffered severe and often painful set-backs within their own community leadership and the larger Canadian radical movement.

Because the history of Finnish-Canadian radicalism has been documented by several scholars,[6] this paper concentrates only on women's activity within the Finnish-Canadian left-wing communities and organizations, and their attempts at co-operation with non-Finnish socialist women. In the process it will also examine the role of sex, culture, and class in the political life of the Finnish immigrant women in Canada prior to 1930. First, however, I sketch the geographic and demographic patterns of Finnish women in Canada, as well as present some background on the nature of Finnish socialism. This information partially explains the 'exceptional' radicalism of Finnish immigrant women in Canada.

GEOGRAPHIC AND DEMOGRAPHIC PATTERNS OF FINNISH FEMALE SETTLEMENT IN CANADA

The first Finnish women arrived in Canada during the last quarter of the nineteenth century. Many of these women were married and came here with their husbands from the United States or, later, directly from Finland. They settled in the resource areas of British Columbia and northern Ontario, and by the turn of the century accounted for about a quarter of the Finnish population in Canada.[7] Some of these resourceful pioneering women settled in the coal-mining districts of Vancouver Island, in the lumber and mining towns of Fort William, Port Arthur (Thunder Bay), Sault Ste Marie, and Copper Cliff, and – after the turn of the century – in Sudbury, Timmins, Kirkland Lake, and most other smaller northern Ontario settlements. As a rule, Finnish women were reluctant to settle in the prairies, although they were to be found in New Finland, Saskatchewan, in the mining towns of Alberta, and in some smaller farming communities near Red Deer.[8] By 1929, however, newly arriving Finnish immigrants were exceptional in their near-total rejection of the prairie-farming alternative. Instead, in that year, 88 per cent of the Finns were planning to settle in Ontario or Quebec.[9]

Increasingly, Finnish women began to exhibit an independent settlement pattern from Finnish men; they chose to live in the larger urban centres of Toronto and Montreal, where they were able to secure work as domestic servants. In 1931, 42 per cent of Finns in Canada were female, but in Toronto women made up 60 per cent of the Finnish population and on Montreal Island, 54 per cent. The distinctive choice of women's settlement is clearest in Montreal's Outremont and Westmount districts, where 96 and 94 per cent of the Finns were women. Thus, unlike in many other immigrant communities where there existed a severe shortage of females, in some Finnish communities women were actually in the majority, particularly in the age range of 20 to 29.[10]

It is also important to note that thousands of Finnish women were found on the edges of Canadian civilization, in the densest of forests and the bleakest of mining towns. In these communities, where class divisions were clearly visible and where the vulnerability of immigrant workers was painfully evident, women were a minority.

One reason why Finnish immigrant women were able to make independent decisions about where to live and work can be traced to their age, marital status, and time of migration. Census statistics reveal that the majority of Finnish women in Canada were recent, mature immigrants, who had very small families. In fact, for every Finnish woman in Canada between the ages of 20 and 44, there were only 1.2 children, half the Canadian national average and less than one-quarter of many southern- or eastern-European immigrant groups.[11] Finnish women were drastically limiting their families, thus distinguishing themselves from most other immigrant women in Canada. Small families (or no families at all) gave women not only the freedom to work, but also the time to conduct other activities outside the home.

Because so many of the women were recent immigrants who had made their own choice to leave Finland, the cultural and political life of that country was still fresh in their minds. The surge of socialism that had penetrated all corners of Finland and, in 1918, had culminated in a bitter civil war between the 'reds' and the 'whites' had educated and involved many of the immigrant women. The Social Democratic party strongly promoted the political equality of women, the organization of women into unions, the establishment of a women's socialist press, and better educational opportunities for women. It is also important that, with few exceptions, all Finnish women were literate and had received at least a basic education. The platform of the Finnish Social Democratic party before the civil war was strictly Marxist, and was especially critical of the state Lutheran church to which nearly all the Finns belonged. As a result, a more moderate Christian socialist tradition, so popular in many other European countries, never gained a strong foothold in Finland. Hence, Finnish radicalism was tinged with strong anti-church sentiments.

Socialist programs in Finland place a heavy emphasis on community activity and aimed for the total involvement of Finnish workers. Socialist temperance organizations, theatre groups, sports clubs, community halls, newspapers, and youth organizations complimented the more rigorous political organizing of the socialists. Women were involved in all aspects of socialist activity, often forming separate women's branches, sewing circles, education leagues, maid's unions, and newspapers, all of which were in direct competition with the religious or bourgeois women's groups. When the 'reds' lost the civil war in Finland in 1918, many of the disappointed socialist women moved to Canada, bringing with them a clear sense of class consciousness, journalistic and organizational skills, and bitter memories of the wartime atrocities.[12]

It is important to point out, however, that immigration from Finland was mainly from the western coastal area of Ostrobothnia, which was well known for its conservatism. Thus, it would not be accurate to assume that all Finnish-Canadian radical women had landed with their progressive world-view intact. The immigrant women's working and living conditions in Canada and the influence of the established Finnish communities produced new converts to socialism.

FINNISH-CANADIAN WOMEN AND THE SOCIALIST DEBATE BEFORE 1908

The earliest recorded organized activity among Finnish socialist women is found in the temperance society Aallotar minute books in North Wellington, British Columbia. Here the coal-miners' wives, the dishwashers, cleaning women, and cooks of the rooming-houses were concerned with the dangerous working conditions in the mines, the abuse of alcohol in their communities, and the lack of any alternative social activity to taverns. As early as 1894 the first rumblings of socialist discontent were recorded, and by 1896 Finnish women joined the men in protest marches. Within the temperance society the women functioned mainly as an auxiliary, raising funds for the construction of a hall, for the purchase of musical instruments for the brass band, and for ordering books, magazines, and newspapers from Finland. Because the Finnish immigrant workers in the mining communities of North Wellington, Extension, Nanaimo, and Ladysmith, British Columbia, felt vulnerable in the face of sickness, injury, or sudden death, they established a mutual health plan, an insurance that would give the sick enough money to survive, provide him or her with 'nursing,' or – in the worst cases – take care of the funeral costs. Needless to say, much of the 'nursing' was a task for the women.[13]

The leaders of the first group of socialist Finns in Canada were mainly men, usually class-conscious coal-miners. Women were not elected to leadership positions, but they did participate in the executive where they were relegated to the most arduous tasks. They were also vocal in the many socialist lectures and debates held at the temperance hall. They contributed generously not only to their own organization but also to socialist causes and strike victims in both Finland and the United States well before the Socialist Party of British Columbia was ever founded. These socialist women clung to each other for moral support, fined themselves for breaking the temperance pledge, lectured endlessly on the importance of self-help and learning, and tried to organize enjoyable social events.[14]

Similar socialist women's groups, whose prime objective was to assist the men, soon developed in all larger Finnish-Canadian communities. Common to all these groups prior to the 1920s was the important role of women as fund-raisers. This, however, was not the only activity for the sewing circles – established in many Finnish communities at the beginning of this century – took on an educational role for independent women. Finnish women quickly realized that if they were to be full participants in the community organizations, capable agitators for the socialist cause, and able to influence other women, they had first to be knowledgeable about the socialist issues themselves. Moreover, in order to express themselves in public and in writing, they had to overcome their lack of self-confidence, inexperience in procedures of meetings and fear of voicing opinions in public. Some women battled hard against their own sense of inferiority. As one Toronto woman recalls: 'I had made up my mind to speak, in my thoughts at home I had practiced over and over again what I would say, how I would say it. I went to the meeting determined that this was going to be the night. 'Any questions?" I heard the chairman ask. My heart started racing, beads of perspiration gathered on my forehead, and then a big lump gripped my throat. Not a sound did I utter ... next time, maybe next time.'[15]

In Toronto, the Finns had gathered around the Finnish Society as early as 1902 and started their own handwritten newspaper called *Toivo* (Hope). Between 1902 and 1904 this 'fist paper,' as the Finns called their modest publishing effort, featured several articles on 'women and socialism.' Most of these seemed to be written by Frans Syrjälä, an eloquent Finnish socialist leader in Toronto who borrowed heavily from August Bebel and used the pen-name 'Shadow' (*Varjo*). The paper argued that women had to use their own initiative to gain equality with men, showing by their work and behaviour that they were able to fulfil the responsibilities that come with equal rights. A few issues later, 'Shadow' continued his rather paternalistic lecturing: 'It is the responsibility of every single woman, be they housewives or just girls, to obtain knowledge ... It is true that men have noticed how beneficial it is for them to keep women in some kind of state of dependency. The modern enlightened opinion, however, absolutely rejects this viewpoint and demands the same rights for women that men already enjoy in the society.'[16]

Translations provided from Bebel's *Woman* and *Woman in Future Society* predicted that, in the new society, the woman would be socially and economically independent, 'no longer a slave but ... totally free and in charge of her own happiness.'[17] Matti Kurikka, a charismatic Finnish utopian socialist, who succeeded in establishing a colony on Malcolm Island in the Pacific Ocean near Vancouver Island in 1901, echoed similar sentiments. Kurikka's utopian socialist experiment, which lasted from 1901 to 1905 and attracted over 100 women, tried to free women not only from the bonds of the capitalist system but also from the bonds of marriage, sexual obligations, and child-rearing. One of the first buildings to go up in this communal village of Sointula (Harmony) was a child-care centre.[18]

Thus, a few male journalists and theorists had taken up the women's cause in the Finnish-Canadian communities shortly after the turn of the century and had made encouraging predictions. These few enlightened men, however, did not represent the majority, and the daily reality for women was another matter. Women not only needed to reject their own traditional values, but they also had to fight the discriminatory attitudes of most men in these organizations and at home. As one woman activist complained: 'What about us women who attend the meetings and social evenings at the society. We are often treated like some kinds of "toothpicks." Little while ago the subject for debate was announced to be: Is a woman equal to a man? The ensuing discussion was hairy, intended to raise laughter ... these kinds of underhanded compliments and spectacles do nothing to promote women's enthusiasm or increase their involvement.'[19]

Despair was also evident from a Port Arthur woman's article in a US socialist newspaper, *Raivaaja* (Pioneer), in which she angrily asked: 'Are women but pieces of furniture,' in the corners of the hall? Should they be taken for granted or, worse yet, ignored? Should they be used only for practical purposes and at other times remain mute? Were women themselves to blame? In the lively debate that ensued not only men, but 'despicably vain' upper-class (Canadian) women, were accused. The harshest criticism, however, was reserved for the church and the institution of marriage, which was declared to be 'simply slavery.'[20]

These are the earliest recorded debates on the woman question in a Finnish-Canadian socialist context. All took place in or before 1905, just as the Socialist Party of Canada was emerging, and they give an indication of the early awareness of socialist issues among Finnish immigrant women. When the socialist Finns in Toronto decided to expand beyond their ethnic organization and to join the Socialist Party of Canada (SPC), each negotiating team included at least two Finnish women. At first their role seemed to be symbolic, but by 1908, when the SPC held its first Ontario-wide convention in the Finnish hall in Toronto, some articulate Finnish women leaders took the platform while their less confident sisters contributed by baking *pulla* and serving coffee. A bright young domestic, Aino Suomi, clearly defined her feminist goals and revealed her personal struggle with the male leadership in the socialist movement: 'Are men not everyday and every year grinding hundreds even thousands of women to mud? And now as the desire has awakened in women to be progressive they try to show us the reactionary direction. They know that when women become totally enlightened, men will lose their sceptre they now carry. We want to discover what our position as women is.'[21]

Another champion of Finnish Canadian socialist women who came to the fore at this time was Sanna Kannasto. She became a tireless agitator, a paid socialist organizer, and an able leader in guiding the Finnish women into the second, more active, stage of independent women's socialist activity.

FINNISH-CANADIAN WOMEN'S ORGANIZATIONS BEFORE 1920

Sanna Kannasto worked as a socialist organizer for the entire Finnish community, but throughout her many journeys across Canada she made a special effort to encourage women to participate in politics. Born in Yli-Härmä, Ostrobothnia, Finland, in 1878, Kannasto (Kallio) moved first to the United States at the age of 21. In 1905 she had joined the Socialist Party of America and soon after moved to Canada with her partner J.V. Kannasto (true to the Finnish socialist tradition, the Kannasto's refused to be married in a church and hence could not be legally married). She arrived just in time to witness the troubled link between Finns and the SPC, which ultimately led to the ousting of Finns and the many other 'foreigners' and to the formation of the Social Democratic Party of Canada. Finns joined this political party as a Finnish language local in 1911 after having first organized their own nation-wide Finnish Socialist Organization of Canada. The FSOC grew spectacularly and when the First World War broke out, it had sixty-four locals with 3062 members. All these members also joined the SDP of Canada, making the Finns the largest cultural group within the party, while the Ukrainians added 816 members and 'others' 1502.[22]

Women constituted one-third of the membership of most Finnish socialist locals, but in some urban centres they made up half the membership. The recruitment efforts of Sanna Kannasto had not been in vain. She had sent a clear message to women not to hide behind their womanhood or to use children as an excuse to withdraw from politics. Kannasto's own partnership had collapsed and she was a single-support mother. She was fond of publishing 'live examples' of the most unlikely candidates for socialist agitation. One photo showed a strong woman with an army of young tots around her. Sanna Kannasto added: 'This is a poor farmer's wife, Senja Koski. She does all the household work, looks after the animals, sews all the clothes for her seven children and still finds time to be most active in the women's reading circle and is the socialist reporter for her community.'[23] Kannasto herself proved to be of iron will and willing to sacrifice her personal comfort for the cause of socialist women. On her gruelling tours she often tramped through thick forests, faced wild animals, was lost during storms and blizzards, and carried heavy loads of socialist literature in her pack sacks, and upon reaching her 'destination,' she still had no assurance of a friendly welcome. On trains Kannasto saved the society's money by not travelling in sleeping compartments. She was frequently followed by the RCMP and on one occasion, when she was arrested near Manyberries, Alberta, in 1919, she revealed her determined spirit in a letter: 'What makes them [police] most upset is that they don't succeed in making me angry or nervous and thereby in making me cry and confess. I am as if made of iron, I never knew how much I could endure ... God help the people when I can once again be in the middle of a crowd. This is agitation at its best.'[24]

Although Sanna Kannasto remained the only strong national leader of Finnish women and was their ardent spokesperson in all socialist conventions, the Finnish community did develop literally hundreds of grass-roots organizers, many of whom became respected leaders within their own ethnically and geographically confined communities. The separate women's groups and clubs founded by these women reflected Kannasto's independent spirit, her defiance of tradition, and her socialist beliefs. These literate common workers, who spoke English with difficulty if at all, were the strength behind the Finnish socialist women's movement. They were not doctrinaire theorists, but rather immigrant women who sought to improve their social conditions and who believed that by uniting with other workers they could best achieve change.

It is not clear which Finnish community in Canada can claim to be the first to have had a separate women's socialist group that went beyond fund-raising and socializing. The Aallotar temperance society sewing circle, for example, slowly evolved from a religious group of women into a socialist support organization. Sewing circles were traditionally part of all secular and religious Finnish organizations. Women not only felt frequently excluded from male-dominated groups, but also sought out separate space from men, feeling more comfortable in each other's company. The term 'sewing circle,' however, acquired a new meaning in the socialist movement. After 1908 it was often replaced by such titles as 'study ring,' 'discussion club,' or simply 'women's club,' which more accurately reflected its ongoing activity. The by-product of these organizations was still money, but the main aim was to make women into socialist agitators who could hold their own with men. Women, who often encountered ridicule and derision from Finnish men, were determined to improve their skills.

The oldest surviving minutes of such a sewing circle provide a glimpse into the routine of the meetings. Part of the ritual was for every woman to come prepared to give a speech, recite a poem, or read a well-chosen article. Their performances were judged, and by no means gently. 'There was plenty of room for improvement for Aino,' who had recited her poem as if 'hacking away like a lumberjack who is splitting wood.' The performers were not the only people who came under scrutiny. The rotating chairpersons and secretaries were judged weekly for their fairness, accuracy, and efficiency. In addition, the group published a handwritten newspaper and everyone took turns being the editor, journalist, or a poet. Topics for debate in the meetings and in the papers varied from questions of morality, to how religion fools workers, to women's role in a socialist society. The aims of this Toronto sewing circle, as written in the minutes of 23 January 1908, say nothing about sewing: 'Let us develop ourselves so that we can perform freely and vigourously, so that the day will yet come when we can show that a woman is not only the type who gets a heart attack when she should tell a story or speak in some public place. Let's be enthusiastic!'[25]

This form of women's activity was not confined to Toronto. The women in Sointula, British Columbia, had founded a separate speaker's club where they debated such issues as international women's day, women's legal position in British Columbia, and support of the women's socialist newspaper *Toveritar* (Female Comrade), published in the United States since 1911.[26] Geographic isolation did not stifle women's interest in and identification with the larger, world-wide movement of socialist women. Like their *toverittaret* from the tiny Malcolm island in the Pacific Ocean, the women of Fort Frances, Ontario, also hosted debates and speeches on the history of socialism and raised funds for *Toveritar*.[27] A handwritten newspaper, *Piiskuri*, from the tiny village of Pottsville, Ontario (near Timmins), advertised one week in 1912 a 'contest for poetry reading,' and the next week the sewing circle's sale of 'clothes, baked goods and beer.'[28] By the time the First World War erupted, hundreds of women had 'graduated' from the Finnish women's socialist training sessions and were ready to take a more active role in the Canadian socialist women's movement.

THE DECADE OF FINNISH-CANADIAN WOMEN'S SOCIALIST ORGANIZATIONS, 1920–30

The Canadian government's fear of foreign agitators and the red scare during and after the First World War effectively closed the Social Democratic Finnish language locals, which were declared illegal by the government. In the early 1920s most socialist Finns decided to attach their support to the Workers' party, which later became the Communist Party of Canada. Some Finns, especially in Sault Ste Marie and Thunder Bay, Ontario, chose to support the Industrial Workers of the World instead. Finnish women's sewing circles were transferred to these radical Canadian organizations.

During the twenties, the socialist Finnish women's independent activity peaked at an all-time high. This decade also witnessed the full strength of socialist activity in many Finnish communities. Much of this activity, termed merely 'hall socialism,' was not, some historians claim, necessarily evidence of stronger socialist commitments. Many women, for example, agreed with Lyyli Tamminen, who confessed: 'I went to the worker's hall in Kirkland Lake because I was a worker, but if there was a dance held somewhere else, I went there too.'[29] Still, we should not underestimate the general influence of the socialist movement on women.

In 1930 when *Toveritar*, the socialist women's newspaper in the United States, was banned from Canada, it had a spectacular 3000 Canadian subscribers. It can safely be assumed that another 3000 Finnish women (mothers, daughters, friends, and room-mates) had access to the paper. In addition, *Toveritar* was found in all Finnish halls, reading-rooms, and libraries. According to the Canadian census of 1931 there were 12,361 women of Finnish ethnic origin in Canada who were 20 years old, or older. Therefore, at least half the Finnish women in Canada had regular access to a radical socialist women's weekly, and a quarter of them received their very own issue. They renewed their commitment annually and faithfully sent their $2 subscription fees until many communities reported that they could not get new subscription pledges because 'everyone already gets *Toveritar*.'[30]

Toveritar was a very effective tool in disseminating socialist information to its readers. The paper's popularity can be attributed to its feminist stance but also to its down-to-earth articles, which discussed women's issues, gave helpful household hints, and strongly encouraged women to support their separate organizations, to form unions, and to contribute to the paper by filing weekly 'letters to the editor.' At least 122 different correspondents in Canada responded to the call for articles. They wrote about the conditions on isolated prairie farms, described the danger of wolves in their wilderness lumber-camps, complained about bad treatment from their employers in the cities, and shared local news. Their efforts knitted together a network of women who, though distanced by thousands of kilometres, were brought close together by their need to rely on other women for comfort, advice, and information. *Toveritar*, a successful experiment in women's journalistic independence, became an integral part of all Finnish women's socialist activity in Canada.

With the same spirit of independence, Finnish women set out to support their own organizations. In the 1920s this movement received encouragement from a few men, grudging acceptance from others, and ridicule from some. The male leadership had accepted the Communist Party of Canada's platform, which included support for an international women's movement. At a local level, the party's aim was to reform the loosely knit ethnic women's groups into units of a more centralized political structure. While the party line on the 'woman question' took many turns during the era of the Comintern, in the early twenties it was compatible with Finnish women's desire for sex-segregated activity.[31]

In many communities the reorganization of women's activity meant simply a change of name for their existing socialist sewing circle. In other communities, however, the women met with resistance from the male leadership. Women in Finland, Ontario, for example, complained of the mixed messages they were receiving in 1924: 'The Workers' Party and the [Finnish] Socialist Organization has made it the responsibility of the locals that belong to it to establish women's organizations ... in reality nothing has been done to revitalize women's activity, at least not in the organization or the district assembly.'[32]

Since women could not count on Finnish men to further their cause, they had to step up their own educational activities and attempt to train and promote female leaders. Their effort to train writers and speakers was intensified because women wished to be more effective in attracting other women into the movement and to have a larger share in political organizing. 'Women need women organizers because women can understand each other better than a man can understand a woman,' wrote Siiri Wiita from Timmins, Ontario.[33] Helma Laakso described the subjects in an educational course in Sault Ste Marie, Ontario, attended by seven Finnish women in 1921: the woman's place in society and the communist women's movement, economics, the birth and development of nations, class-struggle tactics, the international workers' movement, and the history of Finnish class war. With the exception of the lectures on the political history of Finland, the courses did not reflect Finnish ethnicity.[34]

Along with a new educational program, women's locals revitalized the tradition of handwritten newspapers – fist press – which required women to take turns as editors, writers, poets, and readers. Women found these papers less intimidating and the cost of production was minimal. Several of the women's fist papers were circulated from one community to another and some were bound. Their titles revealed the educational purpose of the papers: *Opin-Ahjo* (Forge of Learning), *Kehitys* (Progress), *Naisten Kehittäjä* (Women's Teacher [lit.: developer]). Having first summoned up the courage to write to the modest fist paper, many women were later encouraged to write to a 'real' newspaper. This stress on education and self-improvement among the already literate women increased the number of capable female organizers, speakers, and writers who could hold their own in their demands for separate organizations or concessions from the parent organization.

Women's independent profile was soon evident in the newspapers and in the minutes of their organizations. Women were still fund-raising, but instead of turning the money over to the men, they now decided where to contribute it. Women took pride in purchasing their own advertisements in North American Finnish-language newspapers. No less than 127 women signed the Christmas greetings from Timmins that urged 'Vigour to the Class War!'[35] In this way, women were simultaneously supporting the socialist papers and declaring their separate activity.

All the Finnish women's locals were ostensibly under the purview of the Communist Party's Women's Bureau, which in 1924 adopted a strategy of broadening its base beyond ethnic activities. Finnish-Canadian women were now urged to affiliate with the newly formed Women's Labor Leagues (WLL), a communist-led organization with locals in a handful of Canadian cities. The affiliation of at least twenty-seven Finnish women's groups with the league, between 1924 and 1929, and reports of their activities in the English-language press testify to their eagerness to forge links with other Canadian women as well as to promote socialist-feminist solidarity.

Feminist solidarity was also articulated by the Finnish women's commitment to the *Woman Worker*, official organ of the WLL published between 1926 and 1929. Finnish women ordered this paper, despite the fact that they often could not read it.[36] They reprinted translated articles and resolutions of WLL conventions from the *Woman Worker* in *Toveritar*, thus assuring that Finnish women could keep in touch with women outside their own ethnic enclave. Among themselves, they were critical of the lack of support from their 'English-speaking sisters' for their own paper. After all, to Finns, newspapers were the workers' 'daily bread.'[37]

Finnish immigrant women faithfully adopted the resolutions passed in WLL conventions, and on the surface, it seems that their own culture did not shape their socialist activity. If we probe deeper, however, it is easy to distinguish which issues were important to the immigrant women and were acted on, and which issues were downplayed. As early as 1922 the Women's Bureau of the Workers' party was defining pertinent issues for socialist women. They stressed agitation, wage equity, conditions of industrial workers (especially piece workers), mothers' allowance, unionizing women, minimum wage for farm and domestic women, and the celebration of International Women's Day. Later, the WLL emphasized the importance of the youth movement, warned against the capitalist influence of public-school education, and promoted workers' co-operatives and the international peace movement. From this list of grievances and plan of action, Finnish women picked out the issues relevant to their daily lives. They did not ignore International Women's Day and petitions for peace, and they continued to collect funds for strike victims, for families of unemployed workers, and for the WLL.

The priorities of Finnish women, however, reflected their culture. First of all, they pledged their continued support for their own Finnish papers and second for the *Woman Worker*. Competent women journalists such as Martta Lehtonen, former editor of a socialist newspaper in Finland, taught courses in journalism and public speaking. Women continued to improve their knowledge of socialist doctrines and to agitate among other Finnish women. Occasionally they reached out to women of other ethnic backgrounds and found most in common with Ukrainian women, with whom they held some joint meetings in places like Sudbury, Timmins, Thunder Bay, and Toronto. Integration of women from several cultures into socialist activity was most successful in areas where the Finns were few in number. Thus, Mary North, a

Finnish agitator from the coal-mining district of Alberta, was able to report successful organization of miners' wives from many ethnic backgrounds. Most agitational work, however, was culturally exclusive within the Finnish community.[38]

Concern over industrial women, piece workers, or the debates over the minimum wage did not receive great attention among Finnish immigrant women, who worked mainly as domestic servants. The call to act on behalf of maids, however, was welcomed with open arms. Finnish women, who had earlier formed loose-knit networks to provide information about employers, to give advice on working conditions, to shelter each other between jobs, now formalized these ties by setting up domestic servants' organizations. Maids' organizations were familiar to them from Finland, where the domestic servants had founded their own organization, school, and newspaper. The first official Palvelijatar Yhdistys (servant's organization) was established in Toronto in 1925. Vancouver, Montreal, Sudbury, Sault Ste Marie, and Timmins had all followed suit by 1930. Montreal domestics were even successful in securing a hostel for domestic servants, while the other communities were able to have offices and meeting rooms. These organizations, which had about 300 paid members, tried to agree on acceptable minimum wages and working hours, kept blacklists of employers, and found information about job openings. By 1930 the separate domestic servants' clubs were reintegrated back into the women's locals, which had found that the splintering of different groups of women was not fruitful for their collective good. The concern for the welfare of domestic servants within the community, however, did not diminish.[39]

The issues of youth organization and public-school education were also of great concern. Not only were mothers worried about the capitalist and religious instructions directed to their children in the public schools but, as immigrants, they were also worried about losing their children's respect. One obviously upset mother complained in a handwritten newspaper from South Porcupine in 1927: 'In the schools children are actually taught to despise us, the immigrants and workers.'[40] The mothers responded by establishing youth camps and Sunday clubs where the children were taught class consciousness together with Finnish culture and language. The first such clubs sprang up as early as 1903.[41] Children's activity closely resembled that of their parents. Much energy was spent on the sports fields and in rehearsing for theatrical plays. The young Finnish socialists of Timmins, Ontario, for example, collected funds for their separate organization, which was founded in 1917, by staging two plays: 'We Will Not Get Married' and 'Mr. God Is Not at Home.'[42]

The church was also seen as a great threat in the assimilation of Finnish children into the Canadian culture. While the Finnish Lutheran church in Canada was relatively weak, the Presbyterians and later the United Church of Canada set up special Finnish congregations in order to provide an alternative to the radical activity of the Finns. Finnish socialists fought back. Finnish men, the women said, '[had] tired of doing educational work against the misconstrued teachings of the church, it will be up to the women workers to do so with ever greater enthusiasm. Destroy the Gods from heavens, destroy the capitalists on earth!'[43]

As a protest against the influence of the schools and religion, many socialist parents kept their children out of school on May Day and asked them to boycott the Lord's Prayer; some children refused to stand up for 'God Save the King.' These demonstrations did not go unnoticed by horrified Canadian ministers and the press. In this fashion the Finnish parents were making a statement through their children against capitalism, imperialism, religion, and the pressure of assimilation. However, the impact of the contradictory information provided at the youth camps and clubs and by the public schools may also have confused many children of Finnish descent. The behaviour of the second generation is still unexplored. From today's vantage point, it does seem, however, that for a variety of reasons many parents lost the battle of the socialist souls for their daughters who rarely continued to carry the radical torch as intently or as proudly as their mothers had.

Finnish immigrant women were also dedicated to the fight for mothers' and widows' allowances. As immigrant women who had come independently, Finnish women did not have extended families in Canada. Unlike many southern Europeans, Finns were not family migrants and seldom brought their parents to Canada. Thus, a widowed Finnish woman could not count on help from her family. In addition, many women who worked as live-in maids never did get married and found themselves totally unprotected in old age. Finally, those women who did marry often refused to compromise their strong socialist principles by kneeling in front of the altar. Within the radical Finnish community, common-law marriages were a matter of pride; advertisements in the socialist papers announced clearly that 'No sky pilots were present.' But in Canadian law, these marriages were not legal, a fact which could have tragic consequences for women. The legal problem of widows' allowances surfaced most clearly during the Hollinger mine accident of 1928 in Timmins, when several Finnish women found that compensation for them and their children would be denied because of their illegal living arrangements. The fact that they had clearly announced in front of dozens of witnesses that 'according to the laws of nature [they] united together as comrades for each other' did not influence the Canadian officials. Finns, who had already agitated for civil marriages in Canada, stepped up this activity in 1928 by sending a written protest to the Canadian Parliament. The WLL strongly supported the Finnish women in this fight. In Finland, civil marriages had been a fact of life since 1919.[44]

When the Communist Party of Canada decided to support the establishment of workers' co-operatives, the Finns once again were in full support. The co-operative movement in Finland had spread rapidly after the turn of the century, and Finns in Canada had established co-operative rooming-houses, restaurants, and consumer rings well before the First World War. Although most co-operatives were run by men, women had an extremely important part in them as consumers. By 1930, Finns had established several co-operative bakeries, dairies, and large grocery stores, and women were often called upon to draw in new customers to the movement. The problem was, once again, how to explain to a non-Finn the benefits of co-operatives when one could not speak English. Optimistically, women were advised: 'Don't worry if you can't speak, just give them [non-Finnish women] a cup of our famous 'Red Star Coffee' and tell them from what store it came. Maybe this will get them into the store and later they might even learn what co-operatives mean.'[45]

Finally, a major concern of the Finnish socialist women was bootlegging and drunkenness. Time and again Finnish women swore to fight these great evils in the Finnish communities. The socialist Finnish women typically presented drinking as a male problem with women as the victims, usually the penniless mothers and the abused wives of alcoholic men. Overall, however, a class analysis still predominated and the drinking habits of Finnish men were blamed on the capitalist system. Women lost their battle against drink. Alcohol and alcohol-related accidents were the second-largest cause of unnatural death (after workplace accidents) among Finnish men. Bootleggers flourished in every single Finnish community and along with them came gambling and prostitution. The socialist temperance organizations, which so bravely had fought 'King alcohol' during the early part of this century, had all but disappeared from the Finnish communities in the 1920s, although beliefs in temperance were still strongly supported by the socialist leadership. Nor were the women simply the innocent victims of drunken men. In many Finnish communities they controlled the marketing of the liquor by running illegal taverns or by selling alcohol by the bottle. The curse of drinking, concluded the socialist women of Timmins in defeat, has always been and still is the greatest threat to Finnish workers in Canada.[46]

Alcohol was admittedly of great concern to the Finnish Canadians, but the women had to battle other enemies as well. By 1930 the Government of Canada had declared *Toveritar* – the socialist women's lifeline of communication – illegal. Despite desperate pleas and pledges of support for their own Canadian-Finnish women's socialist paper, the Finnish men failed to agree with the need for separate woman's paper. Instead, women had to be satisfied with a token page in the Finnish-Canadian socialist newspaper *Vapaus* (Freedom). In the early 1930s, Finnish women were also feeling increasingly disappointed with their Canadian sisters. They accused the WLL leadership of discriminatory actions and argued that Finnish women were expected to pay the bills but not necessarily play any part in the formulation of issues or in the decisions on how the money was spent.[47]

The immigrant community was hit hard by the depression, and many capable socialist women left Canada for Soviet Karelia, where Finns hoped to establish a better socialist society. The remaining socialist Finns began to feud among themselves, and the more moderate Finns split from the communist-led Finnish Organization of Canada. Many women who had worked together for years now found themselves in opposite camps. Furthermore, immigration from Finland was effectively banned from 1930 to 1947, eliminating the chance to bring new women to the organization. Although the socialist activity of Finnish women is still evident today in some small senior-citizen groups in the Finnish communities, it never regained the vigour of the 1920s. Women were largely reintegrated into the Finnish Organization of Canada, which also experienced a steady decline of membership. The immigrants who arrived after the Second World War were no longer interested in the same socialist battles, nor did they share the memories of the bitter civil war. They had just lived through the Second World War and fought at great cost Finland's enemy – the Soviet Union. This generation of Finns was hard pressed to sympathize with problems of the radical Finnish Canadians; instead, they proceeded to form new organizations. The conservative and religious Finns had begun to reorganize in the late twenties and when 25,000 new immigrants arrived from Finland after the Second World War, their activity expanded rapidly. Socialist Finns had clearly lost their power and influence in Finnish communities.

Because of the strength of conservative and religious Finns in today's Finnish community, there has been a desire to forget or even to deny the existence of the Finnish-Canadian radical movement. Many Finnish-Canadian women today are unable to understand the earlier women's motives and circumstances, and are ashamed of their sisters of the past. Their history as one of the most radical groups of women in Canada had been deliberately ignored. Yet, the socialist Finnish women showed a spirit and determination as yet unequalled by any Finnish women's group. They refused to believe that they were helpless victims; they refused to leave decisions up to the male leaders; and, despite great odds, they succeeded in forming a strong network of women who shared their culture and socialist beliefs.

Finnish immigrant women's actions were motivated by gender, class, and cultural consciousness. As women whose feminism had been nurtured by their Finnish origins, they rebelled against the generally patriarchal views of male socialists. Because they chose to have small families or no families at all, these women had the time for activity outside the house. Their position as immigrant workers exposed the women to their own vulnerability and gave further encouragement for socialist activity. Those women who had acquired the basics of socialist ideology in Finland were eager to spread the word in Canada. Literate Finnish women were receptive and willing to make their contribution to the Canadian labour movement. In the process they also created an efficient network of communication and women's organizations that could combine to meet their social and political needs. Furthermore, Finnish women activists made attempts to reach out to their Canadian sisters. Ultimately, however, they did not feel at ease within the larger Canadian movement. They suspected that the women from the English-language locals discriminated against foreign women. Understandably, the Finnish women were more comfortable among those who shared the same culture and, above all, among those who spoke their own language. Only a handful of Finnish activist women were ever able to speak English fluently; thus, they were effectively barred from leadership positions outside their own community. None the less, they managed to construct a strong community, dedicated to feminist goals within the Finnish left.

Miina Knutila, a dedicated Finnish woman socialist who arrived in Timmins, Ontario, in 1911, and who passed away in 1986 after a full and active life, never compromised her principles. She concluded on her deathbed: 'At first I could only think of how to get away from Timmins; it was an awful place and then the fire destroyed whatever was left. But now when I think of it, the beauty of the town did not lie in its buildings, in the mineshafts or in the muddy, impassable roads; it was in the hearts of the spirited workers and the women who worked so hard together. We all shared, everything. We cried together, we laughed together, we marched together, and we stuck together to the bitter end. I have no regrets, I never did find the gold I came to look for, but I did find a life full of purpose.'[48]

It is time that Miina Knutila and the thousands of other immigrant women from many different cultures receive their own place in Canadian history.

214 Varpu Lindström-Best

NOTES

1 Interview with Elina Sytelä, Sudbury, 1973.
2 Riitta Jallinoja, *Suomalaisen naisasialiikkeen taistelukaudet* (Porvoo, Finland, 1983); L.A. Puntila, *The Political History of Finland, 1908–1966* (Helsinki 1975).
3 Joan Sangster, 'Finnish Women in Ontario, 1890–1930, *Polyphony* 3:2 (Fall 1981), 46–54; 'The Communist Party and the Woman Question, 1922–1929,' *Labour/Le Travail* 15 (Spring 1985), 25–56.
4 Linda Kealey, 'Canadian Socialism and the Woman Question, 1900–14,' *Labour/Le Travail* 13 (1984), 77–101. See also Janice Newton, 'Women and *Cotton's Weekly*: A Study of Women and Socialism in Canada, 1909,' *Resources for Feminist Research* 8 (1979), 58–61.
5 Mari Jo Buhle, *Women and American Socialism, 1870–1920* (Urbana 1983) XIII, 302; see also Sally M. Miller, 'Other Socialists: Native-born and Immigrant Women in the Socialist Party of America, 1901–1917,' *Labour History* 24:1 (Winter 1983).
6 Mauri A. Jalava, 'Radicalism or a 'New Deal"? The Unfolding World View of the Finnish Immigrants in Sudbury, 1883–1932,' MA diss., Laurentian University, 1983; Edward W. Laine, 'Finnish-Canadian Radicalism and Canadian Politics: The First Forty Years, 1900–1940,' and Varpu Lindström-Best, 'The Socialist Party of Canada and the Finnish Connection, 1905–1911' in Jorgen Dahlie and Tissa Fernando, eds, *Ethnicity, Power and Politics in Canada* (Toronto 1981).
7 Varpu Lindström-Best, 'Defiant Sisters: A Social History of the Finnish Immigrant Women in Canada, 1890–1930,' PhD diss., York University, 1986, 69–122.
8 Oiva Saarinen, 'Finns in Northeastern Ontario with Special Reference to the Sudbury Area,' *Laurentian University Review* 15:1 (November 1982), 41–54 and 'Geographical Perspectives of Finnish Canadian Immigration and Settlement,' *Polyphony* 3:2 (Fall 1981), 16–22; J. Donald Wilson, 'Finns in British Columbia before the First World War,' *Polyphony* 3:2 (Fall 1981), 55–64; *A Chronicle of Finnish Settlement in Rural Thunder Bay* (Thunder Bay 1976); Nancy Mattson Schelstraete, ed., *Life in the New Finland Woods* (Rocanville, SK, 1982).
9 *Dominion of Canada, Report of the Department of Immigration and Colonization for the fiscal year ended March 31, 1929* (Ottawa 1930), 38–9.
10 *Seventh Census of Canada, 1931. Cross-Classification* IV, part III (Ottawa 1933), 558–601.
11 Ibid., 736–9.

12 Anthony F. Upton, *The Finnish Revolution 1917–1918* (Minnesota 1980); Juhani Piilonen, 'Women's Contribution in "Red Finland" 1918,' unpublished research paper presented at 'Women as Builders of Society' Conference in Kuopio, Finland (27 August 1987).

13 Aallotar Minute Books 1891–1912, series C-1, files 1–4, Finnish Canadian Historical Society Collection (FCHSC), Archives of Ontario (AO).

14 Ibid., 9 September 1894, first mention of Women's Sewing Circle.

15 *Vapaus*, 7 November 1924.

16 *Toivo*, 30 September 1904.

17 *Toivo*, no. 6, 1904, refers to two Finnish translations – 'Nainen' and 'Nainen tulevana aikana'; August Bebel, *Woman and Socialism* (New York 1910). The Finnish translation is from *Die Frau und der Sozialismus* (1879).

18 Matti Halminen, *Sointula: Kalevan Kansa ja Kanadan Suomalaisten Historiaa* (Helsinki 1936); J. Donald Wilson, 'Matti Kurikka: Finnish Canadian Intellectual,' BC *Studies*, no. 20 (Winter 1973–4).

19 *Toivo*, 6 March 1904.

20 *Raivaaja*, 23 March 1905.

21 Annual report for the Finnish Socialist League's Women's section, 24 March 1907, MG28, V46, vol. 36, case II, file G, National Archives of Canada (NA).

22 Jalava, 'Radicalism or a "New Deal,"' appendix A, table 8, 299; *Western Clarion*, 22 January 1910; Lindström-Best, 'The Socialist Party of Canada,' 113–22.

23 *Vapaus*, 29 August 1928.

24 Letter from Sanna Kannasto to J.W. Ahlqvist, 6 February 1920, MG28, V46, vol. 3, file 34, NA.

25 Minutes of the Women's Section of the Finnish Society of Toronto, 23 January 1908, MG28, V46, vol. 42, file 22, NA.

26 See Varpu Lindström-Best and Allen Seager, '*Toveritar* and Finnish Canadian Women, 1900–1930,' in Christiane Harzig and Dirk Hoerder, eds, *The Press of Labour Migrants in Europe and North America 1880s to 1930s* (Bremen 1985).

27 *Toveritar*, 29 May 1917.

28 *Piiskuri*, 30 March 1912.

29 Interview with Lyyli Tamminen, Toronto, 1983.

30 For example, see reports from Blairmore and Bingley, Alberta, *Toveritar*, 25 April 1922 and 2 February 1926.

31 Sangster, 'The Communist Party,' 25–56.

32 *Vapaus*, 15 March 1924.

33 Ibid., 25 June 1921.

34 Ibid., 19 January 1927.

35 *Toveritar*, 15 December 1925.

36 'Our Labour Leagues at Work,' *Woman Worker*, October 1927; Sangster, 'The Communist Party,' 29–41.

37 A series of critical articles was published in *Vapaus*, 12 and 18 February, 6 August 1930; P. George Hummasti, '"The Working Man's Daily Bread," Finnish-American Working Class Newspapers, 1900–1921,' in *For the Common Good* (Superior, WI, 1970), 167–94.

38 Correspondence: Concerning the Women's Labour League of Canada 1927–1931, letter from Mary North, 1 April 1931, MG28, v46, vol. 16, file 38, NA.

39 Varpu Lindström-Best, '"I Won't Be a Slave!" Finnish Domestics in Canada, 1911–30,' in Jean Burnet, ed., *Looking into My Sister's Eyes: An Exploration in Women's History* (Toronto 1986), 33–53.

40 *Toveritar*, 22 March 1927. Reprinted article from South Porcupine handwritten newspaper *Virkistäjä*.

41 Interview with Saimi Hormavirta, Toronto, 1978.

42 William Eklund, *Canadan Rakentajia: Canadan Suomalaisen Järjestön Historia vv. 1911–1971* (Toronto 1983), 329–31.

43 *Yritys*, no. 2, 1928.

44 For examples of marriage advertisements, see *Vapaus*, 16 April 1921, 17 June 1921, 25 September 1921, 18 May 1922; *Toveritar*, 8 August 1922, 11 March 1924. On the question of civil marriages, see the *Woman Worker*, March 1928; *Vapaus*, 28 October 1928; *Sudbury Star*, 12 January 1929; *Canadan Uutiset*, 25 April 1918.

45 Published minutes of WLL Northern Ontario District Conference held in Timmins, Ontario, 29 April 1928, *Toveritar*, 5 June 1928.

46 *Vapaus*, 7 March 1922.

47 Ibid., 4 March 1930; the woman's column printed a detailed description of the dispute as seen by the Finnish local in Levac, Ontario.

48 Interview with Wilhelmiina (Miina) Knutila, Timmins, 1983.

From Wage Slave to White Slave

The Prostitution Controversy
and the Early Canadian Left

Janice Newton

'Capitalism systematically manufactures prostitutes' declared the front page of Canada's largest selling socialist newspaper in 1911.[1] The newspaper was responding to a perceived crisis in the changing nature of sexual relations, known as the 'sex question,' that frequently heralded growing concerns about the changing nature of Canadian society. During the first two decades of the twentieth century, public debate raged over the problems of prostitution, the declining birth rate, sexual morality, white slavery, venereal disease, and the sexual customs that were thought to accompany these problems. Prostitution, in particular, drew public attention as it became more visible with industrialization and urbanization. Politicians were increasingly pressured by social reformers to make prostitution a priority on the political agenda and to bring an end to prostitution in Canada.[2]

'From Wage Slave to White Slave' became a prominent slogan in the left's response to the problem of prostitution. In their attempt to explain 'Why Working Women Sell Their Honour,'[3] the left challenged the class bias of social reformers and focused intensely on the economic constraints that led to prostitution. To understand these approaches to the problem of prostitution, I examine both the larger context of debate over the 'sex question' in Canada and how differing views on prostitution were worked out from within the left. I argue that much of the left's analysis of prostitution was a direct challenge to the position of middle-class reformers. The left thus contributed a distinctive and important perspective to the political debates on prostitution.

This class perspective, however, offered limited insight into the sexual oppression of women inherent in prostitution. A few socialists, mostly women, urged the left to adopt a more feminist critique of the problem of prostitution, challenging basic assumptions about male sexuality. In doing so, these women urged the left to acknowledge that matters of sexuality had implications for the private and the public actions of socialists – especially for men. The views of this minority were outweighed by those within the left who refused to consider the broader implications of such a critique for male sexual behaviour. They chose to limit their analysis of prostitution to a class analysis, rather than to integrate feminist concerns with their class perspective. In tracing the contours of this debate over prostitution within the left, we can discern a political struggle over the left's definition of a political agenda.

Social and moral reformers tended to view prostitution, which had been made more visible by industrialization and urbanization, as a direct threat to their social values and customs. They lobbied politicians, formed social and moral reform societies and purity leagues, and undertook investigations to direct public attention to the problem of prostitution.[4] They also proposed reforms they thought would help eliminate prostitution, including prohibition of women from saloons; separate courts, sentences, and jails for women; building of homes for working women; moral reform of working women; sterilization of the feeble-minded; the establishment of purity leagues to drive out brothels; a tax on bachelors; laws to abolish ragtime dancing and joy rides; or even 'the whipping post for white slavers and seducers of women.'[5] Many reformers also argued that woman suffrage and prohibition would put an end to prostitution.[6] Although some reformers were concerned over the economic causes of prostitution and many of them abhorred the sexual coercion and abuse of women, the dominant emphasis in their efforts was often on altering the moral structure of society rather than its economic or social structure.

For the most part, these reformers sought changes that would impose their middle-class concept of 'social purity' upon society. Their ideal was a 'white life for two': a single sexual standard for men and women, characterized by restraint. In a social milieu in which respectable women were not supposed publicly to raise sexual matters, many of these reformers camouflaged their campaigns to educate the public – especially women – about sexual matters by cloaking the entire discussion in the guise of motherhood and female reproduction. This circumspection was not grounded in simple prudery. In the face of both real and imagined dangers faced by women in expressing their sexuality, these social campaigns sought to protect women from the risks inherent in female sexuality. Campaigns, such as the one for 'voluntary motherhood,' which insisted upon a married woman's right to refuse sexual relations with her husband in order to prevent conception, had a twofold impact. They enhanced woman's autonomy over her sexuality, while at the same time they denied women the expression of sexuality as a form of pleasure.[7]

The sex question was also raised within the international socialist movement.

Private property, its impact upon marriage and sex relations, and the sexual oppression of women both inside and outside marriage were the subjects of the work of Frederick Engels in *The Origin of the Family, Private Property and the State*, and of August Bebel in *Woman under Socialism*.[8] Drawing on anthropological evidence of communal societies, Engels's work viewed monogamous marriage as the product of the development of private property and the need for male property owners to determine the legitimacy of their offspring. This drive to legitimate inheritance of property led to the oppression of women within marriage and the imposition of monogamous sexual behaviour on women, but not necessarily on men. Bebel viewed the sex instinct as natural and insisted that women as well as men had such instincts. Capitalist society prevented their full expression because of the reign of private property. Under socialism, satisfaction of sexual instincts would become a private matter, just like eating and dressing. Marriages would be based upon love and attraction, but if 'repulsion sets in ... morality commands that the unnatural and therefore immoral, bond be dissolved.' He anticipated, however, that most marriages would be happy because they would be based on true attraction rather than economic need.[9] Both Engels and Bebel devoted the bulk of their books to the negative effects of private property on marriage and sexual relations. Few pages were devoted to articulating socialist alternatives.

Before the First World War, there were a few radicals in North America who went further than this. Called sex radicals, these people challenged the view that woman's sexuality was restricted to reproductive functions and insisted that sexual pleasure was also part of woman's sexuality. They argued that men as well as women should enjoy sexual pleasure and bear the responsibilities of sexual activity. From this radicalism sprang the early support for birth control led by radicals such as Emma Goldman and Margaret Sanger. These ideas were in direct conflict with those of the social purity movement, which denied woman's interest in sexuality other than for reproduction.[10]

Many sex radicals were initially drawn to the socialist movement in the United States and elsewhere because of the feminist concern for equality in sex relations that was embedded in the communitarian heritage of the socialist movement and expressed through the works of Engels and Bebel. The ideas of these sex radicals, however, never came to prevail within the international socialist movement. Indeed, the mere suggestion that under socialism people may choose to leave unhappy marriages was sufficient to offend the moral sensibilities of many socialists. For example, Daniel De Leon, in the preface to his English translation of Bebel's work in 1904, refused to accept Bebel's rejection of monogamous marriage.[11]

Socialist parties everywhere consistently refused to legitimize these concerns as being a central part of socialism.[12] Despite this official rejection of the sex question, critics of socialism constantly used this issue to discredit socialism, claiming that socialists wanted to destroy the family. Thus, the international socialist movement, though officially unwilling to consider sexual relations as a part of the movement's agenda, was thus nevertheless drawn into a defensive debate over socialism and sexual relations.

The Canadian left both reflected and responded to these ideas. A few individuals connected with the left in Canada shared the convictions of the sex radicals. Through her woman's column in the socialist press, Bertha Merrill Burns argued quite forcibly that socialism should address the sex question and recommended to her readers the works of sex radicals such as Edward Carpenter, and Moses Harman, editor of the journal *Lucifer*. Burns admitted that she was influenced by a talk given by Dr Amelia Youmans of Winnipeg, who had advocated more openness in speaking about sex. Burns acknowledged that some would say this view was not socialism, but insisted that it was 'not less important than socialism.'[13] Another socialist woman, Dora F. Kerr, sympathized with the sex radicals and recommended their work to readers. Kerr lamented that American socialists shirked this subject and were so far behind the Europeans, claiming that 'nearly all the advanced thinkers on the sex question have been driven into the anarchist movement.'[14]

The views of these individuals never gained widespread acceptance within the left in Canada. Although acknowleding these social currents, the two main parties of the left – the Social Democratic Party of Canada (SDPC) and the Socialist Party of Canada (SPC) – took remarkably similar stances on the sex question as a whole. As elsewhere, ever conscious of the charge that socialism would destroy the home, the Canadian left remained defensive in discussing socialist views of sex relations. 'Socialism is not a social reform or a sex reform movement ...' argued *The Western Clarion*; 'It no more criticizes matrimony than it criticizes eating peas with a knife.'[15] The sex question was rejected by the party leadership as having nothing to do with socialism: 'Socialist writers may have individual opinions with respect to the action of economic change upon institutions of which marriage is one. Such opinions however are not authoritative, and they often bring it about that the sex vagaries of individuals are laid at the door of the movement to its hurt. The person who occupies the platform of the Socialist Movement in order to express his individual ideas on the sex question is out of place and should find some other vehicle for the publication of his doctrine.'[16] Thus, neither socialist party in Canada made it a priority to articulate a consistent party line on many of the concerns that sprang from the sex question. Any concern for the sexual oppression of women was clearly viewed as secondary to the primary concern

Figure 1 *Western Clarion*, 2 August 1913, 1 (original archival copy retouched by Avril Orloff)

for the pragmatic survival of the party. While reluctant to take any stand on issues related to the sex question more generally, the issue of prostitution, however, was one dimension of the sex question that the left did address, because often it fit so well into its critique of capitalism.

The left's perspective on prostitution was quite distinct from that of middle-class reformers. Consistently, party papers argued that capitalism was the cause of prostitution (see figure 1). Capitalism and private property made it impossible for men and women to marry and have families; thus, capitalism was to blame for destroying the family and for those social vices, such as prostitution, which sprang from one's inability to marry. Concentrating on the futility and hypocrisy of reformers, the *Western Clarion*, party paper for the SPC, emphasized that reforms would not change a problem if one did not address the cause: capitalism. Women's groups, which demanded the vote in order to end prostitution, were repeatedly criticized as naïve, self-serving reformers. Some socialists directly attacked the class interests of reformers, accusing them of focusing on prostitution and alcohol consumption in working-class districts, while ignoring these issues in the wealthy districts.[17] Although the SDPC did not in principle reject the idea of endorsing some reforms, it similarly rejected the reformers' moral exhortations and attempts to 'reform' prostitutes. One socialist writer declared that morality flowed directly from economic conditions, and unless those were changed there was no point in moral reform.[18] Another writer attacked the Council of Women meeting in Toronto, which had spent hours discussing the social evil: 'While they were moralizing thousands of young girls were being ground into mire.'[19] Typically, this writer made a direct appeal to men of the working class to defend their women by opposing the capitalist system. Although concerned for the working-class women who were drawn into prostitution, this attitude reflected a strikingly limited perception of the role that working-class men might have in the social evil (figure 1). Men were urged to defend women, but this appeal was to men as fathers and brothers; they were not, however, urged to protect women by refusing to be their customers.

Other socialists did acknowledge the role of working-class men as the clients of prostitutes. One man criticized reformers for treating the women – and their clients – as if they were the source of the problem: 'You organize purity leagues and hound the unfortunate women down. You fairly froth at the mouth when you are discussing the 'low beastly man' who may occasionally visit a house of ill fame.'[20] The article stressed that reformers were wrong to attack either the men or the prostitutes. It was the economic system which prevented them from having 'moral' alternatives.

Suspicion of the class bias of the reformers and insistence on fundamental change were sometimes shared by the larger labour movement. In 1913, the Edmonton branch of the United Brotherhood for Carpenters and Joiners refused to lend its support to the National Committee for the Suppression of the White Slave Trade, stating that a generation ago prostitution did not exist in Canada, but that this circumstance had changed with the development of the 'factory system of industry.' According to this view, the extremely low pay for women's factory work, the 'natural aversion of the girls to the damnable drudgery of the factory,' their dislike of unhealthy working conditions, and their reluctance to perform 'dangerous and brutalizing tasks' made women workers 'easy victims to the wiles of the procurer.' The United Brotherhood voted overwhelmingly to circulate their response and it was published by *Cotton's Weekly* and the *Western Clarion*.[21] This underscores the extent to which the left concurred in the view that reformers were profoundly misguided and self-serving. The left's disdain for the reformers is well illustrated in the terse response of *Cotton's Weekly* to the establishment of a government commission to look into the white slave trade in Canada: 'Bah!'[22]

While some reformers tended to view prostitution as stemming from the weaknesses, moral or otherwise, of the prostitutes and their clients, socialists explained that capitalism caused prostitution by underpaying women workers. Because women workers were not paid wages adequate to support themselves, they had to seek an additional source of income to survive.[23] When the campaign to prosecute prostitutes in Montreal came to the attention of *Cotton's Weekly*, the paper criticized the prosecutor, Recorder Wier, for bringing these women to court. Instead, the paper urged him to 'go to the departmental stores' proprietors, the mill owners and other employers of girl labour, and force them to pay a living wage to the girls who work under them.'[24] Employers justified the payment of low wages by arguing that many working women lived at home and were supported by male family members. This argument was rarely acknowledged by socialists. Rather they stressed the need to pay women wages that would enable them to be self-sufficient. Interestingly, this demand for a living wage for women, which arose in discussions of prostitution, was never reconciled with the more prevalent demand that men should earn enough wages to support a family.

The emphasis on women's low wages as the cause of prostitution was not always posed in the extreme terms of a woman choosing between starvation and prostitution. A few articles alluded to prostitution as the 'only way' for women to get clothes and adornment, such as the shop-girl who 'likes pretty things and cannot afford them and finally barters her purity and good name for money.'[25] Those articles were quite sympathetic to these desires, but many moral reformers were not, viewing such desires as evidence of a woman's wickedness. In one respect, the socialist emphasis on women's low wages as the cause of prostitution reflected an acknowledgment that some working women made a reasoned choice to engage in prostitution because the alternatives were so limited. Although seen as victims of the capitalist system, the women were also seen as acting subjects who made choices from among limited alternatives.

Socialists believed that by ensuring women equal wages or establishing minimum-wage laws, prostitution might be curbed.[26] More frequently, they called for abolition of the wage system itself, thus giving women workers the full value of their labour. Under socialism, 'whoever works would be given the full value of whatever he or she does' and, therefore, prostitution would 'cease automatically with abolition of class ownership of the tools of production.'[27] With economic independence, socialists hoped the working woman would be free to act as arbiter of her own sexuality.

The wage system was also seen to cause prostitution in another way: it created the demand for prostitutes. The left distinguished between two types of customers: working-class men and capitalist or wealthy men. The low wages paid to working-class men were often cited alongside women's low wages as a

The Dream of Home

Figure 2 Gordon Nye, 'Who Destroys the Home?' *Cotton's Weekly*,

'cause' of prostitution: because men were paid such low wages they could not afford to marry. Thus, working-class women who could not find men to marry and support them were driven into the wage market and exposed to the choices described above. More directly, the men who were prevented from marrying became the clients of prostitutes. Like the prostitute, the working-class man was depicted as a victim of capitalism: deprived of sex within marriage, he was 'forced' to resort to prostitution.[28] The best example of this common perception of prostitution by the left is expressed in figure 2.

A number of important assumptions were embedded in this illustration. First, it seems blind to the different forces that capitalism exerted on men and women. Women faced starvation if they had no husband or family and

But Capitalism Gives This Instead

7 September 1911, 1 (original archival copy retouched by Avril Orloff)

subsisted on women's wages; men could survive on their wages and did not face starvation, but they could not support families. Yet both men and women were portrayed as equally victimized by capitalism. Second, the proposed 'solution' resorted to the idea that men should earn enough wages to support a wife and a home. Socialism, by giving the male worker the full value of his labour, would make this possible. This 'solution' (implied by figure 2), placed less emphasis on the autonomy of women than did the 'solution' (implied by figure 1) that women be paid a living wage that represented the full value of their labour. Third, there was a presumption that once the working-class male was married, he would no longer seek out the services of a prostitute. Although never openly stated, a wife was also seen as necessary for a man's sexual gratification. None of these arguments questioned whether the working-class man who used a prostitute (or his wife) in this spirit was exploiting his working-class sister. In short, the left's class analysis of prostitution failed to acknowledge that the sexual oppression of women by working-class men was integral to the problem of prostitution.

Failure to reflect upon sexual exploitation by the working-class male is well illustrated in those articles, written by men, that insisted that the *male* sex drive was a strong, 'natural' hunger requiring satisfaction.[29] Men who used prostitutes were not to be viewed as immoral or beastly: 'The so-called bestial behaviour of men is but the perverted strivings for expression of the divine INSTINCT OF FATHERHOOD.'[30] Once deprived of the chance to marry, a man would inevitably seek out the services of a prostitute: 'But of course, he has, as a normal healthy animal, certain desires. Since society – or the ruling class in society – prevent the satisfaction of those desires in one way [marriage], the *normal man* satisfies them in another' (emphasis added).[31]

Wilfred Gribble, a socialist who served in the navy and claimed to have treated hundreds of cases of venereal disease, provides us with an extreme example of this male perspective. Gribble claimed that more attention should be paid to the male 'victims' of prostitution, who were only following 'insistent, irresistible … urges.' Recognizing that this argument could be used to justify all men's – including capitalists' – use of prostitutes, he qualified his remarks: 'Understand I am writing this not in defense of the overfed plutocrats, who *being overfed*, go in for excessive sexual indulgence as a *natural consequence*, but in defense of the normal unmarried male of the working class.' Notably, he viewed the female prostitute in a very different light. Although the man is acting naturally, the female prostitute is abnormal: 'The sellers of the sexual commodity are physically abnormal in submitting themselves to all and sundry for pay.'[32] Gribble understood that either the man or the woman could contract venereal disease, but he clearly associated doing so with the abnormality of the prostitute, rather than with the man using the prostitute.

Through these discussions of prostitution we can begin to understand the dominant view of male sexuality among socialists. It was seen as natural and as uncontrollable if not satisfied – as a drive analogous to hunger. The man, in satisfying it, was simply eating a meal. The prostitute as victim disappeared. Given the left's economic arguments about prostitution and the keen sense of capitalism's victimization of the prostitute, these arguments – which absolved working-class men of any responsibility for participating in the sexual exploitation of women prostitutes – are especially striking. Rather than perceiving sexuality as a natural urge – like all other human urges compelling us to interact and enjoining us to mutual responsibility and obligations – these arguments, in effect, justified the sexual objectification of women.

Women became a necessary object for the male sex drive. In this respect, the socialist views of male sexuality differed markedly from the dominant views of the social purity reformers, who stressed that male sexuality should be controlled.

Whatever blindness the left showed to working-class use of prostitutes, they were clear-sighted regarding capitalists' use of their services. The left press repeatedly characterized capitalists as sexually immoral. For evidence it drew upon widely publicized scandals of the sexual exploits of the wealthy: divorce, homosexuality, marital infidelity, 'licentious carousals,' and sexual assault among the wealthy.[33] The rich man's sexual exploitation of working women was described in language that emphasized these women's role as 'playthings of wealthy sports' and as victims of 'the lusts of leisure-class men' and 'tyrannical foremen.'[34] The following describes sexual exploitation at work, arguing that the domestic servant was most vulnerable of all: 'Every male member of the household has a right to insult her. No matter who or what he is – raw and drivelling youth, burly master, or drooling and senile grandpa. Driven to bay by these the gentlemen, she may call for help. But there is no help. Only mistress can hear her cry. She knows that "her boy" wouldn't do such a thing. "You are the brazen baggage." "Leave my house – hussy!" No reference. No "character." When attacked by foreman or employer the factory girl may save her soul at the price of her place and bread, but many a time the "domestic" must give up all on the altar of slavery.'[35]

The profit motive of 'the system' was deemed the cause of prostitution. The employer who paid low wages and the rich who lived off the profits were seen to be no different from a pimp who lived off the proceeds of prostitution. Beyond the procurers, madames, pimps, property owners, merchants, liquor interests, and others were also seen to profit from prostitution. In short, prostitution was depicted as a highly monopolized, concentrated, commercial enterprise, like all business interests under capitalism.[36]

Socialists also discussed the 'white slave' trade as if it were an integral part of the capitalist system. The term itself was first used by factory workers during early industrialization in England and the United States 'to describe their "slavery" to wages and industrial discipline.'[37] But at this time, white slavery was understood to refer to the forcible capture of women – not necessarily white women – and their subsequent sale and forcible initiation as prostitutes.[38] The left echoed much of the existing publicity about white slavery as proof of the immorality and corruption of capitalism. It did not query the validity of such reports, but accepted as fact that women were indeed captured and forced into prostitution. The trade was depicted as part of an international network, with girls and women being kidnapped from Canada, the United States, England, and China.[39]

The idea of white slavery differed from the usual descriptions of prostitution in one important respect. The usual arguments about prostitution, which focused on women's low wages, none the less depicted women as having a subjective being. They could make a choice between starvation, suicide, and a life of prostitution. The left did not condemn women who chose the last. In discussions of white slavery, that small element of choice disappeared. Women were not presented with the alternatives of starvation or suicide. They became the ultimate commodity of capitalism – an object devoid of any human subjectivity. A number of socialists explicitly noted the parallels between wage slavery and white slavery, thus linking the extreme dehumanization of woman as prostitute to the exploitation of men and women as workers. White slavery was described as 'just as moral and clean' as any other business under capitalism because such activities were all based on 'the enslavement and robbery of the working class.' Under capitalism, 'every power, faculty and attribute of the slave is a legitimate article of barter and sale in the market. The money gained by the white slave dealers is as free from taint as any of that which flows from the exploitation of slaves under the rule of capital. The curse of the thing does not lie in the turning of woman's virtue into profitable account. It lies in the enslavement of labour which alone makes the beastly traffic possible.'[40] The issues of prostitution and white slavery provided socialists with a dramatic, compelling, and at times romanticized illustration of the dehumanization of the working class under capitalism.

The above views represented the dominant attitudes expressed by socialists on the issues of prostitution. For the most part, these views were expressed by male socialists. Notably, a few socialist women expressed a strikingly different perception of prostitution. For example, the front page of *Cotton's Weekly* bitterly attacked efforts to reform or punish Montreal prostitutes, contending that one must attack the cause of prostitution – the low wages paid to women workers.[41] In contrast to this economic argument, Mary Cotton Wisdom, editor of the 'Woman's Page,' presented a very different view of male responsibility for prostitution. She declared her indignation that 'a man of God' should bring 'those women made outcasts by a man's sin, up before the courts to be judged by a man, imprisoned by a man, for what? For committing a sin for which man is responsible.' She claimed the man who frequented prostitutes was a 'beast or reptile' and she further argued that such men 'should be punished to the full extent of the law.' She also criticized the laws for being too lax on such men and used this laxity to illustrate the need for woman suffrage: 'Women must stand shoulder to shoulder. Together we must insist upon the right to control the conditions under which we live.'[42] Unlike her brother William Cotton, Mary Cotton Wisdom focused less on the issue of economic exploitation of women than on the problems of male domination, including sexual domination.

Her view that men who used prostitutes were 'beasts or reptiles' also stands in marked contrast to views discussed earlier, which depicted such activity as flowing from 'natural' human urges. Other women concurred with her depiction of prostitution as a male crime stemming from men's depraved nature. One woman insisted that the 'immoral traffic' was not possible without men, who should bear the responsibility of their actions: 'I know of none which drives a man there except his depraved nature. It is certainly not a moment of forgetfulness but deliberate sin.[43] These few socialist women clearly challenged the dominant view among socialists that prostitution could be addressed strictly from a class perspective.

We wonder at the fervour with which these women empathized with the prostitute and deplored the behaviour of the men. Women who expressed these views articulated an important link among the experiences shared by women. Women's status and respectability were dependent upon things beyond a woman's control. Even the 'respectable' woman could recognize how tenuous these virtues were. Illness, injury, or death of the bread-winner might bring respectable women into the world of the prostitute. Furthermore, far from presuming that only single men used prostitutes, some women were concerned that husbands would catch venereal disease and contaminate them and their children.[44] One woman queried how a wife could remain pure and undefiled when she lived with a 'bestial man.'[45] It is clear these women felt the sancity of their homes threatened by the infidelity of their husbands. These views expressed a sense of powerlessness that allowed respectable married women to identify with the victimization of the prostitute.

More important, however, were the indications that such women identified specifically with the prostitute's experience of *sexual* oppression. At this time, there was widespread acceptance of the idea that within marriage women were expected to submit to their husband's sexual desires, an idea that was reinforced by the force of the medical community, religious beliefs, the law, and implicitly by much of the left press.[46] In challenge to this convention, some socialist women discussed marriage as a form of prostitution where women had to sell 'her sex life in return for her keep.'[47] Other articles made veiled reference to the unwanted sexual demands of husbands. For example, one article spoke of how 'we have perverted nature in submitting mothers to the lusts of brute beasts who monopolize the power and means of life under the present system.'[48] Another described a mother who 'suffered from the tyranny and brutality of her husband during pregnancy, and was rebuked and told to submit by a doctor to whom she complained.'[49] While quite circumspect in the description of the husband's behaviour, at minimum the latter article seemed sympathetic to a wife's right to refuse sex when pregnant.

One woman was very direct in describing women's sexual submission to their husbands as 'undescribable torture,' worse than that of a female animal 'which follows sincerely and simply upon the call of nature.' She declared that 'millions' of married women were forced to act against their nature and spoil their health and the health of their children in their tolerance of the 'insane obedience to 'hubby.'"[50] Such depictions of male sexuality as bestial or abnormal led to the demand for woman's sexual autonomy, including the right of a wife to refuse sex. This demand also meant challenging men to change their behaviour. As one woman bluntly put it: 'Go preach to the men and tell them how to control themselves.'[51] Thus, the issue of prostitution became a forum for women to insist upon freedom from sexual exploitation by men – inside and outside marriage.

The above examples link woman's right to refuse sex with her maternal role. At this time, the challenge to male sexual oppression required resort to woman's role as mother – a role thought to carry sufficient force to counter the idea of woman's obligation to submit to her husband's demands. Unfortunately, this demand for woman's sexual autonomy also denied women access to an important dimension of their own sexuality: acknowledgment of sensual pleasure. Although there was acknowledgment, albeit couched in terms of bestial behaviour, that men enjoyed sex, few socialists acknowledged that women might also find sex pleasurable. Moral reformers were, in part, convinced that women turned to prostitution because of their sinful nature, hence the emphasis on moral salvation of the 'fallen women.' 'Sinful nature' was a euphemism for sensual pleasure. The left rejected the idea that women turned to prostitution as an expression of their sexuality. The view that women would never turn to prostitution because of 'attractiveness or choice' or even 'innate wickedness' was reinforced by poems and stories depicting women who had to choose among starvation, suicide, and prostitution.[52] As one writer put it, it was unthinkable that a prostitute had any 'love of the game.'[53] Neither the wife nor the prostitute was depicted as enjoying sensual pleasures. Thus, the women socialists cited above articulated their view of 'free love': given economic independence, women would be free to love as they chose, but *not* in the sensual, libertarian sense that opponents of socialism interpreted. Indeed, as is evident from the above remarks, the socialists rarely expressed any concept of women as capable or desiring of sensual pleasure.[54] Rather, insistence on woman's freedom to love as they choose was a negative freedom: freedom from the unwanted sexual overtures of men.

Male socialists tended to stress the economic roots of woman's sexual oppression and ignored the challenge that women socialists made to male sexual behaviour. Once economically free, woman could 'naturally select the father of her children, and determine when she was prepared to become a mother.' She would no longer be 'compelled by economic necessity to tolerate a drunkard, a bully, or a sensualist.'[55] Woman's economic independence would mean the 'total cessation of marrying for a home ... It means that there will be no more prostitution, either inside or outside of the marriage relation. It means that the sex relations between men and women will be raised to a plane of purity which can scarcely be imagined under the present impossible conditions.'[56] Unlike the women socialists, these male socialists did not envisage that men would be either urged or compelled to change their behaviour towards women. Women would simply be free to leave a 'bully' or a 'sensualist.'

Some socialist women saw that the solution to prostitution and the sexual domination of women required more than economic resolution. They stressed the need for all women to unite to act collectively to assert their freedom from sexual oppression by men and to 'let women make the laws to govern punishment of their sisters and let a woman judge and minister the woman-made laws against women.'[57] These women used their common experience of sexual oppression to urge a common political bond among all women: 'Women must stand by women. Women must go forward to free their sisters from awful conditions imposed upon them by man's brutality and selfishness.'[58]

This examination of socialist views of prostitution lends insight into the struggle over feminist issues within a political movement. A minority of socialists, mostly women, wanted the socialist movement to address the problem of sexual domination as well as economic exploitation inherent in the problem of prostitution. Through their experience and understanding of sexual oppression, socialist women could identify with the plight of prostitutes. Their understanding of the issue differed markedly from that of male socialists. As a result, women socialists posed a serious challenge to male socialists, obliging them to reflect on their own private behaviour in relation to women and to articulate a public stance that would repudiate the sexual oppression of women. The women who voiced these concerns, however, were in a minority within the left. Men controlled the leadership positions and the party newspapers, and constituted the majority within the socialist move-ment.[59] Their unwillingness to accept the challenge of women to reflect upon their own attitudes was in turn reflected in the dominant view of prostitution among socialists.

Prostitution was understood in terms of a class analysis that emphasized the economic constraints leading to prostitution. But this class perspective was also a guise that obscured the unwillingness of socialist men to consider their contribution –as clients of prostitutes or as husbands – to the sexual oppression of women. A few women socialists saw through this guise and challenged socialist men to acknowledge the private and public dimensions of this problem: men's role in the sexual oppression of women, the need for men to forswear such behaviour, and the need to challenge the economic and political institutions that perpetuated the sexual oppression of women. These women were met with the criticism that such concerns had nothing to do with socialism. It is abundantly clear from consideration of the nature of prostitution, however, that the resolution of the prostitution issue would have to address both the economic exploitation and the sexual oppression of women. This, in turn, would require a reconsideration of both the private and public dimensions of the problem.

The issue of prostitution provided socialists with an excellent vehicle to illustrate the class bias and futility of reforms under capitalism. The reformers' proposals were viewed as profoundly inadequate because they did not attack the wage system and the low wages paid to working women. The left's criticisms were, in one respect, well founded. Reform efforts did fail – as prostitutes themselves rejected the attempts to morally reform them. Efforts to disband the red-light districts did not end prostitution; the prostitutes simply moved to other locations. Also, the end of the era of brothels marked a dramatic decline in the quality of life for the prostitute. Devoid of the security and social network of the houses, and pushed out into the streets, women were more vulnerable to exploitation and victimization by pimps and customers. The moral reformers who may have sincerely desired to improve the life of the prostitute failed miserably to do so. Their failure was marked by an inability or an unwillingness to recognize that real alternatives for women, although not the only solution, were certainly essential to solving the problem of prostitution. Women needed viable and attractive alternatives to a life of prostitution.

Rather than blaming women for turning to prostitution, socialists empathized with their plight. The prostitute became a symbol of the extremes of exploitation and dehumanization that capitalism wreaked upon the working class. However sympathetic the left may have been to the economic pressures that forced women into prostitution, there were important lacunae and contradictions in their arguments, and these inhibited the development of a more feminist understanding of prostitution and the sexual oppression of women. Most significant in this regard was the assumption, expressed primarily by men, that wealthy men who used prostitutes were sexually depraved and exploitative of women, while working-class men who did the same were not. In this respect, the socialists did not perceive male sexual oppression as a primary problem to be addressed by the left. Only a few isolated individuals, most of them women, were able to perceive both the sexual exploitation and the economic exploitation inherent in the problem. They recognized that male sexual oppression had no class boundaries. For these few, the issue of prostitution provided an ideal forum to expand the socialist agenda to include a feminist challenge to male sexual oppression.

NOTES

1 *Cotton's Weekly*, 7 September 1911, 1.
2 For discussion of the history of prostitution in various Canadian cities at this time, see Joy Cooper, 'Red Lights of Winnipeg,' Historical and Scientific Society of Manitoba, *Transactions* 27 (1971), 61–74; Lori Rotenberg, 'The Wayward Worker: Toronto's Prostitute at the Turn of the Century,' in Janice Acton, et al, eds, *Women at Work, Ontario, 1850–1930* (Toronto 1974), 33–70; James Gray, *Red Lights on the Prairies* (Toronto 1974); Deborah Nilsen, 'The 'Social Evil': Prostitution in Vancouver, 1900–1920,' in Barbara Latham and Cathy Kess, eds, *In Her Own Right* (Victoria 1980), 205–28; and Tamara Adilman, 'A Preliminary Sketch of Chinese Women and Work in British Columbia, 1858–1950, in Barbara Latham and Roberta Pazdro, eds, *Not Just Pin Money: Selected Essays on the History of Women's Work in British Columbia* (Victoria 1984), 53–78. For a discussion of the American setting, see Ruth Rosen, *The Lost Sisterhood: Prostitution in America, 1900–1918* (Baltimore 1982).
3 *Western Clarion*, 27 July 1912, 4.
4 For discussion of the ideas and activities of such Canadian organizations, see Veronica Strong-Boag, 'Setting the Stage,' in Susan Mann Trofimenkoff, eds, *The Neglected Majority* (Toronto 1977), 87–103; Strong-Boag, *The Parliament of Women* (Ottawa 1976); Carol Bacchi, *Liberation Deferred* (Toronto 1983); Linda Kealey, ed., *A Not Unreasonable Claim: Women and Reform in Canada, 1880s–1920s* (Toronto 1979); Susan Buckley and Janice Dickin McGinnis, 'Venereal Disease and Public Health Reform in Canada,' *Canadian Historical Review* 63 (1982), 337–54; Paul Bator, 'The Struggle to Raise the Lower Classes: Public Health Reform and the Problem of Poverty in Toronto, 1910 to 1921,' *Journal of Canadian Studies* 14 (Spring 1979), 43–9; Norah Lewis, 'Reducing Maternal Mortality in British Columbia: An Educational Process,' Latham and Pazdro, eds, in *Not Just Pin Money*, 337–55; Angus and Arlene McLaren, *The Bedroom and the State* (Toronto 1986).

5 *Cotton's Weekly*, 16 June 1910, 1; 17 April 1913, 1; 15 April 1909, 8; Gerald
 Desmond, 'To the Social and Moral Reformers,' 13 May 1909, 2; Roscoe
 A. Fillmore, 'The Social Evil,' 9 September 1909, 8; 11 November 1909, 1; 17
 February 1910, 4; and 24 December 1908, 2.
6 E.M. Epplett, 'Workers Sit up and Take Notice,' *Western Clarion*, 8 April
 1909, 7, and 'A Surface Skimmer,' *Western Clarion*, 30 May 1908.
7 For a discussion of prevailing concepts of sexuality, see Sarah Jeffreys, '"Free
 from All Uninvited Touch of Man": Women's Campaigns around Sexuality,
 1880–1914,' *Women's Studies International Journal* 5 (1982), 629–45; Ellen
 DuBois and Linda Gordon, 'Seeking Ecstasy on the Battlefield: Danger and
 Pleasure in Nineteenth-Century Feminist Sexual Thought,' *Feminist Studies* 9
 (Spring 1983), 7–25; Sondra Herman, 'Loving Courtship or the Marriage
 Market?: The Ideal and Its Critics, 1871–1911,' *American Quarterly* 25 (May
 1973), 235–52.
8 Friedrich Engel's book, *The Origin of the Family, Private Property and the State*
 (Zurich), was first published in 1884 and was widely read in socialist circles
 by the turn of the century. August Bebel's *Woman under Socialism* (New York
 1904) was first published in German in 1883, and translated into English in
 1904. Like Engels's book, it was also widely read and popular among socialists
 of the time.
9 Bebel, *Women under Socialism* (New York 1904), 79–86 and 343–44.
10 For a discussion of the American sex radicals, see Linda Gordon, *Woman's Body,
 Woman's Right* (New York 1977); Leslie Fishbein, *Radicals in Bohemia: The
 Radicals of 'The Masses,' 1911–1917* (Chapel Hill 1982); Carlos A. Schwantes,
 'Free Love and Free Speech on the Pacific Northwest Frontier,' *Oregon
 Historical Quarterly* 82 (Fall 1981), 271–93; Dolores Hayden, *The Grand
 Domestic Revolution* (Cambridge, MA, 1981), 90–113; Margaret Marsh,
 Anarchist Women, 1870–1920 (Philadelphia 1981).
11 D. DeLeon, trans., in preface to Bebel's *Woman under Socialism*, xviii. DeLeon
 was the leader of the Socialist Labor party in the United States.
12 The free-love group of Victoria Woodhull was expelled from the International
 Workingmen's Association, a branch of the First International, for its feminist causes of 'free love and suffrage' (Hayden, *The Grand Domestic Revolution*,
 101–3. See also Barbara Taylor, *Eve and the New Jerusalem* (London 1983);
 and Mari Jo Buhle, *Women and American Socialism* (Urbana 1981).
13 'We Women,' *Western Socialist*, 8 November 1902, 3.
14 Ibid., 29 November 1902, 3. The Canadian sex radicals who were active in the
 birth-control movement in Canada are discussed in McLaren, *The Bedroom
 and the State*, 54–91. For a more extensive discussion of the debates over sexuality
 within the early Canadian left, including discussions of birth control, mar-

riage, and free love, see Janice Newton, "Enough of Exclusive Masculine Thinking": The Feminist Challenge to the Early Canadian Left,' PhD diss., York University, 1987, ch 5.

15 'Socialist Movement Defined,' *Western Clarion*, 17 June 1905.

16 Ibid. See also 'Economics or Esoterics,' *Western Clarion*, 13 October 1906, 2.

17 For examples of these arguments, see A. Budden, 'Women and Socialism,' *Western Clarion*, 27 September 1913, 1; 25 November 1905, 3; and W. Laurence, 'Reform, Social and Moral,' 25 February 1911, 1.

18 *Cotton's Weekly*, 24 December 1908, 2.

19 Fillmore, 'The Social Evil,' *Cotton's Weekly*, 9 September 1909, 8.

20 Gerald Desmond, 'To the Social and Moral Reformers,' *Cotton's Weekly*, 13 May 1909, 2.

21 'Reform or Revolution: Edmonton Unionists Expose the Inefficiency of Reform Measures,' *Western Clarion*, 16 August 1913, 1, and 'A Crushing Reply,' *Cotton's Weekly*, 4 September 1913, 3.

22 *Cotton's Weekly*, 10 July 1913, 1.

23 For example, see 'What a Girl Can Live On,' *Cotton's Weekly*, 1 July 1909, 7.

24 'Punishment,' *Cotton's Weekly*, 21 January 1909, 1.

25 *Western Socialist*, 27 September 1902, 3. See also, 'Perfect Nonsense,' *Cotton's Weekly*, 3 July 1913, 1.

26 *Cotton's Weekly*, 30 June 1910, 4, and 3 July 1913, 1.

27 'Why Working Women Sell Their Honor,' *Western Clarion*, 27 July 1912, 4.

28 For example, see *Western Clarion*, 11 June 1903, 2.

29 For example, 'The Socialists and the Sexual Relations,' *Western Clarion*, 11 June 1903, 2. See also *Cotton's Weekly*, 1 July 1909, 3, and 13 November 1913, 1.

30 *Western Clarion*, 14 August 1903, 1.

31 Gerald Desmond, 'Prostitution,' *Western Clarion*, 30 April 1910, 1.

32 'The White Slave Traffic,' *Western Clarion*, 14 February 1914, 2.

33 For example, see *Western Socialist*, 11 October 1902, 3; *Cotton's Weekly*, 7 October 1909, 1; *Western Clarion*, 23 May 1903, 1.

34 May Walden Kerr, 'Socialism and the Home,' *Western Socialist*, 11 October 1902, 3; *Cotton's Weekly*, 7 October 1909, 1; and *Western Clarion*, 23 May 1903, 1.

35 Ben Hanford, 'Under Socialism There Ain't Goin' be No Servant Girls,' *Cotton's Weekly*, 12 June 1913, 7.

36 For example, Edwin Simms, 'Betraying and Selling Girls for Profit: One Aspect of Capitalist System,' *Cotton's Weekly*, 24 June 1909, 3.

37 Rosen, *The Lost Sisterhood*, 116.

38 Considerable publicity was given to this issue as government commissions in Canada and the United States were struck to investigate the existence of the

white slave trade in North America. While much controversy exists over the
extent and nature of the trade given the difficulty in establishing reliable
sources, it is certain that white slavery did exist in Canada and in the United States
at this time. Sources cited above on prostitution in Canada cite cases where
women prostitutes were held as slaves.

39 For example, see 'White Slave Traffic,' *Cotton's Weekly*, 16 December 1909,
2, and 'The White Slave Trade,' *Western Clarion*, 24 February 1912, 2.
40 *Western Clarion*, 14 November 1908, 4.
41 *Cotton's Weekly*, 21 January 1909, 1, and 28 January 1909, 1.
42 'Women Judged by Men,' *Cotton's Weekly*, 28 January 1909, 7.
43 Rosa Gabriel, *Cotton's Weekly*, 4 March 1909, 3.
44 For example, see 'Race Suicide with a Vengeance,' *Cotton's Weekly*, 8 July 1909,
7, and 'Isolation for Sufferers,' 21 January 1909, 8.
45 Mrs Jane V. Brown, 'The Woman Who Knows,' *Cotton's Weekly*, 2 July 1914,
1.
46 Wendy Mitchinson, 'Historical Attitudes towards Women and Childbirth,' *Atlantis* 4 (Spring 1979), 13–34.
47 *Cotton's Weekly*, 4 May 1911, 2. See also Mrs Brown, 'Woman Who Knows.'
48 *Cotton's Weekly*, 19 January 1911, 4.
49 R.B. Kerr, *Western Clarion*, 13 October 1906, 2.
50 Mary Nicolaeff, 'Women under Socialism,' *Cotton's Weekly*, 4 June 1914, 1.
51 Mrs Brown, 'Woman Who Knows.'
52 For example, see 'One Way Out,' *Western Clarion*, 26 November 1910, 1; 'Girl
on the Bridge,' 9 November 1907, 3; and Rosa Gabriel, 'Woman's Honour,'
Cotton's Weekly, 18 February 1909, 7.
53 Gourock, 'Simply Socialism,' *Western Clarion*, 10 June 1911, 1.
54 Articles by J.K. Mergler are one exception. He writes of a 'woman's passion'
and 'gnawing desire for vicious recreation,'; see 'What Then Shall They Do?'
Western Clarion, 27 September 1913, 2.
55 F.J. Flatman, 'The Question of Free Love,' *Cotton's Weekly*, 28 August 1913,
4. See also William Scott, 'Socialists and the Sexual Relations,' *Western
Clarion*, 11 June 1903, 2; 'Socialism and Sex,' *Western Clarion*, 14 December
1907, 4.
56 John M. Work, 'Shall Women Work?' *Cotton's Weekly*, 16 November 1911, 4.
57 *Cotton's Weekly*, 17 February 1910, 4.
58 Ibid., 25 February 1909, 1.
59 For a more complete discussion of women's role in the early Canadian left, see
Newton, '"Enough of Exclusive Masculine Thinking."'

PART FIVE

Politics and Community

The Ideas of the Ukrainian Women's Organization of Canada

1930–1945

Frances Swyripa

In February 1924 a 34-year-old Ukrainian woman, Olha Basarab, died in a jail in Lviv, the major city in Galicia in Western Ukraine. Her death followed her torture by Polish police acting for the new Poland to which, in 1923, the Council of Ambassadors had handed most of Western Ukraine. Basarab had been arrested for activities as an intelligence courier in the illegal Ukrainian Military Organization (Ukrainska viiskova orhanizatsiia – UVO), composed of members of the defeated Ukrainian independence armies unreconciled to the new status quo and dedicated to continuing the struggle. She died without betraying her comrades or the cause they championed.[1]

Basarab and others like her became martyrs in the eyes of the UVO and its successor, the militant Organization of Ukrainian Nationalists (Orhanizatsiia ukrainskykh natsionalistiv – OUN), which denounced all compromise with the foreign regimes on Ukrainian soil[2] and master-minded the often violent underground campaign on behalf of a united independent Ukrainian state. The OUN's nationalist ideology was hierarchical, corporatist, militaristic, and totalitarian; it placed the nation and national interest above all; and it exalted the state as the highest form of evolution in the struggle of each national organism for existence. The OUN's influence extended beyond its stronghold in Ukrainian sections of Poland. Ukrainian émigrés in Western Europe not only participated in its establishment, contributed to its ideology, and provided leadership but also acted as diplomatic emissaries. Nazi Germany was presumed to be sympathetic to Ukrainian independence and also judged to be the sole power with sufficient interest and strength to destroy Poland and the Soviet Union to make independence possible.[3]

Across the ocean, other Ukrainian émigrés were equally committed to Ukrainian sovereignty and to their own responsibility for its attainment. In

1934 the Ukrainian Women's Organization of Canada (Orhanizatsiia ukrainok Kanady – OUK) was formed to bring Ukrainian-Canadian women under the umbrella of the two-year-old Ukrainian National Federation (Ukrainske natsionalne obiednannia – UNO), dominated by recent immigrants and closely identifying with the brand of Ukrainian nationalism espoused by the OUN.[4] The women were urged to organize, for only through coherent and well-directed plans could they accomplish the tasks that membership in the Ukrainian nation demanded: to assist, morally and materially, in the liberation of the native land and to propagate the nationalist movement in Canada, not only cultivating it among Ukrainian-Canadian women but also forging links with Canadian women's organizations to publicize the Ukrainian question in mainstream circles.[5] The OUK chose as its patroness Olha Basarab, whose example and supreme sacrifice were to be both an inspiration and a challenge.

The Canadian UNO saw itself as part of the Ukrainian nation in diaspora, more emigrant than immigrant. The columns of its official organ, *Novyi shliakh* (New Pathway), made clear its concern for Ukrainian life in Canada and its immediate problems; the UNO supported the Ukrainian-Canadian co-operative movement, for example, as a means of self-help during the Great Depression. But sporting the slogans 'nation above all' and 'our strength is in ourselves,' *Novyi shliakh* made it equally clear that until September 1939 (when the prudence of stressing loyalty to Canada became obvious), an independent and united Ukrainian state was the UNO's primary concern. 'Nationalists of Canada,' an article marking the OUN's tenth anniversary appealed, 'let our ranks [here] beyond the ocean, beyond the borders, be firmly welded with the nationalist columns of Warring Ukraine, with the cohorts of the OUN in the Fatherland.'[6]

As an émigré organization, the UNO faced the same handicaps as other similar groups or governments-in-exile: an air of unreality about their pronouncements, ambitions, and activities – or their irrelevance to current events in the homeland. Unreality and irrelevance can create a gap between the ideal role such bodies envisage for themselves and the actual role they can play. Their situation is exacerbated if their aspirations fail to enjoy the support of the country in which they exist or if their members as immigrants (like Ukrainians in Canada between the wars) labour under a negative image and low status. Nevertheless, to the UNO, the rights and privileges Canada provided enabled it to serve Ukraine in ways impossible for its enslaved brethren (*v nevoli*) in Europe. It was free to indoctrinate the Ukrainian-Canadian masses in nationalist ideology and responsibility, to propagandize the Ukrainian cause among Canadians and world leaders, and to aid materially the struggle in the native land. Aid ranged from financial, as with the Liberation Fund

(Vyzvolnyi fond), to radio-telegraphy and flying schools, established in 1935 and 1938 respectively, to prepare young Ukrainian Canadians for the Ukrainian campaign in the anticipated European war.[7]

Within the Ukrainian-Canadian community, the UNO's program of Ukraine first created tensions with the more Canadian national organizations crystallizing in the inter-war years, specifically the Ukrainian Self-Reliance League, representing Orthodox laity, and the Ukrainian Catholic Brotherhood. At the same time, its hatred of the Soviet Union pitted it in bitter controversy against the pro-Soviet, pro-communist Ukrainian Labour-Farmer Temple Association. The UNO's anti-Soviet and anti-Polish stance, open admiration of Germany and Italy, belief that an independent Ukraine figured in Reich plans, and physical and spiritual links with the OUN made it vulnerable when the expected European war finally erupted and Canada entered alongside Britain. Stalin (after an interval) was the ally, Hitler and Mussolini were the enemy. All but the communist minority among Ukrainian Canadians found the Soviet alliance and Britain's guarantee to Poland hard pills to swallow. The UNO was not unique in that respect. It fell prey, however, to charges of fascism and nazism.

In 1943 the communist press published 'This Is Our Land': Ukrainian Canadians against Hitler, as a defence of the loyal but mistreated pro-Soviet sector (the 'anti-fascists') and an exposé of the 'fascist' Hitlerophile fifth column, the UNO, quoting extensively from Novyi shliakh to support its argument.[8] The same month, the UNO published A Program and a Record to explain its philosophy and activities. The pamphlet denounced all fascist charges, stressed loyalty to Canada (the enlistment of its radio-telegraphy and flying school trainees, for example, identified the UNO with the Canadian war effort), and 'once and for all' denied affiliation with Ukrainian organizations outside Canada.[9] The interest of Canada's wartime leaders and other well-placed individuals in the UNO justified this sensitivity about its image.[10]

As the UNO's affiliate, and subordinate in matters of general policy and decision making, the OUK shared its philosophy, programs, and fortunes. Initially uniting existing women's clubs with a nationalist outlook, the OUK embraced some 30 branches across Canada and perhaps 1000 members on the eve of the Second World War. Like the UNO, it was spearheaded by recent immigrants and reflected the attractiveness of central Canada and urban life to the new arrivals, compared to the rural prairies destinations of the pre-war Ukrainian immigration. Fully one-half of the OUK locals were located in Ontario, and, with the partial exception of Saskatchewan, they existed in larger urban centres or resource towns as opposed to farming communities.[11] The OUK represented but a fraction of organized Ukrainian-Canadian women and an even smaller minority (less than 1 per cent) of Ukrainian-Canadian women as a whole.[12] But it was a vocal and active minority, one which saw itself as a leading wedge, the conscious élite of Ukrainian womanhood obligated to raise the mass of Ukrainian-Canadian women to a higher level of awareness and commitment to the national idea. Only collective strength and single-minded pursuit of the goal would achieve a united, independent Ukrainian state.[13]

The conviction that all forces – material, spiritual, human – were to be harnessed in the interests of the nation and the state meant that women as well as men had both an indispensable role and unavoidable duty in national life. Through the organization's page in *Novyi shliakh*, the OUK leadership explained for its readers, the women within OUK's ranks and the women it hoped to reach, exactly what that role and duty were.

I

The OUK's position on the relationship of Ukrainian women to national life proceeded from the fundamental belief in the primacy of the nation. It was the principle guiding every action, and it demanded the submersion of the individual in the collective interest and the maximum contribution and effort by all parts on behalf of the whole. Such self-sacrifice and dedication were particularly necessary among peoples striving for the ultimate form of self-expression – their own states – because freedom came through struggle, not as a gift.[14] This thinking produced two directives for Ukrainian women. The first held that motherhood and homemaking were not enough; Ukrainian women had to participate actively in all spheres of life if the goal of national independence were to be realized. The second subordinated women's liberation to national liberation; with Ukrainian men and women both 'enslaved and under the terror of the conqueror,'[15] it could not be otherwise. On closer inspection, the first directive loses much of its radicalism, the second some of its conservatism. Their incompatibility, moreover, proves more apparent than real.

Despite claims that 'fascist' states oppressed women by denying them equal rights, wrote Rozha Kovalska, OUK organizer in central Canada, it was precisely such states that honoured women as mothers of the next generation. The women, in turn, valued this special role as their greatest service to the fatherland.[16] But, Kovalska continued, and others echoed her sentiments, only in nation-states secure in their own strength could women confine themselves to their natural function. Statelessness imposed additional burdens and responsibilities. When enemies threatened or held captive not only a people's soil and wealth but also its soul, women as one-half the nation had to stand shoulder to shoulder with men on all fronts in its defence. In 1933 an agitator for a nationalist organization to unite and propagandize among Ukrainian-Canadian women explained that women, whether in Ukraine or in the emigration, had a dual role. They must, as mothers, rear 'fresh cadres of young nationalist warriors who put Ukraine first,' and they must, themselves, participate actively and directly in the liberation struggle. Their abdication in the past on both counts had proved disastrous.[17]

The women spearheading the OUK placed much of the blame for the failure of the fledgling Ukrainian state to sustain itself in 1917–20 on their sex. Despite the conscious few who had taken up arms, worked in field kitchens and hospitals, and exhorted their menfolk to join the revolutionary army, this decisive juncture in the life of their nation had caught Ukrainian women as a whole unprepared and indifferent. Besides having failed to raise the cadres of nationalist warriors necessary for victory, they had defaulted personally and done nothing at the moment when Ukraine most needed them. A Ukrainian state would exist today, an OUK audience in Edmonton was told, if in 1917 Ukrainian women had grasped the issue at stake – the significance and centrality of 'nation above all' – and recognized their own role and responsibilities.[18] The next decisive juncture in the life of their nation could not find Ukrainian women equally unprepared and indifferent.

The women of those nations that had been successful in their struggles for independence and statehood had lessons to teach. While Joan of Arc figured as the archetype of female heroism in the service of the nation, models came from the era of modern nationalism as well. Italian, German, Polish, and Czech women, for example, had contributed greatly – on occasion with their blood – to the rise of their states: modern Germany and Italy in the late nineteenth century, Poland and Czechoslovakia on the ruins of the Austro-Hungarian and tsarist empires and at the expense of peoples like the Ukrainians.[19] And as the world of the 1930s appeared to be moving toward a major crisis, even the strong nations with their own states prepared their women, ever ready to defend their countries, not only for home-front duties but for the front line itself; they were being taught how to shoot, throw bombs, use gas, and operate tanks. When the crisis broke – the crisis that was also to bring the favourable resolution of the Ukrainian question – Ukrainians would be confronting hostile armies of men and women backed by firm support systems. Such a confrontation rendered victory impossible unless Ukrainian women were equally mobilized and identified unflinchingly with their nation's struggle for a better tomorrow.[20] Preparedness, both in Ukraine and abroad, hinged on the success of the nationalist élite in arousing the political consciousness of the mass of Ukrainian women, uniting them under its banner to work for the common goal and good. 'And when with our active help our Fatherland stands free, and the valiant Ukrainian army secures the borders of the Free, United Ukrainian State,' Rozha Kovalska concluded, 'only then will we have respite from our labours in the environment of our free and happy family.'[21] Participation in all spheres of life was not to overshadow woman's primary responsibility as mother.

If the ultimate dominance of motherhood in defining women's relationship to the nation muted the radicalism suggested in 'active on every front' and 'arm in arm with men,' the insistence on women's full acceptance of the responsibilities of membership in the nation muted the conservatism suggested in 'national emancipation before female emancipation.' This conservatism is little muted from a contemporary feminist perspective and understanding of the equality of women, but it is within the context of OUK thought, for although women were subordinated to the nation's needs, their service in its name required a degree of education, self-awareness, and public conscience. To the OUK, the relationship between the sexes was one of co-operation, not difference or conflict, and equal rights meant the right to bear equal (although not always the same) burdens and responsibilities. To the extent that the majority of Ukrainian women, as the result of centuries of national subjugation, did not feel themselves the equals of men, ready to assume equal burdens and responsibilities, they had to be emancipated – awakened to the full conscious-ness of themselves, their people, and the world that would herald national emancipation. Such women understood their tasks before their families, community, and nation, and directed their abilities, knowledge, and labour to their benefit. The emancipation of women as persons or individuals, in contrast, was equated with efforts to assert female superiority or to serve selfish individual interests, and was assumed to appeal to women seeking to shirk their national obligations.[22] Self-fulfilment came through national service.

The OUK's perception of female emancipation, in both its positive and negative meanings, reinforces the impression that woman's 'natural' function was her most important. Liberated women in the positive sense possessed the tools to raise their children as 'upright, honourable, conscious and industrious citizens' who loved their nation and freedom, women's 'major and most important task.' Liberated women in the negative sense avoided their 'greatest natural and national responsibility,' which was to bear and rear children.[23]

In combining a public role with women's first role in the nursery, the OUK was not advocating anything novel. Nations have traditionally asked more from their subjects or citizens in times of emergency, which has often meant a temporary broadened scope of activity or heightened profile, but without any built-in intention of formalizing these changes upon return to normalcy. Claudia Koonz describes how Nazi ideology placed extra demands on German women while the movement was struggling, but after Hitler's consolidation of power eased them back into their traditional stabilizing role in the family; then again, as Germany prepared for war, they were recruited into the labour force to release males for military needs.[24] Canada's wartime approach, as Ruth Roach Pierson points out, was similar: officially sponsored entry into the workplace during manpower shortages, officially encouraged exit when demobilized veterans needed jobs and women were to resume their proper place in the home.[25] Women in both Germany and Canada were impressed with the necessity to sacrifice for their nation during crisis, and women in both countries acquiesced in the return to domesticity once the crisis ended.

What distinguished the OUK in the period under discussion was the absence of normalcy, in which the nation and the state were synonymous and mutually secure. The question of physical and political-cultural survival has been a permanent feature of Ukrainian history. The medieval princedom of Kievan Rus', the seventeenth-century Cossack state, and the Ukrainian People's Republic of 1917–20 were separated by longer periods of rule by more powerful neighbours unsympathetic to the Ukrainian population and Ukrainian national aspirations. The OUK's interpretation of the past emphasized the virtue and fortitude of the Ukrainian nation and the nationalists' role as the vessel of the national idea: the glorious times when Ukrainians controlled their own destiny, and justice and equality reigned; the terrible times of subjugation in which, however, despite the submission of the masses and opportunism of those who served Ukraine's masters, individuals kept alive the ideas of freedom and struggle; and the heroic times of struggle these individuals inspired and led.[26] This general scheme provided not only a framework for the Ukrainian woman's historical role in national life but also a series of female models, from Ukraine's own past, for the role she should play in the present.

Although the women of other nations could teach Ukrainian women many things, their own heroines were the true source of inspiration. Ukrainian history offered contemporary Ukrainian women evidence of women's vital and honourable participation in nation building, together with their love for their people and identification with its struggle; and it proved them capable of great deeds and sacrifice. Women had the right to be proud of their foremothers, as well as the obligation to honour their memory and the cause they served.[27] In keeping with the OUK's priorities, the female figures held up for veneration and emulation came from Ukraine's periods of glory and struggle. With two exceptions, they were women of action (rulers, warriors, militants); the exceptions were women of the nineteenth-century renaissance and mothers. The OUK's pantheon of heroines highlighted the interrelationship and essential sameness of Ukrainian women's public and domestic roles.

The Great Heroines of Kievan Rus' and Cossack Ukraine were women of influence, the 'powers behind the throne' or the occupiers of the throne during male absences, and women in military situations.[28] The prototype, uniting all the qualities of the ideal Ukrainian woman, was the Kievan princess Olha. As a wife, she was devoted to her husband, the prerequisite for happy family life, and she counselled him wisely in matters of state. After his death, as ruler, she governed in the state's best interests during her son's minority and avenged her husband's murder at enemy hands. As a mother, she raised a son, Sviatoslav 'the Conqueror,' and a grandson, Volodymyr 'the Great,' who converted Rus' to Christianity (both he and his grandmother were canonized). The sooner all Ukrainian women followed Olha's example of national service, the readers of *Novyi shliakh* were told, the sooner Ukraine would be free.[29]

Its view of Ukrainian history also gave the OUK the explanation for women's weakness in the great test of the twentieth century. The dismantling of the Cossack state in the eighteenth century and subsequent overlordship of Ukraine by Russia, Poland, and Austria had inaugurated women's darkest hour and continued to haunt their mentality. The reason? Ukraine's conquerors knew that Ukrainian women were the key to their control. Slave-mothers raised slave-children, and as long as Ukrainian mothers were oppressed, their sons and daughters would never become conscious Ukrainians prepared to fight for their people. The result? Instead of the rights, equality, and active role the OUK saw women enjoying in natural Ukrainian society, women were confined to the home, denied education, and had their creativity smothered. Moreover, to enhance the masters' grip, Ukrainian men were encouraged to regard women as weak and inferior.[30] This perspective conveniently absolved Ukrainians of self-blame for the subordination of women in the nineteenth- and twentieth-century Ukrainian peasant societies, and it precluded the need or desire for OUK sympathizers to analyse what was perceived as a temporary phenomenon, destined to disappear with national liberation. This view also dispensed with female rulers and warriors, and elevated motherhood to women's supreme role in national life. On the quality of the 'Ukrainianness' of mothers hung the fate of the nation.

The OUK's interpretation of recent Ukrainian history, with successive generations of indifferent and servile women lacking national consciousness, would have made the fate of the nation despairingly bleak had it not been able to point to individuals who had never accepted their subjugated condition or assimilated with the enemy. In 1884 the Ukrainian women's movement began the process of liberating and organizing women in the best interest of the family and nation.[31] Its efforts bore fruit in the children brought up as Ukrainian patriots by conscious mothers. Olena Pchilka, herself a figure of the national renaissance and a women's activist, raised an even greater daughter, the writer Lesia Ukrainka. The OUK hailed Ukrainka as the precursor of Ukrainian nationalism, popularizing the necessity of struggle and armed insurrection by a captive people.[32] In the twentieth century, martyrs like Sofia Halechko (ensign in the Ukrainian Sich Sharpshooters), Olha Basarab, Vira Babenko (tortured to death by the Bolsheviks), and their sisters of the 1930s had by their deaths gained immortality. These were the Great Heroines – the OUK's 'spiritual mothers,' who had demonstrated that no sacrifice was too large, no task too hard – that Ukrainian women were to emulate.[33]

Mothers themselves completed the pantheon. Like Spartan women of old,[34] Ukrainian mothers had since the days of Cossackdom despatched their sons and daughters to fight for the honour and freedom of the fatherland. Accepting the personal price that placing their nation first exacted, they had nurtured in their children love for their country and liberty, a sense of duty and spirit of sacrifice, and the demeanour of warriors. The adoption of Mother's Day by Ukrainians in the 1930s was a national gesture, to acknowledge Great Mothers of the nation's past who had contributed so much not only to the Ukrainian family but also to national life. Mother's Day speeches and editorials invited contemporary Ukrainian women to follow the example of their predecessors, and by raising their children in the service of the nation, to share their glory.[35]

Great Heroines and Great Mothers not only inspired but also left a legacy. The testament of Ukraine's dead – it is better to die in struggle than to live in slavery – together with their vision, sacrifice, and unfinished work, imposed an obligation on the living. Ukrainian nationalism had to become the idea binding and motivating all Ukrainians.[36] For defeat in 1917–20 had been a result less of weakness in the ranks of the dedicated than of the indifference and hostility of those who outnumbered them. Against heroic individuals were the apathetic masses; and against the millions of mothers who had raised their children as Ukrainian patriots were the many more millions who had not.[37] This knowledge and the blood of the martyrs determined the OUK's work: to continue the struggle by every means available and to bring all Ukrainian women to the national idea.

'An Independent United Ukraine,' Anna Kramar told an OUK meeting in Edmonton, 'is the aim, and the path is implacable struggle against all occupiers of our lands. For Ukraine will rise only when the entire Ukrainian People – all men, all women, and even children – take weapons in their hands and together smite the enemy.'[38] These were rousing words and in the spirit of Ukraine's martyrs. But as emigrants, the women in the OUK also realized that the Great

Heroines of Ukraine, while sources of inspiration and pride, had limitations as practical models. One could not throw grenades or carry secret messages when living in Sudbury or Saskatoon. But neither – when women in Ukraine had died for their beliefs, and were suffering under occupation – did living in Sudbury or Saskatoon permit women to think they could not help their nation; nor could they think that meetings and their associated tasks were a 'great sacrifice' even though they impinged upon family responsibilities.[39]

In fact, Sudbury and Saskatoon possessed certain advantages over Ukraine. Ukrainian women in Canada could freely organize, which provided the basis for material aid to the homeland, the popularization of nationalist sentiment, and an enlightened womanhood conscious of its duty. The OUK contributed to the Liberation Fund and it urged members to support the Ukrainian-Canadian co-operative movement, so that by improving their own material circumstances they could better assist Ukraine. It urged its members to support the many nationalist press fund-drives; and it urged them to read the press and to pass issues along to others to read. It sponsored information evenings, where women learned about their role in national life, past and present; and it had an annual agenda of concerts honouring Ukrainian national heroes, male and female, and marking Mother's Day.[40]

Great Mothers had more potential than Great Heroines as practical models. They were also perceived as more necessary, for mothers raised the nation.[41] To the leadership of the OUK, Canada was a mixed blessing. On the one hand, and unlike the situation in Ukraine, it gave Ukrainian women the freedom to raise their children in a nationalist spirit; on the other hand, it was itself an assimilationist society.[42] Before 1939, mothers were told that their sons and daughters must be made to realize that the country in which they lived was not their Fatherland; Ukrainian-Canadian youth were to be raised as 'national heroes, ready to sacrifice everything, including their lives, for Ukraine.'[43] After 1939, mothers were told that they must raise good Canadian citizens as well.[44]

II

When Canada went to war in 1939, it was to help the mother country, Great Britain, defeat Nazi ambitions for European hegemony. For Ukrainian Canadians, the issue was more complex. As an immigrant group with memories of enemy-alien status from one war and a reputation for political and labour radicalism, they were anxious that their loyalty to Canada be unquestioned. As Ukrainians, they hoped the conflict would redress the injustices of the inter-war settlement in Eastern Europe. But the unlikelihood that Britain, and therefore Canada, would support the dismemberment of allied nations that Ukrainian sovereignty required affected Ukrainian activities. The situation was further complicated by the fact that the war in the East crossed and recrossed Ukraine, taking a heavy toll among the civilian population and arousing widespread animosity to both Soviet and German regimes, despite initial reception of the Nazis as liberators. The nationalists, spearheaded by the OUN and represented by the Ukrainian Insurgent Army, led an underground resistance, pursuing the inter-war goal of a united independent Ukrainian state. The Soviet Union's final western offensive left Ukraine united after 1945, but under Soviet domination.[45]

The war was the event that the UNO and the OUK had awaited, when the renewed Ukrainian liberation struggle would be crowned with victory. But they had not anticipated Canadian involvement or the international alignments that emerged. From being absorbed with their emigrant role and responsibilities, they had suddenly to consider their immigrant situation as well.

Before the war, the OUK had stressed the duty of Ukrainian women in Canada to the Fatherland. Ukraine continued to be important, particularly given the urgency the imminent revolution lent to preparation.[46] Although the diaspora was to be ready to answer Ukraine's call in whatever form it came, the OUK acknowledged that it would contribute to the liberation struggle primarily from a distance. Women in Canada could not carry the burden of women in Ukraine, but they could launch projects and appeals impossible or difficult for Ukrainians at home.

Both the Ukrainian Gold Cross and Ukrainian First Aid were to represent a major part of the OUK's work in readiness for the Ukrainian campaign. As the war progressed, however, the destruction in Ukraine shifted the focus of fund-raising towards more humanitarian ends, aid to a war-ravaged civilian population once the restoration of contacts permitted.[47] Ukrainians in North America also had a propaganda service to perform. The 'Chinese wall of their own erection' that separated Ukrainian from other women's organizations, especially Anglo-Canadian ones, had to be broken down and the mainstream platform used both to counter the propaganda of Ukraine's detractors and to educate Canadians in Ukrainian history and national aspirations. OUK women had to convince their audiences that the Ukrainian nation of 50,000,000 deserved its 'place in the sun.'[48]

Much of the rhetoric used to argue for Ukraine's place in the sun came from Canada's own war. At a time when 'good' in the world was fighting for the freedom, equality, and rights of all peoples, could Ukrainians be faulted for wanting the same?[49] It was because they valued freedom, and felt loyalty and gratitude for the country that had given it to them, that Ukrainian-Canadian boys responded to Canada's call for their blood sacrifice; that Ukrainian-Canadian mothers willingly sent their sons; that Ukrainian women's organizations directed their energies to war work on the home front; that Ukrainian-Canadian mothers would teach their children not only about the Ukrainian struggle for freedom but also how, in the present war, their adopted homeland was fighting for the freedom and rights of all peoples.[50] Ukrainian women in their past had proved themselves worthy Ukrainians, lovers of freedom and ready to take heroic action in its name. Here in Canada, where they had acquired broader rights and, liberated from their servile mentality, a better understanding of women's responsibilities as members of the nation, they would also prove themselves worthy Canadians.[51]

As responsible and loyal citizens of Canada, the women in the OUK added duty to the adopted homeland to duty to Ukraine. Although Stepaniia Savchuk told the UNO convention in 1943 that creating loyal citizens prepared to serve Canada whenever necessary had been a long-time OUK plank, Canadian emphases had received little attention prior to the war.[52] During the war this changed, on paper and in fact. The OUK early identified co-operation with and support of the Canadian Red Cross as the most important aspect of its war work. It also encouraged Ukrainian-Canadian women to make financial sacrifices, endorsed and promoted national registration, and operated a parcel and correspondence service for Ukrainian-Canadian servicemen overseas.[53]

The pressure of the wartime responsibilities falling on Ukrainian-Canadian women impressed the OUK's leadership with the necessity for better and greater organization. Only the united strength of all members of the community – dedicating their full physical, moral, and material support to the Canadian war effort and Ukrainian cause – could guarantee victory. As a result, the OUK agitated throughout the war for increased activity by its branches and members, improved planning and co-ordination, recruiting campaigns to bring more Ukrainian-Canadian women within its orbit, and accelerated educational work to alert them to their manifold tasks.[54]

Emphasis on collective organized action brought a broadened perspective and greater openness to a group hitherto not only absorbed by its Ukrainianness but also impatient with other Ukrainian-Canadian women's organizations whose nationalism was less intense. Participation in the Canadian war effort, like Red Cross work, and propagandizing for Ukraine among their fellow citizens increased the formal contacts of the OUK and its members with Canadian women and Canadian women's organizations. If to this are added individual contributions to home-front success – working in war industries, buying war savings bonds, cooking with rationing – then probably for the first time many immigrant women felt part of Canada in a meaningful sense.

Emphasis on collective organized action also turned attention to the Ukrainian-Canadian community, where inter-war religious and political rivalries had prevented co-operation and wasted energy, goodwill, and resources. In 1940, with prodding from official circles concerned about Ukrainian identification with the Canadian war effort, the non-communist organizations formed a superstructure, the Ukrainian Canadian Committee, to co-ordinate their wartime activities. Besides giving Canada 'every assistance,' the Ukrainian-Canadian Committee undertook 'to explain and to interpret the problems facing the Ukrainians both in Canada and in Europe.'[55] The UNO was a founding member. Ukrainian women and their organizations, as Stepaniia Savchuk, OUK delegate to the committee's first national congress in 1943, complained, were excluded from its central executive and local branches. This was unfair, Savchuk said, given the war record of the women's organizations and women's individual sacrifices, particularly of their sons.[56] The women's organizations were not to be accepted as equal partners in the male-dominated umbrella organization and formal group mouthpiece, and in 1944 they formed a parallel superstructure, the Ukrainian Canadian Women's Committee.[57]

Maintaining relations with other Ukrainian-Canadian women's organizations, to discuss common Ukrainian concerns and 'draw closer to our Ukrainian sisters,' and establishing ties with Anglo-Canadian women's organizations remained OUK post-war goals as well.[58] Shortly after the armistice, an OUK district convention in Regina heard a speech on women in national life. It reflected both the continuity and the change in OUK attitudes. Continuity was found in the emphasis on enlightened and conscious motherhood; women's dual public and domestic role to work for a better future; the necessity of organization, commitment, and maximum effort for women whose people were still without control of their own destiny; and the advantages for Ukrainian work that accrued from living in Canada. Change came in a greater consciousness or acknowledgment of Canada. The OUK, the speaker insisted, had worked since its inception not only for Ukraine's liberation but also for the benefit of its new homeland; it had shouldered its wartime responsibilities in Canada as well as remembering its brothers and sisters in Europe; and Ukrainian-Canadian mothers were raising children who were both conscious Ukrainians and model Canadians.[59]

III

The Second World War took the OUK from an émigré organization concerned above all with Ukraine to one that increasingly took into account its new environment. It was not that its activities and attitudes before the war had been anti-Canadian or that its members had held aloof from Canadian society; for the immigrant generation, Canada was often simply secondary. It is probably partially correct to say that protestations of loyalty and identification with the Canadian war effort were perceived as a prudent course. But an ideology that stressed the primacy of the nation's interests, individual and collective responsibility to the nation and state, and service and willing sacrifice was admirably suited to wartime Canada and facilitated the transition from Ukrainian to Ukrainian Canadian.

The OUK philosophy had always combined the militant and activist with the maternal and traditionally feminine in defining women's role in national life. The heroines of Ukrainian history adopted as models reflected both strains; the bond that united these women, identifying and dominating them, was their Ukrainianism. Their emigrant and immigrant condition severely limited the militant and activist option for women in the OUK. As emigrants, they could not be Olha Basarabs, dying for the ideal of a united independent Ukrainian state. As immigrants, both women and members of a socio-economically handicapped minority, they could act, whether for the Ukrainian cause or for Canada, only within the parameters permitted their sex and ethnic group. The traditionally feminine tasks – fund-raising bazaars, the Canadian Red Cross, the Ukrainian Gold Cross – remained open to them. They could promote self-help and self-education through their organization, working to elevate the national consciousness of Ukrainian-Canadian women and to bring them under the OUK's umbrella. And they could be mothers, raising sons and daughters prepared to serve the Fatherland, easily expanded in wartime to include the adopted homeland as well. Given the ultimate subordination of woman's public to her maternal role in OUK philosophy, this emphasis seemed both logical and natural and was one that did not diminish the significance of the Ukrainian woman in emigration.

NOTES

1 This is the Ukrainian version. See Oleksander Luhovyi, *Vyznachne zhinotstvo Ukrainy: Istorychni zhyttiepysy u chotyrokh chastynakh* (Toronto 1942), 220–1; and his play, *Ol'ha Basarabova: Drama v 5-okh diiakh* (Saskatoon 1936). Polish authorities denied torturing Basarab and maintained she hanged herself in her cell.

2 Woodrow Wilson's self-determination of nations did not apply to Ukraine in redrawing the map of Europe after 1918. By the mid 1920s, Western Ukrainian territories had been divided among the emergent states of Poland (receiving

the largest, most prosperous, and most nationally active portion), Romania, and Czechoslovakia; larger Eastern Ukraine was incorporated into the Soviet Union.

3 See Alexander J. Motyl, *The Turn to the Right: The Ideological Origins and Development of Ukrainian Nationalism, 1919–1929* (Boulder, CO 1980); and John Armstrong, *Ukrainian Nationalism*, 2nd ed. (Littleton, CO, 1980), 1–45.

4 Both the UNO and the OUK had their roots in the Ukrainian War Veterans' Association, established in 1928 by former soldiers of the Ukrainian revolutionary armies. The OUK dates its beginnings from 1930, with the founding of women's branches of this organization; see Michael H. Marunchak, *The Ukrainian Canadians: A History*, 2nd ed. rev. (Winnipeg and Ottawa 1982), 398–401, 413–15; and Irena Knysh, ed., *Na sluzhbi ridnoho narodu: luvileinyi zbirnyk Orhanizatsii ukrainok Kanady im. Olhy Basarab u 25–richchia vid zaïsnuvannia (1930–55)* (Winnipeg 1955), 5–80.

5 *Novyi shliakh*, 28 August 1934.

6 Ibid., 9 February 1939.

7 See, in particular, the youth page in *Novyi shliakh* for information on the two schools.

8 Raymond Arthur Davies, *'This Is Our Land': Ukrainian Canadians against Hitler* (Toronto 1943), especially 19, 21–2, 26, 31, 61, 64–70, 75–9, 87–139. Davies treats another inter-war émigré group, the United Hetman Organization, as a second fifth column. See also *Saturday Night*, 28 June 1941 and 12 July 1941, for an exchange between Davies and UNO spokesman Wasyl Swystun.

9 Ukrainian National Federation of Canada, *A Program and a Record* (Winnipeg and Saskatoon 1943).

10 Among Watson Kirkconnell's many wartime publications on the Ukrainian Canadians, see, for example, his *Canada, Europe and Hitler* (Toronto 1939), 38–61, 74–90, 137–52; see also Bohdan S. Kordan, 'Disunity and Duality: Ukrainian Canadians and the Second World War,' MA thesis, Carleton University, 1981.

11 In 1935 the OUK had 18 branches (Quebec 2, Ontario 8, Manitoba 2, Saskatchewan 5, Alberta 1) with approximately 500 members (*Novyi shliakh*, 23 July 1935). In 1937, the last year through 1945 for which the national conference published full figures, it reported 27 branches (Quebec 2, Ontario 14, Manitoba 2, Saskatchewan 7, Alberta 2) and 610 members (*Novyi shliakh*, 6 July 1937). The following year, 5 new branches were formed (Quebec 2, Ontario 2, Manitoba 1) (*Novyi shliakh*, 16 and 23 August 1938). Marunchak, *Ukrainian Canadians*, 401, gives 33 branches in six provinces on the eve of the Second World War.

12 By the end of the Second World War, all major Ukrainian-Canadian organiza-

tions had women's affiliates. In addition to the OUK, they included the Women's Section of the Ukrainian Labour-Farmer Temple Association (subsequently the Association of United Ukrainian Canadians), the Ukrainian Women's Association of Canada for Orthodox laity, the Ukrainian Catholic Women's League, and the women's section of the United Hetman Organization.

13 See, for example, *Novyi shliakh*, 25 December 1934.

14 Ibid., 11 December 1934, 12 and 19 February 1935, 14 May 1935, 4 June 1935, 13 August 1935.

15 Ibid., 28 December 1937. This article was an attack on the legal mass women's organization in Galicia, Soiuz ukrainok (Women's Union), criticizing it for speaking of the oppression of Ukrainian women by Ukrainian men when both were oppressed by foreign overlords.

16 *Novyi shliakh*, 1 December 1936; see also 3 November 1936.

17 Ibid., 27 June 1933; see also 17 September 1931, 15 November 1932, 11 December 1934, 12 February 1935, 1 December 1936, 1 February 1938.

18 Ibid., 12 February 1935; see also 25 October 1932, 21 May 1935, 4 June 1935, 10 November 1936, 21 December 1937. Criticism of the overall record of Ukrainian women during the revolution should obscure neither the recognition accorded those who had pulled their weight nor challenges to the general criticism itself. One angry male reader wrote to *Novyi shliakh* (13 August 1931) to take exception to a public lecture that had belittled and criticized women's role in the recent independence struggles; at the same time he castigated the women present who had applauded the man's speech. The OUK regretted that women who had contributed to their nation in its hour of need, either personally or through their children, received little acknowledgment in official community ritual, and it instituted February (the month Basarab died) as the month for honouring Ukraine's heroines.

19 See *Novyi shliakh*, 13 August 1931, 17 September 1931, 11 December 1934, 12 and 19 February 1935, 1 December 1936, 1 May 1941. The OUK approved highly of Italian women who had given their wedding rings to help Mussolini finance his Ethiopian war (see 26 December 1938).

20 See *Novyi shliakh*, 3 May 1932, 13 August 1935, 15 October 1935, 21 June 1938, 26 December 1938, 3 April 1939.

21 Ibid., 1 December 1936.

22 For OUK opinion on women's emancipation, see *Novyi shliakh*, 17 May 1932, 5 June 1934, 11 December 1934, 19 and 26 February 1935, 10 November 1936, 23 March 1937, 12 October 1937, 28 December 1937, 17 April 1941, 8 May 1943, 17 March 1945, 10 November 1945.

23 Ibid., 17 May 1932, 10 November 1936, 17 April 1941.

24 Claudia Koonz, 'Mothers in the Fatherland: Women in Nazi Germany,' in

Renate Bridenthal and Claudia Koonz, eds, *Becoming Visible: Women in European History* (Boston 1977), 445–73.

25 Ruth Roach Pierson, 'Women's Emancipation and the Recruitment of Women into the Labour Force in World War II,' in Susan Mann Trofimenkoff and Alison Prentice, eds, *The Neglected Majority: Essays in Canadian Women's History* (Toronto 1977), 125–45; and *Canadian Women and the Second World War*, Canadian Historical Association Booklet no. 37 (Ottawa 1983). See also the *Novyi shliakh* editorial, 8 May 1943, which makes the point that women must not allow their wartime work outside the home to become 'normal' after the war's end.

26 See the three-part article by Anastaziia Pavlychenko, 'Borotba natsionalnykh idei i ukrainske zhinotstvo Kanady' (The struggle of the national idea and Ukrainian womanhood in Canada), *Novyi shliakh*, 14, 21, and 28 May 1935. It maintains that nationally conscious elements have had to struggle against not only Ukraine's external enemies but also servitude and opportunism among their own people. The opinion that Ukrainian society naturally inclined toward equality for women, in the OUK's definition, can be found in *Novyi shliakh*, 6 April 1935, 3 February 1936, 3 March 1936, 6 November 1936, 29 December 1936.

27 *Novyi shliakh*, 19 February 1935, 4 June 1935, 3 March 1936, 29 December 1936. In late 1936 the women's page began to publish biographical sketches of famous Ukrainian women who had contributed to the development of their nation and state.

28 For discussion or biographical sketches of the heroines of Kievan Rus' and Cossack Ukraine, see *Novyi shliakh*, 11 September 1934, 11 December 1934, 19 February 1935, 4 June 1935, 3 March 1936, 22 and 29 December 1936, 5 and 19 January 1937, 21 December 1937, 6 November 1941.

29 Ibid., 24 July 1941.

30 Ibid., 12 February 1935, 31 March 1936, 10 November 1936, 21 December 1937.

31 See ibid., 5 June 1934, 12 February 1935, 31 March 1936, 21 December 1937.

32 Articles appeared on Ukrainka every year to mark her anniversary; see, for example, *Novyi shliakh*, 5 March 1935, 3 March 1936, 22 February 1938. See 21 April 1936 for a sketch of Pchilka.

33 See *Novyi shliakh*, 3 May 1932, 5 June 1934, 11 December 1934, 12 and 19 February 1935, 4 June 1935, 4 and 18 February 1936; 3, 17, and 31 March 1936; 10 November 1936, 30 November 1937.

34 Just as other women could teach Ukrainian women about active participation in the national struggle, so could other women provide examples as mothers. Beside the immensely popular image of Spartan mothers stood the mothers of

Irish independence fighters, the Italian Arditti, and young Nazis, as well as the mothers of such great men as Socrates and Napoleon; see *Novyi shliakh*, 8 January 1931, 13 August 1935, 5 September 1935, 13 October 1936, 3 November 1936, 3 and 10 May 1938, 9 May 1942.

35 Ibid., 7 May 1931, 5 September 1933, 7 May 1935, 1 February 1938, 3 and 10 May 1938, 14 June 1938, 8 May 1943.

36 See, for example, ibid., 3 May 1932, 12 February 1935, 18 February 1936, 3 March 1936, 20 March 1941.

37 Ibid., 7 May 1931, 31 March 1936, 21 December 1937.

38 Ibid., 4 June 1935.

39 See ibid., 28 May 1935, 6 March 1936, 30 November 1937, 21 December 1937.

40 See, for example, ibid., 19 February 1935, 15 October 1935, 18 February 1936, 17 May 1938, 14 June 1938. Local OUK branches regularly published club activity reports on the women's page as well as annual summaries of their programs.

41 *Novyi shliakh*, 6 October 1936, 8 May 1943.

42 See ibid., 8 January 1931, 7 May 1935, 10 August 1937, 14 December 1937, 8 February 1938 for expressions of concern about the assimilation of Ukrainian-Canadian youth.

43 Ibid., 21 December 1937. The suggestion that young Ukrainian Canadians were to be prepared to die for Ukraine was repeated frequently; see 5 September 1933, 19 February 1935, 4 June 1935, 18 February 1936, 31 March 1936, 16 March 1937, 10 August 1937, 6 and 19 October 1937, 30 November 1937.

44 See, for example, ibid., 25 April 1942, 8 May 1943, 16 June 1945, 1 September 1945.

45 On Ukraine in the Second World War, see Armstrong, *Ukrainian Nationalism*, 46–321; and Yury Boshyk, ed., *Ukraine during World War II: History and Its Aftermath* (Edmonton 1986), 3–104.

46 See *Novyi shliakh*, 3 April 1939, 29 June 1939, 20 March 1941, 30 January 1943.

47 Both the Ukrainian Gold Cross and the Ukrainian First Aid existed before the war; see *Novyi shliakh*, 21 June 1938, 3 April 1939, 29 June 1939, 29 August 1940. Ukrainian women were also told to learn what they could from the Canadian Red Cross: how it worked, its relations with other peoples, the extension of its authority, what could be expected of it in Ukraine's time of need (20 March 1941). See 30 January 1943 for discussion of OUK relief work in Ukraine.

48 *Novyi shliakh*, 3 April 1939, 20 March 1941, 24 July 1941.

49 Ibid., 22 May 1943.

50 See, for example, ibid., 23 November 1939, 31 October 1942, 7 November 1942, 23 January 1943, 7 August 1943, 10 June 1944; and Stephanie Sawchuk, 'Our Women in Ukrainian and Canadian Life,' in Ukrainian Canadian Committee, *First All-Canadian Congress of Ukrainians in Canada* (Winnipeg 1943), 164.

51 See *Novyi shliakh*, 14 March 1940, 24 June 1941, 14 March 1942, 31 October 1942.

52 Ibid., 23 January 1943. See 3 August 1935 for an exception to the generalization; alarmed by Anglo-Canadian contentions that East Europeans were particularly susceptible to Tim Buck and his communist propaganda, the OUK insisted that nationalist Ukrainians work to divorce Ukrainian Canadians from association with Moscow and convince their fellow citizens that they were loyal Canadians, conscious of their origins and believers in both Ukraine and their adopted homeland, Canada.

53 See, for example, *Novyi shliakh*, 23 and 30 November 1939, 29 August 1940, 7 August 1943; the OUK also suggested that Ukrainian-Canadian girls who had completed school join the Canadian armed forces, there to contribute to the Canadian war effort and gain experience useful to Ukraine (14 March 1942).

54 *Novyi shliakh*, 29 August 1940, 24 June 1941, 23 and 30 January 1943, 10 June 1944, 10 February 1945; this thrust continued into the post-war period as well (see 10 November 1945 and 15 December 1945).

55 Ukrainian Canadian Committee, *First All-Canadian Congress of Ukrainians in Canada*, 3.

56 *Novyi shliakh*, 31 July 1943.

57 The OUK was a founding member of the Ukrainian Canadian Women's Committee. Both superstructures were retained after the war, their immediate focus being the thousands of Ukrainian displaced persons in Western Europe. While the men lobbied the Canadian government to admit refugees as immigrants, the women concentrated on relief work; see, for example, *Novyi shliakh*, 15 September 1945; Marunchak, *Ukrainian Canadians*, 560–5; Oleh W. Gerus, 'The Ukrainian Canadian Committee,' in Manoly R. Lupul, ed., *A Heritage in Transition: Essays in the History of Ukrainians in Canada* (Toronto 1982), 199–201.

58 *Novyi shliakh*, 20 October 1945.

59 Ibid., 10 November 1945.

Politicized Housewives in the Jewish Communist Movement of Toronto

1923–1933

Ruth A. Frager

Egalitarianism is the touchstone of both socialism and feminism, and many believe that this implies common goals. One who believes this is Sadie Hoffman, a long-time member of Toronto's Jewish Communist movement. When Hoffman was asked recently if the men within the movement had had a more progressive view of woman's place than other men had during the inter-war period, she replied: 'I don't know. They should have. They should have [because] they wanted everybody to be freer.'[1] Her reply highlights the common assumption that because socialists have been attuned to issues of class domination, they would have been sensitive to issues of gender domination as well. Yet the logic of Hoffman's position is undercut by the uncertainty of her reply.

Much of the recent debate about the relationship between socialism and feminism centres on this question of whether there is a close affinity between the two ideologies. The point of view exemplified by Sadie Hoffman's remark suggests that the socialists' radical critique of class relations leads to a radical critique of gender relations, partly as a result of the socialists' willingness to challenge core social orthodoxies. According to this line of thought, the socialists' emphasis on freedom and equality for working people moves beyond class terms and comes to embrace women's equality as well. Proponents of the natural affinity between socialism and feminism also often argue that socialists are led to feminism because the very process of women's political mobilization within the socialist movement entails the breaking down of traditional female roles.

By contrast, opponents of this view argue that socialism's emphasis on the primacy of class struggle undermines the development of feminism, indeed that socialist focus on class oppression precludes a genuine analysis of women's oppression *as women*. Proponents of this view often maintain that socialists regard feminism as a threat that undermines socialist prospects by dividing the working class along gender lines and diverting the energy of sections of the working class toward 'secondary' issues.[2]

The history of the Jewish left in Toronto provides a critical context for the examination of these issues, not only because of the highly developed class consciousness among Jewish leftists but also because of the important participation of women in this movement. The Jewish left in Toronto was a vibrant working-class movement, broadly based in the immigrant Jewish community. Toronto's immigrant Jews had fled to North America in the early twentieth century to escape the horrors of extreme poverty and virulent anti-Semitism in Eastern Europe.[3] By 1931, there were over 45,000 Jews in Toronto.[4] While a significant number of these Jews had been radicalized by harsh conditions in the Old World, others were radicalized on this side of the ocean by the hardships of immigrant life in Toronto, particularly as they toiled in the needle trades sweat-shops on Spadina Avenue. Here, their socialist commitment was reinforced by strong community bonds. The occupational concentration of Jews in the garment industry, combined with a high degree of residential concentration, helped to create a cohesive community basis for the Jewish left.

Although most Jewish leftists were atheists, their Jewish identity was usually very important to them. They saw themselves as secular Jews, and many of them continued such traditional cultural practices as eating kosher meat. They were particularly concerned to fight against anti-Semitism, which they continued to encounter in Toronto. Although there were certainly tensions between the leftists and the Orthodox Jews, the leftists were very much a part of the city's working-class Jewish community.

The early twentieth-century Jewish left divided into several different ideological groups. The Labour Zionists, for example, believed in the creation of a socialist Jewish state in Palestine. The Bundists, by contrast, were non-Zionists who believed in a decentralized form of socialism which they felt would enable Jews to preserve their own culture within multi-ethnic socialist federations. There were also groups of Jewish Anarchists and Jewish Bolsheviks.

During the first two decades of the twentieth century, these different groups co-operated closely within Toronto's immigrant Jewish community. However, the formation of the Communist Party of Canada in 1921, in the aftermath of the Russian Revolution, led to substantial change. In addition to encompassing the Jewish Bolsheviks, the new party also took in some former members of other branches of the Jewish left. Many Jews became strong supporters of the Communist party because they believed deeply that the Soviet Union provided freedom and equality not only for the working class but also for the Jewish people. Other Jewish leftists sharply criticized many aspects of Soviet policy, and a deep split developed between the Jewish Communists and the rest of the Jewish left during the inter-war period.[5]

This division affected both women and men, for the Jewish left was not exclusively male. A significant number of Jewish women had become radicalized for many of the same reasons as had Jewish men, and they were divided along the same political lines. Jewish women's political activism was also related to the nature of women's role in traditional East European Jewish culture. Unlike the Victorian 'cult of true womanhood,' Jewish women were not seen as particularly fragile or docile.

Although East European Jewish women were deeply subordinated within the religious sphere, they had more latitude in those areas of life that were considered less important. Although the women were entirely responsible for looking after the home, Jewish women were not limited to the domestic sphere. In Eastern Europe, dire poverty, together with the traditional emphasis on the male pursuit of religious study, meant that women had a legitimate role to play in the market-place, contributing directly to the family income. Artisanal workshops were often located in or near the home, which meant that women would combine child-rearing with artisanal tasks shared with their husbands. Thus, there was little separation between the private and public spheres in the Old World. Although the increased division between the home and the 'workplace' in the more industrialized New World meant that there was an increasing tendency for married Jewish women to withdraw from income-generating activity, the traditional assertiveness of Jewish women in the market-place helped to prepare a significant number of Jewish women for public activism – an activism that they carried into the Jewish left.[6]

In Toronto, the Jewish Communists formed a special women's organization in 1923, as part of a move to separate the Communists more markedly from the rest of the Jewish left. This organization was known as the Yiddishe Arbeiter Froyen Fareyn (and referred to in English as the Jewish Women's Labour League). By early 1926, the Fareyn had a membership of forty-four, most of whom were full-time housewives.[7]

Through the Fareyn, these women played an important role within the Jewish Communist movement: they were active in the party's electoral campaigns, strike-support work, struggles to reduce the prices of household consumer items, and efforts to socialize the children into the Communist movement. Although these women had some discretion in deciding which activities to promote, they followed the general guide-lines of Communist party policy. There were formal links with the non-Jewish women's labour leagues, but the Fareyn did not operate in close connection with these non-Jewish organizations, largely because of the relative insularity of the Jewish community.[8] An examination of the Fareyn helps to illuminate the critical relationship between socialism and feminism.

Sadie Hoffman, who felt that the Communists 'wanted everybody to be freer,' was one of the founders of the Fareyn and remained a leading activist in this organization for years. Hoffman stressed how deeply she and the other Fareyn members were committed to socialism. Asked if this organization was at all feminist, she replied: 'There wasn't too much talk about that in those years ... There wasn't too much talk like there is today.'[9]

The Fareyn's overriding goal was the political mobilization of women for the class struggle. In a 1927 article in *Der Kamf* (the Communist Party of Canada's Yiddish newspaper), for example, the Fareyn's executive officers proclaimed that the Jewish working-class woman 'cannot and must not remain imprisoned in the narrow four walls of her kitchen.' Why? Because now that 'the working class prepares itself for the decisive struggle,' Jewish women 'cannot remain behind, and must enter the ranks of the organized working masses [and] take an interest in both the daily struggle of the workers and in the international revolutionary struggle.'[10]

This meant that the Fareyn was, in part, a consciousness-raising group, devoted explicitly to raising women's class consciousness.[11] The organization sought to educate its members in the basic ideas of class struggle through a program of lectures and discussions and through a special study group on 'the ABC's of Communism.'[12] Within this class framework, the organization's officers proudly announced that 'our Fareyn has also, to a certain extent, called forth in our members the courage to think independently and to express their thoughts. Also the energy to do independent work.'[13] This type of independence was acceptable, provided that the goal of this self-directed activity was to further the class struggle and provided that women continued to fulfil their traditional domestic responsibilities. Thus, when the Fareyn's executive called on Jewish working-class men to encourage their wives to join this organization, the Fareyn assured the men that: 'You will feel much more fortunate when your wife will be *not only a good housewife* but also a good comrade. Help build the working-class women's organizations which take part in the general struggle of the working class for its liberation.'[14]

Becoming a good comrade also meant that women would sometimes need to be more outspoken. In a 1928 article, for example, a representative of the Fareyn declared approvingly that 'women comrades, who were usually too bashful to say anything during a discussion [held by] other organizations, have learned to speak fluently [at Fareyn meetings] and have generally become more developed and conscious.' Describing the many activities of these newly assertive women, the writer explained that 'the whole work had to be oriented to the class struggle.'[15] Reports on the Fareyn continually reiterated this orientation and never mentioned women's equality as a goal.[16]

The Fareyn women did not take up the argument, which appeared in rare articles in *Der Kamf*, that women had actually achieved equal rights in the Soviet Union as a result of the abolition of capitalism. The Soviet Union, these few articles claimed, had liberated women by adopting a whole range of special measures, including equal educational opportunities for females, equal pay for equal work, paid maternity leave, and the use of nurseries, communal kitchens, and communal laundries. One such article declared that this 'should show the women workers of Canada that real freedom for women can only come when the whole working class is freed.'[17] 'Capitalism,' explained another article, is 'the reason for woman's enslavement.'[18]

In another article in *Der Kamf*, the relationship between 'woman's enslavement' and class oppression was described in greater detail. The Communist movement, it was explained, 'struggles strongly against bourgeois "women's rights."' 'Communists,' the newspaper proclaimed, 'do not demand freedom or more power for the capitalist woman and they do not recognize any women's problem which is not bound together with the general working-class problems' because 'women's enslavement is bound together with the enslavement of the proletariat. Both problems can and must be solved as one.' The rest of this article made it clear than any fight against 'women's enslavement' was being subsumed by the class struggle. The party's political agitation among women was explicitly designed to 'bring Communist teachings to the working-class woman so that the women of the country should become an important factor in the class struggle and in the work to win the workers to Communism.'[19]

Whereas the few articles that mentioned women's rights usually adhered to this general pattern, one very exceptional article suggested a more immediate egalitarian thrust to Communist policy. As working-class women have 'been drawn into the struggles of the working class,' the article explained, 'new horizons have opened for the working women.' Thus: 'Joining together with the fighting proletariat, [woman's] whole mental life is changed. She looks already at herself with very different eyes. There is no longer the lightly esteemed conception of themselves. The working-class woman feels herself completely equal to the man. Family life has become fuller and richer. Man and woman now have common interests as comrades and fellow fighters [in the same struggle]. A real revolution has taken place in the class-conscious woman.' The article concluded with an appeal to working-class women to develop their class consciousness and to join the Communist party, which was described as the party 'which fights for the complete equality of man and woman' and 'which fights so that the working women and men should become the masters of life.'[20]

Such an explicit emphasis on women's equality was, however, foreign to the Yiddishe Arbeiter Froyen Fareyn. Members of this organization did not argue that the very process of mobilizing women for the class struggle would help bring about women's equality, nor did they argue that the abolition of capitalism was so crucial because a Communist regime would liberate women. Instead, the Fareyn's 'Declaration of Principles' made it clear that the organization sought to bring women into the class struggle and was not concerned with women's oppression as women. Emphasizing women workers rather than working-class women more broadly, the declaration proclaimed: 'Recognizing that the development of capitalism has pulled the woman into all branches of industry and placed her in the same position as the male workers [sic], and also recognizing that the imminent liberation of the working class as a whole is also tied to the liberation of the woman worker, we are therefore interested in organizing the Jewish women workers and preparing them for the joint struggle of the whole working class for its imminent liberation.' The declaration exhorted Fareyn members to encourage women workers to join trade unions and to 'prevail upon their men' to belong to unions. Fareyn women also had a responsibility 'to take part in all campaigns which are directed by the revolutionary part of the working class, namely to help elect labour representatives.'[21]

An examination of the specific activities of the Fareyn reveals concrete ways in which Jewish working-class women were mobilized for the class struggle. Although unmarried Jewish women were sometimes able to pursue political activities that were less possible for their married sisters to engage in,[22] the Fareyn represented an important forum where Jewish housewives could address political issues of particular concern to class-conscious women. In part, the Fareyn women's particular political roles within the Jewish Communist movement constituted extensions of their traditional domestic responsibilities, thus reinforcing the significant differences between women's and men's roles in the class struggle. Other aspects of the women's political mobilization, however, were less tied to their domestic traditions.

This mix is apparent in some of the work that the Fareyn women did to support Communist candidates for government office. The women used to help with the election campaigns by arranging neighbourhood teas, where women voters could come and meet the party's local candidates. These gatherings were held at various homes, and the Fareyn women baked cakes to serve to the company. The women also used to do house-to-house canvassing as part of the election campaigns.[23] Although one Fareyn member ran for the Board of Education in Ward 5 in 1933, the Fareyn women's supportive efforts were almost always on behalf of male Communist candidates.[24]

The Fareyn's strike-support work also constituted an important contribution to the class struggle. For example, Fareyn members collected food and clothing for the families of striking Nova Scotia coal-miners.[25] The Fareyn also provided picket-line support for local strikers. The women were especially active in their support for the Industrial Union of Needle Trades Workers (IUNTW), a Communist-led union that was established in the late 1920s. In addition to raising funds for the union, Fareyn members joined the picket line when the union went out on strike.[26] Sadie Hoffman recalled the risks involved during picketing and during demonstrations for other Communist causes. She and her friends were arrested on the IUNTW picket line, taken in a paddy-wagon to the Don Jail, and finally released after paying a $10 fine. On another occasion, Hoffman was arrested and charged with sedition for standing in front of a slaughterhouse and handing out leaflets calling for the overthrow of capitalism.[27]

In a period when police officers often beat Communist demonstrators, it took considerable courage – for both women and men – to join in protest demonstrations. Hoffman herself displayed remarkable physical courage and dramatic militancy in trying to stop the police from beating male comrades. She would rush in front of a man who was being beaten and try to shield him with her body, hoping that the police officers would not hit a woman. This tactic was fairly successful.[28] Here was one situation in which the police officers' traditional attitudes toward women could be used to advantage.

In addition to strike-support work and participation in protest demonstrations, the Fareyn helped organize a kosher-meat boycott in 1924 and played a central role in a similar boycott in 1933.[29] A detailed examination of the 1933 boycott illuminates the nature of women's activism. By the time of the 1933 boycott, the Fareyn had been reorganized as a women's branch of the Labour League, a fraternal organization of male and female Jews who were oriented toward the Communist party. During this boycott, the Fareyn women worked closely with members of the only other women's branch in the Labour League.[30]

When the price of kosher meat increased sharply in March 1933, the two groups of Communist women appealed to Jewish housewives to protest. In response, 700 women quickly gathered at a mass meeting and decided to launch the boycott. The meeting chose a committee of fifty women to direct the protest, and plans were made to picket the butcher shops.[31] Bessie Kramer, a member of the Labour League, was one of the leaders of this boycott. She recalled the breadth of support for this protest: 'The Labour League took the initiative. We called the first meeting; we called all the women of other organizations. And we went out on strike; we're not buying any meat 'til the prices are gonna go down ... In this time of the strike [i.e. the boycott], we got *all* our women, left and right, everybody was together.'[32] Approximately 2000 Jewish women joined the boycott, and hundreds of women picketed the butcher shops. The women on the steering committee co-ordinated the boycott efforts, issued leaflets daily, and held frequent mass meetings to discuss strategy. The committee invited anyone interested in cheaper meat to come to these meetings, and 600 to 800 people, most of whom were women, used to crowd into the hall to discuss the issues.[33]

During this boycott, the women protesters took a strong stand on the picket lines, holding their ground when the butchers tried to drive them away. The women were not deterred from picketing even when a group of drunken butchers attacked and wounded several of them with knives.[34] Scuffles also broke out between picketers and customers when, according to Toronto's daily Yiddish newspaper, 'the picketers and their sympathizers wrenched open packages of purchased meat and threw them in the mud.'[35] Bessie Kramer was struck in the face by one of the butchers, and she recalled other picket-line fights:

One evening, on Thursday evening, I was on the picket line with another woman. And a man was going in to buy meat. I say to him: 'Please don't buy any meat. If you wouldn't buy any meat and somebody else wouldn't buy it, they'll have a chance to settle [the boycott].' He says: 'Oh, I can still afford to buy [meat].' A big shot! ... And he snubbed us, and he went into the butcher shop. The other woman with me [said], 'We're going to give him a lesson!' When he came out, ... I grabbed the parcel of meat from him. She grabbed his head. And I took the parcel of meat and opened it up and threw it right on the road, on College Street. He went and called the police [but I was able to avoid arrest by ducking into a friend's nearby store].[36]

Kramer stressed that this boycott was a woman's action; although men supported the boycott, all the leaders and most of the activists were women.[37] Sadie Hoffman, also a key leader of the boycott, added that women did all the picketing. It was a women's action because: 'You know, meat that you have to cook —it's a woman's item ... We had enough women to help.' The women 'showed by action' that they were capable of such militancy, Hoffman explained.[38] Like Hoffman, Kramer stressed that women were given credit within the immigrant Jewish community for fighting against the high price of meat, but, at the beginning of the boycott, there was less confidence in the women: 'The people [didn't] realize that women could do a thing like this – to go on a picket line, have a fight with the butcher, and go to court ... A lot of people didn't think [that women could engage in such militant action]. "What do you mean you're going out on a strike? You're going to fight with the butchers, with the men?" I [said]: "Why not? Why couldn't women do things that men do?"'[39] Many women agreed with Kramer's assessment of their capabilities: they joined the boycott and they were effective. Within a week, the butchers offered to reduce meat prices substantially. The women accepted the offer and ended the boycott.[40]

Like activist men within the Jewish labour movement, the women were protesting in the public sphere, taking a stand against attacks on the working-class family's standard of living. Although trade unionism was, of course, a more orthodox approach to the class struggle, this boycott represented political action around an issue of particular concern to working-class women. Here, women's traditional domestic responsibilities, which are usually seen as limited to the private sphere, became the basis for women's public, political mobilization.

As Dana Frank explains, in her analysis of the Jewish women's food boycott in New York in 1917, the price levels of food shaped housewives' working conditions: 'Scouring the streets for bargains, overhauling menus, satisfying finicky family members, planning to the last penny – all these consequences of rising prices could multiply a housewife's work immensely.' Thus, 'food price protests were these women's way of organizing at their own workplace, as workers whose occupation was shopping, preparing food, and keeping their families content.'[41] Yet, although women went out on the picket lines to defend their own interests, this kind of protest did not challenge women's traditional responsibility for looking after the household.

The Fareyn women's efforts to build working-class cultural institutions were similarly predicated on women's traditional domestic responsibilities. One example was the Fareyn's establishment of a children's camp in 1925 to enable the children 'to spend time in the free air in a working-class and comradely atmosphere.'[42] The women felt that this 'summer home for working-class children' was badly needed as an alternative to the camps run by the charity institutions where, according to a Fareyn spokesperson, they 'influence our children to be loyal, obedient slaves of capitalism and exploitation.'[43]

In addition to providing the children with recreation in a healthy physical environment, the Fareyn's camp provided lectures and discussions 'for the purpose of interesting and bringing the children closer to the working class' so that the children would learn 'who is their friend and who is their enemy.'[44] It was a 'glorious picture,' explained one of the founders of the camp, to see the children decked out with hammer-and-sickle emblems, singing 'The International' at the end of a lecture.[45] So great was the women's interest in socializing the children into the Jewish Communist movement that the camp was described as the Fareyn's 'most important accomplishment.'[46]

This was no small achievement. The women had to go about establishing the camp from the ground up, and they had very little money to work with, particularly because, as housewives, they generally did not have incomes of their own. As they organized the tents, beds, food, games, and educational activities, the women were extending their traditional responsibilities for looking after the children.[47]

Although the camp was, in effect, a collectivized form of child care, the founders of the camp thought in terms of the needs of the children rather than the needs of the mothers. They talked about how the children benefited from the camp; never did they declare that overworked mothers benefited by sending their children away to camp.[48] Moreover, for the founders of the camp themselves, this new undertaking entailed far more work than if they had each simply stayed home to look after their own children.

Women's traditional concern for children's upbringing was also publicly expressed in the Fareyn's support for the Jewish Communist movement's 'proletarian children's school.'[49] As an important alternative to the traditional religious schools that many Jewish children attended, this school performed a crucial task in socializing the children to become good comrades in the movement. Here, the children learned about left-wing politics and the history of the working class, as well as Jewish history and the Yiddish language.[50]

The Fareyn members viewed their support for the school as part of a whole program of class activism. As a representative declared in *Der Kamf*, the Fareyn 'has participated actively in all actions of the revolutionary workers' movement. There was not one campaign in which [the Fareyn] did not take an active part. Whether it was against Section 98 [a section of the Criminal Code that declared an organization to be illegal if it supported the use of force to change society], for the liberation of the victims of class struggle, for supporting Stratford and other strikes, or for the maintenance of [the] children's school – everywhere where the revolutionary workers' movement needed help, was our organization ready to mobilize our members for the work.'[51] The Fareyn also worked to support the Canadian Communist press, particularly *Der Kamf*, by soliciting subscriptions and raising additional funds. In addition, the Fareyn women raised money for the Jewish colonization efforts in Birobidzhan, a remote region of the Soviet Union that had been set aside as an alternative to a Jewish homeland in Palestine.[52]

The Fareyn's fund-raising methods often stemmed from women's domestic traditions. To help pay for tractors for Birobidzhan, for example, the women held a social evening, and, to raise money for the children's camp, they held a bazaar. In addition, they used to hold *latke* (potato pancake) parties to raise funds for the Communist party's municipal election campaigns.[53]

As within the rest of the Jewish community, the conviction that housework and child-rearing were women's responsibilities remained deeply ingrained in family life within the Jewish Communist movement in this period. The rationale lay in the common family situation in which the husband worked full time in the paid labour force, while the wife was a full-time housewife. It is significant, however, that attitudes toward women's traditional domestic responsibilities did not change when the situations did not fit this pattern. Married Jewish women wage-earners came home each night to a second job, unassisted by their husbands. Bessie Kramer, a dedicated Communist who worked in a garment factory while married, was in just such a situation. When asked if people discussed the idea of men's sharing household responsibilities in the inter-war period, Kramer replied: 'I never even thought of it!'[54] Although the many Jewish men who worked in the highly seasonal garment industry had considerable free time during seasonal downturns, they did not use this time to help with the housework.

As a result, female political activists found it very difficult to juggle their political commitments with their domestic responsibilities, even if they did not engage in paid labour. Sadie Hoffman emphasized these difficulties as she described how she used to take her young daughter with her while doing certain kinds of party work, such as canvassing for elections. Hoffman sadly concluded that some children of activist mothers felt neglected and resentful because their mothers were so busy doing political work.[55]

Thus, to a significant extent, conventional assumptions about women's domestic responsibilities shaped the nature of women's political roles within the Jewish Communist movement. Many of the Fareyn's activities – baking cakes for meet-the-candidate teas, collecting food for strikers' families, protesting the high price of meat, organizing a children's camp, and holding fund-raising *latke* parties – stemmed directly from women's traditional household responsibilities. The connection with these responsibilities reinforced substantial differences between women's roles and men's roles in the class struggle. Significantly, it also meant that the Fareyn enabled class-conscious women to mobilize politically to address their own particular concerns.

The nature of the Fareyn's public, political mobilization around domestic issues, particularly during the kosher-meat boycott, calls into question the way in which historians have commonly viewed women's domestic responsibilities as confined entirely to the private sphere. Although immigrant Jewish women experienced more of a separation between the private and public spheres in the more industrialized New World, there was still considerable overlap between the two. For the Fareyn women – and for the many other Jewish women who joined in the kosher-meat boycott – the private and public spheres were intimately linked. Activities such as the kosher-meat boycott also call into question the common historical assumption that immigrant women were passive spectators of the political scene. Finally, the examination of the Fareyn's activities suggests that women's political interests were often significantly different from the conventional political issues defined by men.

Yet, while the Fareyn provided an important vehicle for class-conscious women to mobilize around their own political concerns, this mobilization did not lead the women to feminism. The organization encouraged women's political activism not because women needed to be liberated from the oppression they faced as women but because women were needed to help liberate the working class. All the Fareyn's specific activities were developed as contributions to the class struggle. The Fareyn women did not develop a consciousness of women's oppression by men.

The Communist party was clear and insistent about the primacy of the class struggle. Thus, in 1931, the party declared: '[Working-class women] can be drawn into the entire struggle of the Canadian workers for relief from their present misery. The women workers have no interests apart from those of the working class generally. There is no room for "feminism" in our movement. There is only place for unity and solidarity on the basis of the joint struggle against capitalism.'[56] Within the Jewish Communist movement, exceptions to this orientation were rare. Such a definition of class struggle clearly precluded the development of a feminist perspective *within* the class struggle, much less outside it.

Faced with pressing economic needs, the working-class women of the Fareyn looked to class gains to improve their lot, both in the short term and in the long term.[57] There was no effective feminist movement to articulate the special, gender-conditioned, economic hardships that women faced. Yet women encountered substantial discrimination in the paid labour force, where they were systematically confined to the least-skilled and lowest-paid jobs.[58] Of course, married women workers faced the additional burden of a second job at home. Nor was the full-time housewife immune from discriminatory labour practices. In addition to having engaged in paid labour before marriage, the full-time housewife could be propelled back into the paid labour force by the unemployment, illness, death, or desertion of her husband.

Feminist economic issues were obscured, however, by the traditional focus on the welfare of the family as a whole. Instead of focusing on their own disadvantaged position in the paid labour force, women focused on the family income. The authority and privileges of males, predicated on their role as primary bread-winner, were taken for granted and overlapped with a male-centred class analysis.[59]

The heightened ethnic consciousness of the Jewish political activists also undermined the development of a feminist consciousness. Working-class Jewish women, whether Communist or not, were less apt to develop a feminist critique of their position within the immigrant Jewish community because they shared a common sense of oppression with most of the men in this community, not only in class terms but also as fellow Jews. In part, this attitude stemmed from the serious threat of anti-Semitism, which reinforced an interest in the Jewish community as a whole. In addition, the deeply patriarchal nature of traditional Jewish culture meant that Jewish women were heavily conditioned not to question Jewish men's prerogatives. It was less likely that Jewish women would develop a sense of their own oppression as women within a community that felt physically and culturally beleaguered.

The women of the Yiddishe Arbeiter Froyen Fareyn displayed remarkable militancy in their contributions to the socialist cause. They were deeply committed to a Communist vision of freedom and equality for the working class, at a time when Communist-party activity meant taking great risks. It is thus all the more ironic that the great physical, moral, and intellectual strength they exhibited was part of a struggle that left them blind to their oppression as women in a society defined so fundamentally by patriarchy as well as by class.

NOTES

I would like to thank Linda Kealey, Lynne Marks, Janice Newton, Joan Sangster, and Don Wells for their helpful suggestions. I am also grateful to the members of the Labour Studies Group; my disagreements with many of them have helped to clarify my ideas. In addition, I thankfully acknowledge financial assistance from the Social Sciences and Humanities Research Council of Canada.

1 Interview with Sadie Hoffman, 1978. In order to protect the confidentiality of the interviewees, pseudonyms and minimal citations are used in reference to interviews throughout this article.

2 Barbara Taylor's analysis of the historical relationship between socialism and feminism is particularly challenging. Focusing on the Owenite socialists in Britain, Taylor argues that 'socialism emerged, in the early decades of the nine-

teenth century, as a humanist ideal of universal emancipation – the ideal of a communal society free of every inequality, including sexual inequality.' She maintains that, in the late nineteenth century, 'the Owenite call for a multi-faceted offensive against all forms of social hierarchy, including sexual hierarchy, disappeared – to be replaced with a dogmatic insistence on the primacy of class-based issues, a demand for sexual unity in the face of a common class enemy, and a vague promise of improved status for women "after the revolution."' Taylor concludes that 'organized feminism was increasingly viewed not as an essential component of the socialist struggle, but as a disunifying, diversionary force, with no inherent connection to the socialist tradition.' See Barbara Taylor, *Eve and the New Jerusalem: Socialism and Feminism in the Nineteenth Century* (New York 1983), x, and xv–xvi.

For a discussion of the historical relationship between socialism and feminism in the United States, see, for example, Mari Jo Buhle, *Women and American Socialism, 1870–1920* (Chicago 1983); Nancy Schrom Dye, *As Equals and as Sisters: Feminism, the Labor Movement, and the Women's Trade Union League of New York* (Columbia, MO, 1980); and Meredith Tax, *The Rising of the Women: Feminist Solidarity and Class Conflict, 1880–1917* (New York 1980). For a theoretical treatment of these issues, see Heidi Hartmann, 'The Unhappy Marriage of Marxism and Feminism: Towards a More Progressive Union,' in Lydia Sargent, ed., *Women and Revolution: A Discussion of the Unhappy Marriage of Marxism and Feminism* (Boston 1981), 1–41.

3 On the hardships of Jewish life in Eastern Europe, see, for example, Salo W. Baron, *The Russian Jew under Tsars and Soviets* (New York 1964), 52–75, 105, and 113–15. On the emigration of East European Jews, see Irving Howe, *World of Our Fathers* (New York 1976), 5–63.

4 Calculations based on the *Census of Canada*, 1931, IV, 268–71.

5 For a fuller discussion of Toronto's immigrant Jewish community and the nature of the city's Jewish left, see Ruth A. Frager, 'Uncloaking Vested Interests: Class, Ethnicity, and Gender in the Jewish Labour Movement of Toronto, 1900–1939,' PhD thesis, York University, 1986, 10–13, 65–98, and 384–5.

6 On Jewish women's role in Eastern Europe, see, for example, Charlotte Baum, Paula Hyman, and Sonya Michel, *The Jewish Woman in America* (New York 1976), 56 and 67. For a good description of the 'cult of true womanhood,' see Barbara Welter, 'The Cult of True Womanhood: 1820–1860,' in Michael Gordon, ed., *The American Family in Social-Historical Perspective* (New York 1973), 224–51. Welter discusses this feminine ideal for a very specific time period, but aspects of this ideal continued to permeate North American society for quite a while. On the reasons why married Jewish women tended to withdraw from the paid labour force in the New World, see Judith E. Smith, *Family*

Connections: A History of Italian and Jewish Immigrant Lives in Providence, Rhode Island, 1900–1940 (Albany, NY, 1985), 30–1, 44, and 50.

7 *Der Kamf* (Toronto), 1 January 1926, 5; 11 February 1927, 3; and interviews with Sadie Hoffman, 1978, 1984, and 1985.

8 During the Communist party's third period (when the party emphasized the establishment of separate Communist unions within the Canadian labour movement), the Fareyn women devoted considerable effort to supporting the Communist-led union in the garment industry. During this time, these women were also able to continue with the usual Fareyn activities. There were some similarities between the activities of the Fareyn and the non-Jewish women's labour leagues, but there was also some variation. On the non-Jewish women's labor leagues, see Joan Sangster, 'The Communist Party and the Woman Question, 1922–1929,' *Labour/Le Travail* 15 (Spring 1985), 45–53. Sangster argues that the various women's labor leagues had some local autonomy within the Communist movement because of the 'secondary nature of the woman question in the party.'

9 Interview with Sadie Hoffman, 1978.

10 *Der Kamf*, 11 February 1927, 3. (All translations from the Yiddish are my own.)

11 Ibid.; see also 24 February 1928, 4.

12 Ibid., 11 February 1927, 3.

13 Ibid. As an example of their independent work, they emphasized the Fareyn's establishment of a summer camp for children.

14 *Der Kamf*, 24 February 1928, 4 (emphasis added).

15 Both quotations are from *Der Kamf*, ibid.

16 For example, *Der Kamf*, 23 January 1931, 1, and 29 January 1932, 4.

17 Ibid., 10 March 1933, 7; see also ibid., November 1924, 11–13, and 10 March 1933, 5 and 9.

18 Ibid., October 1925, 15.

19 Ibid., April 1925, 9–10.

20 Ibid., 4 March 1927, 4.

21 Nisnevitch's membership card (in Yiddish) for the Yiddishe Arbeiter Froyen Fareyn, at the Multicultural History Society of Ontario.

22 Because unmarried women generally had fewer domestic responsibilities than married women, the former tended to be freer to pursue certain kinds of political activities. For example, unmarried women were more likely than their married sisters to do the kinds of party work that required travelling. Although both types of women sometimes risked arrest to do work for the party, the unmarried woman was generally able to take larger risks because she did not have to worry about who would look after her children if she was jailed.

23 Interview with Sadie Hoffman, 1984 and 1985.

24 On Ray Watson's candidacy, see *Der Kamf*, 30 December 1932, 10, and 6 January 1933, 1. On the fact that Watson was a member of the Fareyn, see, for example, *Der Kamf*, 1 January 1926, 5, and interview with Sadie Hoffman, 1978.

25 *Der Kamf*, 24 February 1928, 4.

26 *Worker* (Toronto), 18 January 1930, 2; *Der Kamf*, 16 January 1931, 1, and 23 January 1931, 1.

27 Interview with Sadie Hoffman, 1978. The charge of sedition was finally dropped after the Communist party mounted a big defence campaign.

28 Interview with Sadie Hoffman, 1984. Hoffman even tried to protect men whom she did not know at all. For example, during a demonstration she attended in New York City, she flung herself on top of a stranger who was being beaten by the police. The tactic worked, the police stopped the beating, and the man never found out who had helped him.

29 The kosher-meat boycott of 1924 was undertaken as a protest against the high price of the meat. The decision to launch this boycott was made at a meeting of women from a wide range of Jewish organizations, including representatives from the women's auxiliaries of various benevolent societies, as well as women from the Yiddishe Arbeiter Froyen Fareyn and other socialist groups. Some of the women were beaten up while picketing the butcher shops. The boycott was effective, for, within two weeks, the butchers were forced to agree to the prices set by the consumers' negotiating team. On this event, see *Der Yiddisher Zhurnal* (Toronto), 22 May 1924, 1; 30 May 1924, 1; 2 June 1924, 1.
   In addition to the kosher-meat boycotts of 1924 and 1933, Toronto's immigrant Jewish women had participated in a number of other kosher-food boycotts earlier in the twentieth century; see 'Uncloaking Vested Interests,' 67, 99.

30 The Fareyn was reorganized as a women's branch of the Labour League in October 1932. The first women's branch of the Labour League had been established several month's earlier (*Der Kamf*, 27 May 1932, 8; and 21 October 1932, 1).

31 *Der Yiddisher Zhurnal*, 28 March 1933, 1; *Der Kamf*, 31 March 1933, 1.

32 Interview with Bessie Kramer, 1969. Kramer usually referred to this kosher-meat boycott as a strike. The use of the word 'strike' emphasizes the fact that the women played a very active role in this protest.

33 *Der Kamf*, 31 March 1933, 1, and 7 April 1933, 1. *Der Yiddisher Zhurnal*, 30 March 1933, 1; 2 April 1933, 1; 3 April 1933, 1 and 5. *Worker*, 1 April 1933, 1.

34 *Der Yiddisher Zhurnal*, 30 March 1933, 1. *Der Kamf*, 31 March 1933, 10, and 7 April 1933, 1.

35 *Der Yiddisher Zhurnal*, 30 March 1933, 1.

36 Interview with Bessie Kramer, 1984.

37 Ibid.

38 Interview with Sadie Hoffman, 1984.

39 Interview with Bessie Kramer, 1984.

40 *Der Yiddisher Zhurnal*, 3 April 1933, 1; *Der Kamf*, 7 April 1933, 1. At the end of this boycott, it was decided to establish a permanent women's council to monitor the prices of groceries in order to prevent further price increases.

41 Dana Frank, 'Housewives, Socialists, and the Politics of Food: The 1917 New York Cost-of-Living Protests,' *Feminist Studies* 11: 2 (Summer 1985), 282–3. For an examination of another similar food protest, see Paula E. Hyman, 'Immigrant Women and Consumer Protest: The New York City Kosher Meat Boycott of 1902,' *American Jewish History* 70: 1 (September 1980), 91–105.

42 *Der Kamf*, 11 February 1927, 3.

43 Ibid., October 1925, 18.

44 Ibid., 10 and 18.

45 Ibid., 10.

46 Ibid., 24 February 1928, 4.

47 On the difficulties which the Fareyn women faced in establishing and running the camp, see *Der Kamf*, October 1925, 18, and 24 February 1928, 4 and 6.

48 For example, interviews with Sadie Hoffman, 1978 and 1987; *Der Kamf*, 30 December 1932, 5. Hoffman was one of the managers of the camp when it was first established.

49 Nisnevitch's membership card (in Yiddish) for the Yiddishe Arbeiter Froyen Fareyn. See also *Der Kamf*, 29 January 1932, 4.

50 For example, *Der Kamf*, 27 October 1933, 6; Labour League, *Souvenir Book of Ten Years Labour League* ([Toronto] 1936); and interview with Bessie Kramer, 1969.

51 *Der Kamf*, 27 October 1933, 6. The Stratford strike was a dramatic, Communist-led strike of furniture workers in 1933 (see Charles Lipton, *The Trade Union Movement of Canada, 1927–1959* [Toronto 1973], 256–7).

52 For example, *Der Kamf*, 11 February 1927, 3; 24 February 1928, 4; 30 December 1932, 5; 27 October 1933, 6.

53 Ibid., 1 January 1926, 4; 2 December 1932, 10; 24 November 1933, 10; 15 December 1933, 10.

54 Interview with Bessie Kramer, 1984; see also interview with Sadie Hoffman.

55 Interview with Sadie Hoffman, 1985. The difficulties of juggling these different demands are apparent in the interview with Bessie Kramer 1984. A 1984 interview with Molly Fineberg stresses similar difficulties faced by women in other branches of the Jewish left.

56 *Worker*, 28 February 1931, 1.

57 In the 1985 interview, Sadie Hoffman emphasized the way in which their poverty led them to focus on working-class economic struggles. The 1984 interview with Bessie Kramer stresses similar themes.

58 In Toronto's garment industry, where so many Jewish women and men were employed, the average woman earned between one-half to two-thirds of what the average man earned. Women garment workers often did not even earn enough money to enable to them to be self-sufficient, yet many women struggled to support dependents as well (see 'Uncloaking Vested Interests,' 220–1).

59 This emphasis on the family as a whole is especially apparent in the interview with Bessie Kramer, 1984.

Women's Peace Activism in Canada

Barbara Roberts

Canadian historians have only recently turned their attention to the Canadian peace movement. Although documentation of their activities is still skimpy, it is clear that women working in women-only and mixed women/men groups have made a significant contribution to twentieth-century peace movements at the national and international level. Women's peace activism is noteworthy in several different but overlapping settings. Many Canadian women were active as members of women-only groups that devoted some attention to peace as a subsidiary issue, such as the Woman's Christian Temperance Union or various women's church societies. Many were the mainstay of mixed male/female peace groups such as the League of Nations Society in the 1920s and 1930s, or the Canadian Peace Congress, Toronto's Church Peace Mission, or the Canadian branch of the Fellowship of Reconciliation, during the post–Second World War era. This article focuses primarily on the activities and ideas of individuals and organizations involved in women's peace activism in women-only peace groups, such as the Women's International League for Peace and Freedom (WILPF) and Voice of Women (VOW). These women were a minority of those involved in peace activities. Nevertheless, they represent a consistent and ongoing feminist-pacifist tradition that is of considerable historical and contemporary interest.

Not all peace activists have been 'pacifists.' Fair-weather or peacetime pacifists have been many and visible during this century. To promote peace in peacetime is, generally speaking, to take a position in the mainstream of public opinion. To promote peace in wartime, in contrast, is radical, certainly unpatriotic, and perhaps subversive or treasonous. This is doubly so if pacifism refutes loyalties to male kith and kin and their institutions (such as government), turning instead to a higher loyalty to the sisterhood of woman (and perhaps of man), and is visible as an assault on patriarchy. The women's peace movements in Canada during the twentieth century have spanned these positions. When peace has been respectable, most women's organizations (and for that matter, most mixed and men's reform or progressive organizations) have been for it. During wartime, when peace advocates have been seen as betraying their country, most women (and men) have swung into line and supported their fatherland, leaving only a handful who have insisted that, as Virginia Woolf put it, as women they had no country. During peacetime booms in membership and activity, for example before the First World War and from the early twenties to the mid thirties, when peace ideas were widespread and appear to have been more generally accepted, many peace activists hoped that governments would not be so foolish as to have another war. Of course, they did, and during each wartime, the women's peace-movement membership shrank to the absolute pacifists – usually strong feminists, often socialists, often Christians. At war's end the women's peace movement grew again to include the mainstream women who may have thought war wrong or stupid, or been opposed to particular features of a given war, but were neither absolutely and unconditionally opposed to the use of force to solve conflicts nor willing to 'abandon' or 'betray' their country in wartime.

Women as a potential majority of voters and citizens have for some decades had the capacity to direct democratic decision-making processes as we see fit. Moreover, women have for decades been responsible for most of the work of caring for people and creating the personal relationships and many of the institutions that make up the human community, yet, they have not used the power of numbers to take control of the decision making that determines the allocation of resources needed for those activities. Despite the hopes of our turn-of-the-century feminist forbears that the world's mothers would rise up to pacify society in order to protect all women's children, despite the relatively widespread popularity of a pro-peace stance during peacetime, and despite the stakes at risk, peace has not become a central or mobilizing issue in most women's political behaviour, however 'political behaviour' is defined.

Although pre-war beliefs that women's nature was immutably pacific and maternalism was inevitably a pacifistic force no longer held sway after the First World War, women's organizations still spoke in the post-war period about women's roles as mothers of society's children and therefore guardians of social morality. Although no comprehensive study has been carried out of the rhetoric and ideology of Canadian feminist-pacifists in the first half of this century, a recent study of their US counterparts indicates that most believed as early as the eve of the First World War that differences in women's and men's moral, social, and political priorities arose from their different training and life experiences, rather than from any immutable and inherent biological factors. Intellectual historian Linda Schott provides new insights into the maternalism of the pacifists, identifying three imperatives: social priorities should be to preserve human life, to allow each person to enjoy her right to a decent quality of life, and to sustain human relationships and community. Maternalism was used in feminist peace rhetoric, but it was the concrete rather than the mystical that was called upon. This type of maternalism redefined patriotism that would send men to 'go out and kill' for their country. These women wanted to protect the homes and families of all people, rather than send out men to destroy the homes and families of 'enemy' women, ostensibly to protect those of their own. The statements of these feminist-pacifists often suggested that women's training for and experience in mothering provided valuable knowledge about how to resolve conflict peacefully. A common rhetorical point was that war confiscated the product of women's labour without their consent: women bore, raised, and taught children, and carried out most of the humane and nurturing activities that created and maintained the community. As Schott points out, women's claim to a distinct but socially derived morality was consistent with their single-sex group work for peace and social change. Their ultimate objectives were twofold: to develop a balanced society by integrating women fully into decision making about how it was to be run, and at the same time to train men to be more like women in their values and thus less likely to endanger human life and community by pathological decisions and behaviours. In the peace context, feminism meant that giving women an equal say in running society would greatly eliminate the causes and thus the inevitability of war. Women need not be biologically peaceful to transform society, only humane, responsible, caring, nurturing, tough-minded, and committed.[1]

The erasing of women's historical record is nowhere more evident than in the recurring disappearance of our knowledge of our peace heritage. In Canada as in other countries, women have always, or nearly always, worked to end war, injustice, and human suffering. Feminist-pacifists have usually been a minority; most women have supported or at least tolerated the policies and outlook of those in power, so their participation in peace activism has waxed and waned with the times. Although women often began with a single issue (opposition to a war, or to nuclear-weapons testing), they usually widened their goals as they came to see the causes of war as systemic: economic, political, psycho-social, and so on. It is striking to see the extent to which the analysis of early twentieth-century feminist groups such as the Women's International League for Peace and Freedom echoes the conclusions of the feminist-pacifist movement of our own times. Peace-activists' ideas of women's nature, of what affairs are appropriately the concern of women, and of what women might or must do to gain control over those affairs have repeatedly returned to the necessity to claim power, and to feminize society, if women (and men) are to live according to humane or feminist values or, indeed, to live at all.

Peace had an important place on the agenda of the progressive women's reform movement. Peace work was considered normal and respectable. 'World peace is ... preoccupying ... governments and thinking people more than ever before,' reported the World Woman's Christian Temperance Union's (WCTU) Hannah Bailey in 1910.[2] An influential minority of upper- and middle-class progressives, often influenced by social-gospel views, supported a large and rapidly growing peace movement in North America and in Europe. Peace organizations discussed the economic and social costs of the arms race, the settlement of international disputes by arbitration or other peaceful means, and among the more radical reformers, the disproportionate and bellicose influence of arms manufacturers and (the contemporary equivalent of multinational corporations) the 'interests' and 'trusts' on international relations. Women, however, had little influence in formulating policy or directing activities in mixed-gender mainstream peace groups, and the connections between militarism, women, and an unjust social order were discussed primarily in women's organizations. In this optimistic climate of the anticipated feminization of society, where feminist internationalism was growing rapidly, many took it for granted that women's international commitments to the cause of women and humanity were of a higher order than loyalties to their national states.[3]

THE GREAT WAR

The advent of the First World War shattered peace-women's hopes, world-view, and organizations. The women's movement in all belligerent countries split between a pro-war majority and an anti-war minority. Patriotic leaders rushed to proclaim their support for the war and only a minority were outraged that the war caused cancellation of the Berlin meeting of the International Woman Suffrage Association (IWSA), representing some twelve million women. A handful of IWSA members decided to organize a congress of women from belligerent and neutral nations to take counsel and see what women could do about the war but, as in most belligerent countries, Canadian women's groups were hostile and refused invitations to send delegates to The Hague.

But not all Canadian feminists abandoned their presumed pacifist principles. As in other countries, pacifist women used their existing networks to find and work with others who shared their views. Anti-war feminists thus far identified cannot be simply labelled urban middle-class progressives, for they include women from a variety of backgrounds and circumstances. By definition their anti-war stance cast them as radicals, and their shared social-gospel perspective is noteworthy. Laura Hughes and Gertrude Richardson exemplify the feminist anti-war movement of this period. Richardson was more deeply religious than Hughes, but both were socialists inspired by a belief in a decent, just, and humane social order. Indeed, beyond the period of the Great War, the social gospel has continued to inspire, and its institutions to train ensuing generations of Canadian feminist-pacifists, whose affiliations ranged from Christian to Communist, up to the late 1980s. Deep religious commitment and the social gospel have thus tended to be a radical and activating rather than a conservative and privatizing influence. Women's peace history also challenges our assumptions about the radicalism or conservatism of previous generations of feminists. Feminist social historians in Canada have tended to take maternalist rhetoric at face value and accept the notion that Canadian feminists of the late nineteenth and early twentieth centuries were a conservative lot. Perhaps, though, we need to develop a more complex analysis of the various ways maternalism was used rather than taking at face value the public and official pronouncements our feminist forbears made as rationales and justifications for their actions. A conventional and feminine justification may have been used as a tactic in situations of hostility or backlash. Thus, conservative rhetoric may reflect pragmatic strategies rather than reactionary beliefs and objectives. This is not to deny that maternalism has functioned as a repressive and limiting ideology, but rather to remind us that is has also been used to embolden women to challenge and attempt to eliminate the most profound forms of injustice and violence.[4]

Laura Hughes's activities illustrate the social passion of the anti-war feminists of the Great War period. The daughter of prominent educational and social reformers James L. Hughes and Ada Marean Hughes, and niece of Minister of Militia Sir Sam Hughes, she attended the Women's International Congress at The Hague as an unofficial Canadian delegate. On her return, she worked with her suffrage, socialist, and labour associates in Toronto to organize a woman's peace party affiliated with the Women's International Committee for a Permanent Peace (WICPP), in 1919 renamed the Women's International League for Peace and Freedom (hereafter referred to as WILPF) in Canada. She and Elsie Charlton sent out hundreds of letters to prospective sympathizers, asking them to send away for and study internationalist material, form discussion groups, and work for sanity. The Toronto group organized private and public meetings on peace issues, some of which attracted a good deal of hostility and name calling, and lobbied government to consider the mediation plan, developed by Canadian Julia Grace Wales, a professor at the University of Wisconsin, and the other principles adopted at The Hague congress.

In fall 1915, at her mother's urging, Hughes and her friend Gertrude Graydon carried out undercover investigations of the conditions of women workers in war contract factories for the Trades and Labor Council. The resulting sensational exposés in Toronto dailies helped to convince her uncle Sir Sam Hughes of the necessity to remedy abuses. Hughes subsequently stumped southern Ontario speaking to women's, socialist, and labour groups on topics such as woman suffrage, the economic causes of war, trading in strategic materials by the arms trust (whose members included British officials), war profiteering, labour conditions in war factories, and various other abuses exacerbated by jingoistic patriotism and militarism.[5]

Like most anti-war speakers, Hughes was harassed; in one incident, pro-war bullies tried to incite a crowd to overturn a car in which she and three other pacifists were sitting. Hughes later said that she had been the target of surveillance during the war, and was told she would be debarred from the United States because of her activities and political views.[6] Her connection to social-democratic women's organizations offered support for peace work. The Toronto Women's Social Democratic League, organized in September 1914 with thirty founding members, was open to 'all progressive women,' but most were SDP members. They discussed a wide range of feminist and socialist topics. Hughes was a signatory of the SDP 1917 May Day manifesto and prominent in Toronto festivities on that occasion. Such actions were especially risky for her non-'British' fellow opponents of the war; seventeen Ukrainian workers were arrested the following year at the Ottawa SDP May Day celebration and taken to Kapuskasing internment camp in northern Ontario, from which many trouble-makers were deported at the end of the war. Hughes was also involved in the Ontario Independent Labor party, serving on the founding provincial executive of that body after 1916. She was active in the anti-conscription campaign, and urged the Trades and Labor Congress to organize a protest march on Parliament to demand the repeal of the Military Service Act.

Western anti-war feminists and socialists were enthusiastic about Hughes's ideas and knowledge of economic issues, and her fiery speeches. They persuaded her to plan a prairie lecture tour under the auspices of labour councils in Winnipeg and Calgary. But the tour was cancelled when she married US conscientious objector Erling Lunde, whom she had met in July 1917 while a keynote speaker at a conference to found the Chicago branch of the People's Council for Peace and Democracy, a left-populist US organization concerned with civil liberties and other peace issues. Hughes continued her involvement with the Canadian feminist-pacifists during family visits to Toronto, and spoke at Toronto peace meetings throughout the 1920s. In Chicago, she became a well-known speaker and organizer and was greatly respected as a civic, political, and educational reformer in her adopted city.[7]

Gertrude Richardson's anti-war activities also provide a fascinating glimpse of the impact of the war on feminist-pacifist perspectives. Born Gertrude Twilley in Leicester, England, to a working-class family, she received a high-school education supplemented by home study of the classics, and trained as a fancy seamstress; her father and brothers were in the boot-and-shoe industry. Deeply religious, the Twilleys were part of the tiny minority who opposed the Boer war. She left the Melbourne Hall Evangelical Nonconformist church over the war, to join socialists who followed Christian pacifist principles. Her father died in 1900 after being hit on the head while speaking at an Independent Labour party anti-war meeting. Her own health broke down for several years after a disastrous first marriage, difficult childbirth, and the death of her infant. She was involved with the local Peace Society in 1906, and published poetry, mostly of a devotional nature, in the local press.

Her 1911 move with her widowed elder sister and widowed mother to Swan River, Manitoba, where her brother and sister had established homesteads, led to increased opportunities as a writer after her travel letters, published by a Leicester daily, were enthusiastically received. To her poetry she added regular columns about pioneer life and described her activities in feminist and farm politics, founding a branch of a woman suffrage society and initiating community discussion groups. Her regional political reports to the *Woman's Century*, the National Council of Women of Canada journal, resulted in invitations to publish historical fiction serials. In 1912, she married Robert Richardson, an early settler from Ontario, and they adopted a son, Eric, in 1917. Her vivid and moving wartime columns described the war's impact on the area's families and her own activities in opposition to the war. Despite her heavy domestic responsibilities as a prairie homesteader, she found time to carry out an immense correspondence with like-minded socialists and pacifists from several countries. Through these letters and her writings in the labour and socialist press, she functioned as a clearing-house of information about peace activities.[8] Richardson had found allies in Winnipeg labour circles, where she had spoken on her peace crusade at the Labor Temple. Those closest to her were socialists, such as Helen and George Armstrong, Winona and Fred Dixon, and fellow Christian pacifist S.J. Farmer. Her articles and letters appeared in the western Canadian, national, and British labour press after mid 1917, bringing a strong response from their readers.

Her writings illustrate the shock and sense of loss felt by anti-war feminists as they struggled to rebuild their political and personal lives. She had taken for granted that the peace commitment was a necessary foundation of feminism. Her faith in sisterhood was badly shaken by women's support of the war.

Woman's Century ceased to publish Richardson's contributions after they became too openly anti-war. When pro-war ('British') women in Canada were given the vote by Prime Minister Borden after feminist leaders such as Nellie McClung blatantly betrayed their 'foreign' (non-'British') sisters, in order to gain support for his pro-conscription government in the 1917 election, Richardson commented: 'As a suffragist of many years, I always believed that the coming of women into electoral life would be the end of wars. I am saddened beyond measure to find that, here at least, such is not the case.' Richardson's major contribution to the feminist anti-war movement was her Women's Peace Crusade, publicized through the Canadian and British newspapers columns, modelled after the British Women's Peace Crusade, which sponsored anti-war vigils, demonstrations, and parades. Letters of support for her crusade came from British friends and relatives and Canadian sympathizers, many of them social-democrat women and men. Noting men's support, she said: 'My soul is going out from the "Women's Movement" ... I have discovered that not only women, but men, have great tender hearts, strong courageous souls, beautiful minds ... I shall be among the number now who will not be looking for the miracle I once hoped would come "when women voted." Instead, I shall hope to be counted worthy to cast my vote as one of the brotherhood and sisterhood of the New Humanity.'[9]

Although she had redefined sisterhood to include male supporters, her own women's peace-crusade manifestos were addressed to 'Sister Women' and 'women with mother hearts.' Crusade material spoke of the 'brotherhood and sisterhood of the great family of humanity,' opposed 'all war, conscription, slavery,' and pledged members to campaign and vote only for candidates who worked for peace and against 'militarism under all forms.' With other anti-war feminists and socialists, Richardson supported the 'Workers' Council,' which grew out of the Anti-Conscription League and tried to field non-partisan anti-conscription candidates for the December 1917 federal election. Like its US and British counterparts, the Workers' Council platform demanded civil liberties, repeal of conscription, equal suffrage for men and women, the restoration of freedom of speech and the press, and 'the right to discuss international questions with the workers of other countries'; it protested industrial conscription and the disenfranchisement of Canadians whose countries of origin were now 'enemies.'[10]

Wartime repression illustrated on a daily basis the interconnections between questions of peace and social justice, and Richardson's range of activities are representative. She was a charter member of a Women's Labor League (WLL) branch in Winnipeg. WLL organizer Helen Armstrong was also a key figure in the anti-conscription campaign in the summer of 1917. Often the only woman on the platform at the open-air meetings, Armstrong several times defused violent confrontations, receiving bruises for her trouble. Armstrong also picketed and distributed leaflets at pro-war women's meetings, organized wartime strikes of women workers (which the pro-war Local Council of Women harassed and scabbed), and was often arrested. Hundreds of miles northwest of Winnipeg, Richardson could not often participate but greatly admired this heroine of the 'New Humanity' and she also commended Laura Hughes's work in eastern Canada. The respect was mutual.

Anti-war activists had to piece together information from a variety of sources; in this service WILPF played an important role. As an executive member of the provincial suffrage society, Richardson had been one of the Canadian women to whom invitations to The Hague congress were sent in 1915, and she continued to receive WILPF correspondence and monthly newsletters during (and after) the war. The WILPF newsletter *Internationaal*, issued more or less quarterly beginning January 1916, was an important source of news of peace efforts, official repression of peace activities, the impact of the war upon civilian populations, and reports of the activities of various WILPF groups in the neutral and belligerent countries. Personal contacts supplied other information; in Richardson's case this included letters from women nursing at the front, other overseas and US and Canadian correspondents, and reports in various feminist, farm movement, anti-war, socialist, and labour newspapers and other publications she regularly read. Although unable to participate directly in many events, anti-war feminists, even in isolated areas, could be well aware of events and issues elsewhere and pass on information to others.[11]

Like many of their international associates, Richardson and Hughes were both involved in support for conscientious objectors (COs). Richardson's brother Horace Twilley was brutalized with other COs in the Leicester prison. Their mother, who had returned to England, took part in a weekly prayer and song vigil outside the prison gates. Richardson's columns speak of the treatment of COs in Canada and other countries, and of Manitoba families whose boys were dragged off to military service or prison. When Hughes's husband Erling Lunde was jailed as a conscientious objector shortly after their marriage, she joined her father-in-law in lobbying, protest, and organized efforts to offer COs and their families legal, spiritual, and material support. CO support in Canada was less well organized; in Manitoba, a branch of the Canadian Freedom League (other branches were in Victoria and Toronto) was established to assist COs, but little is known about its activities, and it seems likely that individual efforts such as Richardson's were more typical. In 1918, Richardson circulated a British women's appeal for women to volunteer to take the place of the cos in prison so that the men might be allowed to regain their health. A few did so. Francis Beynon, who had fled the previous year to New York to avoid persecution for her pacifist activities, offered to pay her own way to England if accepted as a substitute.[12]

Richardson continued in her writing and her peace work until 1921, focusing on women's issues and European child relief. She had hoped for a New Humanity, but the governments and citizenry of the victorious powers demonstrated little interest in changing their ways. She had never been robust, and as the stress of the war years was exacerbated by her despair over the cruelty and needless suffering she saw prolonged beyond the war's end, she pushed herself to exhaustion. Her health broke down and after the early 1920s she no longer published or participated in public affairs. Her illness represents a tragic loss for the Canadian women's movement, for she was a gifted poet, journalist, and political activist.[13]

The end of the war, so long awaited, brought its own problems; pacifist women in the victorious, defeated, and neutral nations tried to influence the terms of settlement to avoid planting the seeds for another war. Through WILPF and other women's networks, they reiterated the principles of the 1915 Hague congress for a just settlement, and in addition wanted a charter of equal rights for women in the treaty. Few outsiders cared to hear their message, and many women as well as men in the victorious countries wanted revenge, not justice or peace. There were attempts by some western Canadian women to get women (not necessarily pacifists) to the negotiating table, but to no avail. The government would no doubt have agreed with Winnipeg LCW's Christina Murray, who had scoffed: 'Are the women of each country to ask for representation? Surely that would be impossible!'[14]

As British WILPF co-founder Helena Swanwick later commented: 'When I hear that women are unfit to be diplomats, I wonder by what standards of duplicity and frivolity they could possibly prove themselves to be inferior to the men who represented the victors at Versailles.' These men refused to lift the food blockade behind which women and children of the defeated countries were known to be starving. Although some women, too, were alleged to have objected that 'Huns' wives' should be helped, the pacifists believed that most women would now return to compassion and common sense. The women's peace movement of the ensuing decades would try its utmost to, as German pacifist Lida Gustava Heymann said, 'make good the wrong-doing of men.'[15]

THE TWENTIES AND THIRTIES

The brutality, injustice, and stupidity of the terms of the peace settlement strengthened the conviction of feminist-pacifists that a just and lasting peace required a drastic reshaping of society. As the New York state branch of WILPF declared in 1919, women had failed to halt the war or bring about a just peace settlement 'not because we were wrong, but because we had no power.' Women's cause could best be served by peace work. 'By aiding men to release themselves from their bondage to violence and bloodshed we shall also free ourselves, for women can never know true liberty in a society dominated by force.' These women rededicated themselves to educate the public about the political, economic, and social causes of war, and to educate women to 'gain their share of control in the church, the schools, industry and the state.'[16]

Canadian WILPF members said nothing so radical, but those who had opposed the war continued to be labelled extreme radicals and traitors. Hostility to peace and to radical internationalism lingered for several years, and hostility to a gender analysis of the causes of war exists to the present day. Militarists and extreme nationalists attacked peace activists; in March 1920 they forced the cancellation of WILPF International President Jane Addams's invitation by the University of Toronto's Department of Sociology to give a public lecture. Margaret Perceval from Vancouver WILPF wrote in 1923 of the British Columbia situation: 'I am afraid you will think me a pessimist, but really I am understating the facts.' In the current atmosphere, anyone who was a pacifist 'would not dare to say so, as it would be a criticism and a condemnation of our special brand of imperialism ... [and those few who have spoken out cautiously feel] the cold shadow of disapproval hanging over them because they dared to say even a little. So that we are not free.'[17]

A modified version of internationalism, stripped of its commitment to radical social change, regained some respectability in Canada by the mid twenties. In this moderate climate, European WILPF members carried out a successful speaking tour following the 1924 International Congress held at Washington, DC. As the social and political context of women's peace activism changed, the characterization, and to some extent the character, of the women's peace movement also changed. The spectrum of groups where women could work for peace in this period ranged broadly from radical (WILPF, Women's Peace Union) to conservative (National Council of Women of Canada [NCWC], WCTU, United Church Women), from religious to secular, each with a different focus, definition of peace issues, level of commitment to social change, and analysis of the causes of war, violence, and inequality (if they mentioned the latter at all). Some women's organizations remained indifferent or hostile, but the WCTU, United Church of Canada women, and the NCWC joined with women in mixed internationalist groups such as the League of Nations Society to work with feminist peace groups such as WILPF on various peace issues. The plethora of peacetime peace supporters exhibited varying degrees of commitment to pacifism. Some of them were returning to peace convictions they had abandoned at the onset of the First World War, while others were newly – and temporarily – involved. The core group of radical and Christian or secular, socialist feminist wartime peace activists neither changed their perspective nor ceased their efforts, but they were numerically and ideologically overwhelmed by the more conservative mainstream during the 1920s and 1930s. This pattern of a small radical core supplemented by mainstream newcomers was to be repeated in the ensuing decades, as more conservative women moved into the women's peace movement in relatively tolerant times, and out of it in repressive periods, as the ideological climate and international situation changed.

The new respectability of peace work in the 1920s also increased the numbers of women who wished to be associated with WILPF, which quickly expanded beyond its small radical core. Although there had been scattered activity in western Canada and Nova Scotia during the war, Toronto had remained the centre of organization. Now, WILPF groups were established from Victoria to Newfoundland. Wartime member Violet McNaughton was a key post-war figure, working through farm organizations and the rural press to rally farm women for peace projects.[18]

As WILPF groups were formally organized in the various provinces, vice-presidents were chosen to represent them at the national level. One of these was wartime sympathizer Laura Jamieson, regarded by the mainstream women's and mixed groups as 'radical' and 'even ... a "dangerous woman."' She was a central figure in the Vancouver WILPF, by then the strongest and most active Canadian branch. Most Canadian WILPF work continued to be carried out at the local level, relying on women's organizational and personal networks for support and inspiration. Characteristically, Canadian WILPF continued to link peace, economic and social-justice issues, and women's rights, and campaigned for all. Some branches allowed men to join (in the absence of a mixed national peace group), although not to hold office; most remained women only. Even in the mixed League of Nations Society, women did nearly all the work and eventually transformed the society into a de facto women's organization, which caused a male backlash, a recurring problem. This issue is germane because most women peace workers, including those women-only groups, were also involved in mixed organizations or joint efforts with other women's and mixed groups. Partly because WILPF was more radical in its social, economic, and political views than the mainstream women's organizations and mixed peace organizations, and because WILPF was red-baited in the

1920s (and later through the 1950s), WILPF campaigns were often carried out in co-operation with, or indeed through, other groups.[19]

Most peace activities of this period in Canada were not threatening to the status quo and emphasized preventive measures: education, internationalism, co-operation. Social and economic justice was seen by the more radical as a means to prevent war, but this view had little impact on government policy. Radical or not in their analysis, most women's peace efforts took a broad approach. For example, women's missionary society groups in the Protestant churches tried to teach children about the experiences of minority groups in Canada and the harm that racism did at home, in order to prevent xenophobic bellicosity later in life. Nor were Canadian women's peace groups challenging the status quo on gender relations. The issue of working in mixed groups is worth a brief discussion here. European WILPF groups consistently insisted on keeping WILPF a women's peace organization, while North Americans held a variety of views. Some US women had given up on working with men, others had enjoyed more positive experiences. Canadian feminist-pacifists had been forced to recognize like-minded men as allies. The pre-war and wartime farm movement had given many western women an opportunity to work in harmony and occasional equality with their menfolk. Moreover, feminist separatism was a reactionary rather than a radical movement in Canada during the war years: the Canadian feminists who had promoted the idea of a woman's party near the end of the war were militarist, not pacifist. After the war, some Canadian WILPF members felt that now that women had the vote there was no need or justification for women-only groups. Women's experience in de facto mixed WILPF chapters in the United States and Canada has not yet been explored by historians, but it is an important issue. A recurring factor in the periodic re-emergence of women-only peace groups through the century has been the problem of dealing with authoritarian and sexist male colleagues and leaders in mixed groups.[20]

In the women's peace movement in Canada and internationally, there was disagreement over the question of absolute pacifism, centring around the issue of the use of revolutionary violence and, by the 1930s, violent resistance to repression or fascism. Although WILPF did not require a peace pledge, some prominent WILPF members belonged to other groups that did. One such group was the Women's Peace Union of the Western Hemisphere (WPU), founded at Niagara Falls in August 1921 at the initiative of Christine Ross Barker, a pre-war suffrage activist and Toronto WILPF member since 1915. Key wartime WILPF organizer Laura Hughes, now in Chicago, her mother Ada Marean Hughes, and perhaps at its height a few dozen other Canadian women were members. Although few in number, WPU members were assiduous workers. There were connections between WILPF and WPU-type groups in many countries through the individual members of both groups, but there was no official affiliation. There were also WPU sections in Mexico, and through War Resistors International, organizational links with absolute pacifists in women-only and mixed groups in other countries. In the United States, the WPU promoted an amendment to the Constitution that would make it impossible for the government to prepare for or declare war. The Canadian parliamentary equivalent was WPU member MP Agnes Macphail's attempt to vote down the appropriation for school military training each year when the estimates were brought down.[21]

More typical was the work carried out by groups such as the NCWC, affiliated with the League of Nations Society. By the mid twenties, forty-two of fifty-six Local Councils had league committees. In fact, by this time the society was a women's organization, 'effectively feminized' at the rank-and-file level, and the pro-feminist society head, Sir George Foster, turned over to women's organizations all responsibility for recruiting members. Alice Chown, for example, formed a Women's League of Nations Association as an affiliate of the mixed branch (the former was absorbed by the latter in 1932). But work-horses like Chown were a mixed blessing for the conservatives in the league. An anti-war activist who had been vilified by militarist women and men alike a decade before, she took care not to flaunt her ongoing radical connections and sympathies. She wrote to WILPF International: 'My good Methodist name carries me far, and I have opportunities that another radical might not have. I am severely proper but the day may come when I am thrown out of the League of Nations Society. In the meantime I sow my seed. I am a [WILPF] member (tell it not in Toronto).' The importance of women as peace workers was given a token recognition after 1929, when most Canadian delegations to the League of Nations included a woman, and Mary Craig McGeachy was appointed to the league secretariat.[22]

Most groups concentrated on education. Peace education for young children was aimed largely at mothers' child-rearing methods, persuading mothers to promote lessons of co-operation through play, stories, settling disagreements, and family discipline. Anti-war toys campaigns and other efforts to 'Disarm the Nursery' were a regular feature of WILPF and other groups' activities. For older children, the objectives were to demilitarize the schools and community activities (such as Boy Scouts), and promote 'world-mindedness' in youngsters. In the community, church women made sure that Canadian Girls in Training (CGIT), the United church girls' group, discussed peace themes, and carried out internationalist activities. NCWC and Local Councils used a wide range of methods, from lectures and study sessions to organizing pen-pals and speaking contests. Peace educators sought to inform teachers about peace-education resources and organizations and to train them in peace education. A WILPF survey of militarism in school textbooks attracted much attention, and much energy was expended on opposing cadet training in the schools. Peace workers wanted physical education for both girls and boys, to promote self-discipline and group co-operation rather than military authoritarianism. WILPFers and other peace activists all across the country discussed the issue in existing women's organizations, passed resolutions, organized public meetings, petitioned, and in some communities, succeeded in making cadet training an election issue. Their side usually lost, because the federal government funded military training and thereby relieved the schools of a substantial part of the cost of any sort of physical education program, and because many patriotic organizations (including the Imperial Order, Daughters of the Empire) still retained considerable influence in shaping government and school-board policy and public opinion.[23]

In addition, WILPF and its sister organizations carried out ambitious adult-education programs, ranging from 'No More War' parades to peace conferences, workshops, public lectures, study groups, and internationalist displays in store windows such as the one by Edmonton WILPF in 1930 that stretched ribbons across a world map to show origins of trade goods and to emphasize the importance of Canada's economic connections in the global economy. Groups organized displays in libraries, participated in popular-culture events (such as the Vancouver Folk Festival), and put on peace festivals, fêtes, and pageants, especially popular in the late 1920s. They also attempted to publish information and peace propaganda in the mainstream media, believing with Laura Jamieson that 'get[ting] people reading along progressive lines ... is even better than getting them out to meetings.' In rural areas, farm newspapers were the main vehicles of peace and internationalist education, particularly the *Western Producer*, McNaughton's paper, whose editors were returned soldiers (one, Harris Turner, had been blinded) and strong peace supporters. Personal contact was also an important method of outreach. McNaughton travelled 4000 miles throughout Saskatchewan in 1930 promoting the work of WILPF.[24]

Although peace education and support for the League of Nations continued to be major themes, disarmament became increasingly emphasized in the 1930s. An indicator of great interest in peace and internationalist issues in Canada is the response to the international WILPF disarmament campaign of 1931. Violet McNaughton twice published an international WILPF petition for general and total world disarmament in her *Western Producer* column, and sent copies out by request to readers who circulated them in their organizations and communities. By these means, and 'without any central organized effort at all,' prairie WILPF supporters collected 15,000 signatures, 7000 from Saskatchewan alone. The Newfoundland WILPF group in 1931 distributed

5000 copies of a non-partisan 'International Declaration on World Disarmament.'[25] Other women's groups promoted the campaign, such as the Halifax LCW and the Nova Scotia WCTU, at the initiative of Ella Murray.[26]

NCWC president Winnifred Kidd was appointed by the government as one of the Canadian delegates to the 1932 Disarmament Conference (probably as a result of women's groups' lobbying for Canadian support for the aims of the conference); her subsequent cross-country tour sparked interest in the issue. More than 103,000 United Church women signed a disarmament petition in 1932. When the CCF was formed in 1933, it became a vehicle for peace activity by groups representing political opinion from left to centre. Although, generally speaking, WILPF had the most radical analysis of the causes of war, and consistently advocated redistribution of resources as a necessity for peace, some more traditional women's groups such as the WCTU also supported a similar analysis in the 1930s. Women were active in most of the mixed groups, but mixed-groups' policies did not identify gender issues as peace issues, and women still relied on their own organizations for effective action consistent with their understanding of what changes were required to bring about peace.[27] New issues arose. Like many other peace women, Sen. Cairine Wilson became involved in refugee work in the 1930s, and was among those Canadians who fought a losing battle to get Jewish refugees admitted to Canada. Wilson was unable to rally women's groups to apply enough pressure to overcome the anti-Semitism of politicians, policy-makers, and the general public.[28]

As the depression of the thirties intensified, western farmers' support of peace issues was supplanted by attention to day-to-day survival, and a 1932 farm press survey showed that large numbers of prairie farm readers had ceased to participate in peace campaigns and no longer wished to read about peace issues. The commitment of mainstream women's groups to peace issues, never central, had also begun to wane: by 1933, only sixteen of forty-four Local Councils of Women still had active League of Nations Society (LNS) committees, despite the continued support of the society at the NCWC official level. Canadian women's lack of enthusiasm for peace issues was a bitter disappointment to peace women, who knew that their fellow countrywomen had the power to create a strong public demand for a government 'peace policy,' if only they would decide to make this issue a priority. Committed peace women still tried to change public opinion and create a demand for peaceful methods of solving conflict. They initiated, for example, a Peace Action Project in the Maritime provinces in 1936. As late as June 1939, the WCTU annual meeting passed a resolution that 1 per cent of the defence budget be used to promote international understanding, and recommended that member groups undertake the study of the arms industry and of Gandhi's non-violent methods.[29]

But by the late 1930s, increasing deterioration in the international situation, frustration with the League of Nations' inability or unwillingness to act effectively, and concern with the virulent anti-woman and anti-Jewish policies of fascist governments made it more difficult to generate widespread public enthusiasm for even the tamest women's peace projects. The National Councils of Women of Germany and Austria were eradicated by their governments; the NCWC was horrified when it learned of fascist attacks on feminists and Jews. WILPF internationally opposed anti-Semitism, and many members concluded that war might be less dreadful than Europe under fascism, but WILPF remained convinced that war was not an effective way to achieve just resolutions of the problems at hand. Once again, women were being affected by events they were nearly powerless to influence and being pulled into a war caused by policies over which they had virtually no control. Until war actually began, WILPF continued their peacemaking attempts at the international level.[30]

The start of the war did not eradicate the peace concerns of the women who had been working on these issues for decades. Most were willing to support the war effort, but not at the expense of the ideals that the war purportedly was intended to save. Retired newspaperwoman Ella Murray, who had been an anti-militarist during the First World War and was by the 1940s confined to her bed but still active in the Halifax Council of Women, commented in her December 1939 report that 'if we were really fighting to establish democracy in the world, we must see to it that it was fully established at home.' Listing a range of social and economic justice and equality issues, including rehabilitative rather than punitive prison policies, Murray asserted: 'This work is too important, too imperative, to be side-tracked for years. We have to prove that democracy means what we profess, equal opportunities to all; the one form of Government which establishes and maintains the *rights* of all the people, not merely of a favoured class.'[31]

THE COLD WAR

There was virtually no strong women-only national peace group during the late 1940s and most of the 1950s. Canada was a stodgy and conservative country, socially and politically, in this period. The prevailing post-war ideology sent women back to the kitchens to preoccupy themselves with family life. Not coincidentally, this freed up all those jobs for returning men veterans, now expected to resume their positions of authority in the family and other social institutions. Of course, traditional women's groups continued their activities, but these were unlikely to challenge the status quo. Many of the reforms they had sought had been only partially achieved, but times had changed, reforming club-women had little real impact on society, and their social passion had faded. And many Canadians were in a state of shock after years of war followed by the mid 1940s spy trials, which legitimized the cold war.[32]

The growing red witch-hunt labelled as agents of a hostile foreign power those Canadians who held internationalist or 'communist' views. Reinforced by McCarthyism from the United States and the increasing US domination of the Canadian economy, culture, and media, our home-grown reactionary political climate was intensified by our participation in NATO and NORAD defence agreements, and the Korean war. Critics of injustice or inequality in Canadian society were easily intimidated or silenced; feminists were cranks, socialists were commies. Many companies routinely carried out security checks of employees, and any company doing 'secret' work was required to undergo screening by the RCMP. Former or potential activists saw friends go to jail, or lose their jobs or place in the community because of red smears.[33] Speaking out, dissenting from mainstream bellicose opinion on peace issues, or advocating even a tame internationalism, all of which had been unremarkable in the twenties, were in the fifties, by definition, radical stances and probably a danger to public safety and national security.

After the atomic bombs (built with Canadian uranium) had been dropped by the United States on Hiroshima and Nagasaki in 1945, many people had believed there could be no more wars because weapons had become too terrible to use. By the time this hope was dispelled, many women who might otherwise have become involved in the peace movement were deterred by the virulent anti-communist climate that made peace groups suspect. These included mixed groups such as the religiously based and absolute-pacifist Fellowship of Reconciliation, in Canada since the thirties. The largest and most active mixed group, which included large numbers of women, was the Canadian Peace Congress, founded in 1949 and led by return Methodist China missionary James Endicott and Ontario CCFer Eva Sanderson. Mary Austin Endicott was a key participant.

Mary Austin had met fellow Methodist Jim Endicott at the University of Toronto through the Student Christian Movement (SCM), under whose auspices many of Canada's most effective peace activists received their early training. As newly-weds they went to China, where they remained until the war forced them to return to Toronto in 1941. When he returned to China in 1944, she remained behind to strengthen the social justice and internationalist message in Christian education programs that she revitalized for the CGIT, and to serve on the York School Board. She resigned when she returned briefly to China in 1946; although her subsequent peace work focused more on banning the bomb, she continued to see peace as rooted in profound social change. Like many

Canadian radicals, she was inspired, guided, and sustained by the social gospel and a Christianity made immanent and immediate.[34]

The Peace Congress originated from and had strong ties to mainstream churches and many of its individual participants were church women, although it was not until the mid 1950s that church groups found it comfortable to co-operate on issues. Socialists and communists also made up a substantial proportion, but not necessarily a majority, of its membership. While many members of the Canadian Peace Congress were inspired by religious conviction, the group's activities were mainly secular. They held rallies, demonstrations, and family peace picnics, and attracted large crowds to hear speakers such as the 'red' Dean of Canterbury, whose 1948 tour launched the organization. Shortly thereafter, the Canadian Peace Congress started a ban-the-bomb petition that collected 200,000 signatures before it was merged with an international petition (the 'Stockholm appeal') begun by Moscow-oriented international peace groups in 1950, after which another 300,000 Canadian signatures were collected.[35]

Despite support by prominent clergy and laity, the congress was attacked as 'Communist' by most of the political leaders of the mainstream parties, including the CCF. For a time, government-supported or government-tolerated bullies and hecklers disrupted and broke up meetings. The RCMP initiated smear campaigns and used agents provocateurs to make flaming 'red' speeches, posing as congress members. By 1952, various university heads and civic officials had banned congress speakers. 'Soviet-puppet' accusations were strengthened in 1952 when Endicott won the Stalin Peace Prize (the Eastern bloc Nobel equivalent), and attacks on him and the organization intensified. (Mary Endicott suffered stink-bomb and incendiary-bomb attacks at home during a meeting of fifty women peace workers.) The congress certainly criticized the Western powers more than it did the Soviet Union or China, until revelations by Khrushchev of Stalin's abuses (including mistreatment and murder of Jews) were published in the *New York Times* in June 1956, after which criticism became more even-handed.[36]

By the mid 1950s, the peace movement was again broadening its base, as public concern grew about the dangers of the nuclear arms race. The H-bomb tests that contaminated a Japanese fishing boat crew in 1954, or the Hungary, Suez, and Middle East crises a few years later, may have propelled more women into action, which may in turn have made it 'safer' to engage in peace activities. Although media coverage of Peace Congress activities focused on anti-red sensationalism, respectable mainstream women such as Toronto Tory club-woman Greta Andrew and her friend Mrs Shook, widow of a British military officer, participated in ban-the-bomb marches. By 1956 the Peace

Congress membership had severely shrunk, and as local groups fell into arrears on their financial pledges to headquarters, offices had to be closed, staff cut, and activities curtailed. The causes are unclear. Red peace activists, who were among the most reliable workers and fund-raisers, might have withdrawn from the congress to end all connections with the party after the Khrushchev revelations, but this possibility does not seem sufficient to account entirely for the decline. Many of its members moved into other older (and more respectable) organizations, including the Society of Friends, Fellowship of Reconciliation, and WILPF, and into the new anti-nuclear groups. Despite the overall decline in membership, some Peace Congress locals remained very active, sponsoring speakers and, by the late 1950s, showing British and European anti-nuclear films about Hiroshima to large audiences and loaning the films to other groups.[37]

Despite the fact that WILPF was the oldest women's peace organization in Canada, it did not attract a large membership during the cold war. Internationally, WILPF had been devastated by the war, and communications between various national sections had become nearly impossible. In 1939, its journal *Pax International* (later *Pax et Libertas*) was suspended for ten years and replaced by a quarterly newsletter during the wartime 1940s. Many European WILPFers fled or went into exile; others were persecuted; some were killed in extermination camps or simply executed. The papers of the international headquarters were sent to the United States. An overseas bureau of the headquarters itself was set up there to carry out some international business, but the membership (and the executive) had no clear position on the use of force or violence in this situation. Some had long believed that it was acceptable to use force or violence to resist oppression; others were absolute pacifists. The international executive (or at least those able to attend the sole wartime executive meeting, convened in late 1939) reaffirmed the principles articulated at their 1915 Hague conference as guide-lines for the present-day organization.[38]

Although the Canadian WILPF section is described as being the 'least affected by the war' of the non-European sections, it did not easily regain widespread public support. Vancouver, Edmonton, and Ottawa chapters had continued to function in the early days of the war, organizing study meetings on current events, but the Vancouver chapter may have been the only one that survived. By 1950, Vancouver WILPFers were in full swing. A small but determined group, they organized meetings, made statements, lobbied governments, and participated in peace-movement activities on domestic, foreign-policy, and social-justice issues. Vancouver WILPF reports mention the red-baiting tactics used against them; despite some successful attempts to get retractions, the group remained under fire. One irate woman actually destroyed the group's records, intending to destroy the local WILPF chapter by eradicating its history.[39]

Although the easing of cold-war tensions after 1956 and growing alarm over radiation hazards should have enhanced WILPF's ability to attract more members, the Vancouver branch never regained its pre-war popularity. Nevertheless, the small core of committed members continued their work. Reports in the international WILPF periodical during the next few years are scattered (national section reports ceased altogether in the magazine after the early 1960s), but they indicate that Canadian WILPF focused on a variety of peace, foreign-policy, and social-justice issues, including status of women, civil liberties, immigration, racism, penal reforms, and school strapping. Vancouver reported in the May 1959 issue that a group of heretofore inactive young mothers had formed a 'World Affairs Club,' and hopefully concluded that 'things are moving ... towards a public consciousness of need for action to save the world from annihilation.' That January they reported a substantial increase in membership.[40]

Marion Kerans (then Kellerman) was one of the women who became active toward the end of the decade. Her friends from a bridge-playing group made up of young West Vancouver matrons organized the Mother's Committee on Radiation Hazards in 1958. She says that, at the time, she just wanted safe milk for her children. Mary Van Stolk organized a similar group in Edmonton in 1959; the national male-dominated Committee on Radiation Hazards grew out of the early local mothers' groups. These groups initially tried to get government action on monitoring radioactive strontium 90 in milk. Although there was media coverage of contamination and some discussion of the dangers of exposure to radiation, the government claimed there was no danger. But the only way to get safe milk was to get rid of nuclear weapons. Fear of radiation dangers to children apparently began to outweigh the pressures of political climate, women's constrained role, and the heavy demands on time and energy of housework and child care, as increasing numbers of women turned to exert pressure and to protest on nuclear and peace issues in the late 1950s. An early such group, the National Council against Nuclear Weapons Tests, had been formed by several women's organizations in Britain after the 1955 H-bomb tests, when it was learned that new-borns had strontium 90 in their bones. The Committee on Nuclear Disarmament (CND) was formed by a coalition of women's and mixed organizations in January 1958 after Britain got its own bomb. By then, it was no longer possible to dismiss peace groups as 'red' fronts, or women peace activists as 'red' dupes.[41]

EPILOGUE

The founding of Voice of Women/Voix des Femmes (VOW) in 1960 marked an important turning-point for women's peace activism. At the height of the cold war, when schoolchildren practised ducking beneath their desks in anticipation of nuclear war and debated 'better dead than red' or the reverse, when a US spy plane was shot down over the USSR, when the Summit Conference broke down, and when radioactive fallout from tests was contaminating the air, water, and breast milk, Toronto journalist Lotta Dempsey asked what women could do. 'It seems to me that if we had a summit conference of women dedicated to the welfare of children all over the world, we might reach an understanding.' VOW was founded at Massey Hall on 28 July 1960.[42]

Women flocked in; membership reached 10,000 in less than a year. Some 'Voices,' as they were called, were previously active in red-smeared groups such as WILPF or the Peace Congress, and were attracted by the opportunity to continue peace work in a respectable women's group without hostility and harassment. The majority were previously uninvolved 'housewives.' In the early days, VOW's non-partisan policy meant not attacking or supporting political parties, but when Liberal leader Lester Pearson reversed Liberal policy in 1963 and as prime minister caved in to US and NATO pressure to accept nuclear weapons in Canada, VOW responded with criticism. One thing led to another; soon Voices were getting arrested at anti-NATO demonstrations and internal disputes were reported in the media. By 1965, membership had fallen by half; the organization rapidly evolved into its present non-respectable form.

From its earliest days, VOW was an important training ground for inexperienced women to become effective activists and organizers. Members learned how to work with the media, get coverage of issues and events, lobby government representatives, organize public meetings, national and international conferences, international visits, Canadian tours by foreign women (Soviet, Japanese, Vietnamese), collect and send shipments of clothes and medical supplies to 'enemy' nations, and plan and participate in demonstrations. Two of their most spectacular early nation-wide projects were collecting baby teeth to be analysed for strontium 90, and knitting dark-coloured baby clothes (to assure invisibility to US bombers) to send to Vietnam. Until the 1970s, VOW's structure was formal, with hatted and gloved presidents and parliamentary procedure. VOW offices were full-time jobs. At present, the organization is run by steering committees and a co-ordinator – still virtually full-time jobs. Participation in formally run meetings provided neophytes with valuable experience and the chance to build skills and confidence to speak out and act in public in ways that the newer structures cannot provide. But VOW activities continue to grow out of individual initiative, and opportunities have always existed to develop someone's good idea into a full-blown project.

Although the initial impetus for VOW was to get rid of nuclear weapons and the main focus has been to eliminate war or the threat of war as a means of settling disputes, VOW has also been concerned with eliminating the causes of war and violence. Voices rapidly developed a broad definition of peace, encompassing not only nuclear issues, but social justice, and gender and racial quality. Insisting that Canada should develop an independent foreign policy, VOW has been a strong supporter of the United Nations. VOW pressure helped to bring about the 1963 partial Test Ban Treaty, and played a large part in the declaration of the United Nations International Year of Cooperation (originally conceived by VOW as a year of peace). Voice of Women was founded as a bilingual organization, and early brushes with unilingual anglophone Ottawa arrogance led VOW to work for the appointment of the Royal Commission on Bilingualism and Biculturalism. VOW also was among those women's groups who forced the government to appoint the Royal Commission on the Status of Women.

Many Voices were active in the women's liberation movement of the late 1960s and early 1970s, and were prominent among the women who founded the National Action Committee on the Status of Women (NAC) and a host of other feminist organizations. The more recent establishment of the Survival Committee of NAC, at the behest of Voices, is an indication of the current acceptance that peace is not only a women's concern but a feminist issue. VOW had organized a large international women's peace conference in Montreal in 1976. In 1984, VOW members in Montreal and Halifax, who were infuriated by the lack of women 'experts' in a television panel commenting on the implications of the anti-nuclear film *The Day After* and by the constant and continued exclusion of women from peace negotiations, decided to undertake the development of the Coalition of Canadian Women's Organizations (as it came to be known) that planned the June 1985 Halifax International Women's Conference on Women's Alternatives for Negotiating Peace, which brought women together from over thirty countries. In the late 1980s, Voices are involved in various projects to prod the government into implementing the Forward-Looking Strategies Agreement that Canada signed at the 1985 Nairobi United Nations End-of-the-Decade Conference to achieve the 'equality, development, and peace' objectives of the UN Decade of Women (1976–85) by the year 2000.

When VOW was founded, 'normal' (middle-class) women stayed at home and raised their children. 'Nice' women did not publicly criticize, make fun of, or disagree with (male) political leaders (or for that matter, any men). But in order to do the work of VOW (for example, to assure the physical survival of their children by getting rid of radioactive fallout and ultimately getting rid of nuclear weapons), women had to step outside the confines of what they were supposed to be doing. Voices had to abandon 'ladylike anonymity' for the 'limelight' of public action in order to promote their cause. Some could not overcome their distaste, but others loved it and were never ladylike or anonymous again. Some husbands provided support services (food, baby-sitting, envelope stuffing, chauffeuring and luggage conveyance, message centres, moral support), others were opposed and eventually divorces resulted. As Voices moved into explicitly feminist issues and into broader social-change movements, some family members moved with them. The politicization of individual Voices reveals patterns of political awakening representative of the experience of many middle-class Canadian women. VOW today is in many respects reminiscent of WILPF and other feminist-pacifist groups of earlier decades of this century. One shared feature is that a religious or social passion, and the social-gospel tradition, are strong influences for several prominent Voices. For example, feminist activist, citizen-advocate, and several-time NDP candidate Muriel Duckworth, from a United Church family, was trained in the Student Christian Movement at McGill in the 1920s, active in the Fellowship of Reconciliation in the 1930s, and (through her Voice of Women contacts) became a Quaker in the early 1960s. Ursula Franklin is a Quaker; Rosalie Bertell is a nun. Religious commitment seems to inspire rather than diminish political activism. The Voice of Women has had a 'multiplier effect' on Canadian society out of all proportion to its size and the middle-class character of its membership. With its sister organizations of the 1980s, it is part of a long-standing tradition of women's peace activism.

NOTES

Particular thanks to Diana Chown, Frances Early, Gloria Geller, Linda Kealey, Anne Lunde, David Millar, Anne Molgat, Deborah Powell, Jo Vellacott, Edith Wynner, some of whom have given me expert advice as well as access to impor-tant material, and to various other named in footnotes, for generous assistance; and also to Joanne Oldring Sydiaha whose inspiration was a crucial factor in the early stages of this research. Linda Kealey and Joan Sangster have provided sustained and crucial editorial help.

1 On nurture versus nature, see Linda Kay Schott, 'Women against War: Pacifism, Feminism and Social Justice in the United States, 1915–1919,' PhD diss., Stanford University, 1985; see also Jo Vellacott, 'Images and Models of First Wave Feminism: In 1910 All Things Were Possible,' unpublished CRIAW paper, Montreal 1984; Catherine Marshall, Mary Sargant Florence, and C.K. Ogden, introduction by Margaret Kamester and Jo Vellacott, *Militarism versus Feminism: Writings on Women and War* [1915] (London

1987); Jill Conway, 'The Woman's Peace Party and the First World War,' in J.L. Granatstein and R.D. Cuff, eds, *War and Society in North America* (Toronto 1971).

2 Report of the Eighth Convention of the World's WCTU, 1910, Mrs Hannah J. Bailey, Peace and International Arbitration Superintendent. Bailey was a Quaker from Maine who had headed WCTU peace work since 1887. See Margaret Hope Bacon, *Mothers of Feminism* (San Francisco 1986).

3 On the liberal pre-war Canadian peace movement and some Canadian organizations, see Tom Socknat, *Witness against War: Pacifism in Canada 1900–1945* (Toronto 1987), ch. 1. For women in nineteenth- and early twentieth-century mixed movements, see Sandi Cooper, 'The Work of Women in Nineteenth Century Continental European Peace Movements,' *Peace and Change* 9:4 (Winter 1984), 11–30, and 'Women's Participation in European Peace Movements: The Struggle to Prevent World War I' in Ruth Pierson, ed., *Women and Peace: Theoretical, Historical and Practical Perspectives* (London 1987), 51–95; Frances Early, 'The Historic Roots of the Women's Peace Movement in North America,' *Canadian Woman Studies* 7:4 (Winter 1986), 43–8.

4 For Canadian refusals, see Adelaide Plumptre, secretary of the National Committee of Women for Patriotic Service, to Jane Addams, 15 April 1915, and the anti-Hague Congress pamphlet circulated by Plumptre's group in WILPF Papers, University of Colorado at Boulder, III 4–7; the invitation itself is in I 13–1. For a representative selection of club-women's attitudes, see 'What Twelve Canadian Women Hope to See as the Outcome of the War,' *Everywoman's World*, April 1915. On the devastating impact of the war on the mainstream peace movement, see Tom Socknat, 'Canada's Liberal Pacifists and the Great War,' *Journal of Canadian Studies* 18:4 (Winter 1983–4), 20–44. On the issue of conservatism, maternalism, and religious quietism, see my *Why Do Women Do Nothing to Stop the War? Canadian Feminist Pacifists and the Great War, 1914–18* CRIAW Papers no. 13 (1985), and Ernest Forbes, 'The Ideas of Carol Bacchi and the Suffragists of Halifax: A Review Essay on *Liberation Deferred? The Ideas of the English-Canadian Suffragists, 1877–1918*,' *Atlantis* 10:2 (Spring 1985), 119–26.

5 See Toronto *Daily Star* articles, 19 November 1915, and Toronto *Telegram*, 19 and 20 November 1915. For a fuller account of the feminist anti-war movement in Canada, 1915–8, see B. Roberts, *Why Do Women Do Nothing to Stop the War?* and also 'Women against War, 1914–1918: Francis Beynon and Laura Hughes,' in Deborah Gorham and Janice Williamson, eds, *Women and Peace*, forthcoming. Information on Hughes and the Congress is also based on WILPF Papers at the Norlin Library, University of Colorado at Boulder, her

family papers and interviews in Edison Park, Illinois, with her son Chester
Lunde and granddaughter Anne Lunde, and discussions with Edith Wynner,
consultant to the New York Public Library for the Schwimmer-Lloyd collection. I have apparently erred in repeating elsewhere the claim that Alice Chown
was the second Canadian delegate; Julia Grace Wales may have been counted as
Canadian for political purposes in the Congress report.

6 On the car incident and surveillance, see Toronto *Star*, 18 January 1923; on
exclusion, Scott Nearing, chairman of the People's Council of America for
Democracy and Peace, to Hughes, 26 October 1917. Unless indicated otherwise
all references to Hughes are from the Lunde Family Papers, Edison Park,
Illinois.

7 On the People's Council, see Harriett Alonso, 'A Shared Responsibility: The
Women and Men of the People's Council of America for Democracy and
Terms of Peace, 1917,' MA diss., Sarah Lawrence College, 1982. On the
western trip, see Hughes to Balch, 7 November 1919, WILPF Papers, III 4–7,
and the *Voice* (Winnipeg) 19 October 1917, which also mentions her proposal to
march on Parliament. On SDP women, see *Canadian Forward*, 28 October
1916, 24 April 1917, 24 August 1917, 10 September 1917, 10 October 1917.
On Maydays, see 'Mayday Manifesto, Toronto 1 May 1917' in the Toronto
Public Library collection, given to me by Linda Kealey, and report of the 1918
arrests, *Canadian Forward*, 24 May 1918, 7. For political deportations, see
my 'Shovelling Out the "Mutinous": Political Deportations from Canada before
1936,' *Labour/Le travail* 18 (Fall 1986), 77–110.

8 Research on Richardson was partly funded by a CRIAW research grant, 1986. In
my CRIAW article, I erroneously identified her husband as James Richardson,
Robert's brother. I am grateful to Linda Kealey for leading me to some of
Gertrude's Canadian publications. Subsequent research draws on material held
in various Leicester, England, sources, particularly the Local History Library,
where librarians Mike Raftery and Aubrey Stevenson were helpful, and the
British Library, Colindale, England, as well as material in the Swan River Valley
Museum, and upon interviews with Twilley and Richardson family members
and friends. I am grateful for their hospitality and kindness, as well as for their
help in providing information, to Eric Richardson, Dorothy Shewfelt, the
late Joan Wallcraft, Connie MacDonald, and John Booth, and to Isobel
MacKay, who identified key informants and arranged and facilitated most of
their interviews. For her father's death, see obituary of James William
Twilley, *Midland Free Press* 7 April 1900, and the report of the anti-war rally,
ibid. Gertrude says his death was caused by a broken heart, but family members
say it was his head. For anti-Boer war events, see Richard Rempel, 'British

Quakers and the South African War,' *Quaker History* 64:2 (Autumn 1975), 75–94.

9 'Canadian Women and the War,' *Leicester Pioneer*, 31 August 1917. Also on the women's crusade see the *Voice*, 19 October 1917, 30 November 1917, 22 February 1918, 31 May 1918; *Western Labor News*, 9 August 1918; and 'The Women's Crusade,' 2 November 1917, *Leicester Pioneer*.

10 See her *Leicester Pioneer* articles: 31 August 1917, for the passing of conscription and the western political parties' response, 7 September 1917, 2 November 1917, 9 November 1917. Her 'Harvest Time in Canada' describes the impact of war deaths and mentions the Workers' Council, 16 November 1917. On the Workers' Council, see also *Voice* articles, 17 and 21 September 1917.

11 'Progress in Canada: The Women's Labour League,' *Leicester Pioneer*, 14 December 1917. Also on Armstrong, see 'Helen Armstrong and Mrs. Queen at Mass Women's Meeting,' Winnipeg *Voice*, 31 August 1917; a letter from Helen Armstrong, ibid., 30 November 1917; description of her arrest, ibid., 21 December 1917. On Hughes's views of Richardson, see Hughes to Eva Macnaghten (then visiting in Vancouver), 9 August 1919, and on the planned visit to Winnipeg, see Hughes to Balch, 7 November 1919, WILPF Papers, III 4–7; and 'Laura Hughes Lecture Tour,' *Voice*, 19 October 1917. The Winnipeg group in 1919 was still pressing Hughes to come out to speak; she commented, 'As [Winnipeg] seems the center of peace ideals among the men so it ought to pass among the women.' Presumably she meant the women of the left, as the Winnipeg Local Council of Women (LCW) had been strongly militarist. See Linda Kealey, 'Prairie Socialist Women and World War I: The Urban West,' paper presented at the Annual Meeting of the Canadian Historical Association, June 1986, and 'Women and Labour during World War I: Women Workers and the Minimum Wage in Manitoba,' in Mary Kinnear, ed., *First Days, Fighting Days: Women in Manitoba History* (Regina 1987), 76–99.

12 On the CO substitution, see Richardson's pieces in the *Western Labor News*, 9 August 1918, describing harsh treatment accorded COs at Stony Mountain, 16 August and 20 September 1918, and her poem 'In Prison,' 2 November 1917. On Hughes's CO work, see letters in WILPF Papers, Hughes to Balch, 7 November 1919, III 4–7, and extensive correspondence and clippings in the Hughes and Lunde family papers.

13 Interviews with family members, Swan River, Brandon, and Somerset, Manitoba, September 1986.

14 The Violet McNaughton Papers (hereafter VM Papers) contain telegrams and correspondence related to this attempt, Saskatchewan Archives Board, University of Saskatchewan, folder E 52.

15 From Anne Wiltsher, *Most Dangerous Women: Feminist Peace Campaigners of*

the Great War (London 1985), 201–17, describing the 1919 WILPF Zurich conference. The 'Huns' wives' comment reported in her account is unsubstantiated.

16 Schott, 'Women against War,' 99–100, citing WILPF statement 1919, in records of New York Women's Peace Party, intended to clarify the group's position, Swarthmore College Peace Collection.

17 See correspondence in WILPF Papers, especially Jane Addams to Emily Balch, 30 April 1920, II 2–16. US WILPFers were targeted as an enemy by the US War Department because of WILPF attacks on increases in the military budget (Joan Jensen, 'All Pink Sisters: The War Department and the Feminist Movement in the 1920s,' in Joan Jensen and Lois Scharf, eds, *Decades of Discontent: The Women's Movement, 1920–40* [Westport 1983], 199–222).

18 This account draws from Jennifer Webber, 'Women in the Canadian Pacifist Movement: Pacifism and Feminism Intertwined,' undergraduate paper, 1983, University of Saskatchewan; the WILPF folders (passim) in the VM Papers and the WILPF Papers.

19 See Veronica Strong-Boag, 'Peace-making Women, 1919–1939,' in Pierson, ed., *Women and Peace*, 170–91. For an autobiographical sketch (ca 1926) of Jamieson, see WILPF Papers I 25–8. Jamieson to McNaughton, 27 March 1929, VM Papers, E 95. The WILPF Papers in Boulder suggest that WILPF was more widely established and active in Canada than we had before realized. For an overview of some of the women and peace activities in the inter-war period, see 'Women Unite: Story of the Women's Peace Campaign, WILPF,' *Western Producer*, 7 October 1929; Deborah Powell, 'Women's Peace Organizations in Canada 1920–1970,' unpublished honours essay, Carleton University, 1983.

20 See Forbes, 'The Ideas of Carol Bacchi.' On mixed groups, in the US, see Schott's discussion, 'Women against War,' 19–20. In Canada, see, for example, the postcard from Mrs G. Horton to Harriet Prenter, 17 November [1919], WILPF Papers, III 4–7, and Prenter to Balch, 17 June 1921, WILPF Papers, III 4–8, and Alice Loeb to McNaughton, 27 March 1929, VM Papers, E 95. See Gertrude Bussey and Margaret Tims, *Pioneers for Peace: The Women's International League for Peace and Freedom, 1915–65* (London 1980 [1965]), 124, for a discussion of a 1934 US attempt to make WILPF a mixed group internationally, firmly rejected by the Europeans, who said they had found it virtually impossible to work with men.

21 The Women's Peace Union (1921–41) Papers at the Swarthmore College Peace Collection include correspondence from Barker about Canadian activities. For Macphail, see Barker to Mrs Babcock at the WPU head office, 17 September 1924, and Barker to [Ms] Van Slyke, 8 May 1926, WPU Papers, reel 88.1. Information on WPU was given me by Frances Early.

22 Strong-Boag's 'Peace-making Women' discusses missionary societies' peace

activities. McGeachy was a University of Toronto graduate and a former teacher; it was she whom the Halifax Society male leaders so disliked. Chown was detested by some of the Toronto area men. The quote is from Chown to Doty, 9 February 1929, WILPF Papers, II 7–4.

23 On CGIT, Margaret Prang, '"The Girl God Would Have Me Be": The Canadian Girls in Training, 1915–1939,' *Canadian Historical Review* 66:2 (June 1985), 154–84. On war toys, see Violet McNaughton's columns, for example, her 'Disarm the Nursery,' *Western Producer*, 9 October 1924. Her papers contain several war toys pamphlets. On the schools, and anti-cadet training efforts, see Webber's 'Women in the Canadian Pacifist Movement,' 9–11, and in the VM Papers, see, for example, the Canadian WIL pamphlet, 'What Can I Do for Peace? An Appeal to Teachers,' n.d. [1923], VM Papers, AI H32.

24 On Vancouver WILPF's interest in creating international and multi-ethnic festivals and pageants as peace activities, see Jamieson to Balch et al., passim, WILPF Papers, III 4–9 and 24–10. McNaughton's activities and use of the rural and farm movement press are described in Webber, 'Women in the Canadian Pacifist Movement' and passim in VM Papers, WILPF files.

25 Violet McNaughton to Alice Chown, 11 December 1931, VM Papers, cited by Webber in 'Women in the Canadian Pacifist Movement.' For the international campaign see Gertrude Bussey and Margaret Tims, *Pioneers for Peace*, 94–6, and 'The Story of the Disarmament Declaration,' pamphlet in VM Papers, E 95.

26 The effort is typical of the provincial WCTU's activities in these decades. See LCW Minutes, 19 December 1931, 1 January 1932, Public Archives of Nova Scotia (PANS), MG 20, vol. 353.9.

27 On church women and club-women in the 1930s, see Strong-Boag, 'Peace-making Women.' Prang, 'The Girl God Would Have Me Be.'

28 Franca Iacovetta, 'The Political Career of Senator Cairine Wilson, 1921–62,' *Atlantis* 11:1 (Fall 1985), 115–7. On Canada's refusal of Jewish refugees, see Irving Abella and Harold Troper, *None Is Too Many: Canada and the Jews of Europe, 1933–1948* (Toronto 1983).

29 On farmers' diminished interest in peace issues, see Donald Page, 'The Development of a Western Canadian Peace Movement,' in Susan Trofimenkoff, ed. *The Twenties in Western Canada* (Ottawa 1972), 100, citing a survey of *Western Producer* readers. On NCWC and general apathy concerning peace issues, see Strong-Boag, 'Peace-making Women.' On WILPF views about economic issues as part of peace issues, see Early, 'Historic Roots,' 47; on the changing tenor of peace discussion in the 1930s, see Thomas Socknat, 'Waging Peace,' *Horizon Canada*, November 1986, 2104–5.

30 These are described by Bussey and Tims, *Pioneers for Peace*; WILPF publications provide further details for the period.

31 Citizenship committee monthly reports, E.M. Murray, convenor, Halifax
LCW, 21 December 1939, MG 20, vol. 536.9, PANS.

32 On new norms of withdrawal by women from political involvement, Dorothy
Livesay, 'Women in Public Life: Do We Want Them?' *Saturday Night* 64,
19 July 1949, 17, lists complaints by women activists that most women are
apathetic and don't 'stand together' and work as a group to support women's
interests. See also H.M. Neatby's article in the journal of the Canadian Associa-
tion for Adult Education, 'Are Women Fulfilling Their Obligations to
Society?' *Food for Thought* 13 (November 1952), 19–23; her answer is, no. But
for some exceptional women who were active during and after the Second
World War, see for example Kathryn Ogg, '"Especially When No One Agrees":
An Interview with May Campbell'; and Susan Walsh, 'The Peacock and the
Guinea Hen: Political Profiles of Dorothy Gretchen Steeves and Grace
MacInnis'; and Connie Carter and Eileen Daoust, 'From Home to House:
Women in the BC Legislature,' in Barbara Latham and Roberta Pazdro, eds,
*Not Just Pin Money: Selected Essays on the History of Women's Work in British
Columbia* (Victoria, BC, 1984). Steeves and Jamieson were strong in the
Vancouver WILPF. None the less, Sen. Cairine Wilson was virtually the only
Canadian woman in public life working to support the UN; see Franca
Iacovetta, '"Respectable Feminist": The Political Career of Senator Cairine
Wilson,' in this volume. Veronica Strong-Boag's new research on women,
1945–60 promises to fill out our sketchy knowledge of women in the 1950s.

33 Even those mainstream writers who somewhat daringly criticized the witch-hunt
atmosphere accepted the basic necessity of getting rid of reds. For example,
C.W. Woodside, 'McCarthyism: Is It American Hysteria?' *Saturday Night*, 11
April 1953, 16–18; Blair Fraser, 'How We Check on Loyalty,' *Maclean's*,
1 January 1952. Most members of the CCF national council accepted the witch-
hunt view and blamed the USSR as the cause of the cold war and threats to world
peace, and they cheerfully participated in red-purge and red-baiting activities. On
this, see Stephen Endicott, *James G. Endicott: Rebel out of China* (Toronto
1980), 266–72. Angus MacInnis, Grace's husband, was among this anti-red
group; her views are unknown to me. For a Communist-party insider's view
of this period, see Merrily Weisbord's remarkable oral history, *The Strangest
Dream: Canadian Communists, the Spy Trials, and the Cold War* (Toronto
1983). See also Betty Millard, *Women on Guard: How Women of the World Fight
for Peace* (New York 1952), describing the international disarmament petition
campaign.

34 See 'In Memory of Mary Austin Endicott,' special issue of the *Canadian Far
Eastern Newsletter* 19:198 (August 1967). I am indebted to Stephen Endicott
for material on Mary Endicott and other Congress members, and to James Endi-

cott for access to his papers at the National Archives, which include family and Peace Congress material.

35 For reds as a minority of membership, red-baiting journalist Gerry Waring could only identify 19 of 100 National Council members as reds; reported in his series 'The Canadian Peace Congress,' syndicated in the Montreal *Star* and other papers, 16–18 August 1950, cited by Endicott, *James G. Endicott*, 387n7.

36 See William Bourne, 'Peace Movement Now Uncovered,' *Saturday Night*, 5 December 1950, 8, for a typical attack on World Peace Congress affiliates as dupes of Soviet and Comintern policy. Because women were among the groups specifically identified by the congress for recruitment drives, any women's peace groups were by definition 'Soviet puppets' and unwitting agents of communism. On the activities of the Endicotts and the Peace Congress, see also Gary Moffatt, *History of the Canadian Peace Movement until 1969* (St Catharines 1969), 70–81. The CCF leaders who did not attack the congress, and who refused to abide by the CCF national office's sanctions against peace-movement participation, included William Irvine of Alberta, Eva Sanderson and Rae Luckock of Ontario, and Tommy Douglas of Saskatchewan. Luckock was sister-in-law to the then-minister of immigration Walter E. Harris, who was among those involved in planning vigilante bully-boy attacks on meetings: see Moffatt, *History*, 286. In Weisbord's account of the impact of the Khrushchev revelations on Canadian communists, she says that the Montreal membership of that time dropped from 900 to 300 almost overnight (see Weisbord, *The Strangest Dream*, 204–23).

37 For Greta Andrew, interview with her granddaughter Marian Binkley, Halifax, 27 April 1987.

38 The newsletter (called *International Circular Letters*) discussed various proposals for peace settlements being developed by members in belligerent and neutral countries, anti-war feeling on the civilian front, economic, social, and political conditions, and other matters; thus, as in the First World War, WILPF readers had a glimpse into the situation in 'enemy' countries, as well as behind-the-scenes activities in their own and allied nations. *Pax International* 14:8 (November 1939) discussed these issues. Unless otherwise cited, the account of the activities of the Canadian chapters above is based on reports and discussions in *Pax International*, 1935–50, and *Pax et Libertas*, 1951–60. For the international context and an overview of WILPF during the 1950s and 1960s see Bussey and Tims, *Pioneers for Peace*, 190–240 passim; for the debate over the use of force, see 160–5; on the WILPF view of the WIDF-WILPF conflict, 196–8, and on co-operation, 198, 214, 239.

39 Deborah Powell, 'Women's International League for Peace and Freedom,' *Canadian Encyclopedia* (Edmonton 1986), 1959, states incorrectly that

Vancouver was the only surviving WILPF branch until Ottawa started one in the late 1970s; the WILPF magazine contains late-1950s' reports from a Toronto chapter. For the 'least-affected' comment, see Bussey and Tims, *Pioneers for Peace*, 187. They attribute the small numbers to geographical handicaps. Destruction of records: personal communications, Sheila Young, Vancouver, July 1987. Powell, 'Women's Peace Organizations,' is based partly on interviews with Sheila Young and other WILPF activists.

40 *Pax et Libertas*, May 1959 and January 1960.

41 Descriptions of 1950s activities and climate based also on interviews with Muriel Duckworth and Marion Kerans about their own experiences. For discussions of radiation hazards from fallout, see, for example, Norman J. Berrill [McGill zoology professor], 'Have We Gone Too Far with the Atom Tests?' *Maclean's*, 9 July 1955, citing evidence of danger to the general population from increased background radiation and fallout from US tests in particular, and future dangers from contamination from nuclear wastes from power plants. The article is next to a boxed AECL (atomic energy regulatory body) statement claiming there is no cancer problem as yet with uranium miners, and extolling the safety methods used in mines. See Moffat's description of the formation of the British groups, *History of the Canadian Peace Movement*, 86–8, and on the radiation hazards and early CND groups in Canada, 88–91. Marion Kerans moved to Toronto in 1960, shortly after she had helped organize a women's public-affairs committee at the local YWCA. She had her fifth child in Toronto and did not again become active until 1964, when she worked in parent/teacher organizations; although involved with housing and welfare issues, she did not become active in the peace movement again until the late 1970s when, living in Halifax, she became concerned with Voice of Women projects at the instigation of visiting Norwegian feminist peace activist Berit As.

42 Accounts of the formation and activities of VOW are taken from Kay Macpherson and Meg Sears, 'The Voice of Women: A History,' in Gwen Matheson, ed., *Women in the Canadian Mosaic* (Toronto 1976), 71–92; Kay Macpherson, 'The Seeds of the Seventies,' *Canadian Dimension* 10:8 (June 1975), 39–41, and 'Persistent Voices: Twenty-Five Years with Voice of Women,' *Atlantis* 12:2, (Spring 1987), 60–72; Candace Loewen, 'Mike Hears Voices: Voice of Women and Lester Pearson, 1960–1963,' *Atlantis*, ibid., 24–30; Moffat, *History of the Canadian Peace Movement*, 114–30; my own participation in some later events, and discussions with many members and interviews with Muriel Duckworth and Marion Kerans, Halifax. Moffatt suggests that VOW's policy of promoting personal contact was an important difference between it and the mainstream (mixed) peace groups that emphasized political issues and actions; this policy may have been a factor in keeping VOW

a strong group when others faded during the 1960s. VOW's membership slumped in the 1970s but many *Voices* apparently merely transferred their activities to other women's organizations and issues. If the broad definition of peace is used, then peace promotion did not suffer so great a decline as is usually supposed. Duckworth biography based on interviews with her, discussion with her biographer Marion Kerans, and Muriel Duckworth, *On Becoming a Friend*, Canadian Quaker Pamphlet no. 24, Argenta Friends Press (Argenta, BC, July 1986).

The Politicization of
Ontario Farm Women

Pauline Rankin

Housed in Canada's National Gallery is an 1890 painting by Ontario artist George Agnew Reid entitled 'Mortgaging the Homestead.' In sombre tones, Reid's canvas depicts a disheartened farm family huddled together to witness the signing of the mortgage documents. While other members of the discouraged gathering peer downwards, only a young woman clutching a baby and seated in the centre of the scene meets the viewer's eye as if looking beyond the farm for a solution to her family's financial woes. Although almost a century old, Reid's poignant portrayal of this farm wife still serves as an appropriate symbol for Canadian farm women who have repeatedly looked beyond the family unit for amelioration of economic emergencies and attention to rural social issues. In the last decade, Canada has seen a nation-wide proliferation of organizations intent on channelling the political energies of farm women; such activism among Ontario's rural women, however, has a long and varied history. Associations have existed with differing degrees of success and longevity since 1897 and the formation in Stoney Creek of the now internationally based Women's Institutes.[1]

Mobilization among farm women in Ontario may be described as occurring in two waves, peaking first in the years immediately following the extension of the provincial franchise in 1917 and re-emerging in the mid 1970s. Throughout this period, politically motivated farm women have experimented with an array of organizational arrangements, working in an auxiliary capacity with the United Farmers, later acting as relatively silent partners in male-dominated agricultural pressure groups, and, today, opting for single-sex associations. Regardless of the nature of the alliance, the struggle to reconcile their interests as women with their loyalty to the rural community at large has posed an agonizing dilemma for contemporary farm women and their rural foremothers. Influenced by early western farm leaders, such as Irene Parlby, who vowed that 'first and foremost as organized farm women we stand shoulder to shoulder with the men's organizations,'[2] Ontario farm women involved in the Progressive movement initially emulated such rhetoric by submerging their commitment to women's issues and rallying with their husbands and fathers, a strategy that eventually contributed to their limited impact and subsequent demise. Willing neither to ignore gender inequities in the name of rural solidarity, nor to forsake farm allegiances in pursuit of feminist principles, today's mobilized farm women are refusing to choose between labels of 'farmer' and 'farm woman.' Current grass-roots groups are moulding strategies and structures that seek to incorporate analyses of both gender and economic oppression, the result being a noticeable increase in their political participation and influence. A corollary to this mobilization has been a long overdue process of introspection on the part of established rural interest groups and a gradual transformation in the philosophy and approach traditionally pursued in agricultural politics. An overview of the barriers that have precluded farm women's political participation, when combined with a comparative examination of farm-women's organizations active within Ontario during this century, illustrates the commonality of problems confronted by politicized farm women of both today and yesterday. Such an inquiry also raises questions about the potential for long-term viability of the contemporary farm-women's movement.

TOWARDS AN UNDERSTANDING OF FARM WOMEN'S POLITICAL BEHAVIOUR

As a rural woman herself, Nellie McClung understood well the pervasive and potentially debilitating mythologizing to which farm women have long been subject. Writing in 1915, McClung commented that the mere mention of a farmer's wife might well conjure up images of a 'poor faded women [with] hair the colour of last year's grass and teeth gone in front.'[3] Remnants of such stereotypes persist today, counterpointed by the notion of farm women as idealized self-sacrificing nurturers privileged by a peaceful, undemanding life-style. State policies, bolstered by popular culture, have mistakenly identified farming as an exclusively male endeavour, despite the fact that it is, perhaps, the one occupation in which there exists the greatest amount of interdependence between the sexes. With responsibilities ranging from baling hay to maintaining the financial records, the farm-wife's simultaneous involvement in the productive and reproductive realms of the family enterprise renders problematic those analyses that attempt to differentiate arbitrarily between 'public' and 'private' farm tasks, defined in terms of a sexual division of labour. As findings from Saskatchewan research have shown, contemporary farm women actually retain almost exclusive control over the flow of financial and agricultural information crucial to the decision-making process on the farm.[4] A recent survey of the role played by eastern Ontario women in agriculture confirms the Saskatchewan data and forwards evidence of women's activity in all aspects of farm life.[5] Like their pioneer predecessors, Ontario farm women continue to be integral participants in the field work associated with crop production and the care of livestock. In contrast to her western sisters whose homesteading work was acknowledged in government and land policies, however, the influence of urbanization on Ontario culture minimized the social and economic value attributed to the rural Ontario woman of the early twentieth century, a situation still prevalent in modern times.[6]

Despite their indispensability to the farm, women's economic contributions to agriculture have been omitted from state ledgers. As Christine Delphy explains, this occurs because farm wives assume responsibility for productive tasks such as dairying for their husbands, who then exchange this appropriated and unpaid labour in the market-place; the non-value ascribed to this work is then exacerbated by the disparity between the marketable value of the services rendered and the remuneration received by the farm woman, who is limited in her ability to exchange her own labour, or to change her employer/husband.[7] The androcentricity of the agricultural industry as a whole has been legitimized in this country by discriminatory procedures such as Statistics Canada's practice of permitting only one member of the household, the one who claims to make the daily decisions regarding the farm business, to be designated as the farm 'operator,' thus discouraging recognition of the wife's role.[8]

The multiplicity of duties juggled by farm wives, coupled with their economic invisibility, has impeded their opportunity for political visibility. While early farm lobbyists, particularly in the prairie provinces, did lend invaluable support to the suffrage cause, similar male-controlled eastern associations utilized women much like a reserve army of labour, encouraging their participation only when female support became critical to the realization of specific goals. In Ontario, the political mobilization of farm women was sanctioned by the United Farmers only when women's votes became necessary to ensure the movement's electoral success. Throughout this country, resistance to the representation of women at the élite levels of agricultural unions has meant that, until quite recently, women have been restricted to social housekeeping tasks. Women's input into rural farm groups has been masked by customs such as issuing a single membership per family, with that membership generally listed in the husband's or father's name.[9]

Farm-women's political voices have also been muted by what has been termed the 'myth of rural cohesiveness,' which conceals the many cleavages within the hierarchical nature of rural society.[10] Rural residents of both sexes have historically identified themselves as a 'class' distinct from the urban 'class,' whom they accuse of lacking sufficient appreciation of the contributions of the farm population. Using the term 'class' in this context refers not only to a shared set of economic relations, but also to the sense of unity existing between farm men and women that stems from their perception of themselves as guardians of an endangered life-style.[11] The ardent commitment of the entire rural population to their farms is captured by Nancy Painter, who writes that 'farming is more than just a job; it's a way of life for those of us who have chosen to work the land ... our land is as much a part of us as an arm or a leg.'[12] Socialized by agrarian society to encourage solidarity with their communities, rural women have been confronted with a conservative perspective dictating that political action by farm women was justifiable only when understood in the context of a service or duty to be performed on behalf of their families or country.

This combination of opportunity barriers and role constraints has thwarted the development of farm-women's political participation and has conflicted with the marked degree of activism traditionally associated with agrarian culture. Since Confederation, Canadian farmers have retained a high level of political efficacy, regarding their work as fundamental to the nation's economic and social well-being. Farmers have, in fact, often incorrectly assumed that they have a ready-made constituency just because everyone has to eat.[13] The reluctance of legislators to support this sentiment, however, has engendered widespread cynicism among farmers towards politics. Such a mixture of high political efficacy and low political trust has fostered the optimum environment for mobilization among farm men; for farm women incited to action by their environment, yet denied access to key positions within male-controlled rural pressure groups,[14] it has generated little more than frustration.

Geographic variables have also affected farm-women's political responses. In Canada, where generalizations about the regional bases of economic activities are commonplace, agriculture is typically associated with a prairie setting. Western farmers have historically wielded considerable clout within their provincial economies and still capture the majority of attention from government, media, and the academic community when agricultural issues are debated.[15] Conversely, Ontario farmers have been largely overlooked. Since the days of the United Farmers movement, the progressive encroachment of urbanization has precipitated a decline in the 'industrial heartland's' rural population and a concomitant diminution of their economic and political power. Such a trend has strengthened ties among Ontario's rural communities, which maintain that they must protect themselves against the urban 'class' that is gradually destroying their livelihood. Contemporary farmers in Ontario grapple with feelings of alienation and powerlessness within a province where electoral outcomes hinge on the decisions of one urban metropolis and the government's leader is enthusiastically hailed as a 'progressive urbanite who understand[s] the Yuppie culture of the 1980s.'[16]

Faced with these external pressures, male farmers insist that independent political action by farm women, which concentrates on exposing the gender inequities endemic in rural life, constitutes a betrayal of the larger issues, that of rural survival. Like the women of the United Farmers movement, farm women are today encouraged by provincial farm association leaders to think of themselves as 'farmers first and women second.'[17] This plea for unity between the sexes has been complicated by Ontario's role as focal point for the nation's women's movement. Although feminism has received much criticism from farm women on the basis of its perceived urban bias,[18] the feminist presence within the province has aroused farm-women's consciousness of women's issues and alerted them to the commonality of their problems and those of their urban counterparts, making farm women more reticent to overlook gender-based inequality.

In her study of women's participation in party politics, Sylvia Bashevkin cites the tension between political independence and conventional partisanship as the central dichotomy in English-Canadian women's political history.[19] A similar model of autonomy versus integration is useful in describing the political legacy of Ontario farm women. Initially, rural women organized autonomously within the government-sponsored Women's Institutes. Later, rural interest groups urged women to consolidate their energies behind a single, united lobby, intimating that failure to support their platforms would precipitate the disappearance of family farms. Farm women who chose to integrate within such forums soon discovered, however, that conventional associations held little interest in exploring issues of particular relevance to rural women and were unwilling to distribute decision-making power equally. In the first wave of their politicization, farm women were faced with either subservience within male-dominated alliances or independent development in affiliations such as the Women's Institutes, which did not effectively challenge the division of labour by sex characteristic of Ontario's agricultural politics.

'SISTER DIANA' AND THE UNITED FARM WOMEN OF ONTARIO

During the years immediately preceding the First World War, Ontario's shrinking rural population sensed what it believed to be a gradual dislodging of its previously central position in provincial society.[20] Feeling deprived of the respect to which it considered itself entitled, the farm community found itself 'sliding into the second rank in society [with] the first rank occupied by the urban and middle classes who felt a certain condescension for the farmer.'[21] In reaction to the increasing hegemony of industrialists over the economy, an exodus of farm youth to urban centres and a general decline in rural self-esteem, the United Farmers of Ontario (UFO), organizing under the motto of 'equality for all, special privileges for none,' consolidated its efforts in an attempt to reverse these troubling trends. Although the memoirs of co-founder J.J. Morrison reveal that, from the time of its incorporation in 1914, the UFO received inquiries from women anxious to be involved in this newest manifestation of agrarian activism, Morrison's papers also demonstrate that movement leaders ignored such requests until the mobilization of farm women became expedient in ensuring the electoral fortunes of farmer candidates.[22]

The principal lobby behind the creation of the United Farm Women of Ontario (UFWO) came from the women's page of the Toronto-based journal, the *Weekly Sun*. In a November 1917 edition of the popular rural newspaper, 'Sister Diana' was welcomed as a new columnist whose 'letters will invite discussion among the readers.'[23] Indeed, the debate generated by the writings of Collingwood farmer and teacher Emma Griesbach triggered the widespread politicization of the paper's female readership. Serving as primary strategist for Ontario's rural women, Griesbach piloted the 'Sun Sisters' Page' from a collection of domestic-science articles into an arena for debate over the implications of the franchise and women's potential for power within the farm movement. Inspired by the vitality of western farm-women's organizations, Griesbach envisioned a similar role for her Ontario sisters. Initially, Griesbach used her column to furnish the newly enfranchised women with role models for their political activity, a favourite being the United States House of Representatives' Jeanette Rankin. Preferring to be addressed as 'farmer' rather than 'farmer-lady,' Griesbach repeatedly challenged her women readers to acknowledge their positions as partners in the farm unit.[24] Frequently using vitriolic attacks on the indifference of urban dwellers towards rural residents, Griesbach's tactics·quickly succeeded in attracting attention. Across the province, women began to question their negligible role within farm politics and by June 1918 the 'Sun Sisters' Page' reported that a 'seasonable courtship' was flourishing between women and the UFO. Later that same month, in the parlour of the Elm Street Toronto YWCA, sixteen women formed the nucleus of the United Farm Women of Ontario, electing Emma Griesbach as provincial secretary. Under the terms of the December 1918 agreement, women were eligible to join men within existing UFO clubs or to create their own auxiliaries. A member of the UFWO executive was to represent the women's section at all directors' meetings of the UFO and the executive of the UFO would send a representative to all meetings of the UFWO directors.[25] While Griesbach personally discouraged their segregation, small groups of women quickly organized throughout the province, perhaps because of their unfamiliarity with mixed-sex forums. At the local level, the women's auxiliaries were expected to combine a strong social function with the study of contemporary issues such as rural modernization, educational reform, and temperance. Membership within the UFWO reached 2000 within its first year of operation and peaked in 1921 at 6000.

As the UFO turned its sights towards securing electoral power, calls for solidarity between farm women and men intensified. Echoing the rhetoric of UFO leaders, contributors to the *Weekly Sun* insisted that UFWO members 'must cease to think of themselves as a unit and must get the class idea.'[26] Although Griesbach herself had earlier advanced such sentiments, disillusionment over the treatment received by women within the UFO began to override her desire for rural cohesiveness. Her editorials increasingly focused on exposing the sexual discrimination that women had suffered since joining the movement. In addition to refusing to open the doors of their Toronto headquarters to the women for their organizational meeting, party leaders had denied the UFWO an independent treasury, arguing that the 'women would spend money so freely that the treasury would be depleted.'[27] Other directors insisted that the prestige of their association would decline if women were granted active membership. Such antagonism was not easily dissipated. Letters to the paper continued to cite examples of the blatant hostility that greeted women who chose to attend male-dominated meetings. In reaction to such stories, Griesbach would sarcastically retort that 'these poor men are to be pitied ... accustomed to riding the high horse around the domestic premises, they are unable to see wife or children, [their] chief symptoms being swelled heads and ornery dispositions.'[28]

Articles on feminism and the lack of respect afforded women's labour began to appear regularly within Griesbach's writings as the columnist apparently decided that the political awakening of farm women must also include development of their gender consciousness. Exhibiting her commitment to the principles of collectivity on which the United Farmers was founded, Griesbach proposed community laundries and collective housekeeping as methods of emancipating rural women from their drudgery and freeing them to assume influential positions within the farm movement. Although it is difficult to assess the impact of Griesbach's prescriptive literature, resolutions were adopted by UFWO clubs that reflected her ideals. Proposals such as wages for farm wives, advocated by some UFWO clubs, illustrate that Griesbach's calls for reform of rural society did not go entirely unheeded.

Despite its growing preoccupation with gender-related issues, Griesbach refused to endorse the other major rural women's organization. Already popular throughout Canada, the Women's Institutes (WI) had many staunch supporters who combined WI membership with UFWO participation. Griesbach's plan, however, was to present the UFWO as an alternative to the Women's Institutes, which had alienated many farm women with its pro-war stance. While the UFWO's first president accused the WI of having a 'decided tendency to stifle any sign of independent thought on the part of women' and UFWO secretary Griesbach openly declared that she hoped to see the WI 'scrapped to the junk heap,'[29] UFWO clubs continued to attract women unwilling to sever ties with the first organization that had offered them support and respect for their domestic duties. Inevitably, the question of the WI became a divisive one within UFWO ranks: some members, sharing the opinions of prairie rural leaders, scorned the Women's Institutes as being manipulated by an urban-biased government,[30] while other members found such criticism unacceptable and begged Griesbach to end her scathing attacks on the WI. The antagonism between the groups subsided by 1921 as the agendas of the two associations began to merge and as UFWO members found themselves lobbying for hydroelectric power for rural areas and the extension of social services, concerns long prioritized by the increasingly outspoken Women's Institutes.[31] Anti-WI rhetoric nevertheless remained, perpetuated by Griesbach and Agnes Macphail, who both persisted in criticizing the WI for its conservative perspective.[32]

Griesbach's harsh indictments against the WI, UFO leaders, and UFWO members themselves, whom Griesbach chided for failing to capitalize on their opportunity for equality within the movement, eventually led to her dismissal from the paper. The controversial writer was removed without warning from the 'Sun Sisters' Page' in 1922, only to be succeeded by Violet Dickens who promptly restructured the women's section into the 'Sunroom Page for Women,' promising a renewed attention to domestic interests. Dickens vowed that her column would only 'occasionally glance out of our broad windows and look at the world outside,'[33] a position directly antithetical to that espoused by Griesbach during her tenure. The firing generated heated responses. Griesbach alleged that the unwarranted action was 'undemocratic' in that she was denied an opportunity to discuss her removal with the UFO board of directors, adding that with their actions, 'the directors of the *Sun* have defaulted on the very principle [democracy] that they have announced to the world they would stand for.'[34] Writing to party leaders in protest of the move, UFWO members asked if 'you think the women of this country can put any faith in the sincerity of the UFO when you talk of giving equal rights to women after you have cut us off from our leader?'[35] Directors of the UFO defended the firing by explaining that the approach adopted by Dickens would be one 'more appropriate' for the women's section.[36] Yet even without Griesbach's often contentious leadership, UFWO clubs survived for the next twenty years, the last club being dismantled in 1943. Margaret Kechnie's research documents that those clubs with the longest history existed in localities in which the Women's Institutes were inactive;[37] in contrast to Griesbach's vision, then, the UFWO eventually acted as a substitute for, rather than an alternative to, the larger and better-organized WI.

The UFWO's limited success is substantially attributable to the structural relationship that existed between the UFO and its women's auxiliary. Tied to movement purse-strings, farm women were denied the freedom to set their own agenda, being forced to rely on the benevolence of UFO executives for funding. Such a dependence on the UFO meant that the women's clubs could not escape damage from the erratic leadership that plagued the UFO during its brief term in power. The potential of the UFWO's autonomous development was further constrained by the paternalism of movement leaders towards its women's organization. In entrusting supervision of the United Farmers Young People's Organization to the UFWO, the United Farmers further restricted farm-women's political development and reinforced traditional stereotypes about women's primary responsibility for children. In silencing Emma Griesbach, UFO leaders demonstrated that they had little intention of allowing women the opportunity to analyse and debate their secondary status both at home and within farm politics. The support extended by the UFO to the candidacy of Agnes Macphail should not be construed as a departure in UFO policy vis-à-vis women's subordinate role in the movement; unlike Griesbach, Macphail concentrated on farm economic issues such as tariffs and rural credit, and, as her biographers indicate, gave secondary consideration to issues of gender.[38] Indeed, early in her political career, Macphail 'blamed women as much as men for the inferior position of the female citizen,'[39] a position that reiterated the one espoused by her male colleagues within the United Farmers.

Griesbach's goal of liberating rural women from their dismal working conditions in order to have them assume key leadership positions within farm politics proved too ambitious for her time. While they were still reeling from the realization that their social roles were little valued by the urban population, the demoralizing experience of the conscription debate left farm women without the confidence necessary to demand an active role within a movement that was openly apathetic towards problems of particular relevance to women.[40] It has been suggested that, in her aggressive approach, Emma Griesbach obviously 'forgot, ignored or knew nothing of rural values and the uniqueness and individuality of rural people.'[41] Admittedly, Griesbach's perspective as an unmarried working woman may well have rendered her unsympathetic to the pride farm women took in their domestic chores. Nevertheless, Griesbach's campaign to modernize farm homes and 'get rural women out of the kitchen' was quite consistent with the priorities of Ontario farm women themselves.[42] Recent research by Veronica Strong-Boag shows that, during the 1920s and 1930s, prairie women directed their attention towards the politics of the private sphere, a move that Strong-Boag terms a manifestation of a 'feminism of the workplace, of day-to-day life.'[43] Such a trend was largely replicated in rural Ontario because Griesbach's columns had made farm women cognizant of the power imbalances inherent in their everyday life. Noting no extension in rural services under the Drury-led farm-labour government, farm women's experience within the UFO had also made them acutely aware of the high price of integration with male-controlled organizations. With characteristic pragmatism, UFWO members made their way back into the ranks of the WI, an organization dedicated to legitimizing rural-women's domestic pursuits and already engaged in reformist initiatives. Perhaps, like Emma Griesbach, Ontario farm women had decided that lightening their double work-loads was a necessary prerequisite to raising the socio-economic position of all farmers. The trend of farm women to renew their association with the Women's Institutes was, ironically, a move of which Emma Griesbach could be proud.

BETWEEN THE WAVES

Gender divisions within farm politics intensified from the time the UFWO disbanded in 1944 until the emergence of activism among Ontario farm women in the 1970s. Out of the economic chaos that gripped the agricultural sector during the depression years arose what would become the most powerful Canadian agricultural lobby forum. Organized in 1935, the Canadian Chamber of Agriculture, later renamed the Canadian Federation of Agriculture (CFA) consolidated the myriad of commodity groups struggling to gain government attention. Using a hierarchical and complex institutional design, the CFA established nation-wide satellite groups at the county level, which then fell under the jurisdiction of provincial associations. While the CFA did provide an extremely effective instrument for agricultural representation, it proved indifferent to women's participation. Even though women were never expressly prohibited from the federation, they were not mentioned in the CFA constitution until 1964. A 1970 initiative by two female directors, designed to increase women's representation at the national level, met with the suggestion that women's involvement in the CFA was more appropriate at the local level;[44] leaders did welcome participation by women, most particularly when it included the provision of meeting refreshments or the co-ordination of social events. The 'real work' of politicking remained a male bastion.

The rationalization behind women's exclusion from the front lines of the federation hinged on the continued success of the Women's Institutes. Because the CFA maintained a formal affiliation with the WI, it was believed that women's interests were sufficiently accommodated. Certainly, the WI enjoyed enormous popularity among Ontario women, boasting a membership of 42,000 by 1935. Farm women remained intensely loyal to these clubs, which had encouraged them to expand their knowledge of organizational strategies and to develop their leadership skills, opportunities denied them by male-dominated pressure groups. For several decades, the Federated Women's Institutes of Ontario and the Ontario Federation of Agriculture adequately fulfilled the needs of the province's farm population. Members of the federation concentrated on influencing state food policies while the Women's Institutes expanded beyond their original purpose of elevating the standard of homemaking to draw its membership into all aspects of social welfare.

It was not until 1973 that rural women were jarred into recognizing that their preoccupation with social issues had not been matched by adequate attention to their own legal and economic vulnerability. The Supreme Court's decision to strike down Irene Murdoch's claim to half-ownership in the farm she had helped operate for twenty-five years made only too clear the inequities that persisted on the farm.[45] While the Women's Institutes had largely retained traditional notions about the place of farm women within the home, and male-centred rural organizations continued to organize fashion shows and cooking demonstrations for farm wives while educating their husbands about lobbying tactics and tax legislation, the role of Ontario's rural women had been undergoing metamorphosis because of a shift towards capital-intensive farming, the modernization of the farm home, and the necessity for off-farm waged labour.[46] A reform of rural organizations was long overdue.

ON THEIR OWN

Appropriately, the second wave of Ontario farm-women's activism began in International Women's Year (1975). Like the UFWO experiment, this revival in farm-women's political participation was spearheaded by a single woman who sought an expanded role for women in agricultural groups and an improvement in the recognition afforded farm-women's social and economic contributions. In contrast to the earlier movement, however, this wave would develop autonomously from existing pressure groups and would spread in an ad hoc manner across the province, allowing for the incorporation of regional and economic variations. Old tensions over gender-versus-occupational loyalties remain problematic in this new phase of politicization. The rejection of integration within male-dominated lobby groups, and a similar abandonment of rigid bureaucratic procedures, have allowed farm women to fashion a movement whose viability is increased by its capacity to incorporate an equal commitment to the elimination of both gender-based oppression and economic and social oppression.

Finding herself shouldering responsibility for farm tasks while her husband pursued off-farm employment, Winchester farmer Dianne Harkin had grown weary of hearing herself and other rural women constantly referred to as 'just farm wives.' Harkin was no stranger to agricultural politics, having often attended Ontario Federation of Agriculture (OFA) meetings with her husband at which she would be the only female present, except for what would invariably be a female secretary. Sensing that her presence at such gatherings was not entirely welcome, Harkin decided that farm women deserved greater visibility within groups that claimed to represent their interests. In an unprecedented move, Harkin addressed the 1975 annual meeting of her county Federation of Agriculture, urging that farm-women's work be acknowledged by the organization and that farm women themselves realize the extent to which they lagged behind urban women in terms of services available to them. Bolstered by the interest expressed by twenty-five women that evening, Harkin's Women for the Survival of Agriculture (WSA) was set in motion. Initially, Harkin's venture elicited strong negative reactions from both rural men and women who dismissed her as a 'crazy radical' and judged her ideas to be divisive and even 'anti-rural.' But Harkin wouldn't listen. Acceptance for the group slowly grew as Harkin, now joined by other committed farm women, countered such criticisms by arguing that a mobilized, well-informed, and articulate lobby by farm women would provide invaluable assistance in elevating the socio-economic status of all rural residents.[47]

Harkin describes herself as a feminist, and, not surprisingly, her sensitivity to issues of gender spilled over into the philosophy adopted by the innovative group. Her own personal familiarity with urban life made Harkin aware of the similarity of problems confronting all women, regardless of their locality.[48] Consequently, she purposely avoided mobilizing farm women through appeals based on anti-urban rhetoric. Within five years, WSA had generated national attention and capitalized on it by co-ordinating the first National Farm Women's Conference. Held in Ottawa in 1980, the conference attracted 200 farm women from across Canada, who met to discuss issues such as the portrayal of farm women in the media, the economic position of farm women, and the discrimination encountered by farm women attempting to secure credit.

Within the Winchester area, WSA focuses primarily on the provision of continuing-education opportunities for farm women. Working in conjunction with provincial government ministries, WSA has designed and led literally hundreds of seminars for farm women, covering topics such as stress reduction and farm financial management. Government lobbying has been targeted at the federal level because of the group's proximity to Ottawa. The association has established links with individual members of Parliament and public-service officials, in addition to appearing before agricultural standing committees and parliamentary task forces to address problems of child care, family violence, and pornography. The group's most ambitious research project has been a survey of eastern Ontario farm women entitled *What Are You Worth?*, which details the financial value of the work performed by farm women, many of whom function within a 'triple ghetto'[49] of on-farm labour, off-farm waged employment, and domestic responsibilities. WSA has also lobbied in co-operation with other established rural groups on issues like capital-gains taxes and legislation such as the Farm Creditors Arrangement Act and farm-parity bills. Appointments of WSA members to boards and commissions such as the Canadian Advisory Council on the Status of Women, the Task Force of the Ontario Institute of Agrologists, and the Ontario Right to Farm Advisory Committee ensure that the opinions of farm women reach a diverse and influential audience.

What is most noteworthy about WSA's efforts is the small number of women responsible for such a vast number of projects; a nucleus of approximately fifteen women assume the bulk of the organization's agenda. Structurally, little attention is given to organizational maintenance. WSA has largely rejected traditional hierarchical design in favour of what Harkin describes as 'tinker-toy tactics.'[50] Using a collective approach to decision making, the group does have a chairperson, newsletter editor, and treasurer, yet no elections are held for these positions and neither are terms of office predetermined. Members lend their energies to whatever issues are of interest to them, unencumbered by a formal committee structure. WSA does not engage in fund-raising activities, explaining that they have 'more important things to do than sell cookies.'[51] While WSA offers itself as a model for other farm women wishing to organize, it encourages offshoot groups to act autonomously, planning and developing strategies according to the conscience of its own membership and without restrictions imposed from outside leadership.

WSA's preoccupation with gender-based issues contrasts with the perspective embraced by another major farm-women's group, Concerned Farm Women (CFW). The relative economic stability enjoyed by eastern Ontario WSA members, whose incomes largely derive from the government-regulated dairy industry, freed them to explore issues of gender prior to involving themselves in debates over agricultural legislation. Conversely, the precarious financial position of western Ontario farm women, whose incomes fluctuated dramatically because of their participation in the unregulated beef industry, necessitated their primary concentration on economic issues which was only later matched by an examination of areas in which gender was a variable. Situated in the Bruce peninsula area of western Ontario, CFW first organized in autumn 1981 in response to an economic crisis precipitated by falling commodity prices and escalating interest rates. An initial 'kitchen table' meeting arranged by Beth Slumskie and Doris Sweiger attracted an unexpected fifty-one women, anxious to discuss potential strategies for lowering the unprecedented interest rates that had burdened their families with unmanageable debt loads. Two weeks later, at an open county meeting, 250 women jammed a local community centre and CFW was officially launched.

Realizing the marginal role assigned to women in farm politics, the women of CFW were eager to create a forum in which women's opinions could be freely debated and action initiated with minimal organization. Although members were acutely aware of their secondary status within the rural community, they did not define their efforts to mobilize women as feminist activity. A resolution passed at their introductory meeting stated that CFW would not allow itself to be described as part of the women's movement; the original intent was to operate in an ancillary role with male-dominated rural groups, providing emotional support for families who were faced with farm foreclosures. Arguing that their economic woes must be resolved before attention to gender-related concerns was possible, the women of CFW, reminiscent of their foremothers in the UFWO, tried to reinforce their sense of agrarian solidarity by referring to themselves as 'farmers' rather than 'farm women.'[52] The threat of financial insolvency, which acted as the organization's catalyst, also influenced the group's philosophy and is reflected in the five general goals chosen to serve a rubric for their endeavours: the achievement of affordable credit for farmers; better commodity pricing; improved understanding of farming by the consumer; survival of the family farm; and greater recognition of the contribution farmers make to the Canadian economy.[53]

After utilizing a series of successful theatrical demonstrations designed to capture media attention,[54] CFW settled into more formal lobbying tactics through submissions to the provincial government and the Ontario Federation of Agriculture. During the summer of 1982, the group conducted a major research project exploring the impact of financial stress on farm families. Results were compiled the following year in Gisele Ireland's book, *The Farmer Takes a Wife*. A second publication, *To Have and to Hold*, appeared in 1985; it discusses the implications of property, credit, and family law on farm families. While protest marches and farm-gate defences[55] still constitute an important element on CFW's agenda, efforts have expanded to include sponsorship of workshops targeted to meet the needs of all members of the rural community. Current areas of research include consumer education, credit legislation, and the preparation of farm women for re-entry into the paid labour force.

CFW subscribes to the belief that the support of all elements of the rural community is vital if the family farm is to survive. In a region in which one-half to two-thirds of all farms are experiencing severe financial stress, CFW maintains that an institution as influential as the church cannot remain neutral in farm politics. Members have, therefore, pressed religious leaders to join lobby efforts on issues such as credit negotiations and have turned away from those parishes unwilling to co-operate. The group has also approached municipal politicians for assistance in garnering the support of provincial and federal officials.

Despite CFW's initial subordination of women's issues and its commitment to working co-operatively with existing agricultural interest groups, the women of Bruce and Grey counties met with more overt hostility from male farmers than was encountered by their eastern-Ontario counterparts. Founders of CFW received anonymous mail deriding their work and husbands of CFW executives were pressured to curb their wives' outspokeness.[56] Traditional rural-interest associations expressed little enthusiasm in forming liaisons with CFW, leaving the women relatively alienated from farm politics circles. Such isolation forced CFW to confront the pervasiveness of gender bias within the rural community and, in fact, motivated the membership to pursue issues such as wife battering, women's access to credit, and rural day care. Although concentration on economic matters has remained paramount to CFW, the group now recognizes the special needs of women and is no longer willing to have its agenda subsumed under those of male-stream agricultural organizations.

Interaction between CFW and WSA has increased in relation to the gradual meshing of their distinct perspectives. Because of their different patterns of development, the two groups are now well prepared to work together to forward cogent economic and gender-conscious analyses of whatever issues they may confront. Members of both groups share similar conclusions about the benefit of participation in farm-women's politics. Citing an elevation in self-confidence gained as a result of their experience in single-sex organizations, members previously reticent to appear before male-dominated audiences now feel more comfortable within such settings. Farm-women's organizations have enabled them to study agricultural legislation and test their analytic capacities within a supportive, non-competitive environment, a situation that has intensified their political efficacy.

Although the autonomous development of today's farm-women's movement contrasts with that of the United Farm Women of Ontario, several dominant themes from the earlier movement have resurfaced. Almost half a century later, many farm women still resent what they perceive as condescension on the part of urbanites towards the rural community and find themselves continuing the battle for recognition of their social and economic contributions. What is more striking about the similarity between the first and second waves is the perpetuation of criticism levelled against the Women's Institutes. In a style similar to Emma Griesbach's attacks, some farm women of today characterize the WI as little more than an outlet for 'tea and trivia' that has failed to address issues relevant to the younger farm generation.[57] Activists charge that the WI's conservatism is inappropriate within a province in which one-third of the entire farm community finds itself in economic crisis. They argue that the WI's complex institutional design alienates the individual member and inhibits the organization's overall effectiveness; dissatisfied farm women consider the Women's Institutes to be 'so preoccupied with membership drives, fee collections, by-laws and constitutional problems that they no longer have the capacity to think creatively about farm policy matters.'[58]

Such harsh criticism of the WI has caused an estrangement between the two groups. WI adherents resent censure of the organization that they believe has long provided farm women with the knowledge, confidence, and leadership necessary to launch this current movement. Newly mobilized farm women complain that the WI's traditional views about the domestic role of the rural woman only perpetuates stereotypical images of the farm wife and constrain her political potential. While the onslaught against the WI has been unpopular among the province's 26,000 members, the charges made against the organization have not been ignored by the WI executive. As new rural women's groups continue to form across the province, and WI branches simultaneously disband, WI officials have been forced to recognize the urgency of radical reform if their clubs are to survive. The WI finds itself 'torn between tradition and transition,' and debates now rage within the WI concerning the pressing need for structural reorganization.[59] Provincial journals are filled with suggestions for revitalizing local branches and members debate whether or not they should abandon the WI motto – 'for home and country.'

Despite involvement in issues as diverse as farm aid, child pornography, nuclear disarmament, and international development, the WI has received little recognition for its achievements and is realizing the inadequacy of a quiet, non-confrontational approach to rural reform that has rendered it virtually invisible to the general public. Impeded by agendas scheduled a year in advance and a reform process that takes up to a year for resolutions to pass from the local to provincial levels, the WI lags far behind newer farmwomen's groups in the ability to capitalize on media exposure through quick responses to current issues. Challenged by the growing popularity of these more flexible associations, the Women's Institutes are reconsidering both their platforms and procedures.

Male-controlled rural pressure groups have also been unable to disregard the impact of farm-women's latest forays into politics. Like their UFO predecessors, leaders of established farm organizations have initiated a second 'seasonable courtship' of women's groups, recognizing that associations like WSA have succeeded in gaining the government's ear and are now considered by the state to be respected members of the agricultural lobby. Industry groups, which previously dismissed women's input, now consult regularly with women on a wide range of subjects. Armed with an improved understanding of legislative procedures and pressure tactics, farm women have infiltrated the élite levels of many rural organizations, including the Ontario Federation of Agriculture.[60] Ontario farm women now participate in a provincial liaison committee that co-ordinates the work of eight agricultural interest groups. Although respect from male farmers is most gratifying for groups such as WSA and CFW, farm women agree that they are unwilling to abandon their own organization in favour of integration with male-dominated alliances. Farm women remain open to co-operative politicking with their male counterparts, but they are fiercely protective of their independence.

A similar stance has been adopted by farm women in their interactions with urban women. Farm women are willing to unite their efforts on issues of common concern, but they are hesitant to create formal links with urban associations. Members of groups are, however, conscious of the need for urban support of rural initiatives. Rejecting what continues to be the often virulent anti-urban sentiment prevalent within predominantly rural areas, farm-women's groups accept every opportunity to reach an urban audience. A videotape produced by CFW in 1986 entitled *Rural Roots – Urban Connections* highlights the interdependence of the rural and urban populations and represents a major step towards improving the frequently strained relations between rural and urban dwellers.

Nevertheless, for many rural women, the prospect of open identification with the women's movement remains untenable. Aside from the atypical example of WSA,[61] farm women generally view feminism as intent on establishing a gender-neutral society in which women would replace men within existing power hierarchies. As Angela Miles observes: 'Feminism has been interpreted as a message of individual one-*upmanship*,'[62] a message that fails to elicit support from rural constituencies. Miles postulates that rural women consider urban women to have gained equality at the high price of a loss of specificity, something that the farm woman is reluctant to sacrifice.[63] Indeed, rural women consider themselves to be fundamentally misunderstood by feminists. The espousal of public-sphere participation by the women's movement as integral to alleviating women's oppression holds little appeal for the rural woman who does not experience a physical separation between her productive and reproductive responsibilities and is unconvinced by arguments that stress the liberating potential of participation in the public sphere. The perceived mono-dimensional nature of feminism has also proved unattractive to rural women: 'When asked, 'Are you a feminist?'', it appears that an affirmative answer is translated to mean that one is concerned with no political issues other than feminism.'[64] Feminism is judged by many farm women to be a form of organized politics that, like partisan arrangements of any kind, offers certain ideological guide-lines to which one is required to adhere. The jaundiced view of party politics exhibited by the entire farm population translates into a reluctance on the part of farm women to join what they regard as a hybrid form of political party. Contemporary farm women thus continue to be relatively unenamoured with what they understand to be 'life-style feminism,' a movement that appears interested in attracting only those women who are 'slender, intelligent, upwardly mobile,' and, one might add, urban.[65] Although the women's movement has gained an appreciation of the oppression to which rural women are subject through encouraging their participation in lobbying work and including their experiences within research projects,[66] farm-women's groups such as CFW have, to date, displayed little enthusiasm towards membership in umbrella organizations such as the National Action Committee on the Status of Women.

The current mobilization of farm women in Ontario has met with enviable success. With their persistent efforts, farm-women's groups are altering women's status in the rural home and community as they fight to eradicate women's legal vulnerability and economic insecurity. In choosing to work outside both male-controlled farm lobby groups and single-sex affiliations such as the Women's Institutes, farm women have also challenged the sexual division of labour that has long been entrenched in agrarian politics. Through their action-oriented strategies, they are overcoming the 'Joan of Arc syndrome,' which traditionally minimized their willingness to politicize on their own behalf.[67] The independent course selected by these women has permitted them to shape and reshape their groups and goals according to the requirements of their membership.

A collective approach to learning and decision making has allowed farm women to pursue their individual strengths, resulting in empowerment for each member. The collective decision to discard conventional organizational patterns has meant that rural women are free to take immediate action on urgent issues and may circumvent barriers such as lack of time, education, and money through creative strategies. Farm-women's associations have afforded their membership the chance to assume an equal role in the agricultural lobby process without compromising their priorities in the name of rural solidarity. The have created a 'female design for political living' similar to that developed by many women in non-élite, non-partisan political bodies.[68]

Despite their success, the challenges facing the Ontario movement remain formidable. At the insistence of representatives from Ontario, farm women from across Canada established an informal network in 1986. This network will forge national linkages targeted towards augmenting the resource and research potential of existing groups and facilitating communication between rural women. Participants at the Second National Farm Women's Conference held in Charlottetown in 1985 decided that the burgeoning farm-women's movement required a system that would act primarily as a gatherer and distributor of information. Organizers of the new network promise that there will be no attempt made to dictate agendas to member groups but do admit that the co-ordination of national lobbying will now be possible. The network will accept membership from non-farmers but will safeguard its rural perspective by limiting the voting privileges of those women not actively farming.[69]

This latest venture marks a distinct shift towards the institutionalization of the movement, a trend which will inextricably alter the future of farm women's politics. Leaders of the new network insist that it will not interfere with the policies employed by individual groups, yet demands for co-ordinated efforts will undoubtedly increase once the network is in place. Individual groups with larger memberships may well require more formalized procedures like those they have so vigorously opposed in other organizations. Associations may also confront a decline in numbers as the groups become increasingly formal, a trend common among organizations that had originally attracted their members with alternative structures.[70] Groups now expanding their agendas far beyond initial goals may experience dilemmas similar to those of WI clubs, whose mandates are so varied that significant initiatives on specific issues prove problematic. Of immediate concern to farm women is the overwhelming media attention they are currently receiving.

Movement leaders fear that farm women are being characterized as 'super-women' by the press with inadequate analysis being given to the socio-economic problems they face. Perhaps heeding the message of Emma Griesbach, farm women realize that a long-term commitment to the amelioration of rural-women's multiple oppression is necessary beyond short-term headline coverage.

Pressure on farm-women's groups to coalesce with larger rural organizations will certainly intensify as Ontario's farm population continues to decline with the intrusion of corporate agriculture. Agricultural lobbyists will encourage farm-women's support as they cope with the constant demand for professionalism and institutionalization within the competitive arena of the province's interest-group politics. As the movement grows and the dynamic leadership that has been substantially responsible for the development of the politicization changes, farm women will be forced once again to respond to the familiar problem of reconciling 'class' and gender allegiances while searching for solutions that will not demand a compromise of either loyalty. As almost a century of mobilization among Ontario farm women illustrates, this effort may well prove a 'tough row to hoe.'[71]

NOTES

Special thanks to Marilyn Barber, Lesley Bowles, Annette Costigan, Tunde Nemeth, Gaby Levesque, and especially Jill Vickers for their encouragement and helpful comments on an earlier draft of this paper.

1 For further information on the formative years of the Women's Institutes, see Annie Walker, *Fifty Years of Achievement* (Toronto 1948).
2 As cited by Carol Bacchi in 'Divided Allegiances: The Response of Farm and Labour Women to Suffrage,' in Linda Kealey, ed., *A Not Unreasonable Claim: Women and Reform in Canada, 1880s–1920s* (Toronto 1979), 103.
3 Nellie McClung, *In Times Like These* (Toronto 1915), 180.
4 See Seena Kohl, 'Women's Participation in the North American Family Farm,' *Women's Studies International Quarterly* 1 (1977), 47–54.
5 See Susan Watkins, *What Are You Worth?* (Ottawa 1985) for complete results of this study.
6 Prairie land policies dictated that twice as much land be allotted to colonists who were married as to those who were single, thus acknowledging women's economic contributions. For a discussion of these policies, see L. Rasmussen, C. Savage, and A. Wheeler, *A Harvest Yet to Reap* (Toronto 1976).
7 Christine Delphy, *Close to Home: A Materialist Analysis of Women's Oppression* (Amherst, MA 1984), 80–91.
8 See Canadian Advisory Council on the Status of Women, *Women in Agriculture* (Ottawa 1985).

9 Take, for example, the membership structure of the Ontario Cattlemen's Association, an organization whose very name excludes those women active in beef production.

10 Alison Hayford coined this phrase in 'Different Routes to Different Places,' *Resources for Feminist Research* 11 (March 1982), 17.

11 Bacchi makes a similar observation about the difficulty of using a class analysis in 'Divided Allegiances,' 99.

12 Nancy Painter, 'Hard Times on the Homestead,' *Herizons*, June 1986, 17.

13 Carole Giangrande, *Down to Earth: The Crisis in Canadian Farming* (Toronto 1985), 177.

14 The male-dominated farm associations to which I refer include commodity groups, breed associations, and marketing agencies, many of which segregate women employees into areas such as public relations and advertising while men retain control over more 'vital' areas such as policy making and government liaison work. One national interest group utilizing this structure is the Canadian Cattlemen's Association. A noteworthy exception is the National Farmers Union (NFU), which has maintained a long-term commitment to meeting the needs of farm women. The NFU has not, however, enjoyed great popularity in Ontario.

15 'Farm women' have often been made synonymous with 'prairie farm women' in agricultural literature. The lack of existing work on women's participation in agriculture east of Manitoba is evidence of this tendency.

16 Robert Collison, 'The Politics of Style,' *Chatelaine*, August 1986, 60.

17 Remark made by OFA executive, Brigid Pyke, to the Second National Farm Women's Conference, Charlottetown, 1985.

18 See Pauline Rankin, 'Farm Women and Feminism,' unpublished paper (Ottawa 1986).

19 Sylvia Bashevkin, *Toeing the Lines: Women and Party Politics in English Canada* (Toronto 1985), 3–33.

20 'Sister Diana' was a pseudonym used by Emma Griesbach during her tenure as columnist with the *Weekly Sun* (later renamed the *Farmers' Sun*). For a more detailed discussion of the United Farm Women of Ontario, see Margaret Kechnie, 'The United Farm Women of Ontario: Development a Political Consciousness,' *Ontario History* 77 (December 1985), 266–78, to which this discussion of the UFWO owes much.

21 Jean Macleod, 'The United Farmer Movement in Ontario, 1914–1943,' MA diss., Queen's University, 1958, 41.

22 Memoirs of J.J. Morrison (National Archives of Canada [NA], Ottawa), 60.

23 *Weekly Sun*, 7 November 1917.

24 Ibid., 12 December 1917.

25 See Kechnie, 'United Farm Women,' 269, for a more detailed explanation of the UFWO structure.

26 *Weekly Sun*, 25 December 1917.

27 Morrison memoirs, 42.

28 *Farmers' Sun*, 11 June 1919.

29 *Weekly Sun*, 19 June 1918, 12 June 1918, 14 January 1920.

30 A similar opinion of the Homemakers' clubs was expressed by leaders of the prairie farm women's movements, such as Irene Parlby and Violet McNaughton. See Bacchi, 'Divided Allegiances,' 104.

31 Kechnie, 'United Farm Women,' 275.

32 *Farmers' Sun*, 17 December 1921.

33 Ibid., 11 February 1922.

34 E. Griesbach to W.C. Good, 5 March 1923, W.C. Good Papers (NA).

35 A. Webster to W.C. Good, 4 February 1922, ibid.

36 J.C. Ross to E. Griesbach, 8 February 1922, ibid.

37 Kechnie, 'United Farm Women,' 277.

38 Margaret Stewart and Doris French, *Ask No Quarter: A Biography of Agnes Macphail* (Toronto 1959).

39 Ibid., 39.

40 Ontario farm women were outraged at a suggestion made in the Toronto press that urban women might enter rural kitchens, while farm women continued the field work that would be unattended to once conscription was extended to include farm youth. See Kechnie, 'United Farm Women,' 269 and also W.F. Gatsby, 'The Sons of the Soil,' *Saturday Night*, 1 June 1918.

41 Kechnie, 'United Farm Women,' 276.

42 *Weekly Sun*, 25 December 1918.

43 Veronica Strong-Boag, 'Pulling in Double Harness or Hauling a Double Load: Women, Work and Feminism on the Canadian Prairie,' *Journal of Canadian Studies* 21:3 (Fall 1986), 34.

44 See Blair Williams, 'The Canadian Federation of Agriculture,' PhD diss., Carleton University, 1974, for his discussion of women's minimal role in the early days of the CFA.

45 See Suzanne Zwarun, 'Farm Wives 10 Years after Irene Murdoch,' *Chatelaine*, March 1983, 59, 176, 178–80, 182.

46 These trends are discussed more fully in Molly McGhee, *The Changing Scene* (Toronto 1983), 7–24.

47 Information on Women for the Survival of Agriculture (WSA) was gathered through a series of interviews conducted with group members in November 1986.

48 Harkin had spent several years as an urban resident, a fact that she admits later influenced her approach to farm-women's politics.

49 Watkins, *What Are You Worth?* 10–16.

50 Dianne Harkin has adopted this term to describe the highly flexible structure utilized by WSA groups across Canada.

51 Interviews with WSA members, Winchester, 1986.

52 Information on CFW was gathered through a series of interview conducted with group members in February 1986.

53 Membership brochure of Concerned Farm Women, Chesley, 1982.

54 For example, CFW members launched a letter-writing campaign in which individuals outlined their specific farm financial difficulties. These letters were then sealed in a coffin built by CFW members and painted black to depict the death of the family farm. The coffin was presented to then-Minister of Agriculture Eugene Whelan at a demonstration in Port Elgin, Ontario.

55 A farm-gate defence is a tactic used by the farm community to stall farm foreclosures. Neighbours gather at the farm to impede the removal of livestock from the premises through measures such as forming human chains. Such events sometimes result in arrests or even violence, e.g., in the case of Bruce and Grey counties, where vigilante techniques have been used by members of the Canadian Farm Survival Association.

56 Interview with husband of CFW member, Chesley, 1986. Similar harassment tactics were used less frequently in the Winchester area.

57 See Joyce Canning, 'Reflections from Rural Organizations and Services,' *Home and Country*, Summer 1985, 14.

58 Clay Gilson, as cited by Blair Williams, 'Canadian Federation of Agriculture,' 84. While Gilson was not referring to the Women's Institutes, his comments reflect those made by farm women about the Women's Institutes in interviews with me.

59 See Agnes Bongers, 'Torn between Tradition and Transition,' *Ontario Farm Women*, March 1985, 4, 5, and 9.

60 The Ontario Federation of Agriculture recently elected its first woman president, Wolfe Island farmer Brigid Pyke.

61 I consider WSA an atypical example because of the strong feminist views espoused by Dianne Harkin, who has encouraged interaction between her group and the women's movement. Such a situation is somewhat unusual in a rural Ontario community.

62 Angela Miles, 'Ideological Hegemony in Political Discourse,' in A. Miles and G. Finn, eds, *Feminism in Canada* (Montreal 1982), 222. Emphasis in original.

63 See Angela Miles, 'Integrative Feminism,' *Fireweed: A Feminist Quarterly* 19 (Summer/Fall 1984), 55–81.

64 Bell Hooks, *Feminist Theory from Margin to Center* (Boston 1984), 29.

65 Barbara Ehrenreich as cited in Karen Dubinsky, 'Lament for a "Patriarchy Lost"?' *Feminist Perspectives* 1 (Ottawa 1985), 39–40.

66 See, for example, *Women's Involvement in Political Life: A Pilot Study* (Ottawa 1986), which includes discussions of the political behaviour of rural women in Alberta, Nova Scotia, and Ontario in non-élite interest groups. This research was conducted by the Canadian Research Institute for the Advancement of women for UNESCO.
67 Jane Wilson describes farm women in this manner in 'The Feminisation of Farming,' *Herizons*, March 1986, 12.
68 For an analysis of women's political culture, see Thelma McCormack, 'Toward a Nonsexist Perspective on Social and Political Change,' in M. Millman and R.M. Kanter, eds, *Another Voice* (New York 1975), 24.
69 See 'National Network Links Farm Women,' *Farm and Country*, 15 July 1986.
70 See *Women's Involvement in Political Life: A Pilot Study*, 2–9.
71 Victoria Branden, 'A Tough Row to Hoe,' *Canadian Forum*, May 1985, 17–21.

Abbreviations

CCF	Co-operative Commonwealth Federation
CJC	Canadian Jewish Congress
CLP	Canadian Labor Party
DLP	Dominion Labor Party
FNSJB	Fédération nationale Saint-Jean-Baptiste
FSOC	Finnish Socialist Organization of Canada
ILP	Independent Labour Party
IUNTW	Industrial Union of Needle Trades Workers
LCW	Local Council of Women
LSR	League for Social Reconstruction
NCWC	National Council of Women of Canada
NDP	New Democratic Party
NFLWC	National Federation of Liberal Women of Canada
OBU	One Big Union
OFA	Ontario Federation of Agriculture
OUK	Ukrainian Women's Organization
OUN	Organization of Ukrainian Nationalists
SCM	Student Christian Movement
SDPC (SDP)	Social Democratic Party of Canada
SPC	Socialist Party of Canada
TLC	Trades and Labor Congress
UFA	United Farmers of Alberta
UFWA	United Farm Women of Alberta
UFWO	United Farm Women of Ontario
UNO	Ukrainian National Federation
UVO	Ukrainian Military Organization

VOW	Voice of Women
WCTU	Woman's Christian Temperance Union
WI	Women's Institutes
WILPF (WIL)	Women's International League for Peace and Freedom
WJC	Women's Joint Committee
WLFC	Women's Liberal Federation of Canada
WLL	Women's Labor League
YWCA	Young Women's Christian Association

Contributors

Linda Kealey teaches history and women's studies at Memorial University of Newfoundland and is now working on the completion of a book on women in the socialist and labour movements in Canada, 1890–1920.

Joan Sangster is a specialist in women's history and labour history. She has published articles in *Labour/Le Travail* and is the author of *Dreams of Equality: Women on the Canadian Left, 1920–1950*. She teaches history and women's studies at Trent University.

Jill Vickers is director of Carleton University's Institute of Canadian Studies, professor of political science, and has been instrumental in the development of women's studies at Carleton as well as in Canada generally. She is also a past president of the Canadian Research Institute for the Advancement of Women and has been active in many other groups, such as CAUT and the Canadian Women's Studies Association.

Patricia A. Myers holds a master's degree in Canadian history from the University of Waterloo. She is currently with Historic Sites Service, a part of the Alberta government's Department of Culture and Multiculturalism.

Franca Iacovetta recently received her PhD from York University and is currently a post-doctoral fellow at the University of Guelph. She has published in the areas of immigration and women's history, and is currently working on a book manuscript on the Italian working-class experience in post-war Toronto.

Pat Roome is currently on leave from the Department of Humanities, Mount Royal College, Calgary to pursue a PhD in history at Simon Fraser University.

Susan Mann Trofimenkoff is professor of history and vice-rector, academic, at the University of Ottawa. Her special interests are the history of Quebec and the history of women. Publications include *Dream of Nation, Stanley Knowles*, and *The Neglected Majority*, with Alison Prentice.

Varpu Lindström-Best completed her PhD in 1986 and teaches at Atkinson College, York University, in Toronto; she is the author of *Defiant Sisters: Social History of Finnish Immigrant Women in Canada, 1890–1930* and numerous articles on Finnish immigration to Canada.

Janice Newton is a professor of political science at York University. Her research and publication interests are in women and public policy and the role of women in political movements; her doctoral thesis was on feminist challenges within the early Canadian left.

Frances Swyripa has written extensively on Ukrainians in Canada and has been a research associate with the Canadian Institute of Ukrainian Studies. Her recently completed PhD dissertation examines images, roles, and myths in the history of Ukrainian women in Canada.

Ruth Frager is a specialist in Canadian women's, labour, and ethnic history and is completing a book on the Jewish labour movement in Toronto, 1900–39. She teaches in the history department of McMaster University.

Barbara Roberts teaches at Athabasca University, Alberta, and has published in the areas of women's peace history, women's work, and immigration history. She is the author of *Whence They Came: Deportation in Canada, 1900–35*, and co-author of *A Greener Future: Women in the Winnipeg Garment Industry*.

Pauline Rankin, graduate student in Canadian Studies at Carleton University, is researching the political behaviour of farm women.

Index